# ALIENATION

## Concept, Term, and Meanings

# CONTRIBUTORS

# ALIENATION
## Concept, Term, and Meanings

## Edited by *FRANK JOHNSON*

Department of Psychiatry
State University of New York
Upstate Medical Center
Syracuse, New York

SEMINAR PRESS        New York and London

A Subsidiary of Harcourt Brace Jovanovich, Publishers

SEMINAR PRESS, INC.
111 Fifth Avenue, New York, New York 10003


*United Kingdom Edition published by*
SEMINAR PRESS LIMITED
24/28 Oval Road, London NW1


LIBRARY OF CONGRESS CATALOG CARD NUMBER: 72-7702


PRINTED IN THE UNITED STATES OF AMERICA

# Contents

## Part I   OVERVIEW AND BACKGROUND

### Alienation: Overview and Introduction

*Frank Johnson*

### Chapter 1   Alienation: Concept, Term, and Word

*Frank Johnson*

## Part II   CONTEMPORARY PERSPECTIVES

### Chapter 7   Alienation: Contemporary Sociological Approaches
*Eric Josephson and Mary Redmer Josephson*

### Chapter 8   Alternatives to Alienation: A Japanese-American Example
*Colleen Leahy Johnson*

### Chapter 9   Freedom, Order, and Alienation
*Paul Meadows*

### Chapter 10   Prometheus and the Policy Sciences: Alienation as the Decline of Personal Agency
*Manfred Stanley*

Chapter 18   **Alienation: Some Concluding Observations**

*Frank Johnson*

# List of Contributors

Number in parentheses indicate the pages on which the authors' contributions begin.

ROBERT W. DALY, Department of Psychiatry, State University of New York, Upstate Medical Center, Syracuse, New York (339)

THEODORE C. DENISE, Department of Philosophy, Syracuse University, Syracuse, New York (141)

BLANCHE H. GELFANT, Department of English, Dartmouth College, Hanover, New Hampshire (295)

DAVID HERLIHY, Harvard University, Cambridge, Massachusetts (125)

COLLEEN LEAHY JOHNSON, Department of Child and Family Studies, Syracuse University, Syracuse, New York (183)

FRANK JOHNSON, Department of Psychiatry, State University of New York, Upstate Medical Center, Syracuse, New York (3, 27, 53, 369)

ERIC JOSEPHSON, Division of Sociomedical Sciences, Columbia University School of Public Health, New York, New York (163)

MARY REDMER JOSEPHSON, Medina Villa, Hove, Sussex, England (163)

STEPHEN KOFF, Department of Political Science, Maxwell School, Syracuse University, Syracuse, New York (269)

JOHN MACQUARRIE, Department of Theology, University of Oxford, London, England (311)

PAUL MEADOWS, Department of Sociology, State University of New York, Albany, New York (205)

EPHRAIM H. MIZRUCHI, Department of Sociology, Maxwell School Syracuse University, Syracuse, New York (111)

DONALD OKEN, Department of Psychiatry, State University of New York, Upstate Medical Center, Syracuse, New York (83)

GERALD M. REAGAN, Department of Education, Ohio State University, Columbus, Ohio (321)

ALVIN F. POUSSAINT, Department of Psychiatry, Harvard Medical School, Shattuck Street, Boston, Massachusetts (359)

MANFRED STANLEY, Department of Sociology, School of Citizenship and Public Affairs, Syracuse University, Syracuse, New York (221)

A. DALE TUSSING, Department of Economics, Syracuse University, and Educational Policy Research Center, Syracuse, New York (251)

# *Preface*

Despite its generalizability and vagueness, the word *alienation* continues to be advanced as a central concept summarizing salient features of life in contemporary societies. The purpose of this book in regard to alienation is both simple and ambitious. Hopefully, it will offer comprehensive definitions of the term historically, culturally, and in relation to a number of different contemporary contexts and disciplines. Following a definition of the term, there appear contributions regarding the phenomena of alienation as viewed by a philosopher, an historian, several sociologists, an anthropologist, a theologian, an economist, an educator, a literary critic, a political scientist, and several psychiatrists.

It is a source of personal pleasure that the development of this book has proceeded in a very unalienated manner. By and large, selections were sought from individuals with whom I had friendly, colleagial, and scholarly acquaintance. With many of the contributors, the area covered in their writing stems from informal spontaneous discussions held in offices, during conventions, or at informal social engagements.

Some account of my own concern with alienation is probably warranted here. My original interest in the term stemmed from an association with Ernest Becker while I was still a student at the State University of New York in Syracuse. A series of friendly discussions with Melvin Eggers—now Chancellor at Syracuse University—is responsible for reviving my interest in the term as a serious concept some 10 years ago when I had begun to doubt its utility as a scientific or philosophic construct. At a somewhat more remote level, I am very indebted to the writings of Ronald Fairbairn, Harry Guntrip, R. D. Laing, and Richard Schacht for stimulating and clarifying my own thinking. More immediately, I am grateful for a number of discussions and exchange of writings concerning the philosophic and sociological aspects of the term, alienation, with Manfred Stanley, Ephraim Mizruchi, Theodore Denise, Paul Meadows, and A. C. Higgins. Aspects of psychological, anthropological, and literary meanings of the concept of alienation have been repeatedly discussed with Colleen Johnson, Robert Daly, and Blanche Gelfant.

With some of the other contributors, I have had to rely on transcontinental correspondence and cassette tapes to communicate regarding the nature and progress of their contributions. Though this represented a less personal connection, it proved to be very helpful in attempting to create a book of interdigitating observations concerning alienation, rather than the development of an isolated series of essays on a common subject.

The opportunity to develop my thinking on the subject of alienation was fostered when I functioned as Director of an *Institute on Alienation,* held at Maxwell School of Citizenship and Public Affairs during the academic year 1969-70. The assistance of many individuals is acknowledged—notably Roy Price (Project Director), Brian Larkin, Morton Perry, and the students and colleagues who participated in various seminars and meetings.

I am very grateful to the President of my campus, Lewis W. Bluemle and my departmental chairman, Donald Oken (also a contributor) for the arrangement of sabbatical leave during 1970-1971 which facilitated in part the drafting of several of my own chapters. I also wish to acknowledge the help of John McDermott for his gracious instrumental arrangements for me as a visiting professor at the Section of Psychiatry of the University of Hawaii. I am also very grateful to the Social Science Research Institute in Honolulu for preparing the final manuscript of both my own and the contributors' chapters for publication. Many people have been helpful in the actual production of the manuscript. Freda Hellinger, Manuscript Editor, at the Social Science Research Institute has been particularly zealous in assisting, as has Judith Rubano, whose careful indexing will hopefully make the volume more useful for the reader.

A number of people were very patient in working with various drafts of this manuscript both in Hawaii and New York State—notably Marsha Newell, Janet McNair, and Janet Sgroi.

Sandra Ecker Kaplan, Robert Daly, and Eugene Kaplan were especially helpful in a continuing way at various states of the preparation of my chapters.

Finally, I wish to acknowledge the assistance of the State of New York, Department of Mental Hygiene, through their provision of a supplemental training stipend, which was helpful during my sabbatical year in Honolulu.

# Part I

# OVERVIEW AND BACKGROUND

# Alienation: Overview and Introduction

*Frank Johnson*

State University of New York

## ALIENATION AS "PANCHRESTON" AND VOGUE TERM

Alienation is an atrocious word. In its use as a general concept, scientific term, popular expression, and cultural motif, alienation has acquired a semantic richness (and confusion) attained by few words of corresponding significance in contemporary parlance. Few concepts have been subjected to as long a history of association with diverse disciplines, each contributing its own emphases and meanings. Moreover, although popularization of technical terms is common, the plethora of contexts in which alienation is cited on a colloquial level seems extravagant when compared to other vogue expressions.

Most terms which possess scientific bite are characterized by a reasonable specificity of denotation, a clarity of meaning within particular disciplines, and an absence of serious internal paradox or ambiguity. None of these adhere to the word, alienation. Alienation is used to denote a great variety of often quite dissimilar phenomena. Moreover, its meanings within separate disciplines are confusingly interrelated, and the word, of course, is stricken with severe inconsistency and vagueness.

Hardin (1956) has analyzed the status of overgeneralized, scientific concepts through coining the term, "panchreston."[1] He defines panchrestons as

---

[1] Hardin's (1956) term "panchreston" is put to use in an illuminating essay by Szasz (1959) on the vagaries of psychiatric nosology.

those words which, in attempting to explain all, essentially explain nothing. His term has particular applicability for the analysis of archaic constructs in the physical sciences (e.g., protoplasm, elan vital, ether) where an originally heuristic concept evolves over a period of time into a generic expression connotating much but signifying little. The history of the physical sciences and medicine are replete with such panchrestons which are either currently assigned to lexographic museums or retained in contemporary jargon out of inertia or sentiment.

The anachronistic meanings connected with the word, term, and concept of alienation are not so readily disentangled, however. Its older denotations in theology and philosophy are not as easily separated from its current range of meanings within the social sciences. And the meanings of alienation stemming from Hegel, Marx, and Weber are in no sense altogether distinctive from the meaning of alienation within existential psychiatry or, for that matter as the term appears as popular political phraseology.

In an extensive survey of various phenomena of alienation, Schacht (1970) has recently discussed the central semantic connected with the term. Stripped to its essence, the word signifies separation (or distance) between two or more entities. The fact of separation, however integral to its definition, does not in itself convey the full meaning of the word. Equally basic is the connotation of anguish or tension accompanying such separation—usually the quality of estrangement or loss, but also accommodating to the connotation of relief at the interposition of distance. The variety of meanings capable of being added onto this deceptively simple denotation is extravagant. It is the purpose of this overview to look into most of these meanings through an historical review of alienation as concept, term, and expression, within various disciplines.

Before doing this, it should be asked if the word is worth elucidating at all. Perhaps those disciplines which have found the term of some utility in the past should substitute newer terminologies and abandon the word alienation to the ambiguity of its colloquial and vogue usages. For example, Feuer (1963), in a thoughtful analysis of the use of the concept, is led to the conclusion that while alienation (as a condition) is ubiquitous, attempts by sociologists to operationalize its various meanings have been largely unsuccessful. He adds that the preoccupation with the subject in sociology and other fields carries along an implicit presupposition—namely that the cultural, social, and economic systems which have produced widespread alienation are accepted as givens. Therefore, much of the research and rhetoric regarding alienation is directed at the identification and alleviation of symptoms, rather than at the basic sickness (i.e., the disease of technicism and the need for "basic economic reconstruction"). He asks this interesting question:

> Is "alienation," however, a useful concept for analysis of these modes of human unhappiness and frustration? Is it more than a dramatic metaphor which for reasons peculiar to intellectuals' experience has become their favorite root-metaphor for perceiving the social universe? Is it less, however, a tool for understand-

ing than a projection of the psychology of intellectuals disenchanted with themselves? [Feuer, 1963, p. 138.]

McDermott (1969) advances a similar case for the complicity of scientists in perpetuating the status quo in an article called "Technology: The Opiate of the Intellectuals."[2] Through the analysis of an institutional report (from the Harvard Program on Technology and Society[3]), he attempts to show that critiques concerned with the symptomatology of the system lead to obscuring ". . . the systematic and decisive social changes, especially their political and cultural tendencies, that follow the widespread application of advanced technological systems." McDermott's (1969) indictment may seem overdrawn, partly since it is based on the analysis of an institutional report (whose styles, by design, are euphemistic and selfjustifying) rather than on a consideration of the actual scientific work of the contributions to the project. One of his conclusions, nevertheless, seems well established—namely that ". . . technological rationality is as socially neutral today as market rationality was a century ago [p. 33]." Such neutrality is meant to suggest an unconscious and unwitting complicity present among intellectuals serving the government or "Establishment." Others, although aware of these implications, may not believe in the need for fundamental social reconstruction and, hence, continue to seek understanding and remedy through the study of alienation.

Also, in reply to Feuer (1963) and McDermott (1969), the fact that the intellectuals feel alienated in their own personal, professional, and institutional lives does not necessarily invalidate their scientific preoccupations with alienation. Such awareness, for that matter, may more urgently press them to discover personal and social prescriptions for the relief of these conditions.

At any rate, evading the term is not possible; attempting to contribute to the elucidation of its various meanings seems a reasonable enterprise. The purpose of this volume is to inspect and elucidate the various meanings of alienation—as concept, term, and popular expression. This introduction is concerned with definitions and applications of the concept as they appear in the following fields: theology, history, philosophy, psychiatry, sociology, anthropology, education, economics, political science, and literature. This essay is concerned with the usage of the term alienation. The chapter which follows will examine the etymological derivations and meanings of the word.

## SOME DEFINITIONS AND APPLICATIONS OF THE TERM ALIENATION

The purpose of this section is to introduce the concept of alienation through an operational description of its meanings and uses within particular disciplines.

[2] McDermott's (1969) article reviews Mesthene's (1969) essay.
[3] Two subsequent reports are available (*Program*, 1970, and *Final Review*, 1972).

Given the limitations of space, this cannot be done comprehensively. Since the design here is to introduce rather than exhaust the meaning of the concept within these fields, certain critical happenings and important commentary will, of necessity, be omitted. Another problem appears in relation to establishing the relative importance of the concept of alienation within these several disciplines. Obviously the centrality and importance of the concept not only varies widely between these different fields but is a matter of controversy within separate disciplines themselves. Opinions concerning the vitality of the concept are, of course, included in this presentation, but the editor does not propose to adjudicate the particular claims of various specialists. The importance of the term will be established indirectly, through depicting its extensive and manifold connections, both in the past and on the contemporary scene.

The format for the presentation of each of these disciplines will be, first, to review the historical meanings of the term within each field and, second, to inspect selected phenomena of alienation in the contemporary scene which are connected with the perspective of each field. In doing this, an inevitable unevenness will be introduced in the exposition of contemporary concerns within various disciplines. This unevenness is partly a result of the bias connected with having to select out certain salient features of contemporary life which the author feels are particularly germane to the subject of alienation.

Finally, this overview serves as a key to the entire volume. As noted in the Preface, the design of this book is to present basic definitions of the term alienation along with chapter-length commentary from a number of disciplines which illuminate the meanings of this elusive term. This overview and the subsequent chapter hopefully will provide a map of the term in its various meanings and contexts.[4]

## Use of the Concept in Theology and Philosophy

If there were such a thing as proprietary ownership of words as well as things in Western culture, theologians would have little trouble in establishing their priority for the term alienation. As a human drama, Genesis is a story of separation—creation and the fall, closeness followed by estrangement. Even in this original revelation, the quality of existential loneliness is portrayed in the enigmatic, almost Kafkaesque, nature of the story concerning Man, the Serpent, and the Forbidden Fruit. Perhaps the flimsiness and mystery of the allegory are deliberate: alienation is meant to be portrayed as arbitrary and unanticipated; Man is fated to suffer cosmic losses for what on the face of things are peccadillos. Absurd or not, Man is driven from Eden to the importunities, anxieties, and duality of life outside of an integrating Paradise. Alienation is his chronic mortal state, possibly his eternal condition. Particularly in the Christian adumbrations of this drama, the basic issue of alienation remained cen-

---

[4] For another kind of map, the reader is referred to Kaufman (1970).

tral: not only was mortal man reminded of his degradation and estrangement of himself as a species, but his energies on Earth were continually turned toward the reestablishment of union with his Creator in the hereafter. And within Christian theology, the concept of alienation spread from its focus on the separation of man from God to include man's separation from his own body (regarded as an impediment or, at best, a distraction), separation from his fellow man (insofar as temporal relationships were ephemeralized by the emphasis on the hereafter), and alienated from temporal institutions (which, aside from the Church, lacked ultimate connection).

The concept of alienation, therefore, has enjoyed great vitality in Christian theology and consequently has continued as an ontological theme pervading Western culture. It is, of course, fashionable to review the alienating quality of the theological emphasis on guilt, dualism, and sin from our contemporary perspective, and see these as having essentially negative and coercive implications. Such a reconstruction, however, omits the positive aspects of an emphasis on individual consciousness, the transcendental outlook accentuated by such an orientation, and the stability that the promise of euphoric, futuristic reconciliation possessed for the individuals who believed in it.

It should not be overlooked that the theological focus on a personal alienation directed attention to the phenomena of man's inner existence: his cognitive life, moods, impulses, attributes, dispositions, and attitudes. These explorations into the nature of individual man served as rudiments for later psychologies and personologies concerned with man's relatedness, not to an abstract Being, but to himself and others. Western theology and philosophy have been concerned with depicting man as a discrete, internally complex soul involved in an interpersonalized, dyadic relationship with his ultimate Creator and, paradigmatically, his fellow man.[5] Separation (discreteness) was the basic condition; transcendental dealienation the object of existence. Secularized or not, the writings of theologians and philosophers have accentuated this same theme: the primacy of individual existence, along with a focus on anxiety which accompanies the recognition of estrangement and powerlessness.[6] Of course, the interpretations, meanings, and significance of estrangement have differed, but the quality of the experience of alienation has been expressed in nearly identical ways.

[5] A report from a recent conference has discussed some of the differences inherent in the term alienation as viewed by Western and Eastern philosophers. It was generally conceded that the explicit Western sense of alienation has more personal individualistic connotations, whereas the Eastern model is more implicitly a sense of disorder in terms of Nature or some abstract scale concerned with rule-following. Strain resulting from transgressions of rules as an Eastern experience, however, is not connected with the hostile, dissociative quality of alienation explicated in Western Judaeo-Christian traditions (see Manley, 1969).

[6] In a survey of this kind, it is impractical to cite particular sources for each idea which is briefly reviewed here. The reader is referred to citations in the footnotes accompanying subsequent chapters in connection with specific disciplines.

## Alienation in Current Philosophy and Religion

The fundamental importance of alienation as a theme in Western culture also lacks dimension unless reviewed in the context of events occurring in modern philosophy and theology. One might, for example, pursue the current status of the effect of Existentialism on organized religion, or look into some of the phenomena attendant on the popularization of derivations of existential philosophy both within religion as well as in cultural developments among the young, the disenchanted, and the revolutionary. Obviously the possible topics for examination are vast, particularly since the theme of alienation in theology has taken on a thrust incorporating contributions from philosophers and social scientists as well as theologians—the latter from Jewish, Catholic, Protestant, and even Eastern religions.[7]

Alienation, both as concept and experience in contemporary religion is a considerably more complex subject than even thirty years ago. Modern theologians see alienation not simply as a cosmic theme, but as a set of phenomena with compelling secular implications. Man is seen as not only separated from God but as separated from meaningful experience with other men, institutions, Nature, and himself. Furthermore, theologians wrestle with man's relationship to God as a paradigm for his relationship to man, God, himself, being seen as an abstraction whose real existence is, at times, seriously questioned.

On a more mundane level, contemporary men find sources of alienation in their churches and temples—paradoxically because of the recent vitality and relevance in organized religions. Like other contemporary social organizations, churches are in the process of self-examination and change. In many ways, they have tried to discard insularity and detachment to become socially experimental, cultivating new liturgies, seeking ecumenical commonalities, questioning the social structure of their own institutions and society in general. These changes are received with mixtures of both surprise and applause. Some parishioners and clergy are bewildered to find flux in place of certainty, humanity in place of fatalistic acceptance of inequity, ecumenism instead of cultural bias. Such change in function and outlook connotes a loss of attachment and certainty (formerly halcyon qualities of religion). These events portend a loss of meaning, both for some clergy as well as the laity.[8]

There is a parallel ambivalence in the field of philosophy where ordinary men, when they rouse themselves to be interested, again expect to discover evi-

---

[7] The comprehensive attention given this concept by secular, philosophic, social, and theological commentators itself is remarkable. The fact that the concept is viable in theological thought emanating from various denominations lends additional evidence toward establishing alienation as a central cultural theme in Western society.

[8] Since the term alienation is afflicted with an unusual number of internal paradoxes, situations frequently occur in which the same conditions (e.g., the secularization of religious organizations) reduce alienation for some (e.g., the avantgarde among clergy and parishoners) while intensifying alienation for other more traditional clerics and laity. These semantic peculiarities of the word alienation will be confronted in the chapter which follows.

dence of permanence or, at least, exceedingly gradual change. Unlike religion, which is so visibly cultural, human, and pragmatic, philosophy is usually viewed as a rather Olympian enterprise, promising illumination and considered responses, when such are sought, and now and then generating an idea that has an impact on a particular practical endeavor. Philosophy is, of course, not considered a dead or even necessarily sedate field. In general, however, professional philosophers live in Academe, communicate largely with each other, and make contributions which have only remote or delayed effects upon individuals or society. Existentialism in the postwar period, however, has had an almost unprecedented impact on the public (at least the intelligentsia) to the consternation of many philosophers. As Barrett (1962) has commented:

> The important thing was that here was a philosophy that was able to cross the frontier from the Academy into the world at large. This should have been a welcome sign to professional philosophers that ordinary mankind could still hunger and thirst after philosophy if what they were given to bite down on was something that seemed to have a connection with their lives. Instead, the reception given the new movement by philosophers was anything but cordial. Existentialism was rejected, often without very much scrutiny, as sensationalism or mere "psychologizing," a literary attitude, post-war despair, nihilism, or heaven knows what besides.

He adds:

> Such matters as anxiety, death, the conflict between the bogus and the genuine self, the faceless man of the masses, the experience of the death of God are scarcely the themes of analytic philosophy. Yet they are the themes of life: People do die, people do struggle over lives between the demands of real and counterfeit selves . . . [pp. 8-9].

Clearly, the "encounter with Nothingness" and the tenuousness of existence emphasized in Existentialism highlighted certain alienating features of contemporary life. It is not surprising that intellectuals living in postwar Western democracies seized on these observations for explanation and illumination.

The question is, of course, whether such a global term is capable of scientific incisiveness, or whether it is an expression of a universal *Weltschmerz* symptomatic of those intellectuals (philosophers and scientists) who unconsciously promote the very disease they bemoan. Barrett (1962) is concerned with this, both in regard to the sensationalism accompanying the acceptance of Existentialism as well as in regard to the surplus negativity that adheres to the subject deriving from the popularization of the French School (passed on through literary as well as hard nosed publications in America). As Barrett (1962) suggests, however, perhaps this very negativity is expressed because it is prototypical of contemporary life, and not merely as a projection of the gloominess of Sartre, de Beauvoir, and Camus. However that may be, the profusion of existential themes in American life has been notable, both in literature, theatre, and popularizations of theology and philosophy (as well as in cartoons, comic strips, folk lyrics, and speech).

The effect of this has been to deepen the public consciousness concerning alienation, as well as to glamorize, in some ways, the condition of estrangement, much as Bohemian life was romanticized earlier in the century.

The different levels at which a philosopher might choose to examine certain contemporary aspects of alienation, are, of course, most extensive. In this volume, Theodore Denise has selected to dissect the applications of the term—principally within academic philosophy.

### Alienation from the Standpoint of History

There is a very strong tendency in the popular and scholarly literature to identify alienation as either a Postreformation or Postindustrial phenomenon. It is apparent, however, that throughout recorded history men, as individuals and in groups, have actively or passively been cut off from significance, meaning, and power. Potential meaninglessness of human existence is certainly not a Postindustrial phenomenon. Nor did being treated as a "thing" await the development of larger cities, the factory system, or the rise of Capitalism. Slaves, obviously, were indentured "things." And "cultural pseudospeciation" (Erickson, Lorenz) did not await the explication of this recent term, but presumably operated as a dynamic in the aggressive adventures of individuals, tribes, and nations throughout all of history.[9]

The historical perspective is included in this volume, then, for two purposes: first of all for emphasis—the fact that social alienation has an ancient history and that this is very commonly overlooked. Second, it is included for a strategic reason. Part of the problem of misrepresenting alienation as a posttechnological disease is that it leads to a distorted portentiousness concerning its causes and alleged malignancy. The implications of alienation are sufficiently ominous without being made melodramatic through the suggestion that it is a twentieth century version of the Black Death. The point is, of course, that alienation is an antique term, not only in its psychological, religious, and philosophical connections but in the social implications that have been both inherent and manifest in these former meanings. (Such a reflection is not intended to suggest that since alienation has been around for so long it must simply be endured, nor is it to suggest that the modern alienating conditions do not pose some terrible, special hazards. It is suggested, however, that an overdramatizing of the terrifying aspects of modern technology, which, after all, are of our own manufacture and are just possibly capable of our mastery, can only lend an hysterical aura to a subject hardly in need of surplus excitement.)

It is therefore instructive to slip back into previous centuries to examine those species of alienation—intellectual, spiritual, and familial—manifested there. Study-

---

[9] See Lorenz (1970) for a recent discussion on the enmity between generations, cultural groups, and divergent species.

ing the outcomes of the "alien," heretical and "insane" as they have lived in the past, may be used to aid in the selection of genuinely dangerous and terrifying aspects of alienation, in contrast to some of the cyclical, innocuous, and creative features of some of the contemporary manifestations of alienation.

A consideration of history, therefore, can assist in developing a strategic focus on those phenomena which are particularly threatening. Regrettably, there is a very evident tendency to dramatize alienation as being globally threatening to the fabric of society (almost equally in all of its forms), when such is clearly not the case. For example, the enormous amount of attention given to the "generation gap" seems misdirected, as is the concern with the relative permissiveness sponsored by Postdepression, Postfreudian (American) life in the past thirty years. Of course, generation differences are a signal element in alienation within families as well as in society generally. However, as Mannheim, Eisenstadt, de Ortega, Lorenz, Herlihy, and others, have demonstrated, this gap has been a ubiquitous vector affecting social organization among men as well as some higher animals.[10] Similarly, while the qualitative (permissive) changes in educational and cultural training within the last thirty years unquestionably bear on the understanding of the character of contemporary forms of alienation, it is difficult to see how these particular manifestations are either special to these times or crucial. (I am suggesting that needless confusion is engendered when all states of alienation are endowed with a grotesque, and specifically contemporaneous quality of malignancy.)

This not only appears in the overdramatization of certain social factors which enhance alienation, but in the personal and psychological factors as well. Both the academic and popular "psychological" literature present embellished descriptions of the terrible possibilities of personal alienation in the latter half of the twentieth century. Although accurate, these observations are misleading if they perpetrate the idea that personal alienation in the past was necessarily less authentic, or even qualitatively different than now. Some of this commentary would suggest that contemporary man, because of his distinctively different alienation, is more dangerous than alienated man in the past. Such advocates would argue that men in the Pentagon or in the Kremlin are more dangerous pushing a button (rather than throwing a spear or firing a gun), on the basis that they are unusually alienated. Contemporary man is dangerous, not because of the possible qualitative features of his state of alienation, but, rather, because of the incredible destructiveness inherent in his

---

[10] The entire volume cited above (*Psychoanalytic Review,* 1970) is devoted to a number of essays on the conflicts between generations, including a reprinting of Mannheim's "The Problem of Generations" (1970). Also, in addition to articles available in scientific periodicals, some interesting studies have enjoyed popular publication—notably by Yankelovich (1969). A very fundamental treatment of the issue is also available in Eisenstadt (1956). A critical article separating the differences between "trivial opinions versus central opinions" has approached the problem of generation gap from the standpoint of systematic research in examining behaviors connected with politics, values, and pleasure (Adelson, 1970). Herlihy, in this volume (see Chapter 5), discusses evidence for both intergenerational conflict as well as significant hostility to the family as an institution in medieval Italy.

technology. The danger of such formulations is that they focus on the quality personal separateness of the individual (which is a genuine but somewhat incidental issue). This can distract attention from the more central issue of the moral, technological, and political processes through which such massive destructiveness is assembled and deployed.

## Alienation from the Standpoint of Psychiatry and Psychology

The emphasis in western culture on the role of the individual (alienated) existence and consciousness has constituted a milieu in which the need for a "mediatorial elite" (in Nelson's (1965) use of the term) has been imminent and continuing. Although the more specific historical sources of contemporary counselling professionals stem from medieval Christianity, the need for oracles, prophets, and demigods to act as intermediaries in transacting with the divine stems from even older western traditions (Nelson, 1965). This status of an extrafamilial, professional advocate is a predominantly western creation. The need has been clear. The advocate should function to mediate for the (alienated) individual in terms of his relationship to his Creator, himself, his fellowman, and his contemporary institutions. Nelson (1965) analyzes the generic activity of these diverse professionals (advocates, confessors, shaman, or, more latterly, psychotherapists) as a function of double agency. He sees their mediatorial roles to be simultaneously concerned with exonerating the individual in relation to the prevailing society, as well as rescuing the person from his own internalized demonology. There is no suggestion, however, that these various mediators have necessarily been uniformly benign, humanistic, or conscious of their own purposes. Sometimes none of these has obtained. Nevertheless, these counsellors have been available for kings and peasants, clergy and heretics, although, obviously, not equally available. Some of the socially or personally alienated have found thier own way to these counsellors; others have been forced to accept their counsels.

The fact that psychiatrists and their predecessors have functioned as typical rather than exceptional members of the societies in which they worked has received all shades of self justifying, documentary, and acrimonious attention from historical critics within and outside of the field. The compassion and courage shown by some members of the profession has been sporadic, depending upon particular individuals' aptitudes as well as upon the cultural and political climates in which they have functioned. Displaying typical western scientific zeal, psychiatrists have made important contributions to the understanding of Man through the description and categorization of human behavior. Although it is difficult to see how they could have avoided doing so, they have, at the same time, unwittingly contributed to the reification of cultural variation as "illness." They have also impressed a biological, taxonomic stamp onto social, behavioral phenomena.

As an outgrowth of their pastoral and medical origins, psychiatrists have continued to focus on the individual as an idiodynamic "soul." As practitioners, they have close association with persons who find themselves unusually estranged, depressed, or eccentric. Their empathy for such patients, however, is not unlimited. Their double agency has implicated them in the creation of various forms of alienation. They have stood by to carry out various forms of secular excommunication for those persons whose disturbances will not yield to their ministrations or show evidence of being suppressed by the pressures of the normative order.

Like other encapsulated professional groups, many psychiatrists seem unaware of the cultural milieu in which they work. Nor do they see the "ethnicizing" (as Leifer, 1969, depicts these) socially suppressive nature of some of their functions.[11]

Currently, the institution of psychiatry comprises a number of dissimilar sectors, practicing in diverse modes and settings. These sectors (psychoanalysis, hospital psychiatry, academic psychiatry, etc.) pursue separate goals within the general society. As in other contemporary institutions, there is evidence of a higher degree of consciousness concerning such pluralism and sectarianism than in the past. Furthermore, an awareness of the convert purposes of psychiatry as an institution, both in relation to itself as well as other institutions (e.g., law, medicine, government), is refreshingly explicit. Such insights, of course, are not always flattering or eagerly received. However, the analysis of covert, self-protective institutional purposes is in no way unique to psychiatry. The awareness of the existence of unconscious self-protective mechanisms in both individuals and groups was, of course, promulgated through psychoanalysis and only later reformulated and applied by social scientists. That such insights should come home to roost in the analysis of psychiatry as a social organization seems particularly fitting.[12]

Within the academic community, psychiatry and (clinical) psychology are often regarded with reserve and suspicion. Publicity about internal dissensions concerning science, practice, and doctrine obscures the potentiality of these disciplines to contribute to the subject of alienation, or, more practically, to the alleviation

---

[11] In general, Leifer (1969) depicts "ethnicizing" as an invidious coercion of the patient in the direction of changes that are in society's or the family's best interest (and this often may be the case). Ethnicizing need not, however, always have this connotation since the range of choices within any psychotherapeutic course (as in any other life situation) are necessarily limited by the restrictions of social reality and, hence, may be "ethnicizing" even in a more subtle or noncoercive sense.

[12] The popularization and application of psychoanalytic concepts (e.g., "repression," "rationalization," "projection") within the scientific, philosophical, and religious community has been an important ingredient in the current general understanding of the operation of inexplicit personal or institutional motivations. A summary of some of these contributions in a variety of disciplines is reviewed in Nelson (1957) and in Seeley (1967a). A description of the dissemination of Freudian ideas through American newspapers during the 1920s is available. This centers on the coverage of the Leopold-Loeb Trial (see Covert, 1970).

of both personal and social despair. Considering the breadth of concerns in these
fields which touch on various aspects of alienation, it is not surprising that several
commentators appear in this volume—speaking not only of the "psychology" of
estranged individuals but also in regard to factors which contribute to the alienation of individuals in society.

## Contributions from Sociology to the Concept of Alienation

The contributions of sociologists to the meaning of alienation have been
most extensive. Some of these will be traced historically in several chapters later
in this same volume.

There are multiple points at which the concept of alienation strayed from
its original theological focus and began to appear in more humanized and secular
versions. The understanding about Man's basic capacity for exquisite loneliness,
licensiousness, and atavistic destructiveness was caricaturized in folklore, literature, and official publications concerning "human nature." These latently secular
outlooks finally became explicitly social through Rousseau, who transliterated the
explanation of Man's loneliness and despair to his relationship with Nature rather
than with God. His conception was that man was separated from his innate goodness not through Original Sin but through living in a denaturalizing social milieu.
A succession of philosophers and social scientists continued the secular use of the
term, searching for potentially scientific meanings within the concept of alienation
(Nietzsche, Fuerbach, Marx, Durkheim, Weber, etc.). Although current scholarly
criticism of the term has run high, sociologists still return to this concept, now further concatenated by their own scholarly writings, to examine it for new meanings, applications, and potentials for empirical research.

There are various shades of commitment to the use of the concept, alienation,
by social scientists, several of which have already been noted. The following is a
list of some of the possible positions and representative spokesmen:

1. The concept is viable as a cultural motif but implies acceptance of the
status quo (Feuer, 1963, p. 146; McDermott, 1969, p. 35).

2. The concept should be confined to the use of its specific components
applied to particular phenomena, for example, "normlessness" in regard to political behavior (Seeman, 1959).

3. The concept is too shifty for use in sociological research, such as in the
above (Feuer, 1963, pp. 140-141).

4. Its inclusion is essential in any (value) science of man—the function of
empirical research being to guide educational and social reconstruction (Becker,
1967, p. 106.)

5. The concept functions as a sop for the intellectual community itself,

already dangerously alienated (Feuer, 1963, p. 146; McDermott, 1969, p. 35).

6. The return to alienation as an animating social theme gives promise for a revised, humanistic socialism (Fromm[13]).

7. The concept is used as an attempt to scientize radical intellectual dissent (Herberg, 1968).

This list could easily be expanded; certainly, other exponents for these positions could be added. Even as it is, however, the controversial nature of the term is quite apparent. Aside from the motives of the spokesmen or the validity of their positions, part of the controversy is most properly an issue concerned with the philosophy of science and the question of whether value free social science is either possible or desirable.[14]

Sociologists have been concerned with codifying, operationalizing, and inevitably expanding the meaning of the term alienation. As Feuer has noted, the term was used by Engels and Marx with a nearly sexual connotation as an outgrowth of the romantic nuances given to the concept in the German philosophical tradition culminating in the writings of Hegel and Feuerbach. Marx's version, of course, was to conceptualize alienation as a state produced by the ravages of a particular economic system—viz, capitalism—which separated the individual from the products of his labor, from the process of work, from the fellowship of his mankind, and, ultimately, from himself. Both Becker and Feuer have discussed the significance of the replacement of the theme of alienation with that of "class struggle" by an older and more seasoned Marx. Their interpretations are similar, although their conclusions are opposite. They both see this as a selection of a more practical and suitable dynamic to galvanize political and economic change. Both cite the fact that the connections between general social phenomena and specific changes in human behavior were not structurally clarified at that time, while the relationship between the economy and social deprivation was more latently evident. Feuer (1963) describes an older Engels' embarrassment with the themes of his youthful writings concerning the loss of love or personal meaning. He concludes that these themes were not, and still are not, practical for creating social change, and indeed, may lapse into counterproductive, narcissistic languishment.

Becker (1967), on the other hand, sees alienation as a central conceptualization boding for social change if properly listened to and directed.

> The Enlightenment paradox, then, is this: It discovered the problem of alienation, the problem of social constraint on human freedom; but, in order to get agreement by society at large on the problem of social reconstruction, one would

[13] Alienation as a dynamic theme is central and recurrent in all of Fromm's work, although especially in Fromm (1947, 1955, pp. 120-121).

[14] See Seeley (1967b, esp. "articles" 6-24); see also Gouldner (1965). The criticisms of both Gouldner and Friedrichs toward "value free sociology" have recently been reviewed by Simpson (1971).

have to have a compelling theory of how society *causes* alienation. One would
want a cumulative body of knowledge that enlists the support of all men of
good will; and not simply the striking ideology that awakens the frustrations
and passions of large groups of dispossessed people [p. 101].

Arguments concerning the utility of the term will be continued throughout
the book, particularly in those disciplines where alienation is used as a definitive
concept. Other contributions to the structural definitions of alienation will not
be comprehensively traced here; however, five relatively recent analytic schemata
will be mentioned at this point.

The first of these is Seeman's (1959) separation of the concept into five components: (1) powerlessness; (2) meaninglessness; (3) normlessness; (4) isolation; (5)
self estrangement.

Feuer (1963, pp. 137-140) divides the phenomena somewhat differently
listing the following modes: "1) the alienation of class society; 2) the alienation
of competitive society; 3) the alienation of industrial society; 4) the alienation of
man's society; 5) the alienation of race; 6) the alienation of the generations [p. 137]."

Barakat (1969) offers another description of alienation, seeing it as stages instead of a "set of variants." These stages are: "1) sources of alienation at the level of
social and normative structures; 2) alienation as a psychological property of the individual; 3) behavioral consequences of alienation [pp. 3-4]."

Josephson and Josephson, in this volume (see Chapter 7), suggest another
operational analysis of the phenomenon of alienation—namely differentiations between states of alienation versus conditions causing alienation.

Samuel Keen, a philosopher (cited in Manley, 1969), divides the phenomena
into "principles of human society," locating varieties of alienation in those human
activities ("foci") involving speech, promises, work, reproduction, civility, hope for
the future and respect for ecology.

Scott (1965) describes alienation in regard to its sources, seen as a series of
deficiencies: (a) lack of commitment to values, (b) absence of conformity to norms,
(c) loss of responsibility in roles, and (d) deficiency in control of facilities.

And, of course, there are other operational descriptions of the term. The point
here is not to list all of these but to suggest the breadth of possibilities for analyzing
and operationalizing this term. Although there are many areas of overlap detectable
in all of these schemata, there are some stubborn differences and suggested deficiencies. Some of the categories are phenomenal and static (that is, are based on rather
specific human behaviors). Others are based on dynamic changes either directly a-
rising from human behavior or epiphenomenal (as in Marx's notions concerning Capitalism). Furthermore, a number of the above categories leave the psychological dimensions of alienation either barely tacked on, implied, or omitted entirely. This
alone accounts for a good deal of confusion, since, at times, the same terms (normlessness, anomie, meaninglessness) are interchangeably used to describe internal psychological states as well as objective social phenomena.

(That confusions and confounding of this term appear even within a specific discipline in no way disparages either the methods of these disciplines or the persons who have created such apparently dissimilar categories. These confusions instead emanate from the multiplicity of meanings inherent in this term itself. A clarification of these will be made in a section in the next chapter through a semantic analysis of the term.)

## Alienation from the Standpoint of Anthropological Theory and Ethnography

The contributions of anthropologists to the concept and phenomenology of alienation have been less concerned with intricate structural analysis than with the phenomenological aspects of relationships within social organizations. In many ways, anthropology has been concerned with describing factors connected with *de*alienation: kinship patterns, ritual, religion, child rearing practices, cultural traits associated with solidarity, analysis of language as a shared meaning system, cultural identity as a collective force for personal value and social integration. A series of insights into the quality of human relationships have emanated from comparative structural analysis of the evolving levels of human organization: folk-urban (Redfield), Gemeinschaft-Gesellschaft (Toennies), status and contract (Maine), primary and secondary relations (Wirth), primitive-peasant-urban societies (Redfield). Although all of these have implications for alienation, and dealienation, the primitive-urban comparison is particularly fruitful in identifying those mutations in roles which occur in complex societies: diminished personal identity, less comprehensibility of meaning, fewer opportunities for transcendence, and a higher potentiality for isolation, deviance, and madness (Redfield, 1953).

At another level, the documentary evidence furnished through decades of ethnographic work in primitive and complex societies has furnished an empirical substantiation for symbolical action formulations developed by George Herbert Mead. As Becker (1962; and others) have commented, man's connection to himself, to his fellow man, and to his institutions, primarily takes place in a symbolical mode, rather than in a biological, or even psychological mode (in the older, closed-system meaning).[15] At this level, all states of alienation become quests for value, significance, meaning, and transcendence within a symbolical reality. [Becker (1964) therefore analyzes psychological depression not merely as loss of an object, or of the lowered esteem connected with such loss, but a temporary crisis in meaning inherent when objects disappear. Similarly, he analyzes schizophrenia as a condition which ensues when an individual's pretense concerning shared meaning undergoes complete collapse.]

---

[15] Becker (1962) has written an excellent resume of the relationship of anthropology, psychiatry, and symbolical action theory. It will shortly be republished in a revised edition.

As an extension of this, social alienation, from a symbolical standpoint, ensues when the symbol systems of individuals or groups lose significance and power in relation to the prevailing symbolical meanings. The alienating results are, of course, meaninglessness, insignificance, and anomie. It is difficult to imagine how such insights concerning the synthetic (and basically symbolical) quality of individual and collective life could have been generalized and publicized without the detailed, empirical observations of anthropologists.

Another point connecting anthropologists to the phenomenon of dealienation is that even in their methodologies, they have stayed closer to a naturalistic and descriptive focus on complicated human events and shown less tendency to succumb to mathematical, actuarial, or segmentalized research popular (and germane) to other social sciences. As a final contribution, anthropologists have furnished refreshing insights concerning the artificialities and paradoxes of the institutions in which they themselves live and work.

Colleen Johnson, in this volume (see Chapter 8), discusses aspects of social alienation which are apparently mitigated by the preservation of a strong system of family, kin, and friendship relationships within a subculture of Japanese-Americans residing in the United States.

## Economic Perspectives on Alienation

Economic considerations have been implicit in discussions in previous sections concerning history, sociology, and anthropology. Many of the individuals that have been mentioned so far flourished in a cross disciplinary manner during eras before the house of the intellect underwent extensive compartmentalization.

Of the fields so far mentioned, economics seems most detached from dealing with the concept of alienation, although there are significant contributions made from some statesmen within the field concerning relationships of larger institutions to the polity or to the individual citizen. Economics, nevertheless, ordinarily remains quite dissociated from the "gut" issues entertained by theological, psychological, and social disciplines. This is due to a number of factors. For one thing, economics is, in the main, concerned with very concrete facts approached through highly discrete criteria. Most of its doctoral diplomates function in specific practical modes serving industries, governments, corporations, and, of course, institutions of finance. Their activities are highly particularistic—making judgments and advising about quantifiable phenomena: natural resources, capital, real property, labor, products, commodities, services, transportation, markets, etc.

Concerned with a universe of quantitative factors, there is a great reliance on empiricism in seeking evidence to describe almost stoichiometric changes which occur in relation to the fluctuation of specific variables. Theories which attempt to relate broader social or psychological phenomena to fluctuations of an economic

nature are looked on as being political, social, or moral and, hence, not in
the realm of the professional economist. Furthermore, the economist's vision begins to sharpen beyond the factor of $10^6$, a point at which phenomena get
blurry for many of his social scientific colleagues. Dealing in a unitary way with
magnitudes of thousands and millions in itself discourages the use of conceptions
based on immediate social, interactional events. (This is not to suggest that economists are not humanistic, nor that their relative aloofness from certain social conceptions is distinctive. The fields of both law and medicine—much more intimately
connected with treatment of individuals—also have shown relatively little explicit
use of social scientific conceptualizations.)

Because of the nature of the subject matter, their disciplinary work (science)
and the relation of broader social issues to this discipline (social philosophy) are
more readily distinguished from each other. When discussing the latter, economists
(e.g. Galbraith, Slichter, etc.) are more clearly speaking *ex cathedra*.

However, the social implications of economics are, of course, extensive. In
all societies the possession of useful resources, real property, and money is regarded
as desirable, with few exceptions, and is seen as providing a basis for the avoidance
of insignificance, powerlessness, or lack of meaning. Despite the ideological pieties
of Christianity or Socialism, the possession or control of capital, real estate, or objects of value is uniformly connected with security, opportunity, and prestige. The
success with which individuals function as workers, consumers, and users of goods
and services in any society is one measure of their potentiality for averting certain
forms of alienation. The manner in which natural resources are used, selective work
roles rewarded, or capital made available have enormous consequences for individuals and groups within any society. Tussing addresses himself to some of these incongruities inherent in participation in contemporary U. S. economy later in this
volume (see Chapter 11).

## Alienation in Contemporary Education

Within education there are two main ways in which the phenomena of alienation are prominent—first, in the inevitable fact of separation inherent in a procedure which is social and institutional rather than familial, and, second, in regard
to more pathological potentialities for separateness fostered by the numbers of
individuals involved in the process, the intricacies of the institution itself, and in
the character of the procedures designed for learning.

Education, as an institution, is concerned with the provision of substantive
information, the learning of crucial techniques that implement some of this information, the inculcation of consensual historical and cosmological conventions, and,
*sub rosa*, the transmission of salient attitudes and formulae concerning expected
public behavior. The learning of these necessarily constitutes a deliberate alienation. The student is separated from his family and the casual pastimes of his peer

group. While in school he must renounce the relative narcissism available to him when with his family and friends. He must subordinate himself to the contential, technical, and formalized interpersonal phenomena of the classroom.

There are aspects of learning that are purposely (some would argue necessarily) obsessional, schizoidal, and abstractified. The pathologies that attend such an alienating focus are not conventionally seen as constituting a serious problem, particularly among those who are destined to succeed through the mastery of these social and intellectual techniques. Even for those who succeed, however, this inculcates a conditioned process through which they learn to become mindlessly adaptive to abstracted bits that have little or no immediate application for them (e.g., the "universe" of base-ten, *Beowulf,* Ponce de Leon in Florida, grasshopper mouthparts, etc.). The alienating quality of this inculcation—which is accentuated by the sheer masses of individuals undergoing it—while serious for all participants, is especially cruel for those whose social destiny is constricted either because of societal or intrinsic subcultural factors. As numerous commentators have pointed out, education for this group often is simply contact with yet another alienating institution within society which threatens them with ascription of inferiority or maladroitness.

From another standpoint, the potential for alienation among educational professionals, themselves, is quite distinctive.[16] Public educators, at all levels (although particularly in primary and secondary systems), are in the position of having to be directly responsive to an unusual number of other institutions and individuals in their society. They are held responsible for nearly all children: the bright, the slow, the average, children of the affluent, the middle class, and the disadvantaged. They are subject to local government in a direct and intimate way, not only through school boards, but through their dependence on tax monies and other support given by municipal government at the community at large. They are responsible to state and federal governments, and to various credentialing societies at various levels. These credentials are related in a complex and intimate way to financial subsidization, the direction of curriculum, and the maintenance of standards promulgated in explicit ways by these organizations. Moreover, schools function in communities where all kinds of extraneous institutional pressures impinge upon them—civic, religious, commercial, associational. These various pressures inflicted on a school system from its community, agencies, credentialing societies, and organs of government, are, themselves, frequently dissimilar and conflicting. The alienating quality that this imposes on (particularly) public education at the primary and secondary level is that the people in the schools adapt their practices and ideologies to external criteria rather than seeing the conduct

---

[16]These statements concerning alienation in education are derived from a number of well-popularized commentaries on the subject by Paul Goodman. It also includes reflections concerning the structural potentialities for alienation covered in writings by Greene and Reagan which are cited in this volume (see Chapter 15).

of education in their own hands, or in the hands of the colleges of education. Both the teachers and administrators in these systems, therefore, tend to have other-directed and fractionated identities in regard to their professional activities.

Another factor which makes this other-directedness difficult to bear is that the recognition of the role of public educators in the operation of a cultural and social institution (as opposed to an educational institution) was, for a very long time, inexplicit. The idea of inculcating particular cultural themes was originally seen as existing only in parochial schools where explicit moral or theological training accompanied the overt educational procedure. Furthermore, in attempting to serve the diverse cultural institutions in the community and not realizing the enormity of the task, educators frequently become the scapegoats for cultural practices that the rest of society deems offensive. With this other-directed orientation, teachers become almost obsequious in accepting blame for diverse social phenomena (dropouts, irrelevant curriculum, drug abuse, overpermissiveness, the extinction of spontaneity in the young, etc.). Obviously, this is not to suggest that educational institutions should not be strongly criticized, but to point out the ease with which the schools can be made to feel somehow responsible for social and cultural factors that are more plausibly related to other institutions in the society, including, of course, the family. Compounding their other-directedness, teachers within public systems, except at a university level, often feel themselves disconnected in a relative way from prestige and importance in the community, compared to other professionals, entrepreneurs, or executives.

Structurally, the possibilities for alienation exist between the following groups in a number of ways: the teachers, the administration, the students, the credentialing agencies, and the polity. Several ways in which these various potentialities for alienation are currently evident will be treated by Reagan later in this volume (see Chapter 15).

## Alienation from the Standpoint of Political Science

Political science, in being concerned with some of the actual behaviors subsumed under the rubric, alienation (notably powerlessness, normlessness, isolation), often finds no need for description of the metaphenomenal level of alienation. In dealing directly with the issues of power and the corollary, real ways of allocating value, advantage, and opportunity, the questions of estrangement and insignificance are continually raised. The specific manner in which groups of people become ascendant or lapse into powerlessness is of central significance for political scientists. The ways in which elite groups or political minorities attempt to polemicize the issue of separateness or attempt to manipulate the normative order through rhetoric and propaganda is so close to the scientific, analytic work of political scientists that it rarely gets designated as alienation, but, rather, is seen as a series of specific behaviors calculated to achieve certain distinct ends. Because interests in the phenomena of alienation are so specifically fitted to the actual behaviors under purview, the concept of alienation seems to have undergone little strain or concatenation within this discipline as compared to the multiplication of meanings generated within theology, psychology, and sociology. Furthermore, the rhetorical use of "alienation" as political cant is transparently different from the meaning of alienation as a structural analytical term and, therefore, is a source of little or no confusion within the field. As in economics, then, the distinctions between science and social philosophy (or practice, for that matter) are more easily seen than in the fields of theology, psychology, anthropology, and sociology.

Stephen Koff's presentation of this subject within this volume is concerned with a historical review of the term, focusing on some processes which occur in response to political alienation.

## Alienation in Modern Literature

The cybernetic nature of the relation between culture and popular art has long been a matter of trite understanding. In the past quarter of a century, the burgeoning of mass communication and the merchandising of various art forms have worked on this dynamism to produce an even more intimate reciprocity between the general society and its artistic products.

In modern American literature, the heroes and themes, along with the stylistic conventions in which these are presented, are detectably more manifold and representative than in the past. Heroes and heroines are drawn from all classes, occupations, races, and even genders (suggesting, obviously, that life is epic in all persons). Correspondingly, themes are more comprehensive, and there are few detectable restraints regarding the presentation of diverse human actions in direct and concrete ways. Criteria for publishable literary styles have also expanded considerably. The combined effect of these changes in style and content, as well as developments in communication and marketing, have given rise to artistic products which are, at once, more diverse, representative, and available. In terms of the themes themselves, there is, of course, nothing novel about the presentation of loneliness, rejection, or normlessness. These have always been the stuff of literature, drama, and the arts. Certainly the portrayal of alienation is not new, although its forms have clearly been broadened since the turn of the century (Taviss, 1969).

This change in focus of alienation themes (from Divine to Human) parallels the secularization of the concept of alienation imparted following the Enlightenment. Doctor Faust, within the older sense of alienation, sought meaning through an illicit, transcendental connection, just as Melville's Ahab searched for revenge and reunion with an abstract absolute. Not so, however, with Kafka's heroes. Abetted not only by the intellectual climate following Rousseau, but more immediately from the felt insignificance of his own life (as disappointed son and lover, faceless insurance executive), Kafka documents the remoteness of the individual's relationship to intransigent bureaucracies, governments, and family (Greenberg, 1966). In both European and American literature, transcendental symbolical themes have given way to a depiction of the ever present potential for injustice, meaninglessness, and violence present in persons and society, rather than in the cosmological order.

As one might expect, the alienated heroes in American fiction and drama portray some distinctively American (cultural) responses to finding themselves alienated. Threatened with defeat these heroes react with offensive, expressive, and aggressive maneuvers. The characters of Kafka and Camus, by contrast, seem more resigned to being inexorably trapped and overpowered by the world. Their cavil against the inanity and meaninglessness of society is almost totally subjective—mental, often, not even verbal. Perhaps most dishearteningly, their reaction to increasing stupidity, injustice, and mischance is to define this progressive loss of meaning, itself, as being meaningful.[17]

As Gelfant points out in this volume (see Chapter 13), the Road Novel has acquired special significance in American fiction by using the themes of motion as an antidote to alienating conditions. Other kinds of active solutions are also evident. Some American authors seem to be saying that even if you are alienated you will be o.k. as long as you do something. "Something" has certainly included copulation. An abundant description of frantic sexuality is available (solo, tandem, group), simultaneously portraying meaninglessness and, apparently, a temporary escape from it. "Something" has also included the use of a great variety of drugs and intoxicants by characters in current novels, dramas, and films. While the escapistic use of intoxicants is in no way distinctively American, the frequency with which such themes appear (among the poor, the affluent, the radical, the bored), and the great variety of agents used, testify to a singularly American preoccupation with this species of escape.

Again, it is not merely the existence of these themes, styles, and heroes within American literature, but the availability and marketability of the novels and their ubiquitous merchandising (in drug stores, airports, supermarkets, even vending machines) which establish a more intimate and dynamic relationship between art and the normative opinions and subsequent actions of the reading and viewing public.

## SUMMARY

This introduction has been concerned with sketching the meanings of the word, alienation, as concept and term, as they appear in the disciplines of theology,

---

[17] Knoff (1969) examines Mersault's resignation as an *active* process of resolution when he is faced with the inanities of human existence. Knoff's point is that meaninglessness is (partly) sought after rather than passively accepted. This interpretation is crucial and will be dealt with later in this volume (see Chapter 18).

philosophy, history, psychiatry, sociology, anthropology, economics, political science, education, and literature. An attempt has been made to describe some of the traditional issues within each of these disciplines which are illuminated by the concept, as well as to suggest contemporary manifestations of alienation falling within their purview.

It has been obvious from this presentation that these various fields are not e-qually or similarly concerned with the concept of alienation. Position statements have been listed which indicate the nature of some of the controversy concerning the meaning and importance of this elusive concept. The importance of alienation as a concept, term, and cultural motif has been established here by way of annotating its diverse uses in these many fields. More rigorous arguments concerning the usefulness of the concept of alienation will be presented in subsequent chapters.

## REFERENCES

Adelson, J. What generation gap? *New York Times Magazine,* 1970, January 18, 10 ff.

Barakat, H. Alienation: A process of encounter between utopia and reality. *British Journal of Sociology,* 1969, *20,* 1-10.

Barrett, W. *Irrational man: A study in existential philosophy.* Garden City, N. Y.: Doubleday, 1962.

Becker, E. *The birth and death of meaning.* Glencoe, Ill.: Free Press, 1962. Chs. III & VIII.

Becker, E. *The revolution in psychiatry.* Glencoe, Ill: Free Press, 1964. Chs. II, III, & IV.

Becker, E. Beyond alienation. New York: Braziller, 1967.

Covert, C. Freud on the front page. Working paper, Newhouse School of Journalism, Syracuse University, 1970.

Eisenstadt, S. N. *From generation to generation.* Glencoe, Ill.: Free Press, 1956.

Feuer, L. What is alienation? The career of a concept. In M. Stein & A. Vidich (Eds.), *Sociology on trial.* Englewood Cliffs, N. J.: Prentice-Hall, 1963.

*Fortune Magazine,* (entire issue) A special issue on American youth, 1969, January.

Fromm, E. *Man for himself.* New York: Holt, 1947. Ch. V.

Fromm, E. *The sane society.* New York: Holt, 1955.

Gouldner, A. W. Anti-Minotaur: The myth of a value-free sociology. In I. Horowitz (Ed.), *The new sociology.* New York: Oxford University Press, 1965. Pp. 196-218.

Greenberg, M. It's a Kafkaesque world. *New York Times Review of Books,* 1966, May 29, 12 ff.

Hardin, G. Meaningless of the word protoplasm. *Scientific Monthly,* 1956, *82,* 112-120.

Herberg, W. Alienation, "dissent," and the intellectual. *National Review,* 1968, July 30, 738-739.

Kaufman, W. Introduction. In R. Schacht, *Alienation.* Garden City, N. Y.: Doubleday, 1970.

Knoff, W. A psychiatrist reads Camus' "The Stranger." *Psychiatric Opinion,* 1969, *6,* 19-25.

Leifer, R. *In the name of mental health.* New York: Science House, 1969. Pp. 158-165.

Lorenz, K. The enmity between generations and its probable ethological causes. *Psychoanalytic Review,* 1970, 57, 333-337.

McDermott, J. Technology: The opiate of the intellectuals. *New York Review of Books,* 1969, *XIII* (July 31), 25-35.

Mannheim, K. The problem of generations. *Psychoanalytic Review,* 1970, *57,* 383-384. (Reprinted from *Essays on the sociology of knowledge.* New York: Oxford University Press, 1952.)

Manley, J. C. *Report of the fifth East-West philosopher's conference.* Honolulu: Department of Philosophy, University of Hawaii, 1969. Pp. 390-392.

Mesthene, E. *Program on technology and society: Fourth annual report 1967-8.* Cambridge, Mass.: Harvard University, 1969.

Nelson, B. (Ed.) *Freud and the 20th century.* New York: World Publ. Co., 1957.

Nelson, B. The analyst as mediator and double-agent. *Psychoanalytic Review,* 1965, *53,* 375-390.

*Program on technology and society: Fifth annual report 1968-9.* Cambridge, Mass.: Harvard University, 1970.

*Program on technology and society: A final review,* Cambridge, Mass.: Harvard University, 1972.

*Psychoanalytic Review,* 1970, Vol. 57, No. 3.

Redfield, R. *The primitive world and its transformations.* Ithaca, N. Y.: Cornell University Press, 1953.

Schacht, R. *Alienation.* Garden City, N. Y.: Doubleday, 1970.

Scott, M. B. The social sources of alienation. In I. Horowitz (Ed.), *The new sociology.* New York: Oxford University Press, 1965. Pp. 239-252.

Seeley, J. R. *The Americanization of the unconscious.* New York: Lippincott, 1967. (a)

Seeley, J. R. Thirty-nine articles toward a theory of social theory. In K. Wolff & B. Moore (Eds.), *The critical spirit.* Boston: Beacon Press, 1967. Pp. 150-171. (b)

Seeman, M. On the meaning of alienation. *American Sociological Review,* 1959, *24,* 786.

Simpson, R. L. System and humanism in social science. (Book Reivews) *Science,* 1971, May 14, 661-664.

Szasz, T. The classification of "mental illness." *Psychiatric Quarterly,* 1959, *33,* 77-101.

Taviss, I. Changes in the form of alienation: The 1900's vs. the 1950's. *American Sociological Review,* 1969, *34,* 46-57.

Yankelovich, D. *CBS Report: The generation gap,* 1969, May & June.

# Chapter 1

# Alienation: Concept, Term, and Word

## Frank Johnson
State University of New York

## DEFINITIONS

In the Introduction, the etymology of the term alienation was reviewed, in some of its historical and contemporary connections, in a number of disciplines. This present chapter is a continuation of the examination of the concept. Alienation will here be described more analytically in terms of its various specific meanings, structural characteristics, and operational applications. The inevitable inconsistencies present in these various usages will also be elucidated. Finally, a more detailed description of the uses of the term in psychiatry and the social sciences will be presented, along with a consideration of those factors held either to account for or to occur in conjunction with processes and states of alienation.

The implications of the banal overgeneralizations connected with the term have been confronted in the Introduction under a discussion of the use of the word as a panchreston. As noted there, panchreston is Hardin's (1956) word for any scientific concept which, in attempting to explain all, explains nothing. Another characteristic of panchrestons—their unusual capacity to communicate feeling—is easily met by the word alienation. Especially in its use as a vogue or "fetish" word, alienation is capable of conveying more feeling than denotation. The various emotional components present in its connotations will be analyzed in this chapter.

Before discussing this, however, it is worthwhile to review one other confusion inherent in the etymology of alienation—namely, the problems that are encountered when a word is used variously as a concept, as a scientific term, as a specific construct, and as a popular expression. In some fields (e.g., theology, philosophy, psychiatry) the word alienation is used as a concept denoting the element of separation of two entities, with resulting tension and frustration. These same disciplines, however, may, under other circumstances, employ the word alienation as a specific scientific term suggesting rather special aspects of separation. For example, alienation in theology may be used to signify a sense of separated existence either from a Creator or from other existences. Similarly, its use in sociology (as a general scientific term) might be to define the separation of the individual from aspects of his personal or material environment.

In these same fields, however, the word alienation may be used more as a delimited, theoretical construct depicting salient and specific aspects of behavior which are artificially separated by design, definition, and methodology from other phenomena of alienation.[1] For example, schizoid personality may be established as a symptom cluster consisting of exaggerated shyness, autistic thinking, heightened self-concern, emotional withdrawal, and other symptoms related to psychological estrangement. Focusing on these temporarily sets aside a consideration of social factors which, of course, may or may not be related to the concept of schizoid personality.

Finally, the word alienation enjoys a great popularity in colloquial conversation as a vogue or fetish word where its meanings are not specifically restrained. Reference to alienation in literature and in the news media, for example, often falls into this category. For that matter, social philosophers, politicians, and educators often use alienation in a way that seems designed more to convey passion than to suggest specific meaning. In this latter usage, the word is clearly a panchreston (Hardin, 1956) and, while capable of carrying a great deal of feeling, manages to *do* this in an inexplicit, perplexing, and deeply annoying way.

---

[1] The term *construct* is used here as Rapoport (1953) describes it: that is, "a term which can be defined by operations on symbols alone, for example, mathematic entities [p. 266, 238]." The distinction between "observational" terms and "symbolical" terms is also discussed by Kaplan (1964). He distinguishes between scientific terms on the basis of the phenomena studied, the mode of analysis used, the character of observation, and the logical relation of the term to the phenomena it depicts. Concerning *construct* he describes: "Hence these terms are sometimes called 'explanatory terms' (as contrasted with the 'descriptive' ones), or 'hypothetical constructs' in recognition of the ideational (as contrasted with the empirical) component in all theory formation [pp. 56-58]."

## Definitions: Denotative and Connotative

It is interesting that the definitions of alienation available in the major unabridged dictionaries fail to suggest the richness and confusion inherent in its etymology. They, first, denote alienation as a "conveyance of property to another party, second, relate the term to the "estrangement of a person" (or of his affections), and, third, define it as "mental derangement" (*Webster's*, 1968).[2] In the *Dictionary of Social Sciences*, Kurt Lang defines alienation as "an estrangement or separation between parts or the whole of the personality and significant aspects of the world of experience." He describes the term in its references to (1) objective states, (2) states of feeling accompanying alienation, and (3) "motivational states tending toward estrangement." In these latter states (3), separation is possible between self and the objective world, self and factors within the self, and, finally, between self and (total) self (Lang, 1964).

In *The International Encyclopedia of Social Sciences*, Lichtheim (1968) has described the concept of alienation as a basic ontological theme in Western culture stemming from a Neoplatonic doctrine of emanation. Through this doctrine, finite, existent beings are depicted as creations springing from some ultimate source. He traces the fusion of this concept with early Christian interpretations of Creation. These connections are complex and need not concern us here. The effect of these doctrines of creation (emanation) has been to emphasize the discrete, finite nature of all forms of creation. An immediate implication of such discreteness is of course, separateness.

In an excellent historical review of the concept of alienation, Schacht (1970) has listed the various meanings of this "separateness" in the philosophical writings of Hobbes, Rousseau, Fichte, Schiller, and, most importantly, Hegel. In *The Phenomenology of Spirit*, Hegel's use of the word alienation (*Entfremdung*) is analyzed by Schacht (1970, pp. 7-60) as being used in two distinct ways. According to Schacht, Hegel's first use of alienation is connected with the notion of "becoming alien." This is similar to its popular, contemporary meaning and refers to the state or process through which an individual becomes separated, in various degrees, from the social reality (Hegel's "social substance"). This conception would suggest that all individuals are only partly aware of the social reality, and participate only fractionally with other objects in the social universe. Hence, in this sense all humans are, at least, partly estranged and alien. Corollary to this meaning is the recognition of frustration and discord in the realization of the discrepancy between the actual condition of the individual, and those broader potentialities which are latent in his essential nature.

[2] The word alienation has some specialized uses which are so delimited that they do not bear on its current social and psychological meanings. For example, alienation is used in statistics to describe the appearance of separated clusters of data.

Again, according to Schacht (1970), the second meaning of *Entfremdung* that Hegel intends is the more active condition of "making alien." Alienation, in this sense, is a deliberate "surrender or transfer of a right to another," and is connected to a more hostile, inimical, and deliberate separation of individuals from parts of the social substance (including, possibly, their own essences).

Against this background, Schacht sees Marx's use of the concept of self-alienation as remiss, insofar as Marx did not always distinguish between these two meanings, that is, between aspects of ubiquitous separation versus enforced surrender. Schacht (1970) illustrates this in the following way:

> Because this syndrome (i.e. of alienation) comprehends very different relations, however, the use of the term "alienation" to designate all of these severely limits its descriptive content. My relation to my product is one thing; my relation to other men is another; and the degree of correspondence of my actual condition to my essential nature is yet another. Since the term "alienation" is employed in connection with all three (and others besides), and since they share little more than a common origin and the idea of separation, it cannot convey anything very specific [p. 112].

Schacht's (1970) criticism of Marx's use of the term applies equally to the contemporary uses of alienation as a scientific concept, when distinctions in these various basic denotations are either confused or ignored. This can be illustrated by listing three basic, contemporary meanings.[3]

### Alienation as Separation

This describes those processes or states of alienation devolving from the (inevitable, ontological) separation of two or more entities. Along with separation, the notion of a tension existing within or between these entities is integral in this denotation. (As Schacht (1970) points out, this meaning is in Hegel's notion of the universal sense of "becoming alienated.")

### Alienation as Transfer

When alienation is connected to deliberate (contractual) renunciation or relinquishment, a significantly different meaning is suggested. This is closer to the historic English meaning of alienation as transfer (or expropriation) of property or of rights belonging to an individual, which are either renounced or given over to others. Although tension may accompany such alienation, feelings of anger or resignation would more usually be connected with these surrenders.

### Alienation as Objectivity

This meaning depicts alienation as being aroused by the basic, subjective "awareness of others." Here, man's capacity to perceive "the other" as discrete

---

[3] My listing of three contemporary meanings of alienation is derived from Schacht's analysis of the term.

from himself (irrespective of the quality of relation to the other) is identified as
alienation. The affective concomitants of this condition are mainly those of loneliness and isolation, rather than tension or frustration.[4]

In much current writing and speech, distinctions often are not made between
these three meanings (with their separate denotations and altogether varying emotions). The result is that statements using the word alienation are at once ambiguous (since they ignore these distinctions) and emotionally powerful (because they
carry along the orchestration from these diverse, emotional connotations). Being
exposed to this very common, inexplicit use of alienation, the reader is stirred and
aroused but, given a moment of reflection, perplexed and hard put to account for
his feelings.

The various shades of meaning connected with this term are broad, inconsistent, and paradoxical. Parallel to the inconsistencies in denotative aspects of the
etymology of alienation, those affects which are part of its meaning range from
positive to negative, joyous to despondent, festive to pessimistic. (These polarities
will be examined shortly.) Although admitting these broad polarities, it is the author's opinion that the word is usually accompanied by *negative* affects (pessimism,
despair, hostility) presented in situations where the individual is the recipient of
alienating conditions pressed on him either by relentless social circumstances or by
the hostile acts of specific forces.

These predominantly negative connotations of the word are also inherent in
the English language meaning of its stem, alien. As noted by Brinkman (1930),
the word alien has been used since antiquity to define foreign groups of people,
usually in a hypercritical, pejorative way. Generally, the word is applied to groups
with allegedly inferior status, significance, and cultural achievement, for example,
"barbarians," "savages," "gentiles [pp. 633-634] ."

Also, in the more archaic denotation of alienation as loss of affections or
transfer of property, the negative connotations again predominate. Vance (1930)
has traced the development of the concept of what was alienable versus what was
inalienable (or unremovable) in English law. Alienable things consisted of property,
chattel, or real estate which was potentially separable from a person or persons,
either voluntarily, through an act of transfer or sale, or involuntarily, through being claimed or expropriated by others. Conversely, those things which were inalienable were objects which could not be divested from individuals or groups. Vance
recalls the distinction between property ownership in primitive and contemporary
societies. In primitive societies, many objects and properties were not private. Things
were owned by the group, could not be separated from the group, and were passed
on in a communal way to successors in the same society. In primitive societies, goods

---

[4] This serial arrangement of connotations presented here is on the basis of an approxi-
mated frequency of occurrence in usage (in the author's opinion). The term alienation could
also be logically categorized into "neutral," "positive," and "negative" loadings for all *three*
of the catigories I have listed ("separation," "transfer," and "objectivity"). This would highlight other interrelationships—notably the similarity between "objective" and (neutral) "separation."

and products were, of course, limited. As societies become more complex, the emphasis on individual possession increased simultaneously with the increase in the number of commodities, products, and services available. Correspondingly, the concept of what was hypothetically alienable became expanded. Here again, the concept is connected to the invidious aspects of separation from property (or loss of affections). The emotive connotations in these situations is clearly negative and hostile, connected to the threat of being forcibly separated from property or affection (recall the use of "inalienable rights" in the *Declaration of Independence*).

This is cited here to suggest that regardless of the etymological, good-bad bipolarity of the term alienation, the connotations usually are those of a hostile separation, rather than a benign, optional loss. Alienation of property also contributes to the contemporary meaning underlying states of alienation by way of the diminution in personal significance inherent in mass society where individuals may be considered to be units or things. As "things" they can more easily be expended, exchanged, or transferred. They are more readily conceptualized as having actuarial rather than existential selves. They are more potentially negotiable, as if they were property (or factors) rather than real people.

At any rate, negative affects seem to predominate in the current meanings of alienation. In the meaning of alienation as basic "separation of two entities accompanied by tension" (cited before), it is difficult to ignore the frustration theme which accompanies the recognition of such separation. Of course, one can find instances where separation and isolation lead to integrity, creativity, and serenity. Yet, the connotation of "tension regarding separation," is not usually connected with these conditions. Hence, the condition of alienation is rather inaccurately attributed to such states. These latter states of voluntary isolation and creative eccentricity are much closer to the notion of Romanticism than to alienation. The notion of separation is, of course, inherent in Romanticism, but separation is usually associated with suspense, rather than tension. Although frustration is common to both conditions, Romanticism emphasizes the notion of a constant unfulfilled "becoming" (or lessening of the separation). Furthermore, the Romantic is separated from the complete fruition of his personal destiny, but enjoys this state. The tension concerning his real or potential separateness is dealt with more positively. Although the condition of separation is similar, the Romantic appears considerably nearer to connecting with other things: he almost finds eternal truth, he might have married Roxanne, he continues to search for the Holy Grail. The popular versions of the subjective experiences of the Romantic differ, therefore, from the cogitations of the alienated. In the latter, the distances between the two entities are ordinarily very great, and the tension between the separated parties takes on a quality of despair and pessimism over an apparently unbridgeable disconnectedness.

The connotations connected with alienation as surrender and resignation are very difficult to rationalize as positive. Of course, there are occasions when complying with superior forces involves a peaceful acceptance of the inevitable (or even may imply an unconsciously desired capitulation). Usually, however, the etymology of surrender is closely connected to the notion of defeat. Resignation, similarly, clearly connotes a regret in connection with being divested of a previous, desirable state. It certainly does not convey much of a positive emotional condition.

In the third basic meaning of alienation, (the awareness of "the other") such a recognition is often of a negative character. For example, it requires a bit of imagination to detect much cheer in the "encounter with Nothingness." Most of the scholarly and social philosophic literature on "being alone in the world" emphasizes the negative, lonely, and tortuous aspects of trying to connect with others, attempting to integrate with a believable reality, or to find some kind of peaceful communion. Finally, the use of alienation as a neutral term connoting objectification or a basic "spirit of inquiry" (see Kaufman, 1970) is quite exceptional. Admittedly, in this use the term is relatively devoid of emotional connotation. The word is rarely used in this sense, however.[5]

One must also look at the subtle, negative connotations associated with the use of the concept in sociology. Successful attempts to keep the concept of alienation neutral or free of any polemical implication appear only occasionally. Even when the term is used as a delimited hypothetical construct, it is hard to dissociate the moral, hypercritical, and pejorative implications of alienation. For example, it is challenging to try to conceive of instances where powerlessness, meaninglessness, or normlessness might be desirable. (Of course, there could be instances where this might be so, but one wonders how often, and for how many individuals?) It seems obvious that it is mostly disadvantageous to lack significance in one's political and personal connections. Pretending that the term is neutral may, therefore, be quite illusory and (unintentionally) dishonest.

In calling attention to the bipolarity of the term alienation Schacht (1970) notes that a number of commentators (Kaufman, Keniston, Feuer, Fromm, Horney, etc.) have accentuated the negative, invidious connotations of various states of alienation. He discounts this partly, however, pointing out that, after all, the word can be used to describe more creative states of estrangement. He also analyzes the differences inherent in the meaning of alienation in terms of whether the condition being described is one of falling from an actually achieved ideal state or is merely the absence of an idealized existence. He has examined the work of Fromm and Horney in respect to this differentiation (Schacht, 1970, pp. 115-152). This distinction is, of course, important, but seems insignificant when the term is exces-

---

[5] In addition to relating the concept of alienation to its philosophical sources, Kaufman (1970) discusses the relationship of the concept to contemporary culture and literature. Although Schacht (1970) discusses the implications of the popularization of the term alienation, the body of his book is devoted to a careful examination of the specific philosophical connections of the term. His statement concerning the neutrality of the term when used in sociology takes sociologist's statements at face value and, hence, is less critical.

sively cast in the framework of an estrangement from a desirable objective, whether held previously or never attained before. To repeat, alienation is usually used to describe the failure to find certain propitious circumstances which the individual feels should be available to him. It is the absence of certain events in the life of persons or groups that ought to be encountered. Therefore, even though the term permits a variety of meanings, it seems that the overwhelming, emotional connotations of the term are negative, depicting frustrated and hostile separation from various desirable (and deserved) ends.

Similarly, the use of the term alienation in psychiatry is hardly value-free. The implications of the uses of the concept in psychiatry are complex and will be discussed later. It will suffice here to note that, again, the terminology is almost uniformly pessimistic—"inauthenticity," "autism," "existential anxiety," "ontological insecurity," etc. These comments on the negative connotations of the term are not stressed here to suggest that all forms of self-alienation are inevitably negative. Furthermore, it is obvious that investigators can account for these negative implications either through their methodology (where these affects, themselves, might be studied) or through a sophisticated interpretation of their findings. However, it should be acknowledged that the predominant connotational concommitants of alienation are hostile and negative. Attempts to ignore this run the risk of fulfilling Feuer's (1963) and McDermott's (1969) observations—namely, that some current research is unconsciously endorsing the very system it purports to investigate.[6]

## INCONSISTENCIES IN THE TERM
## (ETYMOLOGIC, SEMANTIC, AND STRUCTURAL)

The inconsistencies in the word alienation will be reviewed here in terms of the etymological, structural, and empirical applications.

### Confusions Inherent in the Etymology of the Word Alienation

Although the basic meanings of separation and tension persist in the many usages of alienation, there is an exasperating ambiguity that is connected with the severe bipolarity to which the term accommodates. This ambiguity is further compounded by the capacity of the term to switch its polarity depending on the context in which it is employed. For example, its explicit usage as an active transitive verb ("one person alienates another") is clearly eclipsed by its use in passive con-

---

[6] The observations of Feuer (1963) and McDermott (1969), and others concerning the complicity of social scientists in perpetuating the theme of alienation are covered in the Introduction.

structions ("something or someone is alienated," or "is being alienated"). Here again, the contrast with Romanticism is suggested where the state of tension between the hero and his remote object reflects the estranged individual's passionate attempts to approach the remote object. Quite differently, in his state of alienation, the hero is generally passive and unstriving, having accepted the inevitability of being cut off by overpowering, external forces. This distinction, however, is not consistent, as a review of the various bipolarities of the term will reveal.

Some of the following polar categories obviously overlap, but are listed separately here since the particular connotations of some of these bipolarities deserve to be separately examined. Israel (1971) distinguishes between the "ambiguity" and "vagueness" of the term alienation. He quite correctly shows ambiguity as being "defined as (logically) accidental identity of words standing for different ideas." In contrast, he notes "vagueness" as connected with an uncertainty which "cannot be removed by appealing either to (further) facts about the case or to existing *criteria* for the application of the concept."[7] I have selected the more operationally oriented word, "inconsistency," to describe some of these same conflicting meanings.

### Inconsistencies Inherent in Individual versus Collective Meanings of Alienation

The state of alienation can, of course, be applied to specific individuals, as well as to groups of individuals. There is a difference in meaning between these two applications that is not merely the difference between singular and plural categories. The phenomenology and the meaning connected with individual states of alienation are different both in quality and significance from those connected with the social, interactional, and collective applications of the term. The statement that "all blacks are alienated" prompts different imagery and connotations than the statement "a particular black person is alienated." The statement "all blacks are alienated" is hardly very precise, although it does call to mind relatively specific social conditions (e.g. deficiencies in prestige, power, opportunity), and the feeling states that plausibly accompany such conditions (anger, resignation, futility). However, the statement that "a particular black person is alienated" is more deeply perplexing. There are two ways in which this statement may be construed. It can suggest that the experience and behavior of a specific black person is an instance of the collective experience of black alienation (which would call to mind the social conditions and affects described above). This statement might just as conceivably intend to say that a particular black person is alienated in terms of his personal life, as if his alienation is connected with his own particular social relationships irrespective of the experiences of other blacks.

[7] Israel's (1971) examination of the term centers on the sociologically oriented analyses of the term alienation. His conclusions concerning the contemporary use of the term will be presented in Chapter 18.

As vague as each of these statements may be in communicating explicit aspects of the state of alienation, one could hardly fault the usage in either instance for failing to communicate a feeling concerning the process. Both statements suggest depression, discontent, discomfort, etc.

### Inconsistencies in Regard to Objective and Subjective Frames of Reference

This is similar to, but slightly different from the polarity of the "individual versus collective" meanings.

Alienation may refer to objective social conditions, directly observed by others, and ascribed to individuals or groups (in terms of separation from crucial experiences or persons). However, the term may just as readily be employed to describe two rather different subjective states, the first being states of self-alienation inferred to be present by outside observers. Second, by contrast, it may also refer to subjective states of alienation not detectable to outsiders, but felt by the person himself.

Because of the comprehensive generic meaning of the term alienation, distinctions between subjective and objective, even when established, often do not hold. This, alone, accounts for the fact that most structural classifications of alienation include both frames of reference simply out of the necessity of acknowledging that the meanings in objective situations may potentially shift to subjective frames of reference. For example, one may objectively establish "powerlessness" in relation to a minority group's incapacity to participate in an electoral process. This may be illustrated in regard to the issues of a campaign, control of communications media, characteristics of political organizations, etc. It is very difficult, however, to hold the analysis at this objective level. Whenever the question of attitude or feelings about the state of being powerless is introduced, it is hard to ignore the attendant emotions of apathy, chagrin, or hostility. Furthermore, although these emotional attitudes may themselves be surveyed within the study sample, a question about the meaning of such feelings, in terms of specific individuals in the sample, may be raised, either in terms of criticism or in quest of substantiation. Such potential slippage of meaning may in no way reflect directly on the methodology or workmanship of the investigator, but, rather, is intrinsic in the ambiguity of the concept of alienation. Feuer (1963) illustrates this in a criticism of some of Seeman's work:

> Seeman, for instance, gives an operational definition of "meaninglessness;" it is a mode of alienation which is characterized by lower expectancies that satisfactory predictions about future outcomes of behavior can be made; the person senses that his ability to predict behavior outcomes is low. But, contrary to Seeman's standpoint, a great deal of contemporary thought finds a state of alienation precisely in those ideologies which profess to predict with high confidence the outcome of people's behavior [p. 140].

Note the switch from "objective" meaninglessness intended by Seeman to Feuer's (1963) speculation about "the person," followed by his (Feuer's) contrary statement concerning social aleination. In noting this, I am not critically examining either Seeman's or Feuer's logic, but illustrating some results inherent in the bipolarity of the word, alienation.[8]

## Inconsistencies in Unilateral versus Bilateral Meanings

Given that separation of two entities has taken place, the directionality of the subsequent tension (or of the original cause of separation) is in no way clearly indicated by the term alienation. As pointed out in the distinction between the quality of estrangement in romantic separation and alienation, alienation, generally, has the connotation of separation occurring as a result of oppressive external conditions imposing themselves on the individual or group. Any situation of separation, however, is reciprocal. Individuals or groups may in some way be implicated in either their inability to prevent alienation, or in their conformity to alienating conditions.

Obviously, the meaning of separation that is bilaterally agreed upon, and enacted mutually, is qualitatively different from the meaning of conditions of alienation that are contrived and carried out unilaterally. Many descriptions of alienation simply do not clarify this polarity. This produces two kinds of confusion. First, if these bilaterally different, and often opposite, meanings are not explicated, then they are merely left vague. Second, if the bilateral meanings are clarified, the reader has, then, to tolerate the ambiguity of two separate and conflicting meanings of alienation inherent in what is suggested to be a unitary phenomenon.

## Inconsistencies in Real versus Potential States of Alienation

There are qualitative differences between establishing that certain states actually constitute alienation and the depicting of certain potential states of alienation. This vagueness may more often be encountered in colloquial rather than scholarly usage of the term. The difference, however, between incipient and real conditions of alienation is significant. Potential or almost separated states are closer to the notion of romantic estrangement. Using the expression in this way stretches the meaning of an already vague term to include potentially alienating situations which, strictly speaking, do not qualify as states of alienation.

## Inconsistencies in Volitional and Nonvolitional Meanings

Alienation can be viewed as a condition of separation of two entities produced by a series of actions performed by one or both parties, either deliberately

---

[8] Part of both Seeman's and Feuer's position on the concept of alienation is presented elsewhere in this volume. Seeman's operational "modes of alienation" do not evade the potential for ambiguity unless stringently defined and interpreted. His own awareness of this is evident in his work (Seeman, 1969).

or unintentionally. Alienation, therefore, can be seen as a result of a series of deliberate actions which result in eventual separation. On the other hand, states of alienation may occur where none of the participants directly intended such consequences, and the separation is incidental, or secondary to other actions enjoined by one or both parties involved in the separation.[9]

### Inconsistency between Conscious and Unconscious Meanings

In its comprehensiveness, the term alienation readily accommodates to states of separation in which both parties are consciously aware of separateness (and, perhaps, similarly aware of the actions and events leading to this state). It also can refer to conditions in which the separateness is not accompanied by awareness on the part of one or both parties depicted in a particular state of alienation. Ordinarily, an element of consciousness is an important characteristic of the experience of alienation both in individual and collective instances. However, alienation is frequently depicted as occurring in individuals or groups who are either unaware of the fact of separation (powerlessness, meaninglessness) or, if aware, are apparently oblivious of the significance. It is more than a mere etymological curiosity that this word can simultaneously accommodate to conscious and unconscious states of alienation. The implications of consciousness concerning separation (either in group or individual situations) suggest important differences in the qualitative nature of different states of alienation, as well as differences in the motives of the participants.[10]

### Inconsistencies in "Good" and "Bad" Meanings

As one would expect, the moral and ethical connotations of a term so viable in theology and philosophy, continue, in a very explicit way, to categorize and ethocize the qualities of various states of alienation. It is difficult to find much literature concerning alienation in which the good-bad qualities are explicitly accounted for. Even when explicated, the good-bad polarity, like several of these already listed, remains exceedingly shifty and ambiguous in application. For example, one can easily find support for the statement that a degree of alienation for intellectuals, artists, poets, and prophets is central to their function, and therefore "good." It is not good, however, for corporation executives, politicians, or even ordinary people in the society to be alienated.

[9] Mizruchi (1964) has discussed confusions stemming from the implicit bipolar nature of the term in regard to motive and intentionality.

[10] The two bipolar categories, "volitional versus nonvolitional," and "conscious versus unconscious" may superficially seem to be the same, but they are not. "Unconscious" suggests much more than unconsciousness of a (specific) motive or intention. "Unconsciousness" (and "consciousness") are therefore much broader terms than "volitional" and "nonvolitional" as they are used here. Also, "unconsciousness" in the contexts here, is not equivalent to "false consciousness" (Marx) or to the "System Unconscious" (Freud).

However, it is not difficult to find instances in which the intellectuals' or artists' separation from real experience can be counterproductive for both the individuals and society. Similarly, it is not difficult to find examples of politicians or ordinary individuals who defied the expedient and normative to stand by personal convictions, and later were exonerated for their "idiosyncrasies."

Also, the moral bipolarity of the term alienation may be ambiguous even when it refers to a specific, static instance. One might consider the case of alienation of a subcultural minority due to different linguistic, educational, physical, or other features. These peculiarities can be viewed as "bad" insofar as they may lead to an almost reflexive exclusion by members of the dominant culture. However, they may be simultaneously viewed as "good" insofar as they substantiate personal identity within the subculture.

At any rate, irrespective of its potential ethical bipolarity, the condition of alienation is overwhelmingly connected with "badness," in spite of efforts either to neutralize the concept or cite an occasional positive connotation.

## INCONSISTENCIES IN THE MEANING OF THE TERM DUE TO DIFFERENT STRUCTURAL CONTEXTS

In addition to the vagueness and ambiguity inherent in the bipolar nature of the term, the structural ambiguity of the term (already mentioned in several connections) compounds the inconsistency in meanings because of dissimilar applications. For example, the term alienation currently can be applied to relationships between the following entities.

### The Relationship of Self to Factors of Self

This refers to a closed system approach and describes the relation of the overall person (personality, self, or ego) to components of his own experiential or psychological being (cognition, feeling, memories, etc.)

### The Relationship of Self to Self

This is essentially an open-system psychological approach where the person relates to himself as another social object in a universe of social objects.

### The Relationship of Self to Environment

Here alienation is depicted in terms of the relationship of a person to other persons and objects in his environment (including social institutions, the physical environment, bodies of knowledge, etc.).

## The Relationship of Groups to Individuals or Other Groups

The possibilities for the relatedness or unrelatedness of groups is structurally as complex as those listed for "selves." Alienation can, therefore, occur in the following conditions: (1) group to part of group; (2) group (in its entirety) separated from itself as a social or historical entity; and (3) group separated from other groups, from individuals, or from aspects of the symbolical or physical world.

From a structural standpoint, the worst ambiguity is inherent in the capacity of the term simultaneously to accommodate to the personal meanings (psychologic, intrapersonal, existential, individual) and the equally important social denotations (interpersonal, interactional, collective, mass). This provides a basis for an especially deep confusion since these two categories are, from an analytic standpoint, arbitrarily kept distinct.


# INCONSISTENCY IN MEANING AS A SCIENTIFICALLY TESTABLE TERM

Some of the ambiguity of the term is not only based on the various social configurations in which alienation can occur, and the varying processes and states in which it is manifested, but also in the varying categories and constructs used to test and examine these various manifestations.

## Behavioral Terms

Some processes or states of alienation can most readily be described in mundane descriptive terms concerning distinct, observable, interactions. People are, after all, specifically exiled, killed, abandoned, or ignored by specific, other persons. Such behaviors are ubiquitous and can readily be shown to be actions which account for and produce states of separation or estrangement. Hence, they can be held to be examples of alienation at a *phenomenal* level.

## Epiphenomenal Terms

Alienation is frequently, however, connected not only with distinct behavioral acts but also with epiphenomenal categories, that is, as (secondary) phenomena accompanying these other phenomena or caused by them. Alienation, therefore, may be seen as an *epiphenomenal abstraction,* collectively summarizing a series of specific behaviors and categorizing them as "loneliness," "normlessness," "isolation," etc.

## Metaphenomenal

Confusingly, however, alienation just as commonly refers to an abstraction subsuming other abstractions which are themselves epiphenomenal to real behaviors.

To illustrate this, alienation (as a *metaphenomenon*) can be held to be present when the presence of certain epiphenomena are demonstrated. For example, normlessness may exist in a society when (1) a particular society lacks reasonably explicit principles for the establishing of meaning, value, or significance for human actions; or (2) when these principles, although explicit, are in a state of flux and uncertainty; or (3) when the discrepancy between the normative and factual is so great that the normative becomes useless as a guide for the meaning and value of actions; or (4) when, perhaps, the normative order is explicit but accommodates only to an elite minority.

The problem of relating actual behaviors to the construct, normlessness (given these, above, broad criteria) is methodological. Through the use of description and measurement, actual behaviors may be employed to demonstrate whether normlessness is present or absent. Since normlessness is logically related to alienation, it therefore follows that, given "normlessness," alienation is either present or, at the very least, latent, in such conditions. The problem with such a conclusion is that the epiphenomenon, "normlessness," is only one ingredient in the larger category "alienation" (Seeman, 1959). It cannot be construed as equivalent to alienation.

This, hopefully, illustrates the inconsistencies which derive from the structural ambiguity of the word alienation, which can be held to be equivalent to simple behaviors, equivalent to epiphenomena based on these behaviors and, at the same time, equivalent to a metaphenomenon subsuming a number of epiphenomena.

## PSYCHOLOGICAL AND PSYCHIATRIC ASPECTS OF ALIENATION[11]

The separation of psychological alienation from social alienation is convenient from a descriptive, structural, and analytic standpoint. The dichotomizing of behavior into subjective and objective levels of analysis in no way suggests that behaviors are not unitary phenomena, but, rather, that subjective-objective references are selected as points for descriptive analysis.

Psychological depictions of alienation center on two levels of experience: first, that level which involves judgments concerning the subjective life of individual persons made by observers external to the person, and, second, that level involving judgments made by individuals who comment on aspects of their own subjectivity. Psychological alienation is close to the state of self-alienation (*selb-Entfremdung*). This refers to the awareness of separateness from one's own inner reality.[12]

---

[11] The division of the phenomena of alienation into "psychological" and "social" categories is preserved in the exposition in this chapter because it is traditionally and popularly divided in this way. In doing this, I have chosen to ignore the many problems inherent in holding these dimensions separate.

[12] The description of self-alienated states is present in many philosophical writings, notably within that group designated as existentialists. The complexities of the development of specific meanings of self-alienation in sociology and philosophy are beyond the scope of this volume, but are well covered in both Schacht (1970) and Israel (1971).

The qualities of self-alienation will be listed here according to deficiencies which are, themselves, of course, interrelated, but, for descriptive purposes, are considered separately.

Alienation will here be described in terms of experiences of deficiencies in existence, cognition, conation, feeling, recalling, and behaving. The word deficiency is not used in a pejorative sense, but seems preferable to "imperfections" (which connotes that persons have "fallen" from some ideal, exalted state) or "omissions" (which suggests that functions have capriciously been lost or not originally allocated).

## Deficiencies in Existence

The recognition of existential states of disappointment, isolation, and meaninglessness has received notable publicity from psychiatrists, novelists, theologians, and philosophers. Individual Man is portrayed as estranged from a rejecting God, and thrown into fragile, temporal associations within a denaturalized social milieu. He is overwhelmed by inexorable social procedures which grant him slight significance, and little option in the control of his own destiny. Particularly in populous, civilized societies, he finds himself surrounded by personal and manufactured objects whose separateness from him appears to outweigh their relevance to him. Surrounded by a surfeit of superficial ideologies (religious, commercial, nationalistic, scientific), he selects from these as if they were costumes donned to portray certain agreeable states of conformity, rather than used to nurture or refresh a sense of conviction.

He feels encapsulated and compartmentalized in roles as spouse, parent, worker, lover—even as a player or recreator. In the usual portrayal of the alienated person, the sum of these roles somehow does not add up to a self. (The person is less than the total of his parts.)

Looking inward for some sense of personal integration, the alienated man is confronted with the inconsistencies and deficiencies in these various roles. From inside looking outward, the synthetic aspects of his social performance and the discrepancies between his various roles elicit feelings of inauthenticity and meaninglessness. Looking further into himself, he discovers a systematically regulated repertory of functions. Some of these moderate his interpretation of the actions of people around him, others function to carry out appropriate reactions to those people on the "outside." However, neither his interpretation of others, or his actions toward others, seem original or meaningful. Fleeting memories of innocence and spontaneity are painful and, when recalled, are ascribed to the delusions of childhood which were later shattered by the recognition of separateness and insignificance.

Ultimately, the alienated man sees himself as just another, standardized, manufactured thing. The very self-consciousness that alienated man has about his own functioning convinces him of his synthetic nature and, hence, his inauthenticity. Sensing these deficiencies in his existence as inevitable, he resigns himself to seeking meaning out of isolation and despair themselves. He makes an attempt to enjoy or appreciate himself as an intriguing system of parts. Ultimately, he ends up sitting in his own private theater, at once the projectionist and the sole audience. In this theater he sees his behavior on an imaginary screen ("social reality") outside of himself, but rarely feels as if he is actually there on the screen, since he is so distracted by the production, direction, casting, and filming of his projections.

In severe schizoidal conditions, the deficiencies in meaning connected with social experiences are transferred from the outside to the arena of internal "reality" where they, ostensibly, may be more carefully modulated. The search for meaning, then, becomes formulated as questions concerning the smooth operation of one's (synthetic) parts. Needless to say, the operation of such "parts" is often unsmooth. Anxieties previously cued from contacts with social reality now are cued when the "internal machine" fails to perform satisfactorily. Recoiling from insubstantiality of outside contacts, the alienated man comes to discover deficiencies in his existence signaled by the imperfections of his internal life.

## Deficiencies in Cognition

Restrictions in synthetic or other abstract, intellectual functions may be experienced as self-alienation. Of course, the category of abstract functioning (judgment, reasoning, concept formation, etc.) is in no sense an autonomous mental operation originating, as it were, from specific topical regions of the brain. These functions occur in intimate conjunction with perception, memory, and association: deficiencies in concept formation are inevitably accompanied by some degree of loss of other mental functioning.

Nevertheless, a number of psychiatric conditions are distinguished by deficiencies in cognitive functions associated with (or due to) physical, as well as psychosocial, insults. The capacity to think, judge, and reason is potentially severely reduced if gross changes in the integrity of the brain occur as a result of hereditary, traumatic, toxic, or degenerative processes. Also, changes in the efficiency of symbol formation and utilization may be striking in a number of psychological conditions (notoriously in schizophrenia, but also in less serious disorders). Finally, deficiencies in perception or cognition, imposed by constrictions of cultural or familial training, operate in similar ways. The idiosyncrasies and omissions enculturated through familial and other social forces readily impose severe narrowness or contradiction which restrict cognitive functioning. Regardless of the cause (structural cellular loss, biochemical insult, restrictive enculturation, conflictual early development), the privative result will be the same—namely, relative deficiencies in cognition facilitating the experience of self-alienation. Such cognitive lacks and the degree of awareness of such deficiency of course, vary widely. Severe defects (structural or otherwise), create a condition where the individual is unable to navigate in any but the least complex symbolical interactions, and, often, then, with only a dim awareness of his haplessness. At the other extreme, mild lapses in cognitive functioning are universal, and likely to be accompanied by flashes of recognition of such minor deficiencies.

### Deficiencies in Conating ("Willing")

Interest in the volitional aspects of individual human performance has recently emerged within psychiatry following a long eclipse. This eclipse stemmed from several sources. The application of logical deductive reasoning to the explanation of physical functioning (including the functioning of the brain) was accompanied by the rejection of teleological causation, and of explanations of behavior which involved concepts of personal agency that smacked of "free will." Within psychiatry, this took two forms: first, in an emphasis on explaining human behavior as regulated by physico-chemical activities, and, second, through the ascendency of psychological determinism, represented in diverse theories, but most notably in those of psychoanalytic psychology. Both the physical and psychological modes of explanation took the form of relating clinical conditions (grand paresis, epilepsy, and classic psychoneuroses) to deficiencies in real or metapsychological "structures." The ingredient of volition in these and other conditions was considered to be relatively insignificant.

The concept of volition in human actions was revived through the work of a number of clinicians and scholars who focused on social interactional explanations of behavior rather than on closed system explanations in physical or psychological terms. The concept of will has been rehabilitated, beginning with Otto Rank's formulations and continuing on through the writings of Sullivan, Fromm-Reichman, Erikson, Hartmann, Karl Menninger, and, of course, the existentialist psychiatrists.[13]

The effects of this long eclipse, however, are still felt within the field of psychiatry. By obscuring "will" as an important element in human experience, the notion of choice or option was, in a very fundamental way, overlooked. Another result of not acknowledging volition has been to ignore questions of human meaning and value, which, of course, are subservient to the notion of choice, personal agency, and option.

Alienation from the self, in terms of internal normlessness and meaninglessness is, however, of great importance, although it is usually considered under the existential aspects of human behavior. This is partly because the phenomenological

[13] Classical psychoanalysis in the earlier decades of this century was primarily concerned with speculations about the control of human behavior through the operation of largely unconscious, inexorable systems. Rank's formulations (along with those of Adler) centered on the effect of contemporaneous consciousness on social actions (including, of course, options). These formulations were chronologically too premature to be incorporated in Freudian theory at the time. However, both Anna Freud's and Heinz Hartman's formulations nearly twenty-five years later concerning nonconflict oriented aspects of personality functioning opened the door for a belated treatment of volition. Much of the early antipathy and misunderstanding of psychoanalytic theory can partly be accounted for in terms of the tardy development of ego psychology. Differences concerning both the existential and volitional aspects of human behavior can be seen to be basic to the theoretical dissention between orthodox psychoanalysis and both the interpersonal and phenomenological schools.

school has been most conspicuous in restoring the significance of human volition. The tendency for psychoanalytic theorists to conceptualize problems of meaning, choice, and volition as existential has the effect of continuing to regard these as less important than intrapsychic dynamisms. In one area, however, psychoanalytic theory has traditionally dealt with individual meaning—specifically in terms of ego and ego-ideal. These have been treated as the internally recognized discrepancies between the individual's perceived state of functioning and his realization of his potential for different levels of performance or completeness. Such discrepancies may constitute forms of self-alienation, as the individual senses deficiencies in his actions stemming from restrictions of his options, based either on his own ineptitude or on constraints imposed by social forces. Internal meaninglessness or normlessness may ensue if ambivalence is so severe that all performances and options lack meaning. Similarly, this loss of meaning may be evident when harsh, perfectionistic standards continually subtract from and undercut the significance of human accomplishment.

## Deficiencies in Feeling

The need to separate levels of urgent feeling from human performance is essential for the development of a symbolical creature who passes through a series of different forms and stages (infancy, childhood, adolescence, adulthood, etc.) as well as one who encounters adventitious crises that temporarily produce intense states of excitement, confusion, and anxiety. When only a selective isolation of feeling accompanies here-and-now actions, the individual can still experience the emotional orchestration, positive and negative, which supplies vitality and meaning to human performance. However, when wholesale and pathologic isolation operates to obliterate feeling entirely, the individual is clearly alienated from crucial dimensions of his own experience.

Notoriously, the isolation of feeling is connected with certain characterologic dispositions, particularly those described as "anal personality," "obsessive character," "depressive character," and, of course, the "schizoid personality." Forgetting momentarily about the generalizations incurred through classifications of this sort, each of these conditions is partly defined by a lack of spontaneity and vitality. In "schizoid personality," the experience of diverse feeling states is often interpreted ("felt") by the person as anxiety rather than pleasure, dread rather than excitement. Many social interactions, which on the face of things might seem to be either emotionally neutral or even positive, are felt by the schizoid individual as painful and threatening. This leads to a reduction of social contact, or to highly selective contact designed to minimize excessive states of feeling.

## Deficiencies in Recalling

Although repression is, of course, both universal and essential in efficient human functioning, wholesale and excessive forgetting imposes delimiting and self-alienating strictures on human behavior. Action is necessarily inhibited when the ability to select freely from one's past performance is so restricted that the past cannot be used as a guide to contemporaneous action, or future aspirations.

## Deficiencies in Behaving

Since human functioning has, here, been analyzed in terms of artificially separated aspects of symbolical functioning, deficiencies in action would be associated with restrictions in existence, cognition, conation, feeling, and memory. All of these fractionated functions are, of course, instantially concomitant with behavior. The ways in which behavioral performance are restricted in terms of deficiencies in other functions are obvious and need not be traced here.

## SOCIAL ASPECTS OF ALIENATION

Six analytic schemata defining social alienation have already been listed in the Introduction. Some of these (and others) are also treated later in the book. The purpose of this section is to portray, in structural terms, the extent to which alienation is applied to social phenomena, and to identify some of the particular junctures at which alienation occurs. Of the many available schemes which might be used to display this, Feuer's (1963) will be used here. His particular modes of alienation are selected because they are comprehensive and their primary focus is on social, rather than social-psychological or psychiatric, phenomena.

### The Alienation of Class Society

Gordon (1964) has described social class differences as being constituted from subcultural factors. This is useful in considering the alienation inherent in being identified with particular states of advantage and disadvantage in the society. Gordon sees a subculture as compounded of factors of ethnic (national) origin, number of generations since immigration, religious denomination, education, occupation, and locality in which individuals reside. Gordon's particular emphasis (discussed and embellished by others) is that the compounding of all these factors amounts to the establishment of class positions as subcultures. Admission to these class positions is predicated on the portrayal of selected characteristics in regard to linguistic conventions, value systems, world view, and actions germane to or expected of members of a particular class position.

Alienation, in terms of class society, then, consists of differential behaviors associated with the various class positions in terms of background and current life style. These differences, moreover, are not merely ascriptive, but encompass communicational, cognitive, existential, and behavioral life styles. These are not easily mastered by individuals not enculturated from childhood in particular subcultures or class positions. The relative openness of American society ostensibly allows for mobility. Such mobility, however, is not effortless—in either direction. Except in magical, fictional accounts, such mobility requires planning, experimentation, and learning, as well as the presence of propitious circumstances. Of course, in the United States, the ideology concerning the relative ease of upward mobility continues to be viable. This is in spite of the publicity about the relatively inflexible limitations placed on individuals from a number of ethnic and subcultural groups (see Reagan in this volume, Chapter 15). (Awareness of the difficulties inherent in the process of upward mobility is indirectly attested to through popular interest in themes concerned with these processes. Such themes furnish the basis for much situation comedy, as well as plots for soap operas and serious drama.)

In the context of alienation, class systems operate as a series of subcultures alienated from each other in terms of their differential participation in institutions, selection of ideologies, and degree of identification with social organizations within the society.

## The Alienation of Competitive Society

Feuer (1963) has commented that "A competitive system makes for a mode of alienation distinct from that in which classes are more fixed [p. 137]." Although the pressures of competitive themes are particularly conspicuous in societies influenced by Calvinistic traditions, the emphasis on the enhancement of personal or national development is clearly enunciated in all technological societies. There is a need for individuals and groups to distinguish themselves in terms of achievement, either for themselves, their families, or their nation. This becomes an alienating factor through providing a universal expectation for unusual accomplishment (and reward) that in no possible way can be uniformly achieved by all members within the society. Discrepancies between aspiration and achievement, therefore, are not only frequent, but obviously inevitable. Recognition of these discrepancies is manifested both by disappointment and frustration with personal performance, as well as by envy toward those who are more successful in the system.

This sense of alienation may be more suppressed in a society where the competitive strivings are collectivized in terms of familial or national achievement. In these systems, personal rewards are sought indirectly in terms of family, corporation, or country—as in Japan or some collective societies. It seems clear, however, that in the United States the notion of individual accomplishment through a competitive process has been integrally connected with prevailing work ideology since colonial times. In this cultural milieu the sense of alienation and failure can be especially keen.

## The Alienation of Industrial Society

The concept of separation of humans from objects in their environment has been discussed in connection with its western theological and philosophical origins. In *Genesis,* a corollary to expulsion from Paradise involved the introduction of Man to Work—portrayed as an urgent necessity (rather than a joy or recreation), and intimately fused to the theme of punishment and reparation (in addition to mere survival). Perhaps in this sense, the potentiality of feeling separated from the process and product of one's labor is very fundamental to western culture. More than this estrangement, however, there has been a distinctive need to look for a transcendental significance in work.

The posttechnological literature on the meaninglessness of work has already been partly reviewed. Rousseau, Marx, Durkheim, Seeman, Henry, and Ellul (and many others) have described the potential for meaninglessness connected with living in a society which is obsessed with production, marketing, and consumption as transcendental virtues. Although the degree of meaninglessness in industrial societies has been shown to be a function of social position, the potentiality for work-alienation exists in all class positions. Of course, individuals in the higher social positions, although potentially alienated from their work, are more easily able to sustain the feeling of personal significance. They are not, after all, alienated competitively (they are being, relatively, rewarded). Also, they sense less discrepancy between their personal ideology and the prevailing norms concerning the "goodness" of the productive ethic in their society. They may, however, be severely dissociated from the products they produce and buy, as well as disconnected from the processes through which they produce, consume, and dispose.

## The Alienation of Mass Society

The notion of "mass" is central to the problem of alienation. This is summarized by Meadows (1965):

> Certainly a very large number of economic historians during the second half of the nineteenth century began to see that they were dealing not merely with transformation in productive techniques or production conditions, but with an interlocking meshwork of transformations revolving around the massed mechanization of men, materials, money, institutions, and communities. Some of them were especially interested in the stages of industrialization, others in its variable institutional and ideational forms, still others in cultural continuities which made it possible, yet others in the cultural discontinuities (or incongruities) which accompany its development [p. 453].

This illustrates two ways in which the adjective, mass, is employed to describe phenomena: first, to depict a quantitative level at which aggregates are combined, and, second, to imply that qualitative changes occur after certain levels of mass are reached.

Mills (1956) has discussed these qualitative differences in terms of contrasts between two types of society: public and mass:

> In a public as we may understand the term (1) virtually as many people express opinions as receive them. (2) Public communications are so organized that there is a chance immediately and effectively to answer back any opinion expressed in public. Opinion formed by such discussion (3) readily finds an outlet in effective action even against—if necessary—the prevailing system of authority. And (4) authoritative institutions do not penetrate the public, which is thus more or less autonomous in its operations. When these conditions prevail they have a working model of the community of publics, and this model fits closely to several assumptions of classic democratic theory.
>
> At the opposite extreme, in a *mass*, (1) far fewer people express opinions than receive them; for the community of publics becomes an abstraction of individuals who receive impressions from the mass media. (2) Communications that prevail are so organized that it is difficult or impossible for the individual to answer back immediately or with any effect. (3) The realization of opinion in action is controlled by authorities who organize and control the channels of such action. (4) The mass has no autonomy from institutions; on the contrary, agents of authorized institutions penetrate this mass, reducing any autonomy it may have in the formation of opinion by discussion [p. 207].

The individual, contemporary man is surrounded by mass institutions and large social complexes. He is a tiny citizen in a huge polity. His relationship to his government, in both totalitarian and democratic societies, is relatively insignificant. His participation in the economy is correspondingly passive and tiny. Of course, in affluent societies, he is distracted by the commodities, services, and manufactured products available to him. The prevalent formulation of culture critics (Jules Henry, C. Wright Mills, Vance Packard) would suggest that the individual in mass society is urged to seek significance in terms of ephemeral products, commodities, and service. Even more insidious, the values placed on these goods and services (and the ideologies attached to their production and consumption) are extraneous to the individual consumer-citizen. Again, he is the recipient of (mass) communications which, in essence, tell him what he should strive for, buy, use, and dispose of.

The (mass) communications media are concerned with the creation of what Mills (1956) terms a "pseudoworld." This pseudoworld is not only constituted by a plethora of products and services, but also certain types of life styles inherent in the buying of these products and services. Participation in this pseudoworld, then, includes not only mass control of behavior of consumers, but also suggests that a whole desirable way of life is available to the user of the "right" goods and services.

## The Alienation of Race

If race or ethnic origin were seen simply as a function of position in a scale of subcultures, and, hence, directly related to class position, the alienating quality of race might be subsumed as a special instance of the alienation of class society. This might seem especially plausible since the concept of "race" within physical and cultural anthropology has led away from the generalizations popular even twenty years ago. Regardless of such changes on the scholarly level, the criterion of "race" still forms a compelling social taxonomy on which very rigid judgments and restrictions are based. The possibilities for alienation are enormous, based upon what is perceived as either physical or cultural idiosyncrasy. Despite the current cautious rapprochements between cultures of equal solidarity and power, less sophisticated or powerful subcultures are virtually guaranteed invidious comparison and nonacceptance by those who make use of the culture of the prevailing majorities. The alienating potentialities based on race, therefore, are obvious, and should not be obscured by considering them as examples of the alienation of either class or competitive society.

### The Alienation of the Generations

This form of alienation not only arises from differences in chronological age, but also from differences incumbent on qualitative features distinctive to certain stages of the life cycle. The alienation secondary to differences in generation is, of course, inevitable. Therefore, the natural tensions inherent in a group composed of adult members at different points in the life cycle, and with different experiential backgrounds, can be seen as a crucial dynamic for influencing the progression of culture. As Mannheim (1970) observes:

> This means, in the first place, that our culture is developed by individuals who come into contact anew with the accumulative heritage. In the nature of our physical make-up, a fresh contact (meeting something anew) always means a changed relationship of distance from the object and a novel approach in assimilating, using, and developing the proffered material.

As Mannheim (1970) further points out, members of any particular age group have only a limited opportunity to have their full impact on the guiding of the historical and cultural process. The alienating potentialities in this arrangement consists of the separation between individuals belonging to particular age groups. Although various age groups may be said to be alienated from one another, the consequences of such alienation are obviously variable. In terms of separation from the sociohistorical process, the very young and the old are most conspicuously alienated on the basis of their "generations."

### SUMMARY

The Introduction and this chapter have been devised to provide the reader with a map of the etymology, derivations, and applications of the word alienation.

This has been done by listing the various disciplines in which the concept has enjoyed some definitive usage. Both the Introduction and this chapter have had the purpose of spreading and developing the manifold meanings of this term, as well as portraying the design for this present volume. The chapters which follow are intended to amplify specific aspects of the term alienation as seen in the contemporary disciplines of philosophy, theology, psychiatry, history, sociology, anthropology, education, economics, literature, and political science.

A final chapter will attempt to respond to some of the questions raised in the rest of the volume.

## REFERENCES

Brinkman, C. Alien. In R. A. Seligman & A. Johnson (Eds.), *Encyclopedia of social sciences.* New York: Macmillan, 1930.

Feuer, L. What is alienation? The career of a concept. In M. Stein & A. Vidich (Eds.), *Sociology on trial.* Englewood Cliffs, N. J.: Prentice-Hall, 1963.

Gordon, M. M. *Assimilation in American life.* New York: Oxford University Press, 1964.

Hardin, G. Meaninglessness of the word protoplasm. *Scientific Monthly,* 1956, *82,* 112-120.

Israel, J. *Alienation: From Marx to modern sociology.* Boston: Allynn & Bacon, 1971.

Kaplan, A. *The conduct of inquiry.* San Francisco: Chandler, 1964.

Kaufman, W. Introduction. In R. Schacht (Ed.), *Alienation.* Garden City, N. Y.: Doubleday, 1970. Pp. xiii-lix.

Lang, K. Alienation. In J. Gould & W. Kolb (Eds.), *A dictionary of the social sciences.* New York: Free Press, 1964.

Lichtheim, G. Alienations. In D. Sills (Ed.), *International encyclopedia of the social sciences.* Vol. 1. New York: Macmillan & Free Press, 1968. Pp. 264-268.

McDermott, J. Technology: The opiate of the intellectuals. *New York Review of Books,* 1969, *XIII* (July 31), 25-35.

Mannheim, K. The problem of generations. *Psychoanalytic Review,* 1970, *57,* 383-384. (Reprinted from *Essays on the sociology of knowledge.* New York: Oxford University Press, 1952.)

Meadows, P. Industrial man. In I. Horowitz (Ed.), *The new sociology.* New York: Oxford University Press, 1965.

Mills, C. W. *The power elite.* London: Oxford University Press, 1956.

Mizruchi, E. *Success and opportunity.* Glencoe, Ill.: Free Press, 1964. Pp. 8-20.

Rapoport, A. *Operational philosophy.* New York: Harper, 1953.

Schacht, R. *Alienation.* Garden City, N. Y.: Doubleday, 1970.

Seeman, M. The alienation hypothesis. *Psychiatry and Social Science Review,* 1969, *3,* 1-6.

Vance, W. R. Alienation. In R. A. Seligman & A. Johnson (Eds.), *Encyclopedia of social sciences.* New York: Macmillan, 1930. Pp. 639-641.

*Webster's third new international dictionary of the English language.* Springfield, Mass: Merriam, 1968.

# Chapter 2

# Psychological Alienation:
# Isolation and Self-Estrangement[1]

*Frank Johnson*
State University of New York

Currently, the term alienation is employed to describe objectively-observ -· able states of separateness occurring in human groups. An historically older usage emphasized alienation as a subjective, individual condition. Within psychiatry, un- til early in this century, the term was used as a loose, generic category, describing various states of pathological isolation and madness. In this chapter alienation will be reviewed in these latter connections as it contributes to the understanding of certain clinical states of disturbance. Some factors which make the experience of introspection threatening will be reviewed. A final section will be concerned with a discussion of clinical conditions in which a malignant self-absorption is conspic- uous—notably the schizoid personality. A critical discussion of some of the for- mulations and explanations of these conditions will also be included.

[1] Even in the title to this chapter the unfortunate, although conventional dichotomy between (subjective) Self and (objective) Social Reality is perpetuated. It should be noted here that distinctions concerning "inside-outside," "subjective-objective," and "psychologi- cal-social," are only phenomenological in character. That is to say that in addition to the conventionality of such distinctions, these (pseudo) polarities will be used here because they are central to the estranged person's explanation of himself as an object in the (social) uni- verse. The immense problems posed by the use of these polarities (as ontological realities) are beyond the scope of this presentation. It might be added that Fairbairn's (1954) conception of an "object relations" personality partly cuts through this dilemma.

## INTRODUCTION

In recent times, taxonomy has been the *bête noir* of psychiatry. A good deal of criticism has been leveled at the categorizing and labeling activities of psychiatrists. Such criticism of classification, per se, seems unwarranted when based on the solipsism holding that all persons are ineffably unique, and, hence, incapable of being categorized. Criticism is genuinely warranted, however, when it is based on the understanding that behavioral classification is monstrously complicated and beset with inconsistency. The need to explain and codify behavior for the purpose of scientific classification is, of course, merely an institutionalized version of the universal propensity to make human behaviors more intelligible and predictable. Many institutions which are concerned with classification (e.g., law, government, religion) are able to delimit their concern to those behaviors that are specific to their institution. Furthermore, to justify their classifications they generally employ unitary systems of explanation for such categories. Classification within psychiatry, on the other hand, is much more comprehensive in its concerns with the behavior of human beings at all stages of the life cycle, in all conceivable situations, and in radically different cultures and societies. And, at the same time, classification in psychiatry is stricken with major conceptual discontinuities inherent in the logically disconnected systems (genetic, biochemical, anatomical, psychological, cultural, social) employed in classifying.

The classifications described in this chapter are confined to conditions of exceptional self-alienation currently subsumed into the diagnosis of schizoid personality. It should be noted here that no serious student of human behavior believes in the "reality" of psychiatric classifications, except as nominal categories. Since the phenomenology of schizoid states in itself accentuates the quality of separateness, a dichotomized and isolated caricature of existence is especially difficult to avoid. The artificially delimited nature of closed-system, psychological classifications should be borne in mind by the reader as this chapter unfolds.

### Schizoid Symptoms

We are, however, not only speaking about a specific syndrome, but discussing a number of conditions in which individuals manifest their suffering in terms of their consciousness of estrangement and idiosyncrasy. The list of symptoms usually connected with these states will be listed here:

1. A tendency to experience exorbitant anxiety and disquietude in relatively ordinary interactions with other people.

2. A tendency toward absorption with ideas and fantasy.

3. An uncertainty at both mental and actional levels of human experience (ambivalence plus hesitation in performance).

4. A gnawing consciousness of a lack of "fit" with other individuals or groups.

5. A tendency to retreat and withdraw from others.

6. An alternating vacillation toward and away from social contact.

In these instances, withdrawal is not used selectively as a strategic maneuver, given specific threatening conditions, but, rather, as a reflex to any situation sensed to be even vaguely dangerous or noxious. The strategy of retreat is concerned with reducing external contact with people. The hope, thereby, is to reduce conflict, and, just possibly, to experience less anxiety. While such a strategy may, in fact, reduce the immediately threatening experience of anxiety, it often engenders anxiety concerning the withdrawal itself. Furthermore, having fled from the disharmony and contention of the external contacts, the individual often rediscovers this same disharmony and conflict within himself.

This tendency toward overly ideational activity in self-alienation does not imply anything about the qualitative nature of such ideation. Depending upon the person's aptitude and previous experience, individuals may ponder ideas either of great significance or triviality. The emphasis is on the fact of an overactive mental life, rather than on intellectuality in itself.

Also, a distinctive characteristic of the withdrawal in self-alienation is that after having withdrawn, such alienated individuals do not stay unobtrusively by themselves. There is an engagement in vacillating moves toward and away from people. As described by Daly (1968), the schizoid individual does not find a comfortable hermitage, but is beset with approach-avoidance conflicts concerning affiliation with others.

## The Phenomenology and Significance of Introspection[2]

Introspection, of course, refers to mental experiences where the individual is both the subject and object of his own conscious awareness. Introspection stands in distinction to fantasy, reverie, or daydreaming, insofar as these latter modes are not accompanied by an intense, conscious focus of self-observation. Introspection also stands in contrast to problem solving, logicizing, or formulating, where the content of thought is concerned with abstractions of phenomena which are conceptually identified as outside of the individual.

As a term, introspection often suggests mental activity concerned with deliberations on important and potentially conflictual choices of action. However, the implication that introspection is usually auspicious is misleading. Obviously, most self-reflection is concerned with fleeting deliberations concerning the personal consequences of options in ordinary, prosaic interaction.

It is apparent that making judgments about the quality and frequency of introspection in other persons is an elusive business. Self-reflection is an intensely

[2] The following remarks concerning introspection are intended to be descriptive. The philosophic and psychological literature on introspection is vast and quite unnecessary for this presentation. The reader is referred to Kohut (1959).

private experience that is only exceptionally communicated to other individuals, even then usually reported retrospectively, rather than contemporaneously. Only a few situations, for example, psychoanalytic treatment and some creative writing, are institutionalized, albeit artifactual versions of public introspection.

Also, the capacity for introspection and the frequency with which people, in fact, introspect varies widely. Most individuals, when they think of it at all, speculate about the introspection of others in terms of the characteristics of their own self-reflection.

Systematic attempts to survey the variations in life styles (including the factors of frequency and nature of introspection) have not been done on normal populations. Global behavioral classifications (designated as nosologies of either "character" or "personality") do take into account certain subjective, cognitive, and emotional experiences of the individuals being classified. In psychiatry, however, the most popular classifications of personality are ultimately based more on the characteristics of social interaction (sociopathic personality, passive-aggressive personality, etc.).

Classifications such as the character disorders, neuroses, and psychoses are, furthermore, concerned with depicting abnormality. The "normal" qualities of cognition, memory, or other aspects of subjective life are tautologically suggested to be the absence of "abnormal mental content." Some classifications of character deriving from psychoanalytic theory (Fenichel, Reich, Frosch, etc.) may be related more closely to the subjective (rather than interactional) aspects of the individual's life. Such classifications, however, although more closely based on subjective life, are, again, concerned with abnormality, and, furthermore, are based on a priori schemes of personality maturation which are both idealized and culture bound. They do not attempt to examine the normal distribution of varying cognitive styles, except by way of speculation, case study, and anecdote. Finally, those groups of professionals currently most devoted to the phenomenology of subjective mental experience (in existential psychiatry and phenomenology) tend toward relativistic interpretation of meaning, and, hence, show little interest in categorization.

In summary, then, the systems of personality classification that are most popular offer designations based primarily on social interactional aspects of behavior, and primarily with reference to "abnormal" individuals. There is little empirically-based research on the occurrence of introspection in ordinary life. For these reasons, introspection remains a poorly defined phenomenon, and is usually regarded as either socially irrelevant, or seen as narcissistic and socially dangerous.


## THE SOCIAL UNACCEPTABILITY OF SCHIZOID SYMPTOMS

### The Mirage of "Sameness"

The capacity to understand the subjectivity of others is limited by the tendency for individuals to project the specific quality of their own mental operations directly onto other individuals. This is parallel to the operations of cultural groups who project their own ethnocentric formulae (for cause and meaning) onto the behaviors of other groups, frequently at the cost of serious misunderstanding. While individuals may intellectually understand that considerable variation is present in the mental activities of other persons, they show a great deal of naivete concerning the nature of this variability. Most individuals cannot either tolerate or assimilate evidence of mental activity in others that differs very much from their own thoughts and formulations. Awareness of the range of the broad variations in the thoughts and actions of individuals is further minimized by most people through their selective and narrowly determined choices of friends, marital partner, church, neighborhood, job, clubs, and organizations.

In these various affiliations, conformity and conventionality are continually rediscovered, thus reassuring individuals that they do think alike (i.e., they appear to endorse the same normative explanations and prescriptions). This means that, in general, people agree to ascribe common explanations for human behavior, and, at least in public, tend to act in similar ways. The fact that the purposes and meanings inherent in such similar actions may in themselves be highly idiosyncratic is usually not noticed except in conflicts which develop in intimate relationships between spouses, parents, children, close associates, and friends. This mirage of "sameness" thus becomes seriously challenged only in dyadic relationships where the vagaries of subjective experience are either strongly inferred or directly communicated between individuals. Such interpersonal difficulties may force the latent awareness of differences in mental functioning into consciousness.

The investigation of one's own purposes through deliberate introspection often is prompted by conflict rather than by casual choice. Introspection regrettably, therefore, becomes associated with a quality of negativity, as a symptom of disturbance. The creative and conflict-free uses of introspection are less obtrusive and more readily forgotten. Unusual self-concerns, obsessions, or ambivalence, especially that which can be seen publicly, are therefore interpreted as threatening (insofar as they disturb the myth of sameness and commonality) and idiosyncratic (through advertising that something is peculiar about the individual who has fallen into such self-absorption). Therefore, individuals who tend to be unusually "dreamy" or self-reflective are in danger of finding themselves defined as eccentric or abnormal.

## The Need for Conventional Explanation

Looked at somewhat differently, conspicuous introspection defies the strong preference for the use of conventional, superficial explanations of human behavior in ordinary social situations. From the standpoint of economy of explanation, most behavior is regarded as self-explanatory: for example, (1) "John went to the drugstore to buy razor blades," or is explained satisfactorily on conventional grounds: for example, (2) "John is working very hard at his job in order to win a promotion." Such parsimonious explanations, however adequate and facile in ordinary situations, place an onus on explanations involving more profound interpretations of behavior:

for example, (3) "Is John buying razor blades because he is suicidal?" or (4) "Is John overworking as a way of competing with his father?"

Introspection—and we must remember we are not discussing daydreaming—is often concerned with attempting to infer or discover more profound and, hence, less conventional meanings for human action. Such pondering may, therefore, be seen as dangerous, since deeper motivational explanations are often reversed for control of behavior through the potential manipulation of individual guilt: for example, (5) "John spends too much time on his appearance," or (6) "John's work keeps him away from his family."

One might comment that conventional explanations are satisfactory partly because they relieve the explainer of imputing anything but the most innocuous of meanings to John's buying razor blades or working hard. Meanings which inquire into less overt motivations suggest that John's mental machinations may not be what they should be.

The final examples [(5) and (6)] simultaneously imply the possible unconventional nature of John's behavior, but at the same time deny and suppress this by criticizing the effects of his actions. The point of this is that four of these statements [(1), (2), (5), and (6)] have very little to do with the person, John, but, rather, reflect on the need of explainer to reassure himself about the uniformity of thought and behavior. Statements (3) and (4) are most threatening, since they acknowledge something of the occult, introspective (inner) life of both John and the explainer.

### Fears of Internal Disorganization

Another impediment to the understanding of introspection and schizoid conditions stems from the possibility of self-reflection giving rise to awareness of conflict. Especially at times of crisis, introspection can lead to the experience of thoughts which are perceived as threatening or dangerous. Adults who deal with critical events in their lives (loss of family members, change in work role, immersion in another culture) may find the introspection forced on them by such catastrophic events to be a confirmation of their own sense of peculiarity. This can simplistically be based on the assumption that the mere existence of such diffuse thoughts, feelings, and fantasies pronounces them deviant, strange, or even mad, insofar as it differs from what other people are thinking.

It is difficult to introspect very deeply without finding inconsistencies in one's recollections, thoughts, and feelings. Since most human actions are based upon portraying a sense of consistency (to self and others), the discovery of ambivalence can constitute a confusing and painful realization. The awareness of contrasting feelings may occasion pronounced anxiety, and, furthermore, interfere with spontaneous interaction. Therefore, many individuals find introspection threatening since they cannot easily assimilate discrepancies in feelings, thoughts, and meanings about which they have hoped to have simple unitarian convictions. By implication, the observation of hesitancy or unusual self-reflection in others would tend to be classified as dangerous, idiosyncratic, and strange.

## The Priority of External Reality

Despite some trends in the current counter-culture and the postwar interest in Existentialism and Eastern mysticism, the message in western cultures seems oppressively obvious: "reality" resides outside of the individual. The accepted orientation is to relate to the world in a direct and discrete way as an external environment. States of cogitation which center on internal phenomena run the risk of being disparaged as irrational and dangerous. As described in the preceding chapter, both Man's consciousness and existence are viewed as corpuscular, with an emphasis on his discrete nature and his ultimate separation from other beings and things. The external world (including, of course, overt interaction) are objective, regular, and predictable. Subjectivity is seen as the antithesis of this: normless, irrational, and bizarre. Except for unusually compelling religious or esthetic motives, a focus on internal phenomena is socially repugnant. Unusual self-preoccupation, trances, or reveries which lack social purpose or consensual meaning are at best amusing, but more commonly are regarded as plainly hazardous. One of the hazards, of course, is that the dreamer, the poet, or the contemplative may not find his way back to "reality" again.

## Some Exceptions in the Acceptability of Schizoid Symptoms

It is useful to divide those situations which place existential stresses on individuals into two categories: those occurring in conjunction with a natural progression through the life cycle, and those which are adventitious, historical, or accidental. In this division, maturational stresses would be those which develop in association with crises encountered at nodal points during normal development and involution. Adventitious situations would be those which are more capriciously encountered by the individual, and would include natural catastrophies, unexpected loss of intimate associates, exposure to severe physical threat, etc. Given the vagaries of life experience, the possibilities of severe isolation due to accident, mischance, and fate are unlimited.

Both maturational and adventitious crises present the individual with an often sudden and compelling need to change. The regular ongoing activity of the individual is challenged and found temporarily inadequate. In these situations, maturational and accidental stresses demand a new adaptation. As mentioned before, the use of introspection as a way of problem solving or handling existential anxiety is obviously distributed quite irregularly. Specific crises or maturational stages in no way elicit uniform deliberations or reactions from individuals undergoing stresses.

Adolescence, however, is partly an exception to this, at least insofar as the radical changes in physical and social functioning which take place force all individuals into states of self-reflection. Adolescents do not, in a linear way, vault from their childhood into a secure adult pattern. Rather, they are involved in a series of almost constant modifications of thought and action according to standards established for rather specific eras of this troubled period. They are involved in what, at the time, appears to be a seemingly endless revision of the relationships with parents, teachers, friends, and associates. Uncertainties and conflicts developing from these ever changing relationships thrust the adolescent into self-reflection.

There are several differences between the introspection forced on adolescents and the potentially more pathological degree of self-awareness confronting individuals at later decades of life by more adventitious circumstances. First, adolescents are expected to be in a process of change and, at least partly, to do this as a group. One is therefore not only expected to change but finds comfort and direct support with his similarly awkward peers. This is not true, of course, in later adult life when the significance of protracted states of shyness, eccentricity, withdrawal, or impulsivity connotes graver meaning—usually some form of deviance.

## SELF-ALIENATION: SCHIZOID CONDITIONS

The foregoing sections in this chapter have been concerned with furnishing a background to a description of states of self-alienation. It should be added that social and institutional factors influencing the classification of normal and abnormal behavior obviously affects the ways these conditions are viewed. Alienated Man, during any particular era, is obviously a creature of the ideologies and classificatory systems that are available to define his estrangement. In the previous chapter, the various possible forms of self-alienation were described as a set of possible deficiencies (in existence, cognition, conation, feeling, recalling, and behavior). Other schemes for defining self-alienation were also discussed before and will not be repeated here.

This section will describe the experience of self-alienation through an examination of the phenomenology and genesis of these conditions.

In any psychiatric description involving broad generalizations about clinical conditions, a tension is encountered in making a choice between conceptual simplicity and the depiction of something more complex and paradoxical which is closer to reality. It is very tempting to describe ideal states and conditions which are neatly dissociated from other conditions. Although such "states" represent caricatures, they are, in their very simplicity, easier to conceptualize. Such simplified categorizations also tend to suggest that the dichotomy between abnormality and normality is reassuringly distinct. Regrettably, behavior is far more complex than classifications, dichotomies, and simplifications would suggest. Some reduction, however, is necessary in order to make description coherent.

In this section, only two versions of self-alienation will be presented. These are alienated states defined as (manifest) schizoid personality where there is a high degree of consciousness concerning estrangement from self and others which is accompanied by copious anxiety and withdrawal. This first species of self-alienation is concerned with severe states of separation which are accompanied by eccentricity, peculiarity, and the experience of symptoms which, at times, are disabling.

The second species of self-alienation are those (latent) schizoid states where such separations are present, but are not evident or manifest in the person's social performance. These individuals do not experience high degrees of anxiety or public idiosyncrasy. Individuals with these latent conditions are more often described in the sociological and fictional literature, rather than in the psychiatric writings, since their intact social functioning would suggest that they are "well."[3]

## Historical Background of Schizoid Conditions

The meaning of the concept of schizoid is connected with Bleuler's original and brilliant conceptualization of schizophrenia published in 1911 (Bleuler, 1950). It is popularly misunderstood that Bleuler used the Greek root "σχιζ" to define a "splitting of personality," observable in a number of severe psychoses previously labeled "dementia praecox" by Emil Kraepelin. Bleuler's use of the concept of "splitting" in these disorders was more complex than this, however. He meant to indicate schism or splitting of a number of psychological functions which he held to be distinctive and common to several different conditions. These conditions not only included the then established varieties of dementia praecox, but also applied to less severe, and even nonpsychotic states in which the features of intense self-concern, exaggerated shyness, and some splitting of personality functions were prominent.

It is of more than passing interest that the basic etymological denotations of the words alienation and schizoid both refer to separation and tension. The word schizoid, however, is more confined to the notion of cleavage of previously integral entities, while alienation suggests an increasing distance between two entities that were not necessarily integrally connected or fused before.

One of these basic cleavages, described by Bleuler (1950), was the mental disconnection between self and the outside which he defined as "autism." He described a variety of splitting (dissociations) between thought and action and held that a severe tendency for such stark dissociation was a primary symptom in a number of psychotic and nonpsychotic conditions which he labeled "schizophrenia."

---

[3] The author regards the adjectives *manifest* and *latent* as unsatisfactory but includes them here since they are commonly used within psychiatry to dichotomize medical and behavioral syndromes. The adjectives *pattern* and *trait* are similarly unsatisfactory but are included because they are in conventional use.

Currently the word schizoid (both as a noun and adjective) is used in a number of ways. "Schizoid," like "schizophrenia," enjoys a nontechnical meaning, in this sense denoting a quality of strangeness, isolation, or peculiarity (*Webster's*, 1968).[4] In psychiatry and psychoanalysis, schizoid has at least three technical meanings. First, it is used by some authors (see below) to refer to an early developmental period when the infant begins to make rudimentary distinctions about the disconnectedness (separation) between himself and his human and nonhuman environment. The second meaning of schizoid is derived from the first, and consists of a topographical depiction of human personality described by Fairbairn and later clarified by Guntrip.[5] Basing their insights on the work of Freud, Melanie Klein, and their own clinical observations, they conceptualize human personality as a series of epigenetic stages which are graphically viewed as concentric, but separated levels of functioning (to be described in somewhat more detail later). Within this scheme, they envision the most central, that is, ontogenetically earliest, ego experiences as constituting a "schizoid core" or position.

The third meaning of schizoid relates to specific, characterologic (clinical) syndromes incorporating features of excessive isolation and withdrawal. In this latter, nosological usage, two major variations are intended. The first of these is "schizoid personality pattern," in which all the major attributes associated with the syndrome are present. The second variation is that of "schizoid personality trait," where schizoidal characteristics accompany other personality configurations and adaptations—including, obviously, "normality."

In the current *Diagnostic and Statistical Manual of Mental Disorders* (1968), published by the American Psychiatric Association, schizoid personality is defined as follows:

> This behavior pattern manifests shyness, or sensitivity, seclusiveness, avoidance
> of closer competitive relationships, and also eccentricity. Autistic thinking with-
> out loss of capacity to recognize reality is common, as is daydreaming and the
> inability to express hostility and ordinary aggressive feelings. These patients react
> to disturbing experiences and conflicts with  apparent detachment [p. 42].

There is a confusion, however, in the usage of the diagnosis, schizoid personality. Consistent with Bleuler's (1912) original view, some psychiatrists currently regard "schizoid personality" as either a precursor, or latent variant of schizophrenia. In a corollary way, it is also considered to be a residual characterologic analogue of schizophrenia that is present, for example, following recovery from an acute breakdown. The terms "schizoid" or "schizoid personality" also are used to depict a borderline condition, again in the sense of an incipient psychosis or following recovery from serious psychological disturbances. (Borderline states within psychiatry are,

---

[4] The definitions of schizoid which follow are taken from a number of psychiatric texts and dictionaries (Lorand, Hinsie, and Campbell).

[5] A number of comments in this chapter are taken from the works of Fairbairn (notably from Fairbairn, 1954) and from Guntrip (1964).

in themselves, a complicated subject and no attempt will be made here to relate schizoid personality to various other borderline conditions that have been described by Grinker, Schmitteberg, Hoch and Polatin, or others.)

It should be said, however, that psychiatrists taken as a group tend to read rather dire significance into the designation of schizoid personality—a significance which is, by no means, commonly substantiated. Clinicians whose therapeutic work centers on the treatment of adolescent or college populations generally attach less portent to schizoidal phenomena, because they are seen as frequent as relatively innocuous elements in their clientele. This is also true of clinicians who work with adults in concentrated psychoanalytic work. There, the discovery of latent schizoidal themes can be found routinely in individuals whose social functioning would in no way suggest (or might even belie) the existence of such "splitting."

The relationship between schizoid states and schizophrenia cannot be comprehensively presented here, partly because the arguments for seeing these as separate conditions versus points on a continuum are very diverse and inconclusive. In a review of the genetic aspects of schizophrenia, Böök (1960) discounts the schizoid-schizophrenia (continuum) hypothesis on the grounds that schizoid trait pattern disturbance is so inclusive that the retrospective establishment of schizoid precursors following psychosis is an inexact way of determining the precondition. Furthermore, he cites prospective studies where close examination of personality characteristics prior to the clinical onset of schizophrenia demonstrated no positive correlation between severe introversion, apathy, or withdrawal, as an even common, let alone invariant, predisposition to later schizophrenic breakdown.

Paradoxically, the hypothesis of a schizoid-schizophrenic continuum (held, for different reasons, by many biologically oriented professionals) has been revived and given weight by scientists and writers of fiction concerned with the contemporary experiences of alienation. These writings suggest that disintegration into schizophrenia is a direct function of social and familial pressures. The commentators who take this position are from various scientific and literary backgrounds, and it is not possible to summarize their point of view here. In a sense, however, they all use a somewhat simplified, symbolical interactional model of "illness." They portray schizoidal states and schizophrenia as simple resultants of noxious social pressures. Their basic contention is that internalized, individual madness is, in a linear way, related to familial, corporate, and national madness.

## Contemporary Interpretations and Formulations of Schizoid Conditions

Classical Freudian psychology presents a description of human personality based on a set of biological drives inherent in all individuals.[6] These are observa-

---

[6] The most succinct description of the classical Freudian position is contained in Fenichel (1945).

ble through life but are most blatantly evident during infancy and childhood. Such infantile drives are depicted as compelling, motivational forces within the personality, which (largely) account for the direction of behavior throughout the life of the individual. The development of conceptualizations concerning the more conscious, adaptive, and executive aspects of (adult) human personality occurred later in Freud's career and was fostered by a second generation of psychoanalytic authors (Anna Freud, Wilhelm Reich, Heinz Hartman, etc.). Within orthodox psychoanalysis, therefore, ego psychology came as a later historical adumbration whose current status within psychoanalysis is still dogged to the primacy of the earlier formulations concerning the nature of unconscious processes, infantile behavior, and biological drives.

With a minimum of clamor, a British psychoanalyst, Fairbairn, and his interpreter, Guntrip, have quietly attempted to establish the ego as the most significant element in human personality.[7] Topographically and dynamically, they picture ego (rather than id) at the center of the personality. Briefly stated, Fairbairn (1954) disagrees with Freud that libido is a biological impulse (an autonomous instinct), energized primarily for the need to reduce tension or to achieve pleasure. Fairbairn sees libido as, basically, object-seeking, rather than tension reducing, even in earliest life. He pictures primitive (prohibitory) superego functions as precursors of later conscious ego attitudes that are concerned with the defense of the organism against its own object-seeking mechanisms, as well as in terms of conflicts of individuals with their external world. Moreover, he visualizes early, infantile (primary) ego states as core experiences of a schizoidal type in which the infant begins to define himself as separate from objects. (In this scheme, "objects" are defined both as persons and other material objects in the environment.)

In the broadest terms, Fairbairn (1954) visualizes human personality as basically an object-relations personality. This is opposed to those who formulate object relations as secondary or even incidental. Fairbairn speculates that at the earliest periods of human life, the rudimentary ego is primarily concerned with the building of internal representations (internal objects) based upon relationships with the outside world (external objects). Since the external world is (to the child) exceedingly complex, the internal representations of these phenomena are, even in precognitive childhood, correspondingly complicated.

The concept of the schizoidal splitting of these internal representations follows diverse courses. To a certain extent, there is a separation or splitting which is basic to the very process of making internal representations of external phenomena. This kind of separation would be similar to the objectification or awareness of others incorporated in one of the meanings of alienation (see Chapter 1). A second, and more pathological, meaning of splitting is that of a process whereby internal representations of the outside world are fractionated or split as a reaction

---

[7] Guntrip's (1964) critique of Freudian theory is done with great care. It quotes the original Freudian sources extensively, and also includes responses to criticisms of Fairbairn's (1954) theory by other psychoanalytic authors.

to extremely threatening experiences with external objects. Typically, such pathological splitting is connected with the deletion of negative, frightening, and baleful aspects of objects encountered in the environment. Paradigmatically, this occurs in internalizing the harsh, frightening, and unpleasant aspects of the mother which are split and separated from the benignant and supporting impressions of the same mother. The goal of this splitting is to allow the infant or child to continue relating in a positive way with his otherwise frightening mother. Splitting of this kind, if done in a wholesale way, is held to account for the presence of an abundance of dissociated, negative, internal "partial objects." These partial objects may later become identified with phenomena other than those in which they were originally encountered. (One might note that this formulation amounts to an altered version of the mechanisms and function of "repression.")

A quantitative factor must be added here to assist in understanding Fairbairn's (1954) concept of schizoid personality. If the infant or child has a surfeit of unpleasant encounters with threatening external objects, he must necessarily engage in a great deal of pathological splitting. It is as if many objects in the environment must be selectively processed and divested of their threatening quality in order for the individual to survive and continue interacting. Phenomenologically, the onus of this excessive use of selective decontamination is twofold. First, the individual—simply because of the frequency with which he must perform these functions—becomes acutely aware of himself as a processor of threatening external phenomena. Second, those negative internalizations which are fractionated from the original external objects accumulate as a frightening series of disconnected noxious feelings, memories, and experiences. Since these are disorganized, through being split from their original objects and contexts, they later become diffusely identified with the Self. As such, they constitute a vaguely substantiated but extremely powerful reservoir of negative feelings concerning the Self.

## Self-Alienation as Described by Laing, Fromm, and Horney

This abbreviated review of Fairbarin's (1954) position is presented here not only as general background, but for the elucidation it offers in regard to the genesis of schizoid conditions. The most important aspect of his theory, for our present purposes, is that it accounts for the prodigious amount of negativity and anxiety present in severely schizoidal individuals.

This brief presentation of schizoid states would be seriously remiss in not noting three other theorists who have contributed to the description and formulations of states of pathological estrangement—namely, Erich Fromm, Karen Horney, and R. D. Laing.[8] Interestingly, all three have had as much or more impact on readers outside of their particular professional audience than they have had

[8] Horney, Fromm, and Laing are prolific authors. Reference made to them in this chapter will center on Horney (1963), Fromm (1955), and Laing (1967).

within their own disciplines. Each has spoken of the relation between psychological and social phenomena. Also, the concept of alienation has been central in all of their writings, although each of them has used alienation in a relatively global way.

Schacht (1970) has analyzed Fromm's (1955) and Horney's (1963) use of the concept. In his able and complicated analysis of their major writings, he acknowledges the importance of their contributions but finds their use of the concept of alienation loose, and its application to diverse human conditions, uncritical. (The various species of vagueness, ambiguity, and shifting polarity of the term have been reviewed in the previous chapter. Fromm and Horney, like many others, have suffered from the outrageously flexible etymology of the word alienation. Their contributions to the popularization of alienation as an experience in contemporary life is immense, however puzzling and apparently contradictory their use of the concept of alienation.)

In the same spirit, the writings of R. D. Laing on the ubiquitous propensity for experiencing alienation have had an extraordinary impact on professional and public audiences. In addition to his lucid descriptions of schizophrenic patients, Laing has added to the understanding of schizoidal conditions through his analyses of the individual's experience of estrangement, particularly in *The Divided Self* (Laing, 1965).

Each of these authors formulates that individual deviations and madness are directly related to the impact of a disorganized society on the individual (Fromm, 1955; Horney, 1963; Laing, 1967). Of course, the implication of social factors in individual deviance and madness in no way is exclusive to these authors, as they readily point out. What is distinctive is the importance given to social factors as *sufficient* explanations of abnormality. Horney (1963) does this least. Fromm (1955) certainly makes this point of view plain, but his focus diffuses over into an indictment of society for its social, economic, and humanitarian shortcomings, rather than delving into a protracted case study of Alienated Man.

Laing (1967) comes down on society much harder, and concludes that the whole question of abnormality is simply social. In a way that appears almost playful (although, it is not), he exonerates the psychotic as normal, and sees conformity and adaptation as psychotic.

In a recent review, the theoretical implications of Laing's (1967) work have been critically examined by Siegler, Osmond, and Mann (1969). Although these critics seem overly perturbed with Laing both for being nonmedical in his orientation and for being seductive in his writing, their analysis is interesting. They submit selections of his writings to three of their analytic models of schizophrenia ("conspiratorial," "psychoanalytic," and "psychedelic"). These models are used by them to inspect a variety of theories of schizophrenia. Their brief against Laing is complicated and cannot readily be summarized. However, of the three models used, they show Laing as viewing schizophrenia largely on the basis of conspiratorial and psychedelic hypotheses. Formulations concerning psychoanalytic explanations are far less consistent.[9]

Even allowing for the venom of his critics, Laing's (1967) work seems theoretically heavy on both the conspiratorial and psychedelic explanations of madness. His conspiratorial emphasis centers on an explanation of schizoid states and schizophrenia as externally manufactured conditions. In his explanation, the patient is formulated as a passive object who is brutalized, constricted, and defeated by the family and society who label him "sick," force him to treatment, and submit him to a series (perhaps a whole life) of degradations, incarcerations, and pressure to conform to the ubiquitous "madness" of everyday life.

Laing's (1967) psychedelic explanation of schizoid states and schizophrenia promotes the transcendental and creative features of madness. In his view, certain psychotic states are regarded as transitions to higher states of functioning. Psychosis is therefore seen as a "healing" or renewal in reaction to the confines of a stultifying "normality." This psychedelic emphasis very directly suggests that estrangement, dissociation, and hallucination are positive, even beautiful, experiences.[10]

## THE ONTOLOGICAL STRUGGLE AND THE PROBLEM OF NEGATIVITY

Currently, there are numerous contributions to social-interactional conceptions of schizoid states. One might divide such writings into three main areas: (1) writings concerning the general oppressive social and cultural factors that account for (some) states of self-alienation and deviance; (2) writings that pertain to certain selective social actions of labelling, suppressing, and controlling that have to do with the designation of madness and deviance; and (3) writings which are primarily concerned with an explication of the conditions of severe estrangement as seen by the estranged.

Much of this present volume is concerned with the first of these, although by no means solely with reference to "psychiatric conditions." The activities associated with labelling have been described, but are not a major focus here. This section is concerned with writings [notably those of Laing (1965, 1967), Fromm

[9] Comparison of his work by four of these critics' additional models of schizophrenia ("medical," "moral," "family interactional," and "social") are not made, presumably because the authors do not feel his theories adapt to these. They do not rigorously show this, however. They do dispute the "family interactional" aspects of Laing's theories because they feel he stresses family members as "schizophrenogenic" rather than seeing madness as a collective interaction, as put forth by Haley, Jackson, Bateson, and others. Presumably, they dismiss the social model on the same basis. It should also be clarified here that my understanding of "conspiratorial" is that it is not necessarily "paranoid" or pathological. Conspiracies, after all, do exist. Conspiratorial hypotheses do, however, tend to suggest unilaterally caused conditions, and often are oversimplified in nature.

[10] The creative aspects of schizophrenic disintegration have been commented on by a number of authors in addition to Laing. A relatively recent exposition of this is available by Dabrowski (1964).

(1955), Fairbairn (1954), and Guntrip (1964)] which describe and "explain" malignant forms of estrangement as reactions to social forces.

R. D. Laing (1967) is currently the most influential writer responsible for the accentuation of ontological concerns present in self-alienated, schizoid individuals. The centrality of "problems of being" should not suggest that these are the only mechanisms operating in these various conditions. It is the case, however, that at a clinical, descriptive level, many phenomena are basically related to the problem of individual existence and "being," and, hence, are appropriately emphasized as ontic.

On the other hand, the issues of fatalism and negativity, which are often connected with the forms of these ontological concerns, have been less frequently confronted in existential writings concerning malignant states of estrangement. This is quite parallel to the implicit, unexamined negativity in many sociological writings. Quite unobtrusively, much literature concerning the Alienated Man carries over the implication that such alienation is really inevitable, even desirable. When the issue of negativity is dealt with, it is usually accounted for by way of projection or externalization. It has become popular to account for madness in simplified terms of negative, malignant families or societies which inflict these conditions on individuals. The fact that the (ultimately) schizoidal individuals, themselves, are active in expanding and deepening their own negativity and unrelatedness seems to escape examination.

(Parenthetically, it must be added that the meaning of "negativity" in this essay is relativistic and conventional rather than ethical, empirical, or statistical. Judgments concerning negativity are made according to the tendency to move toward the conventionally regarded lower, or lesser, pole in choices between opposite positions within a given category, for example, good-bad, optimism-pessimism, more-less, happy-unhappy, beautiful-ugly, etc. The author is concerned with the *style* of choosing the conventionally negative pole, rather than with lending any support to the notion that conventionally, normative, negativity is negative in some kind of "ultimate" or pejorative way.)

Flight from persons or from the "social reality" is generally rationalized as being necessarily due to the malignancy of society. Part of the failure to account for the individual's complicity in this process may be attributable to the lack of a rigorous theoretical (developmental) foundation for examining the genesis of these conditions. It may also be attributable to using the subjective, descriptive (existential) utterances of individual patients as final and exclusive explanations of states of estrangement. Objectification, or critical formulation based on other criteria (interpersonal, transactional, etc.) are dispensed with, possibly through being considered to be yet more evidence of socially opprobrious actions against the individual.

## The Function and Meaning of Inauthenticity in Schizoid Conditions

As mentioned before, ontological concerns are central to the experience of self-alienation. The individual is awed by his realization of the synthetic nature of his own, and presumably others', existence. He is distracted by the sound of his own internal machinery, which diminishes his capacity to know or feel others. He is so concerned with his own interior filtering, processing, and reacting "equipment," that he finds little time to examine the actions, qua actions, of others. He prefers to see these actions as a complex of "blips" on his own radar equipment. Possessed with a high degree of objectification and consciousness within himself, he becomes more beguiled with his own reactions to phenomena rather than with the phenomena themselves. He begins to consider himself a locus of processes which are, themselves, disconnected from other processes, both within himself and outside. This sense of disconnectedness accentuates his awareness of separation from others. Descriptions both from fictional and "real" alienated individuals frequently feature terms such as "capsules," "shells," "coverings," "layerings," etc. Metaphorically, such heroes live in "caves," "niches," "cocoons," "containers," and "bell jars." Separation is commonly perceived as a nearly concretized barrier between persons, as if individuals lived behind walls or communicated electronically with each other while living in adjacent Plexiglas containers.

A corollary feeling of falseness and facsimile pervades this disturbed sense of being. Hence, a whole series of descriptions around the idea of *inauthenticity* are replete, both in fictional and real experiences of alienated persons. People are seen as disguised or hiding behind masks. As Laing (1967) comments, the schizoid feels as if he is an actor, player, or impersonator, but never a person. Concepts of "sincerity," "self-confidence," or "authenticity" seem absurd and irrelevant. Relationship to others is accompanied by such intense self-consciousness that any kind of action seems overwhelmingly synthetic, hence phony or "plastic." Like sincerity, spontaneity appears to be a meaningless word, since the schizoid person is so wretchedly aware of the mechanisms underlying his specific actions. It is therefore inconceivable to him that interaction could ever be construed as spontaneous. Even in situations where spontaneity and abandon are difficult to abolish (such as while playing or copulating) the severely alienated person may still feel that he is always acting as an automaton.

The exquisitely schizoidal person becomes, as it were, an amateur sociologist studying his own operations. He looks on himself as a collection of roles rather than a Self. He is able to expound on the nature of his perceptions, integrations, and reactions. However, the tragedy is that in contrast to the use that sociologists make of role playing (as an analytic device), the alienated person begins to believe that that is all he is—a dessicated structural model.

He sees himself as a puppet cued by social circumstances which exact ritualized performances from him. His irritation about the inevitability of this is counterbalanced by one major consolation. This consists of his affection for his own machinery—that is, his own processes and parts. This becomes the most stable and reliable area in his encapsulated ontological scheme. He enjoys the splendid private awareness of his own internal equipment, which he feels (most of the time) that others cannot see. Life then becomes a series of private mental pictures which generate excitement partly because they are secret from others.

In the poignant short story, *Paul's Case,* Cather (1920) grasps the allure and excitement of these consoling, inner experiences.

> Several of Paul's teachers had a theory that his imagination had been perverted by garish fiction; but the truth was, he scarcely ever read at all. The books at home were not such as would either tempt or corrupt a youthful mind, and as for reading the novels that some of his friends urged upon him—well, he got what he wanted much more quickly from music; any sort of music, from an orchestra to a barrel organ. He needed only the spark, the indescribable thrill that made his imagination master of his senses and he could make plots and pictures enough of his own. It was equally true that he was not stage-struck—not, at any rate, in the usual, acceptation of that expression. He had no desire to become an actor, any more than he had to become a musician. He felt no necessity to do any of these things; what he wanted was to see, to be in the atmosphere, float on the wave of it, to be carried out, blue league after blue league, away from everything [p. 56].

A similarly poignant illustration of the connection between "being" and self-alienation is illustrated by Raskolnikov's planning of a murder in Dostoyevsky's (1950) *Crime and Punishment.*

> He could not imagine, for instance, that he would sometime leave off thinking, get up and simply go there. . . . Even his last experiment (i.e., his visit with the object of a final survey of the place) was simply an attempt at an experiment, far from being the real thing, as though one should say "come, let us go and try it—why dream about it!" and at once he had broken down and had run away cursing, in a frenzy with himself. Meanwhile it would seem, as regards the moral question, that his analysis was complete: his casuistry had become keen as a razor, and he could not find rational objections in himself. But in the last resort, he simply ceased to believe in himself and doggedly, slavishly sought arguments in all directions, fumbling for them, as though someone were forcing and drawing him to it [pp. 71-72].

## Inauthenticity as a Touchstone for Action

Although the problem of ontological insecurity has been beautifully expressed by Laing, the implications of the degree to which falseness and inauthenticity are *goals* rather than concomitants has not been confronted. It would seem that the schizoidal disguise is not a side product or mere resultant of social pressures, but rather an essential ingredient which makes performance possible (as in the illustration concerning Raskolnikov cited above).

The portentiousness of any action, significant or insignificant, is, as it were, divested of its threat by pretending that it never really quite happens. The point of mentioning this here is to expose the negativity that accompanies this state of separateness. Ideas concerning personal change or the initiation of any new action take on the cast of heroic, radical, and terrifying change. This portentious characteristic of change is not only connected with major existential crises, when one might expect such anxiety, but pertains equally to contemplating even the most mundane actions.

One is reminded of Prufrock's dilemma in T. S. Eliot's (1934) poem:

Shall I part my hair behind? Do I dare to
        eat a peach?
I shall wear white flannel trousers, and walk
        upon the beach.

It is as if decisions to eat, part one's hair, or take a walk are beset with the highest consequentiality. The problem is that in severe schizoid states, all actions become auspicious, inasmuch as they call to mind ontological concerns. The fear is that unless a real experience can be modified into a "pseudoexperience," the anxiety called forth by the situation may be overwhelming.

It is striking that in most of the literature (both popular and scientific), this negativity, connected with anticipated change, is projected onto the fickleness or intransigence of others. Because of the nature of his introspections, the schizoid individual's thesis is that all behavior occurs on the basis of reaction to a constantly frightening, malignant environment.

Nelson (1971) has also spoken directly to this point. In a critical review he states:

> Along with the other charismatics of our day, Laing runs away from the problematical and predicamental aspects of human existence. To suppose that every influence exerted by every individual upon any other individual is lethal, is to be trapped in nightmare. Unhappily, as is true of the other pneumatics of our time, Laing's supposition is that of a one-person universe—a universe in which only the Transcendental Self has reality [p. 199].

The way in which this projection of negativity is handled in Laing's (1967), and others', description of schizoid states and schizophrenia has not received much critical attention when contrasted with the enthusiastic response to his sympathetic phenomenological depiction of schizophrenia.

Holbrook (1968), however, has teased out Laing's implicit acceptance of negativity in an essay analyzing *The Divided Self, The Self and Others,* and *The Politics of Experience.* In what he calls the "Death Circuit," Holbrook conducts a literary (alluding to Sylvia Plath and Dylan Thomas) and psychoanalytic (Winnicott, Fairbairn, Bowlby) inspection of the implications of Laing's negative position on ontology. He says:

> Laing's problem, I believe, is that he sees that what is necessary is "dissolution of identification." He misinterprets that, however, as dissolution of the ego. Moreover, he is so terrified of relationship in which genuine feeling is involved that the later stages (of maturation, or the growth of independence) appear largely meaningless to him. He cannot abide mutuality. He would not, I

believe, understand Winnicott's emphasis on the positive, reparative work that
has to go on between mother and child. By contrast, Laing understands disintegration, but seems less to believe in integration. Thus, he cannot emphasize
growth in relational therapy, nor can he see any hope in "contributing in" to
the family and social order. The "rebirth" he offers is an extra-personal cosmic
affair; it is, above all, not "weak" in the recognition that we may after all be
no more than human.

According to Guntrip, by contrast, what is needed is an atmosphere in which,
instead of seeking a Wagnerian territory of transcendental mysticism, we accept
our ego-weakness (as Sylvia Plath cries in a poem, "O love, O embryo")—and begin from there, in our needs for one another and our needs *to be.* Laing's intem-
perate mysticism is in fact a further contribution to the prevalent "taboo on
weakness" which is surely the most dangerous tendency in our era [p. 35].

The problem is that those anxieties about action, called up by the need to
act, are handled in the two ways mentioned before. Either the baleful aspects of
an insane external world are held responsible for such excessive anxiety, or the
"creativity" of these states of terrified withdrawal are depicted as "beautiful,"
in themselves. One need not totally deny the veracity of either of these observations.
However, a problem is encountered when these accounts are offered as sufficient
and complete explanations, conspiratorial and psychedelic, in accounting for schizoid states and schizophrenics. At best, such theorizing is structurally weak in not
examining the interactional dimensions of madness.

## The "Beauty" of Psychotic Disintegration

Imputing beauty to psychotic disintegration is generally done in an impressionistic way, where clinicians or novelists cite exceptional individuals whose creativity manages to shine through and partly sway their psychotic episodes. Even
in these instances, which are certainly exceptions rather than the ordinary experience, beauty is inferred by the outside observer. When not dealing with exceptional
individuals, the depiction of psychosis can be beautified through sympathetic description and, in the hands of Laing and others, communicates the meaning and
significance of psychotic dissolution. As in the portrayal of any character in a well
written tragedy, the author is able to make the central character believable, heroic,
and, hence, beautiful. This amounts to glamorizing psychotic disintegration for
esthetic purposes. The novelist not only has the prerogative but the necessity to
do this.

However, it is more difficult to justify the attempts of scholarly writers when
they uncritically indulge poetic license. One expects a scientist-clinician to be able
to distinguish between writing beautifully about tragedy, and the actuality of experiencing tragedy. When the scientific author fails to make this distinction, intentionally or otherwise, he is engaged in a highly promotive exercise.

Whatever else the experience of madness is, it rarely is beautiful to those involved in it. Those autobiographical depictions of insanity (by Schreber, Beers,
Hannah Greene, and many others) rarely suggest much of comfort, let alone

beauty.[11] Similarly, fictional accounts of madness or poetry depicting depravity and isolation may connote beauty in terms of their organization, style, and poignancy, but hardly in terms of their content. In a quite remarkable way, Laing (1967) concretistically accepts all of the paradoxes and negativity in the experience of psychosis and attributes beauty to the content as well as the style. Again, this seems to be mainly a poetical construction that he, as an outside observer, creates, rather than what is felt by the severely schizoid or psychotic person.

This kind of construction was discussed in the Introduction in terms of the manner in which some continental existential writers (e.g., Camus, Kafka) react to alienation. Their fictional characters do not simply accept the absurd, incongruent, and savage aspects of human society. Rather, they comply with the society, not through a perfunctory conformity, but by apparently relishing and amplifying these incongruencies. The ontological world of these fictional "heroes" becomes substantiated through the very presence of these incongruencies and inconsistencies. As Knoff (1969) has commented, the process of creating meaninglessness then, itself, becomes centrally meaningful.[12] The point is that this kind of acceptance is not a passive process but a very active, dialectical procedure toward self-estrangement.

Mechanisms within these estranged individuals can be seen as concerned with deepening the experience of incoherence and insubstantiality as an actively sought goal, rather than simply complying with inexorable, fatalistic ends pressed on them by an insane society. It is not, as it is misleadingly portrayed, a release into a splendid new world of a starkly isolated self. (A tabular comparison of psychedelic and psychotic experiences constructed by Siegler et al., 1969, clarifies Laing's uncritical beautification of madness.)[13]

## Interpretation of the Negativity in Severe Self-Alienation

A dynamic explanation for the need to foster and emphasize the "beautiful and negative" experience of self-alienation has not been entirely clarified. A theo-

[11] A recent account of a schizophrenic episode has been published by Bowers (1965). This article utilizes a diary written during a person's disintegration and includes corollary observations concerning events in the young man's life as viewed by others. Bowers quotes the patient's later opinion (following recovery) about his diary account of madness as being "so bitter, I really can't see how I ever wrote it. It doesn't bother me to read it because it just doesn't seem like me [p. 358]."

[12] Knoff (1969) examines Mersault's resignation as an active process of resolution when he is faced with the inanities of human existence. Knoff's point is that meaninglessness is (partly) sought after rather than passively accepted.

[13] Although these authors (Siegler et al., 1969) are guilty of "overkill," their contrasts between genuinely psychedelic experience and (the usual kinds of) psychotic experience eloquently make the point that extreme estrangement or madness are ordinarily not beautiful. Their scheme is too complex to display here but takes into account time dimension, space dimension, feeling, cognition, perception, and identity.

retical formulation for the psychoanalytic basis of mechanisms underlying the schizoid position has been laid down by Kelin, Fairbairn, Guntrip, and others. These interpretations take into acount both the individual and his social interactions through "object-relations" theory. The explanation, which follows here, will attempt to account, from the dynamic standpoint, for one aspect of the deepening of the schizoidal position. Here, "dynamic" is used in the sense that Rapaport (1960) has defined it as "(an) ultimate determiner of all behavior . . . [p. 47]."

This is to suggest that the drives toward object relationships are turned inward.[14] This has, of course, been repeatedly posited in virtually all commentaries on schizoid conditions before and after Bleuler (1912). Fairbairn (1954) has attempted to account for the schizoidal dilemma in two distinct ways. Guntrip (1966) summarizes the development of his position:

> Fairbairn at first regarded the schizoid's withdrawal from objects as due to his fear that his unsatisfied needs, which the object failed to meet, had become so greedy and devouring that his love had become even more dangerous than his hate. This phenomenon is clearly met with in analysis, but it is only halfway to the more complete explanation toward which Fairbairn's work developed as he discarded impulse psychology, namely, that it is at bottom a question of an infantile ego unable to cope with its outer world. The schizoid is split in his growing emotional life by the inconsistency of his primary parental objects and becomes a prey to loss of internal unity, radical weakness, and helplessness. While still partly struggling to deal with the outer world, he also partly withdraws from it and becomes detached or out of touch, finding refuge in his internal fantasy world [p. 233].

Underlying both of these explanations, Fairbairn (1954) would presumably see a retroversion of basic drives toward satisfactory relationships with objects Originally craving attachment to the outside, the schizoid later becomes occupied with the objectification of his internal mental life.

This process of self-objectification has many facets and would require an exposition of case material and review of theoretical writings to portray it in a meaningful way here. In lieu of this, only one characteristic will be highlighted—namely, the use of the process of "objectification" to denigrate or constrain the individual. This would be the use of introspection to arrive at what Laing (1965, pp. 39-61) depicts as states of "engulfment," "implosion," and "petrification."

The process of self-objectification (insight) is generally heralded as "good" both in religious, political, and psychotherapeutic contexts. It is, therefore, difficult for some psychotherapists, existentially oriented or otherwise, to grasp the destructive and paralytic aspects of self-objectification when used by the schizoid

---

[14] Presented out of context the importance of drive theory in psychoanalysis may appear to be overemphasized or even a bit atavistic. It should be remembered that Rapaport's (1960) analysis is concerned with the structure of psychoanalytic theory viewed as ten compartmentalizations, only one of which is concerned with *drive*. Discussion of the relationship of drives to other structural elements in the theory is beyond the scope of this chapter.

person. The negativity and terror encountered in such introspections are handled
by the patient in three ways. As mentioned before, negativity can be projected
simplistically onto the external world. Alternatively, the negativity may be posi-
tivized by imputing a beauty to the realization of depravity, as in the artistic creations of Edgar Allan Poe, Hieronymous Bosch, or Jean Genet. A final way to dispose with the problem of negativity is to suggest that all actions are only relative
in significance and value. This last view dispenses with the need to deal with negativity at all.

It is my contention that irrespective of the mechanism, the goal of such severe schizoid introspection is to reify a sense of insubstantiality and disconnectedness—a sense of conditionality and "nonbeing." For the schizoid individual, ontological insecurity becomes the touchstone for all performances.

The formulation might be stated in the following fashion: "If I think that I
am not, then I may be!" The complicated problems of ontology ("being") are
solved by transformation into their opposite ("nonbeing"). Hence, one is "authentic" as long as one is aware of being disconnected or "inauthentic."

Remaining conceptually and ideationally disconnected then becomes the
major (ontological) security operation. All questions of interaction and involvement
are tested in this fundamental security context. The question is "will this action
disturb my nonbeing?" If it does not, then action is possible—whether it be parting
one's hair, eating a peach, marrying, or running for the presidency.

Authentic, spontaneous communion is antithetical and threatening to the
security operations of the alienated person. Security resides in the schizoid person's
capacity to conceptualize himself as just another social object—a mechanism, a
thing. At an extreme, the capacity to visualize his own extinction and death as an
objective (insignificant and cosmic) event gives a schizoidal person the sense of
security that he can portray himself in other (likewise fictional) performances with
"real" individuals. In a manner that nonreflective persons find baffling, the schizoid
person is able to introspect concerning colossal kinds of internal ontological threats,
but pales at notions of union outside of himself. This accounts for how he may
spend an entire morning conceptualizing his own depravity and insubstantiality
(including dramatic fantasies of suicide), enjoying the controlled terror called up
by these reflections, but feels incapable of picking up the telephone to ask a young
woman to attend a concert with him later in the week. Anxiety-free performance
seems to depend crucially on the capacity to believe that events only seem to happen, rather than actually happen.

The relation of these negative feelings to the constraints on performance
can be explained through the use of Fairbairn's (1954) insight concerning the internalization of bad (partial) objects during infancy and childhood. It has been
mentioned that the process of associating with a surfeit of intermittently obnox-
ious social objects during childhood produces a high degree of suspense connected
with the thought of conducting social relationships. The need to filter out, control,

and modulate the behaviors of oneself and others gives rise to an overawareness of the mechanistic nature of future interactions. If afflicted with an overabundance of these experiences, the developing child is left with a residual sense of his own idiosyncrasy, negativity, and strangeness. Anticipation concerning the feelings he will encounter in certain interactions with others tends to be exorbitantly high. Anticipations concerning the negative quality of one's own actions are correspondingly elevated. The ontological security which accompanies the thought that "things do not really happen" or "I am really not here" is used as a protective device against the experience of severe anxiety or concern about failure. It, furthermore, engenders a positive version of his own facsimile. That is to say, instead of saying, "I feel as if I am not being sincere or spontaneous," the person instead declaims, "*All* of my actions are insubstantial." This latter statement is then protective toward the schizoid's own feelings since "things aren't really happening." It also provides an ontological catch-all to justify any kind of subsequent event that might occur in consequence of one's own personal behavior.

Seen in this way, the ontic quest of the alienated is not so much a solipsistic enterprise designed to discover the true and real nature of things. Rather, it is a security device designed to protect the individual from the anticipations of painful interactions and to moderate the potentially strong, negative feelings concerning himself.

Before referring to the interpersonal relations of the schizoid individual, one final aspect of his personal ontology should be developed—namely, the maintenance of a sense of disconnectedness (i.e., alienation) from others.[15] The concentration on Self as a fractionated series of complex private processes leads to an accentuation of idiosyncrasy and differentness and, most important, distance from others. Conceiving of himself as an objectified, social "atom" (like all other social objects), he concludes that his own intricate self is as different from others as if he were a separate species. Through his observation of others (at a distance) he detects banality, triteness, and naivete. His views of the performances of others are used by him as further evidence of his own peculiarity, and at the same time as evidence of the strangeness and superficiality of others.

The differences between himself and others may also be noted in terms of feelings. The alienated person may, therefore, intellectually understand that others are experiencing anxiety, uncertainty, and hesitation in their experiences. However, he only sees their superficial behavior, which appears calm when compared to his own inner state of turmoil. Failing to realize what others may feel, he condemns himself for having such exorbitant states of feelings. He simultaneously disclaims the meaning of the superficial performances of others through smugness, arrogance, or envy.

---

[15] Laing talks of this maintenance of boundary (internal coherence) as "inner honesty" (Laing, 1967) and as the pathological need for control (Laing, 1965, p. 83). While he relates this defensive system to a lack of ontological security, I am taking the *opposite* position that the maintaining of this dividedness is necessary in order to establish ontological security.

The important point is that he maintains a sense of discontinuity between his experiences and the experiences of others. As Daly (1968) has pointed out, however, the alienated person still continues to make attempts to continue to relate despite these discontinuities. Withdrawal does not operate by simply diminishing the kind and number of interactions that the schizoid person hazards. Safety can also be realized through a radical denial of the conventional meaning inherent in various performances with other persons. The individual is, therefore, free to vacillate toward and away from people, depending upon the urgency of his feelings connected with these various polar states. Each strategy, however, controls or constricts feeling, one by reducing contact, and the second through the ruse of consciously denying any personal feeling of significance to interpersonal events.

The notion of overcoming separation from others creates the highest level of anxiety in the alienated person. Again, Daly (1968) has discussed this basic conflict concerning action in terms of schizoidal rule-following in regard to approach-avoidance conflicts centering around attempted communion with real persons, ideas, and emotional supplies.[16] In his analysis, the attempts to connect with gratifying objects, to commit himself to ideational systems, or to satisfy his compelling desires are all met with increasing anxiety as satisfactory resolution approaches. Each of these situations is associated with a mounting terror which signals the loss of his secure isolation and a return of the insufferable conflicts which originally led to the creation of the defensive position. The severely alienated person, therefore, fears dependency gratification because it is visualized as an incorporation into a larger engulfing object (which would obliterate the internal definition of himself, and, hence, would be a kind of death). Similarly, commitment of ideology confronts the schizoidal person with a threatening dependency on certain others who may share his ideology. This again would profoundly upset a person whose ontological security is primarily based upon exclusive communion with his own internal objects.[17] Obviously, authentic relations with others (even idealized persons) are threatening and potentially disintegrating.

Similarly, the spontaneous expression of impulses is threatening insofar as the meaning connected with these behaviors cannot be carefully modulated, and may, therefore, expose the person to feelings which he cannot manage. Such impulsive spontaneity, moreover, is connected with one other idea—namely, the notion of transparency. The severely schizoid person operates as the technician who is busy twirling dials and pulling levers behind the public screen of his social per-

[16] This is discussed in a section entitled "The Ideational Schizoid Way" (Daly, 1968, p. 406). This article (as summarized herein) also discusses dependent and impulsive schizoid styles.

[17] One of the differences between persons labelled "schizoid personalities" versus those labelled "schizophrenic" is the schizoidal persons' reluctance to embrace a radical ideological scheme which might psychotically "explain" himself to others. It is as if the schizoid person continues to be ambivalent about both ambient ideologies as well as explanations concerning his own, and others', actions. The schizophrenic, as it were, finally makes a radical choice and fixedly defends his private ideology.

formances. The supposition is made that the insubstantiality of his own performance might be glimpsed by others if he were to act more casually. Spontaneity,
therefore, would allow the outsider to look in on his disheveled apparatus and see
the frenzy, the disguise, and, worst of all, the "badness" and the loneliness which
are his hallmarks.

## LATENT SCHIZOID CONDITIONS AND THE ADAPTATION TO AN ALIENATING WORLD

The foregoing description of schizoid states has focused on states of severe
estrangement (self-alienation) which, except in the most romanticized and poetical
reconstructions, are usually painful and maladaptive. In emphasizing these particularly gross maladaptations, it may unintentionally have been implied that schizoid
phenomena are necessarily pathological and maladaptive. Of course, this simply is
not true. The trenchant formulations of the existential writers (fictional, "clinical,"
and scholarly) have portrayed the fact that less severe schizoidal adaptations are
all too adaptive to living in a society which itself is severely dissociated and schizoidal.

The chapter has intentionally focussed on the most severe states of estrangement and has been concerned with depicting a psychological explanation for such
conditions, stressing interactional interpretations derived from object-relations
theory. This should not distract from the fact that milder (i.e., nonsymptomatic,
"adaptive") schizoidal mechanisms abound, particularly in persons living in industrialized product-oriented, technocratic societies. Sadly, such adaptations are so
general that they possess the substance of "normality," and escape definition as
"pathology" or "sickness." These adaptations have been richly documented by
others, but will be briefly sketched here.

The foregoing sections have been principally concerned with describing individuals whose "conditionality of being" is exceedingly pronounced, and whose
relationships to others are connected with the potentials for severe, paralyzing
anxiety states. A much more common, but considerably less disabling situation
obtains in those many individuals who visualize the social substance as a series of
intricate, vapid role performances, but who, despite this, are fully capable of mastering the various quadrilles, minuets, and tarantellas dictated by the nature of
their various social relationships. Such behavior, however, is predicated on the
same mechanism that the more malignant, schizoidal person employs: that is, the
condition that none of the performances ultimately matters. This is furthermore
accompanied by the consoling awareness that their "real self" exists at an internal,
subjective level, at a safe distance from the social phenomena in which the Self
participates. Alienated individuals functioning in this way do not ordinarily seek
psychiatric treatment, except as they suddenly become aware of a special sense

of loneliness, or if their performance in the objective social reality is sensed as deficient by themselves or others.

These individuals survive as long as they are able to keep the differentiation between inside and outside clearly separated. They live, as it were, in two worlds, and learn not to expect congruity between the internal self and the social reality. Problems of ethics and questions of integrity are always contextually and operationally determined. Such persons are sustained during their work day by the ethics and goals of their organizations. Measurement of the integrity and accomplishment of their family is similarly ascriptive, externalized, and objective. For example, the family may be evaluated by the way in which individuals measure up to community standards in terms of the appearance of the home, the acquisition of certain kinds of consumer products, and the maintenance of expected social rituals. If the family "fails" (wives slip into alcoholism, sons desert to communes, mothers are sent to nursing homes, or daughters expire of drug overdose) these events are ascribed to deficiencies in the *culture.* This does not imply that individuals do not mourn such untoward occurrences, but that these individuals are ultimately insulated from them. They are prepared to rationalize such unpropitious endings (he paid for his wife's psychoanalysis; he used to go to football games with his son; he took his mother to the social security office; he sent his daughter to an excellent secretarial school).

The alarming fact, however, is that their very schizoidal habitus keeps them (existentially) "well." The culturally sustained dissociation ("splitting") allows them to live with thermonuclear threats, environmental destructions, and nationalized savagery. On a more homely level, such alienation also fosters protean adaptations and a diminished expectation for meaning and transcendence through work, family, friendship, and recreation.

## SUMMARY AND CONCLUSION

Although cultural factors affect all classifications of human behavior, both descriptively and prescriptively, their influence on the diagnosis of "character (or personality) disorders" is especially evident. Two variants of one such "disorder" —schizoid personality—have been described in this chapter. To repeat, these three sources are: (1) writings concerning the general, oppressive, social, and cultural factors that account for (some) states of self-alienation and deviancy; (2) writings that pertain to certain selective social actions of labelling, suppressing, and controlling that have to do with the designation of madness and abnormality; and (3) writings which are primarily concerned with the internally perceived (and explained) experience of severe estrangement.

The "schizoid personality" has been presented as a conventional, nominal category, serving to describe both unusual, and not-so-unusual states of separation and estrangement from self and fellowman. Prior to this century, such states of isolation, withdrawal, and eccentricity were formulated in a highly general way as "madness." Milder varieties of idiosyncrasy were depicted as heresy, scrupulosity, apostacy, or eccentricity. These were conceptualized in terms of *sinning,* deficiencies in spiritual life, or evidence of dislocation in the individual's relation to certain cosmic regularities.

The contemporary explanations for estrangement, while partly incorporating these older explanations, are much more complex.

Alienation is now pictured as ubiquitous—a prototypical "given" affecting the lives of all individuals—especially those who live in technologically advanced societies. Although the word is still used scientifically by several disciplines, its generalizability has led to its becoming the twentieth century version of the panchreston, sin. ("Sin," of course, was not the only behavioral panchreston in the past, but, like "alienation," became a category for all kinds of badness and deviance.)

The interesting and fundamental difference, between alienation and sin, of course, is that sin basically implicated the individual in his specific imperfections, which occasioned a separation (and alienation) from God, temporal institutions, and fellowman. The post-Enlightenment view of alienation is radically different in emphasis. The onus for badness and consequent separation has now been largely displaced onto the terrible incongruities inherent in Man's collective (social) life. Although individual persons are implicated in contributing to these conditions, the overwhelming blame for the malignant separateness, meaninglessness, violence, and thwarting of affection is attributed by Man to his *systems of social organization* rather than to his existence as an individual. Another important difference between the panchrestons, sin and alienation, is that the concept of sin was directly related to an overall, explicit cosmological explanation of existence. Human deficiencies or awareness of anguish were directly relatable to (the then) "existential" conditions. In other words, there was a very specific formula for examining individual morality in terms of ultimate significance. Despite the impact of culture critics, the concept of alienation does not readily lead to connections between individual actions and ultimate values. Questions of an individual morality, if raised at all, are answered scientifically and relativistically in the specific contexts in which they occur. More often, however, questions of individual morality are answered by a nebulous indictment of "society," or "technology," or some other collective cause. Rather than leading to the authentic (existential) experience of "wrongness," guilt, or "badness," such a displacement seems to foster an exoneration or rationalization, and, hence, a lowering of concern about the need for any kind of ultimate "rightness."

In the current literature, alienation is mainly attributed to persons living in congested, manufacturing centers, working in Kafkaesque offices, or tending machines which produce things they neither understand nor can value. These faceless individuals are pictured as living in violent and schizoid nuclear families. Their most benign appetites are centered on the acquisition of meaningless, obsolescent objects and the desire to climb to some position of relative importance in a hierarchy of meaningless positions and statuses. Their worst appetites are evidenced by their ravages against other sovereign groups and their heedless abuse of technology to threaten the lives of themselves and others.

Although the above summary may seem overdrawn, it is meant to highlight the fact that much contemporary social philosophy and social science is devoted to the collective externalization and categorization of negativity ("badness," "sin," and "alienation") as de facto operations of large contemporary technological societies. This unilateral reification of badness, in itself, represents the creation of an arbitrary taxonomy similar to the intricate canons, rules, and rituals developed by the medieval church to define and locate the sources of all depravity.

In a complementary way, the depiction of Alienated Man by psychiatric and existential writers indirectly, if unintentionally, substantiates personal alienation as both an inevitable and even acceptable mode—given these malignant social conditions. Schizoid adaptations are therefore justified (on the basis of a bad society and a dead God), and beatified, as in "Saint Genet," on the theory that even the most depraved estrangement is preferable to a mindless conformity in a psychotic society.

Both the social and existential positions tend, ineluctably, not only to explain madness, but inadvertently to depict alienation as sensible and desirable. The implications of these positions will be discussed in a concluding chapter.

## REFERENCES

Bleuler, E. *Dementia praecox.* (Transl. by J. Zinkien) New York: International Universities Press, 1950.

Böök, J. A. Genetical aspects of schizophrenic psychoses. In D. D. Jackson (Ed.), *The etiology of schizophrenia.* New York: Basic Books, 1960. Pp. 43-46.

Bowers, M. The onset of psychosis. *Psychiatry,* 1965, *28*, 346-358.

Cather, W. Paul's case. In *Youth and the bright Medusa.* New York: Knopf, 1920.

Dabrowski, K. *Positive disintegration.* Boston: Little, Brown, 1964.

Daly, W. Schizoid role following. *Psychoanalytic Review,* 1968, *55*, 400-412.

*Diagnostic and statistical manual of mental disorders.* (2nd ed.) Washington, D. C.: American Psychiatric Association, 1968.

Dostoyevsky, F. *Crime and punishment.* New York: Modern Library, 1950.

Eliot, T. S. The love song of J. Alfred Prufrock. In *Collected Poems of T. S. Eliot.* New York: Harcourt, 1934.

Fairbairn, W. R. D. *An object-relations theory of the personality.* New York: Basic Books, 1954.

Fenichel, O. *Psychoanalytic theory of neurosis.* New York: Norton, 1945.

Fromm, E. *The sane society.* New York: Holt, 1955.

Guntrip, H. *Personality structure and human interaction.* New York: International Universities Press, 1964.

Holbrook, D. R. D. Laing and the death circuit. *Encounter,* 1968, *31,* 38-45.

Horney, K. *The neurotic personality of our time.* New York: Horton, 1963.

Knoff, W. A Psychiatrist reads Camus' "The Stranger." *Psychiatric Opinion,* 1969, *6,* 19-25.

Kohut, H. Introspection, empathy, and psychoanalysis. *American Psychoanalytic Association Journal,* 1959, *7,* 459-483.

Laing, R. D. *The divided self.* Baltimore: Penguin Books, 1965.

Laing, R. D. *The politics of experience.* New York: Pantheon Books, 1967.

Nelson, B. Afterword; a medium with a message: R. D. Laing. *Salmagundi Review,* 1971, No. 16 (Spring), 199-201.

Rappaport, D. *The structure of psychoanalytic theory.* New York: International Universities Press, 1960.

Schacht, R. *Alienation.* Garden City, N. Y.: Doubleday, 1970. Pp. 115-145.

Siegler, M., Osmond, H., & Mann, H. Laing's model of madness. *British Journal of Psychiatry,* 1969, *115,* 947-958.

*Webster's third new international dictionary of the English language.* Springfield, Mass.: Merriam, 1968.

# Chapter 3

# Alienation and Identity: Some Comments on Adolescence, the Counterculture, and Contemporary Adaptations

*Donald Oken*

State University of New York

## INTRODUCTION

Alienation is the catchword of the day. College students are neither unhappy nor bad, wild nor troubled, as would have been said in other times; they are alienated. Factory workers are not exploited, lazy, or opportunistic; they too are alientated. So, also, is the voter, the academic, the black, the executive, the white collar worker. So are we all. It is not just that behavioral scientists increasingly have come to consider alienation as a pivotal concept. It has become a central preoccupation of the whole literate segment of our society. Moreover, we are told that alienation has developed not merely as a deplorable by-product of our modern Western culture, but that it is the very essence of this culture. Lo, verily, this is "The Age of Alienation."[1]

What this preoccupation means and the extent to which it mirrors reality are questions that I will address later. However, it does seem clear that hysteria abounds, and that the problem would benefit far more from a careful analysis (to which, hopefully, this volume will make a helpful contribution) than from anxious bewailing. In this spirit, the purpose of this chapter is to examine alienation from a psychiatric perspective that draws primarily on the concept of "Identity." This concept will serve as a basis for understanding alienation in the context of normal development,

[1] Inevitably, a book has appeared with this very title (Murchland, 1971).

particularly during adolescence, and will provide significant insights into it as a phenomenon both of the "counterculture" and of our society at large.

As with any term of such wide usage, a great variety of meanings have developed. Nevertheless, these have a good deal of convergence, from which it is possible to derive a useful working definition. Let us consider that alienation represents a sense of estrangement from other human beings, from society and its values, and from the self—particularly from those parts of the self that link it to others, and to society at large.

In one sense this is a psychological (as differentiated from a sociological) definition, for it starts from an internal feeling state.[2] However, it is one that can arise in individuals comprising a group, as well as individually. Moreover, the suggested definition is not narrowly psychological. For one thing, it is perfectly amenable to use by those whose interests lie in the structure of social organization, institutions, values, group behavior, role, and the like, as these relate to emotional experience. More important, its breadth lies in understanding the inherent premise that the basic nature of man is social. In infancy, survival itself depends not only upon the biological caretaking activities of others but also upon their psychological interaction (Spitz, 1945). At every subsequent stage, the developmental process takes place in a human environment with its (particular) individual, social, and cultural characteristics. Man is an indissolubly biopsychosocial organism, nothing less. Thus, the definition offered is really a psychosocial one that permits us to expand from a focus on internal processes to social, cultural, and historical phenomena.

Furthermore, the nature of psychological processes makes sharp inside/outside distinctions untenable. Not only is it difficult to untangle the web of causation so as to delineate social versus psychological forces, but the nature of a "complaint" is often misleading. The dynamic phenomenon of "projection" allows an internal state to be experienced, and reported, as one arising outside. (There are, after all, real paranoids—even in anomic environments.) Conversely, one may shut one's eyes to painful reality and experience pain as arising as a product of the self rather than the outer world ("It's all in my head") in order to maintain a modicum of seeming

---

[2] Many authors have examined the problem of defining alienation as a psychological versus a social phenomenon. One way to deal with this is to consider the two as separate phenomena, reserving the term alienation to refer to the psychological event and labeling the homologous social phenomenon as "anomie," the latter being consistent with Durkheim's original use of this term (e.g., Nettler, 1957). For a detailed review of many of the issues involved in the social versus psychological differentiation, see McClosky and Schaar (1965).

The difficulties in developing a fully satisfactory definition in purely sociological terms are beautifully revealed by the fact that the modern classic sociological analysis of anomie (see Merton, 1957) has been criticized by another sociologist for being too "atomistic and individualistic," i.e., that it is actually psychological (see Cohen, 1965). To my reading, however, the schema offered in substitution could itself be criticized on the very same score.

It also should be emphasized that a definition of alienation is entirely distinct from a statement about its causes, as I will shortly develop.

self-determination. This is why the stated definition disregards the perceived or reported source of the feeling of alienation, even if that source is verifiably "real." To take this position is not, as mistakenly thought, to classify alienation as a clinical psychiatric phenomenon, and thus to deny validity to social criticism. On the contrary, only after its existence has been defined is it possible to proceed to identify the particular external sociocultural and internal psychological elements involved in the genesis of a specific occurrence of alienation.

This process of delineation often calls for the unique contribution of dynamic psychiatry (i.e., that which derives from Psychoanalysis) which provides a basis for looking beyond phenotypic behavior to genotypic motivational processes. The lens of psychodynamic interpretation has revealed, for example, that obligate conformity is no less a manifestation of alienation than is deviant behavior, and that deviance by no means necessarily indicates alienation. Of course, the accuracy of this interpretive method is by no means perfect. Given the psychiatric orientation to look beneath plausible explanations for the actual, if unconscious, determinants, the potential for uncovering elements of psychopathology in almost all instances of alienation poses a hazard. Though the problem is real, this error is far less commonly made than is generally believed by those outside the field. Statements about "unconscious determinants," are in no sense necessarily attributions of abnormality, though they may appear to be because psychiatric terminology is most often applied to clinical disorders.[3]

Conversely, all psychiatric illness (psychotic and otherwise) could be considered to represent alienation, for every emotional disorder is associated with at least partially defective connections among parts of the self, and with others.[4] While it may be perfectly valid to apply the term this way, to do so is neither consistent with its present day usage nor heuristically helpful. Both in other scholarly fields and in general currency, alienation is customarily reserved to characterize states in which the particular sense of estrangement exists as a major element, whether or not associated with clinical disorders. This is the way most psychiatrists now use the term, and the way it shall be used here.

[3] There is still another way in which social and psychological factors may become compounded. It is perfectly possible that appropriate social action in response to inadequacies in the real social world are so distorted by the neurotic process as to be rendered ineffectual, misplaced off target, or inappropriately expressed. In these instances the psychiatrist quite appropriately treats the patient for a neurosis even though the sources and resolution of the problems lie outside the patient. Again, this does not imply any relegation of social action to the sphere of a psychiatric disorder. Quite the contrary, once freed from his neurosis, the ex-patient can be expected to be a significantly more effective actor on the social scene.

[4] For a recent example of this generalized definition, see Tietz and Woods (1970). Interestingly, Freud used the term alienation, doing so in the closely general related sense of a turning away from reality. By this he specifically included not merely psychotic phenomena but the subtle reality distortions associated with all neurotic symptoms (see Freud, 1959).

## IDENTITY

The pursuit of further understanding of alienation can be helpfully accomplished by an examination of the concept that is, in effect, its mirror image: Identity.[5] Having a sense of identity, knowing "who one is," represents the polar opposite of felt estrangement from one's self. Furthermore, identity, like alienation, is an inherently psychosocial concept. As a definition of the self, it stands at its boundaries, looking Janus-like both inward toward other parts of the personality and outward to the world. It represents the sense of ongoing continuity of one's meaning to others as well as to the self.

This enduring continuity is, of course, a dynamic one. Coherence, wholeness, and congruence come closer to capturing the quality than does stability.[6] What is meant by a "stable" sense of identity involves the capacity to remain oneself in the face of even radically changing conditions: its hallmark is resiliency, not rigidity. This flexibility provides the capacity to assume a variety of roles with confidence in the ability to maintain one's self-sameness, so that one does not have to fear taking these on and becoming fully committed to them.

From the developmental ("genetic") standpoint, though an individual's identity crystallizes at the close of adolescence, the process begins in earliest infancy and continues throughout life. Identity is a configuration arising out of "constitutional givens, idiosyncratic libidinal needs, favored capacities, significant identifications, effective defenses, successful sublimations, and consistent roles [Erikson, 1959, p. 116]." More than that, it requires the integration of all these factors: all of what one was, and how he got to be what he is. While past aspects of the self may be foregone, they are not, in the healthy identity, repudiated. As the successive developmental tasks characteristic of each stage of early life are mastered, they remain part of the self, and, within limits, accessible to it. Consequently, the mature person possesses the capacity to accept and experience the child within himself: to be naive and open, to be dependent and defiant, and to allow "regression in the service of the ego [Kris, 1952]," etc. Where difficult experiences in childhood preclude adequate mastery, these primitive aspects of the self are sequestered and become unconscious foci of neurotic conflict, leaving their imprint upon the adult character structure. This choking off of the natural elements which link a person to his own less mature past often results in a pseudomature, colorless person who finds rigid conformity the easiest path, or one who takes his lead from others' wishes since he cannot recognize his own ("other-directed") [Reisman, 1961]. In either event, the individual is left with a sense of estrangement from him-

[5] This term, and the complex issues which underlie it, derive from the brilliant work of Erikson. For a fuller understanding, see especially Erikson (1959).

[6] It is significant that "congruence" has been used by Rogers (1957) to describe a-personal attribute of "being one's self" that he feels is essential for a psychotherapist's function.

self as well as others. Lacking a clear identity, such a person feels his self as distant, unknown, and "ego alien." As Karen Horney has conceptualized it, the failure to meet the needs of the developing child leads to his experiencing "basic anxiety" which sets in motion a process of negation of the "real self" and the creation of a substitute, artificial "ideal self" whose characteristics are designed to manipulate the environment to meet these needs. This process of "self-alienation" results in a sense of lost self-determination, and a tendency to become "resigned" (i.e., resign) from the world.[7]

The concern with conformity and similar phenomena as expressions of internal alienation marked a shift in psychiatric thinking which occurred during the twenty years following World War II.[8] This involved a much greater concern with deformations of character structure, rather than with traditional psychiatric disorders. Necessarily, this shift has included more attention to disordered interpersonal relationships, but, even so, the focus tended to remain on these as "symptoms," that is, as intrapsychic difficulties. Only in the past few years has the orientation shifted further to become more truly psychosocial. With this, the usefulness of viewing disturbed behavior in terms of disturbances of identity has become increasingly apparent. The reciprocal interplay between one's concept of himself and his recognition as that particular person by others is an intrinsic feature in the progressive development of an identity. Throughout life, the maintenance of a sense of self is tied to the meaning one has for others. Miscarriage in the process of identity formation inevitably carries with it disturbances in the capacity to relate to other people. Camus' (1946) character, Meursault, though a stranger most of all to himself, had no capacity for feelings in relation to his mother or others, including his almost chance victim (see also Knoff, 1969).

Both confidence in one's self and trust in others arise out of experiences in early life in which (parental) others satisfy basic needs. The receipt of this tangible love provides the matrix for the capacity to give love to one's self, providing a sense

---

[7] Note the relation of Horney's "self-alienation" to Hegel's original definition of alienation as a condition in which man is cut off from direct experiencing of nature, including his own nature. Horney's contributions are not only extremely relevant to alienation, but one might view the entire body of her work to be on this topic. For a detailed exposition of her viewpoint, see her final book (Horney, 1950). Recent considerations of alienation seem largely to neglect her work, perhaps due to its complex jargon as well as its primary concern with intra-psychic processes and clinical psychopathology (neurosis). A number of more recent contributions by her disciples, more directly relevant to the present discussion, are contained in Weiss (1961).

[8] The extent of this trend is so general that it is impossible to cite specific references. Within psychoanalysis, the whole development of the modern "ego psychology" orientation is involved, bringing to mind especially such theorists as Ernst Hartmann, Ernst Kris, and Rudolf Lowenstein. Erickson also has been very influential, as I shall demonstrate. A good deal of the stimulus came also from outside the psychoanalytic movement from such "schismatics" as Horney and Harry Stack Sullivan; and the belated influence of Alfred Adler can be discerned too.

of self-esteem, and to others. The sense of self-esteem is progressively consolidated as each successful mastery of progressive developmental tasks brings both a sense of personal achievement and the confirmation from others that the child is successfully becoming "someone." Out of this self-esteem derives the capacity for the developing bonds of affection for specific others as well as the more general sense of belonging to larger social groups, including, potentially, mankind as a whole.[9] At the core of this phenomenon is the awareness that one's self shares something significant with others: a common humanity and a common experience of living in the world, the fact that "everyone is much more simply human than otherwise [Sullivan, 1953, p. 32]." In this sense, the alienated person is blocked from experiencing himself as fully a member of the human race or of society.

It is obvious that the direct sharing of experience and common personality features provide a basis for the especial closeness of family ties and friendships. But even in larger groups, scrutiny will reveal some of the same sharing of personality features of identity. Shared ideals and rules of appropriate social conduct play a major part in this. Thus, Polonius provides Laertes with an extensive guide for social conduct as a preface to his emphasis on maintaining an authentic identity. Paradoxically, therefore, identity implies the simultaneous recognition and manifestation of one's common humanity simultaneously with one's uniqueness.[10]

Earlier it was noted that the sense of estrangement defining alienation need not be conscious. In parallel fashion, the conscious sense of identity is only one part of what that concept includes, and is ordinarily not experienced as such (Erickson, 1959, p. 102).[11] Rather, the sense of satisfactory identity is experienced only as the vague, general, comfortable feeling of coherent self-satisfaction, without awareness of the sense of self per se. Quite the contrary, the conscious awareness of identity obtrudes only in moments when one's identity achieves a distinct increment of closure, or in those stressful states when there is fear of its dissolu-

---

[9] The extension of this process provides a basis for the feeling of belongingness with "the world" itself. This includes, especially, its other animate inhabitants, but also further involves its physical aspects, that is, all of "nature."

[10] Even in common parlance, the word "identity" denotes both singularity and shared similarity. Some aspects of the coexistence of these seeming opposites are illuminated by Maslow in a discussion of what he terms "peak experiences": that which is shared among such phenomena as love, insight, creativeness, orgasm, parturition, mystic and aesthetic experiences, etc. Such experiences, which he describes as associated with the transient achievement of a maximum sense of identity are characterized both by an intense closeness to others and the acme of individuality and uniqueness. At these moments of being most oneself, one transcends the self. Certain other features Maslow delineates, for example, the sense of being most integrated with, and yet most free of, the past and future, highlight other paradoxes in the relation of alienation and identity (see Maslow, 1961).

[11] Erikson explicitly includes in this concept also "an unconscious striving for a continuity of personal character" (and, I would add, the unconscious measure of success in that effort); "a criterion for the silent doings of ego synthesis"; "a maintenance of an inner solidarity with a group's ideals and identity"; and, implicitly, much more.

tion—which will be considered later.[12] Preoccupation with one's identity, or "self-consciousness," represents an uncompleted stage in its actual achievement, or a failure in that process, that is, some kind of alienation. Identity does not materialize out of a search for the self. It is not to be "found." Rather, it is to be progressively realized in the course of traversing life's viscissitudes. Paradoxically, an overt search for identity only signifies that it has not been realized or that it is temporarily disturbed. This is analogous to good health, which normally is experienced only as well-being, whereas an individual's preoccupation with his health indicates that it is disturbed, that he suffers, at least, from hypochondriasis.

Given their painful quality, feelings of alienation are likely to be repressed from consciousness as much as possible. To be able to confront such feelings takes considerable strength and maturity—and, thus, a firm sense of identity. Thus we discern another paradox: alienation is a product of identity, as well as a sign of its disturbance. Put another way, one knows who he is only to the extent that he can know who he is not. Full awareness of the ultimate fact that one can never completely know himself, or others, depends on this knowing of one's self. Thus, the successful achievement of an identity carries with it the quiet courage to recognize and tolerate one's existential aloneness.


## ADOLESCENCE


The consolidation of identity is the primary psychological task of adolescence. Alienation plays a major role in this process.[13] The adolescent avoids the adult world and seems to use every opportunity to indicate that he has no use for it. This rebellious withdrawal serves a double function. It helps him deny his residual conflict-laden Oedipal and childish ties to his parents by allowing him to keep his distance while he effects their reorganization. On the other hand, it gives him the opportunity to "try on" an array of new roles, responsibilities, and modes of relationship. The need for this alienated withdrawal is recognized in the special status of adolescence as a "moratorium." During this period the adolescent is accorded

---

[12] The former include Maslow's "peak experiences" (see Maslow, 1961), but also those far more common experiences, occurring primarily in adolescence, when one tries out a new relationship, activity, role, etc., and experiences a surge of satisfaction arising not only from success in the effort but from the feeling of fit: an "Aha!" reaction of recognition that the new thing is one's self.

[13] Thus far, alienation has been considered largely as an enduring character trait. In adolescence, it may be seen as a process: a passing stage. Still more transitory situational states of alienation occur, primarily as a way of minimizing or denying responsibility for one's actions in a specific experience, that is, as a "defense mechanism"; but these are not germane to the present discussion and will not be considered here.

unusual freedom and the latitude to test out widely different activities and styles of behavior without the expectation that he will be permanently committed to any of these. Much of the changeability of this stage grows out of these recurring forays whose dramatic character is accentuated by the fact that they include "many necessary elements of a semideliberate role experimentation of the 'I dare you' and 'I dare myself' variety [Erikson, 1959, p. 117]." The particular ways in which adolescents express their alienation arise in large part out of their efforts to stave off the ever threatening possibility that they may not succeed in forging an identity.

> To keep themselves together they temporarily over-identify, to the point of apparent complete loss of identity, with the heroes of cliques and crowds. On the other hand, they become remarkably clannish, intolerant, and cruel in their exclusion of others who are "different," in skin color or cultural background, in tastes and gifts, and often in entirely petty aspects of dress and gesture arbitrarily selected as the signs of an in-grouper or out-grouper. It is important to understand (which does not mean condone or participate in) such intolerance as the necessary *defense against a sense of identity diffusion,* which is unavoidable at a time of life when the body changes its proportions radically, when genital maturity floods body and imagination with all manners of drives, when intimacy with the other sex approaches and is, on occasion, forced on the youngster, and when life lies before one with a variety of conflicting possibilities and choices. Adolescents help one another temporarily through such discomfort by forming cliques and by stereotyping themselves, their ideals, and their enemies. . . . It is difficult to be tolerant if deep down you are not quite sure that you are a man (or a woman), that you will ever grow together again and be attractive, that you will be able to master your drives, that you really know who you are, that you know what you want to be, that you know what you look like to others, and that you will know how to make the right decisions without, once for all, committing yourself to the wrong friend, sexual partner, leader, or career [Erikson, 1959, pp. 92-93].

I hasten to reemphasize that all this refers to normal adolescence. Turbulence and alienation are essential features of the "identity crisis" of this growth stage. A placid, unruffled adolescence is a danger sign, indicating that the struggle was felt to be so fearsome that it was given up before it could be started. "Foreclosure" may lead to the apparent good adjustment of pseudomature conformity, but it dooms the person to a permanent regret (at least unconsciously) for what he might have become, and leaves him prone to later breakdown.

Certain characteristic features of the normal adolescent identity process are directly relevant to our interest: the search for a structured set of guidelines and for people to serve as models for identity, and a struggle to achieve closeness with others. The search to find a "cause" and an organizing social or political philosophy that can make their lives meaningful is a passionate one. Concomitantly, they select and create heroes (chosen from among those free of the taint of the parental role) to serve not only as leaders and models but as a basis for developing a concept of meaningful leadership. By testing their own and others' capacity to be true to these they refine their understanding of what loyalty itself is.

The usual psychiatric view is to assign the achievement of the capacity for meaningful heterosexual intimacy as the task of the subsequent phase of young adulthood. There are good grounds, however, for defining this as an issue of late adolescence. In part this may be due to the vast prolongation of adolescence for many in our society, so that it merges into the age once considered early adulthood.[14] But certainly one of the most visible features of our adolescent subculture is its preoccupation with sexuality, relationships, and love.

Some other relevant characteristics of adolescence are brought into clearer relief by noting the symptoms of those who fail to succumb to their task and develop "identity diffusion." Unable to commit themselves, they avoid choice, leaving themselves empty and apathetic, caring for and belonging to nothing. Their relationships are not enduring and do not involve truly loving others, but are based narcissistically: they choose those who are like them so as to help to define themselves. They have a sense of intense urgency and yet time moves too slowly. Either they cannot concentrate or they throw themselves into unidimensional activities, only to give these up just as impetuously with no sense of accomplishment. Violence against the self or others is a common feature. It is not just that they cannot contain the fury of their childish rage at the parents and world who have led them to this state, but that the expression of violence helps ward off the sense of nonexistence. To be active and destructive is to be something real. To hurt someone else is to clarify that they are someone else. To hurt oneself (most clearly in cutting or burning the skin) is to emphasize that one has definition, for the pain signals that a boundary has been breached.[15] And the experience of pain itself proves that one exists: To feel is to be. Their common attempts at suicide also represent, in part, paradoxical attempts at proof of the reality of their existence, for only the alive can die.

The more transparent function of suicide as an escape from painful realities is, of course, also involved. Identity diffusion is an excruciating and frightful experience, sufficiently so that any definite identity may seem better than none.

[14] It is not stretching the point much to define adolescence in our present culture as extending to the age of 30, one reason why "You can't trust anyone over 30." The relative universality of college attendance as a prolongation of the adolescent moratorium is one cause (although also an effect) of this. However, the causative factors are very complex, and many fall entirely outside the realm of concern here, for example, economic pressures to delay entry into the labor force.

[15] This interpretation receives confirmation from studies of psychiatric patients. For example, the Rorschach responses of delinquents have been described as emphasizing sensations of body damage, and it is suggested that the environmental interaction resulting from heightened mobility and aggression helps define their body boundaries. The head-knocking and self-biting of autistic children has been interpreted as attempts to improve ego boundary definition. At least one therapist has based his treatment of childhood schizophrenia on techniques that increase body awareness. There are also reports that episodes of self-laceration and destructiveness in psychotic patients can be terminated by procedures that reestablish body boundaries. For a detailed consideration of this entire area, with specific references, see the classic review (Fisher, 1970).

Rather than suffer this, most choose a negative or "alienated identity" (Schachtel, 1962). It is less painful to derive an identity out of being completely what one is not supposed to be, than to feel unable to achieve an "appropriate" identity. Thus, desperate adolescents may elect careers as criminals, alcoholics, addicts, prostitutes, nomads, homosexuals, or mental patients. A further element in this negative choice is vindictive retaliation against the excessive and hypocritical ideals of demanding parents by perversely basing identity on the opposite of these tarnished standards: the omega of "adolescent rebellion."

These extreme disturbances are, of course, in the realm of clinically recognizable deviance, not normal adolescence. Yet one can discern behaviors in everyday adolescent life that are clearly derivative, thereby revealing their like origins in alienation.

To be an adolescent may be to be stereotyped and patronized, as well as accorded certain freedoms. But to be thus categorized is to be a specific "something," and hence someone. It provides an anchor for defining the self and one's place in the social sun. In the same sense, to be alienated, especially when this self-definition is confirmed by society, is to have an identity: alienation can be a form of identity. An alienated identity can serve also as a form of relationship to others. Typically, the current style of alienation portrays apathy, "coolness," and withdrawal: "dropping out." Yet this behavior, as often as not, has an engaging, waif-like, elusive charm that is highly seductive—as it is intended to be. Not unlike the coquette playing hard to get, these youths subtly transmit covert messages of appeal masked in surliness and indifference. They are equally provocative in their hostility. True withdrawal is rare. Instead they hang around, stimulating feelings of betrayal in the straight society. They are not simply passive, but passive-aggressive, for it is more comfortable to be intermittently hated than ignored. However else determined, the anger they feel themselves affirms the reality of their existence in the same way that pain does, and the angry reactions they successfully induce in others confirms this.

## THE "NEW CONSCIOUSNESS": A SUBCULTURE OF ALIENATION

Adolescents in our society, as a group, though by no means homogeneous, have a reasonably distinct set of shared values, norms, institutions, leaders, etc., as well as a sense of collective identity that constitutes a definable "subculture."[16]

[16] Although unanimity does not exist on this score (nor even about the validity of the concept of subculture) most social scientists would be in clear general agreement with the notion that there is an "adolescent subculture" in our society. This is not to deny that it contains a number of discernibly different subgroups, for example, the Wallacites and New Leftists. Nevertheless, for the reasons stated, it can reasonably be considered a subculture.

I believe it is helpful to understand this as a subculture of alienation.[17] By this phrase is meant that the sense of being not merely apart or different from, but in opposition to, the mainstream culture lies at its core, and that one of its central values is the maintenance of that estrangement. It is not just different in the way that any culture differs from another. It has a *raison d'être*, the expression of its estrangement, both to its members and those outside. This characteristic serves as a collective manifestation, communication, and support for the alienation of its individual adolescent members, for their rebellion and withdrawal from the adult society. It is the social homologue of the alienation of the normal individual adolescence.[18]

This characterization applies even more to "the new consciousness." Variously entitled, often as the "beat," "cool," or "hip" society, the essential nature of this movement is revealed in its appellation by one of its most perceptive and critical adherents as a "counterculture" (Roszak, 1969). While it shares with many other ideologies a critical view of the existing social order, one of its identifying marks is that it not only proposes no substitute, but consciously eschews doing so. This is an oppositional ideology, not an alternative one. Only after it has succeeded in bringing down the existing culture may it consider the possibility of an alternative.[19]

The overlap between the two subcultures is apparent. It has been noted repeatedly that the "new culture" is a youth culture.[20] Adolescents have flocked to it, and most of its members are in this age group or just beyond. Thus, it has a distinctly adolescent flavor and a preoccupation with the issues with which adolescence is engaged, as these have been touched upon above. But it is more than a simple caricature of adolescence despite the fervor with which it pursues these themes. For one thing, young adults and those still older are involved, seemingly to an increasing extent. And the "movement" has attracted a number of mature thinkers on the social scene who have given their blessing if not actually becoming recruits. Nevertheless, it is most characterized by its sense of alienation: by its intense preoccupation and anxious concern over identity.

[17] I certainly do not want to be misread as implying that this is all there is to the adolescent subculture. Obviously there is a great deal more to it, and it can be described or categorized in many other ways. This is, however, one valid way in which it can be viewed and I so view it here for the instructive light this casts on the subject of alienation.

[18] The term "homologue" is used quite specifically. I believe this is a true homology between two phenomena at different levels of analysis, as differentiated from a merely analogous relationship between them.

[19] As Reich (1971), its commercially successful apologist puts it, "*When* [my italics] the new consciousness has achieved its revolution and rescued us from destruction, it must go about the task of learning how to live in a new way [p. 18]."

[20] For example, Roszak (1969) notes: "What we are confronted with is a progressive 'adolescentization' of dissenting thought and culture [p. 39]."

There is multiple evidence that a sense of lost identity and the attempt at the creation of a new one lies at the core of the "new consciousness." The primary consciousness is self-consciousness. It "starts with the self" and emphasizes "self-liberation." "Individuality" and uniqueness are stressed. Everyone must be allowed to "do his own thing," whatever his "bag," so that there will be "recovery of self."[21] It is all wound up with a concern for the self.

The mode of dress has that typical blend of individuality and instantly recognizable uniformity (so typical of adolescents) that thumbs its nose at conventions by parody as well as direct contravention. But a particular characteristic is its emphasis on, or denial of, the contours of the human body.[22] Jeans and tank tops are skin tight, bras and other underwear left off, and a maximum of skin is left exposed. Everything serves to remind the wearer and his audience of every minor individual characteristic, every prominence, lump, birthmark, pimple, scar, and organ, and of the precise lines of his body boundary. The definition of a particular body different from all others, and of its existence as something apart from its surrounding world, is maximally sharpened. Everything reassures the wearer who he is and that he is. Alternatively, they wear shapeless, oversized, flowing, tent-like, sometimes floor-length garments which almost totally obscure the body outlines. In so doing, one is reassured that there need be no concern over one's precise definition because none exists (much as in the formation of a negative identity). "Unisex" (in hair style, clothing, mannerisms, etc.) is a related variant. Muddling the differentiation between the sexes helps deny that they are different, thereby reducing anxiety about the capacity to achieve a masculine or feminine identity.

The emphasis placed on sentience fits into this same scheme. Like pain, sensation is a signal that something outside has breached the boundaries of the Self, affirming its existence. The stronger the sensation the greater the reassuring proof of self-definition. Music is used this way. Intensely rhythmic, volatile, and unsubtle, at times shattering in volume and overpowering in electronic discordancy, it rocks the listener: its force transcends hearing to become literally palpable as physical vibration. In a word, it is piercing. If this is not enough, multicolored strobe lights

[21] Phrases of this type are so much a part of the literature and conversation of the counterculture that they do not have or require any specific attribution. For example, they can be found in profusion throughout Reich (1971).

[22] There is a danger that the reader will react to this assignment of the same meaning to opposite trends as a contradiction, or with the accusation that one (particularly a psychiatrist) can interpret anything any way one wishes. The point here is that the two trends are both extremes on the same dimension, that they are markedly predominant in the counterculture, and that psychoanalysis has revealed that such polarities do have the "same" meaning. (The latter phrase refers to the fact that the two polar "sides" of the same conflicted issue are both aspects of that same issue.) Thus, thóugh some "straight" individuals may dress in a way that reveals the conflict described, most portray an in-between mode which neither quite highlights nor quite obscures the body contours or is a subtle admixture of the two; and this is the prevailing characteristic of dress of the existing core culture.

are added to penetrate the eyes. And the audience is enjoined to "get into it"—
which means to let the it get into them.

The use of drugs also fits this pattern. Public hysteria about "the drug problem" obscures the fact that the drugs used in this subculture are almost always
stimulants of sort. Smoking "grass,"[23] by far the most common act, produces an
exquisite heightening of ordinary sensory experiences: lights become brighter and
sharper, colors more intense, temperatures more extreme, etc. The same occurs
with internal feeling states: insights seem more profound and emotions more acute
—which, under circumstances where fear, depression, jealousy, or other negative
feelings predominate, can lead to some very adverse reactions. "Acid" produces
varied and intense visual illusions and hallucinations as well as releasing fantasies
and images ordinarily kept repressed. The acute effect of "speed" is an intense
"high" and release from depression; it is a potent central nervous system stimu-
lant. "Downers" are used far less commonly and usually for the "kick" of a new,
unusual sensory experience rather than for their dulling effects. This is true also
for heroin and other opiates whose sustained use is low in the counterculture
(though widespread addiction does exist in other subcultures, notably in ghettos).

The intense "high" sought after often has been compared to an orgiastic experience. Certainly, the counterculture places a high value upon sexual excitation
and orgasm in the usual sense. But, as Eissler (1958) has indicated, the psychological function of orgasm extends beyond pleasure: "Orgasm is endowed with the
power to confirm, create and affirm conviction," in fact, it is "the strongest affirmation possible to men [p. 242] ."[24] The affirmation he refers to is one's own
reality.

The injunctions to maintain "cool," avoid commitment, and "hang loose,"
or to be involved in an activity only as long as it provides immediate rewards, also
bespeak identity struggles. These are like the needs of the adolescent to withdraw
and to have the chance to try something just for the sake of trying it. Their protective nature against the identity-fragmenting effects of fearful feelings is also
clear. Like the catatonic whose frozen immobility shields him from his intense
rage and other emotions, the "apathetic" dropout is, inside, a seething mass of
conflicted feeling. Some of this is manifest in the provocative nature of his non-
commitment, which represents a subtle caricature of the values of the technocratic adult society. For what is this if not what everyone is supposed to be: adaptable, flexible, and imperturbable—with a vengeance.

[23] "Grass" is, of course, Marijuana; and (below) "Acid" is lysergic acid diethylamide,
or LSD, and is used here, by implication, to include the entire group of "hallucinogens";
"Speed" is methedrine; and "Downers" are sedatives, primarily barbiturates. I include this
clarification at the request of the Editor who quite correctly points to the evanescence of
slang but who, not uncharacteristically for the breed, ignores the likelihood that this volume will become obsolescent within the same short time span.

[24] I am indebted to Dr. Heinz Lichtenstein for calling this important paper (Eissler,
1958) to my attention.

Although the subculture has evolved its own brand of politics, the foregoing helps explain why it has been unable to sustain effectiveness or involve more than a fraction of its own membership. To the extent that the radical "New Left" represents anarchy, its alienated nature is self-defined. But relatively few members of the subculture take that extreme position. One of the most gratifying aspects of the counterculture has been its emphasis on positive, progressive sociopolitical programs, reflecting its deep humanistic concerns; and this is hardly alienation. If one focuses, however, on the style of the new politics, rather than its programs, there is further evidence of problems with identity. This is seen in the need to be a zealot or nothing, to polarize issues, and to take the simplistic position: "if you're not part of the solution you're part of the problem." Like adolescent ideologies, their overdefined, uncompromising nature is designed to furnish an anchor to which a drifting identity can be moored.

One of the hallmarks of the counterculture is the value it places on "rapping." Talking is almost endless, valued in itself. These sessions, it soon becomes clear, are a substitute for action, rather than preparation for it. They serve as a way of life in which the participants can try out various shades of ideologies without the commitment that action tends to reify. Much rapping, moreover, consists of self-confirmation through listening to one's own expressed thoughts. Thus it becomes a way of defining identity. And, as in the choice of lovers, partners often are selected to be as much like one's self as possible, to mirror one's own ideas as a method of reinforcing this self-clarification. True discourse with outsiders is even more rare, and, when it occurs, is often disputation in the service of hostility. It is less true verbal intercourse than an attempt conversationally to screw and be screwed.

Some functions of violence have already been mentioned. Although gross violence (in the sense typical of the Weathermen, or even of campus riots) may be exaggerated in the public eye, there is an unmistakable violence to much of the militancy of social action that is characteristic of the counterculture.[25] Its politics is one of confrontation, for nothing is so well suited to define the Self and its differentiation from others than such face-to-face opposition. Even without physical abuse, the verbal violence can be extreme. It is transparent that to call the police "Pigs" is no different than to use words like "Niggers," "Gooks," or "Hippies." It is also clear that much of the verbal dialectic is not designed to persuade or educate but, rather, to anger, and thus to invite retaliatory violence. Even the most passive resistance can be an intended provocation. When alienation thus assumes behavioral expression, its manifestations reveal its nature as such, in part by being actively alienating. Through opposition the self is reaffirmed. Even Reich (1971) notes: "to these youngsters there is . . . only a system that must be fought, if only *to give oneself a sense of reality* [p. 228; the italics are mine] .

[25] This broader definition of violence is entirely consistent with its insightful usage within the counterculture—which has, for example, explicitly referred to the overtly polite social structures that serve to oppress minority groups as "violence." The connections between the words militant and military also are revealing in this regard.

## ALIENATED SUBCULTURES

Just as individual alienation can be a source of (negative) identity, so can a subculture of alienation provide the basis for identity. To be a member of an alienated group is to know to that extent who one is. Provided along with group membership are rules for what to believe in or oppose, how to dress and behave, who to admire and place faith in, that is, an entire prefabricated lifestyle, value system, and social organization. This provides a framework for a definition of self for its members to replace their inner confusion over their identity.

The implications of this type of affiliation are highlighted by contrasting such alienated subcultures with another type of subculture, that of the ethnic and racial minorities. The latter, which may be termed alien subcultures, also provide a base of identity in the group: the "I" is a Jew, Mormon, Black Hutterite, etc.[26] What distinguishes these groups is the presence of a primary positive identity that is different from that of the outer culture, and produces a sense of that difference. In contrast, the alienated subculture arises out of the sense of difference, nonbelonging and alienation of its members, and only secondarily leads to identity via the shared (negative) group identity.

The extent to which a subculture can maintain its distinctness is a major determinant of the strength of the sense of identity within its members. Crucial to the success of this process is the subculture's capacity to maintain its distinctive child rearing activities, for it is these that shape identities that express its particular cultural character (Erikson, 1963). Once safely past an adolescence insulated within reasonably well demarcated cultural boundaries, its members are likely to achieve a staunch group identity resistant to outer influence. Persecution is likely to work paradoxically, serving only to enhance their identity as members of that group. When however, children are exposed to persecution to the extent that it interferes seriously with their emotional security, the results are not so sanguine. Raised in such an atmosphere—whether their tyrants are parents or the outer world—they will tend to develop an identity which contains the very sense of badness and failure transmitted to them. Particularly difficult forms of this self-hate are prone to arise where the subculture shares many of the larger cultural values and aspirations (as, by definition, do all subcultures, to a degree) and where there are internal pressures for assimilation. Thus the American Jew, in contrast to those in the original ghettos, is likely to absorb antisemitism along with other things in his need to be a "typical" American.

Far more poignant on the current scene is the problem of the blacks in our new ghettos who are degraded, exploited, and oppressed from their earliest days.[27]

[26] I use the term "alien subcultures" for its obvious convenience in making the contrast with "alienated subcultures," or as I termed them earlier, "subcultures of alienation." It is probably more correct to refer to them as encapsulated alien cultures, at least to the extent that they maintain their overall distinctive culture, an issue that is considered just below.

[27] This subject is covered more fully by Poussaint in this volume (see Chapter 17).

Sharing so much of the white culture, and driven further toward it by the desperate wish to opt in on its material rewards, the black identity includes all that fury of hate compressed into the name nigger. The new black leadership has intuitively grasped this point in its full acuteness, recognizing that the salvation of the individual and the strength for concerted group action can arise only out of the consciousness that "Black is Beautiful." Moreover, they have worked to sharpen the boundary lines around the black subculture (using hostility as one tool) to forge a separate group identity that can serve as the foundation for a positive individual identity. The slow progress encountered by this effort underlines the depth of self-hate engrained in the existing black identity.

The idealization of blacks expressed by the new left on ideological grounds contains within it the identification of its members with the degraded that occurs in negative identity formation with great typicality.[28] This support has been exploited shrewdly by black leaders to improve their movement's power base, but with a degree of standoffishness that reflects their insight into its hostile, depreciating nature. They also have recognized the crucial difference in the nature of black alienation from that of the counterculture. Black rage comes from their wish to fracture their designation as alien by the larger culture, to opt in on its material and other rewards, rather than being just an expressing of their own sense of alienation.

It would be a mistake to draw this line too sharply. Not only is there an element of true alienation in the black movement, but also the counterculture itself provides a potential for opting back in. Sometimes this is an unconscious part of the motivation for affiliation with it. Precisely because a solid if "alienated" identity can be achieved through membership in the alienated subculture, it provides a process for reentry. Even where the identity achieved is well outside the range of the establishment, the fact of mature identity formation per se often is welcomed by the culture. In the long run, enduring cultures provide substantial if ambivalent support for creative identities: artists, philosophers, social critics, religious and political leaders, and others, and they have a reasonable capacity to distinguish original, authentic personhood from sheer rebellion. Moreover, once such prodigal sons have returned, they are likely to stimulate changes in the core culture in the direction of their own values, and, thus, toward the counterculture: a truly co-opting process.

The microcosm of the counterculture provides a haven for its members to develop mature individual identities. Its separateness structuralizes the opportunity for a moratorium during which this can occur. Conformity to its unconventional conventions reduces the energy required to rebel, while sustaining the illusion of being entirely one's own man. The group's acceptance of rebellious rage reduces the guilt that helps sustain that rage, thereby increasing comfort. Strength in num-

---

[28] See Russell (1950) for a classic description of this process including a perceptive dissection of its intrinsic depreciatory component.

bers provides a bulwark against feelings of vulnerability to the hostile world outside. The shared common enemy links the group and directs its rage outward, enhancing the possibility for positive relationships within it. The emphasis on first names or nicknames, the abhorrence of "titles," and the whole atmosphere of easy social familiarity, though partly representing the most obvious kind of pseudointimacy, provides a nonthreatening path for the development of relationships that may in time come to be very real.[29] Avenues also are opened for attainable success in careers newly designated as valuable—careers as folk singers, musicians, pamphleteers, artists, dialecticians, etc.—or merely as a good citizen of the counterculture. A successful failure may thus become, within the subculture, a genuine success. With this achievement comes group recognition and respect, and, thence, pride and self-respect. Positions of leadership become accessible to the able, further expanding their opportunity for self-growth through the expression of that role.

Certainly all is not so simple. It may be exceedingly difficult to move to a position of true individuality; just as in the conventional society, there are the problems of giving up friends and an automatic, familiar lifestyle. And there is a parallel set of social sanctions to be endured, including accusations of having "sold out." More important, isolation within a group characterized by identity problems accentuates the difficulty in achieving a healthy identity and tends to reinforce the status quo of a negative identity. Shared accusations against the establishment become an all too easy method for the projection of fault, blocking the achievement of responsibility. Individuality becomes a guise for blatant selfishness and exploitation. Action is overtly despised and internally blocked. Dropping out becomes not a moratorium permitting the finding of one's self but an institutionalized reinforcement for apathy and withdrawal. (This negative state is more likely when drug usage has accelerated to the point where brain damage has ensued.) As a consequence, effective social change cannot be accomplished, even where very creative insights have been evolved.

Another factor in this ineffectuality is the lack of sustained leadership. Leadership per se is despised as an "establishment" and as an echo of the parental figures from which rebellion took origin. The counterculture is characterized less by the usual form of leaders than by heroes and models, which is not to deny that those thus chosen are very influential.

The qualities which make for "leadership" are far from known. Those who achieve this role seem to have the capacity to project, in a public dramatic fashion, some new synthesis of the shared aspirations and ideals lying dormant in the unconscious of their followers. Mutual identification among the group members is enhanced by their shared allegiance to the leader who presents, in bold and special

[29] The similarity of this fake intimacy to the superficiality of Madison Avenue relationships (one of the prime, and apposite, targets of the counterculture) is compelling, and is one of the certain signs that the counterculture is the natural child of the prevailing culture rather than representing something apart.

relief, the personification of that unconscious content.[30] Somehow in his style, words, and especially in his "image," is represented what they only dimly perceive of their own understanding of the world. In his identity, this insight becomes crystal clear and compelling truth.

Unfortunately, a leader's appeal may be to the most evil as well as the noblest within his followers, Hitler, Gandhi, and George Washington were all "leaders." This holds also for the counterculture which includes among its heroes not only Baez and Marcuse, but Rubin and Leary. In fact, there may be special dangers in this subculture because the appeal must strike directly to their central shared problems of identity. While an Alan Watts may be admired for his spirituality and learnedness, his impact seems to promote autistic withdrawal more often than spiritual insight. It is this kind of problem which seems to be involved in the phenomenon of a Charles Manson. Especially at the level of small groups, leaders seem often to represent the most negative elements of the subculture.

Under the dominion of such leadership, the individual may move to a position of greater alienation. His own wish to achieve leadership of the group, or at least its recognition, may move him in that same direction. As this becomes concretized in overt behavior, a negative identity becomes more crystallized, and the likelihood of change is reduced. Thus, the force of subculture membership acts progressively to fix the individual in a state of alienation.

## TECHNOCRACY, CHANGE, AND REALITY

But expressions of alienation extend widely beyond the counterculture. To understand the causative factors involved in this mass identity crisis requires a shift to consider the social and cultural characteristics of our modern society.[31] Necessarily, this examination will be restricted to those factors which bear on the issues that have already been raised. Thus, the major focus will be upon the effects of modern "technocratic" society upon identity and upon the related issues of rapid change and the nature of "reality."

The characteristics of the technocratic society have been well described (see, among others, Benis & Slater, 1968; Ellul, 1967; Mumford, 1963; Roszak, 1969, Ch. 1, pp. 1-41; Toffler, 1971). Among its major features are the reliance on complex mechanical and electronic devices and on technical processes; the substitution of technical organizations for interpersonal relationship; emphasis upon utility as

[30] For a discussion of group dynamics and their relation to leadership, see Freud (1955).

[31] My reference to "our" society throughout this paper is in terms of the predominant culture of modern western society, and especially that in the United States. It does not consider the "underdeveloped" nations, the Orient, nor even segments of American society that fall outside the cultural mainstream.

a measure of individual worth, and the need to adopt and shift among multiple roles—both serving to deemphasize personal characteristics and substitute the interchangeability of people; uprootedness and mobility, both geographic and social; a diminished relevance of status descriptors and social rituals; the exposure in rapid succession to increasing numbers of rapidly appearing new products, processes, and behaviors; and the massively accelerated pace of change of all kinds, including social change itself.

In sum, there are a multiplicity of factors that promote dehumanization and which pose the problem of coping with accelerated change. One conclusion that could be drawn from this terrifying array is that no identity formation is possible (and, thus, that the concept of identity itself has become obsolete). The evidence of widespread identity confusion seems to confirm this.

But it will be recalled that some degree of identity crisis is the expected pathway to the crystallization of a new identity; and there are grounds to believe that this is just what is taking place: that a new type of identity is beginning to emerge, shaped by the pressures induced by a technocratic society. Some hints of this inchoate new identity may be seen in the "new consciousness" of the counterculture. It would be mistaken to underestimate this as merely a shift in the content of identity, as one person inevitably differs from another. Rather it is (in part) a new form or style of identity, consonant with existence of unique qualities inherent in a new phase of sociocultural evolution. These discontinuities make it very difficult for any adult to apprehend it. This, I believe, is the crucial feature in what Mead (1970) has described as a shift to a "prefigurative" culture: one in which only youth are expert and must therefore be the source of instruction for the adult society. What adults must learn from youth is not merely a mass of new information to which only the young have acquired access, but their novel ways of organizing that information as a way of understanding the world.

What can we say about the nature of this new identity? If change is so characteristic of the society, it is not surprising that a central feature will be in relation to change. A suggestion of what this is like is contained in what Mead (1960) has referred to as a "situational approach to life": "taking each situation as a single unit [pp. 94-95]." This is closely related to Erikson's (1959, p. 42; 1963, p. 286) term "tentativeness." Both contain elements suggesting the ability to value change itself, in an unchanging way. This involves not only the capacity to tolerate and enjoy change, but a positive evaluation of the general openness of options. Thus, roles are easily slipped on and off like costumes, out of the appreciation that they are in some sense only costumes.

Such a position can be more, not less, "honest"; it is not dehumanization. It frees up the capacity for deeper commitment to each role while fulfilling it, since less of the self is left behind in other roles. In this way, the quality differs from what Lifton (1971) has called the "Protean Style," although there is much overlap. Lifton describes a chameleon-like quality of shifting personality and belief in response to new situations and events. He concludes from this that "the self" (for which term identity might be substituted) "can no longer be considered a fixed concept in Psychiatry [p. 298] ." Yet such a comment seems to neglect the fact that an identity is never a fixed thing, even during times of relative stability. More important, it views role interchangeability from the value perspective of the current form of identity in which such shifts would be dishonest. From the perspective just indicated, this interchangeability has an authenticity and genuineness of its own.

But there is a fundamental problem here that cannot be sidestepped. If the changing nature of the world reaches an extreme, there is no psychological reality: what "was" no longer "is." Certainly identity, as a concept of a stable—if evolving—psycho-social Self, requires that there be a dependable and predictable reality. Moreover, the problem goes beyond psychology.[32] The currently fashionable existential cry (alas, often a whine) about the loss of meaning of life points also to new insights in the philosophy of science. Man, and all life arose as a mere "accident." Thus, his biology cannot be considered real. In modern physics, a most important principle is that of indeterminacy. Events are unpredictable; their specific attributes result from chance. How then can one believe in anything? Belief requires some degree of predictability. God is dead, supplanted by Heisenberg!

To accept this view is to forget that indeterminacy is itself a principle, an orderly statement about, it is true, an aspect of nonorderliness. At a primary level, order remains. What the principle refers to is the unpredictability of a single event, while simultaneously reaffirming the capacity to describe the events of the larger system of like events as dependable statistical probabilities. The system as a whole has a lawful orderliness. Newtonian physics has remained valid, supplemented but not supplanted by post-Newtonian developments. While chance may be a larger factor than once realized, there are laws of chance which describe its operation and which support statistically dependable expectancies. Maxwell's Demon Lives!— but we can predict how he will behave. It seems necessary to shift from a fixed to a stochastic model of reality, but that is quite different from discarding the concept altogether. Not only does it seem to be within human capability to make this shift, but the incorporation of aspects of this new model now can be discerned as a feature of the evolving new form of identity.

Before we despair while reading obituaries for reality based on "advanced" scientific insights, we might remember that their authors wrote them on desks without the slightest doubt that these would remain solid, supporting the weight of their efforts, despite the "reality" that the desk contained more space than matter, and despite the indeterminacy which characterizes any given particle comprising that matter. Everyday conceptions of reality are consensually validated in the most direct operational sense: they "work."

Nor are descriptions of social reality that emphasize a quantum jump in its

[32] For a sophisticated, perceptive presentation both of this psychological viewpoint and of its broader implications, within a psychoanalytic theoretical framework, see Lichtenstein (1972).

unpredictability free from error. It would be foolish to deny the great uncertainties of our day. Yet a critical look will reveal that our futures are at least as predictable as that of the caveman surrounded by carnivorous predators, of the knight in the presence of Plague, or of a Frenchman during the Hundred Years War. I would not for a moment walk the streets of New York alone at 3 A.M. Yet I gainsay that my chances would be better than on a similar walk in Dicken's London, Oliver Twist's good fortune not withstanding. This is not even remotely to suggest complacent acceptance of the world as it is. There is an immense need for confronting our very real problems with action. But it is essential to consider that the biggest change may not be in the amount of uncertainty existing but in our much more sophisticated awareness of its extent. Alienation may, thus, be as much a cause of social disorganization as its consequence.

Before pursuing this last point, let us turn briefly to another quality of the new identity. Just as narrow, fixed roles are transcended, there is a tendency to look beyond circumscribed group identifications to an identification with mankind as a whole. This appears to pave the way for an identity which involves a new modification of the superego (and the ego ideal). Classically, "good" has been defined in terms of individual morality. More recently this has been expanded to require behavior that also does not prevent other men from attaining similar good. The developing newer definition requires actions which actually increase the likelihood of that common good. The glimmerings of this new morality are revealed within some of the sentimentalized humanistic ideology of the counterculture. Its deep concern for "ecology" is a further extension of this.

In this vein, the new standard for individual contacts emphasizes honesty, openness, and helpfulness, along with its spurious familiarity. Together with the efforts at breaking down status barriers, this constitutes a potential counteractant to the dehumanization which technocracy fosters. With the technical triumph over problems of production, this society has shifted to a service economy (Galbraith, 1958). (Labor Department statistics reveal that nearly 60% of workers are now in the service sector, and by 1980 this should rise to 80%.) This produces a sharp rise in the number of personal contacts, but these tend to be increasingly brief and task-oriented. In response, the new identity provides a style of relating that maximizes the personal quality of these contacts, to the benefit of both participants.

To return to the earlier topic, what can be made of the fact that feelings of alienation are so rife. Some insight may be gained by examining a phenomenon in clinical psychiatry. Within the past several decades, there has been a major shift in the kinds of patients psychiatrists see. In general terms, the shift has been from the classical psychiatric disorders to an ever larger number of patients with "personality disorders" whose difficulties affect mainly their relationships with others, and their behavior within society. Within this latter group, there has arisen a whole new diagnostic group, the "borderline states," in which these difficulties reach psychotic proportions, without the presence of symptoms ordinarily associated with the psychoses. What is characteristic of these patients is the presence of a major disturbance in their identity formation. Much of their difficulty can be understood as severe forms of identity diffusion and negative identity. Consistent with this, many of these patients experience deep feelings of alienation in relation to society.

In contrast, fewer people now present themselves with difficulties in the form that can be classified as the usual Neuroses, whose typical symptoms result from intrapsychic alterations. (Hysteria, for example, a common and major concern of the early 1900s, is today a rarity—almost a curiosity.) While the diminishing patients who have these symptoms may suffer intense discomfort, they do not characteristically experience much of that particular feeling that constitutes alienation, as it has been defined earlier. But it should be recalled that the concept of alienation can be used in a broader sense to include all forms of defective communication among parts of the Self. In that broadened sense, these patients too are alienated. Their alienation, however, is localized "within the personality organization" rather than being felt in relation to the outer social world.

Thus, in the realm of psychiatric disorders, what can be concluded is that psychopathology has taken a new turn in the direction of more manifest alienation, that is, more overt, conscious feelings of disturbance in the social realm. Extrapolated to the wider social scene, this finding suggests an hypothesis that seems entirely tenable: that the human condition may be no worse than it was, but man's awareness of that condition recently has become markedly heightened. Thus the "sense" of alienation has increased. Put another way, the significance of the social conditions of modern society may rest largely in their capacity to stimulate conscious feelings of alienation, rather than in their being more "alienating" in the broader sense.

If such an extrapolation from psychopathology seems dubious, there are reasons for accepting it. For one thing, if mental illness is conceptualized as arising out of a psychosocial nexus, it must reflect the characteristic features of the culture in which it appears; and there is ample empirical evidence to support this view. For another, if alienation can be understood in terms of the vicissitudes of identity formation, as has been demonstrated, then all evidence about that process in our society has relevance. And, finally, the weight of the evidence on the social scene itself, as already noted, strongly suggests the same conclusion.

## THE CURRENT SCENE IN HISTORICAL PERSPECTIVE

Potent as are recent social forces, older influences can be discerned that have set the stage for the current epidemic of alienation. Though any concept of an overall "national identity" is, admittedly, an heuristic oversimplification, there are certain shared distinctive features of outlook that exist in a given society. An understanding of the historical evolution of these characteristic features provides considerable insight into the significant forces operating within that society. Our current self-preoccupation is no exception.

This nation started *de novo*, free of tradition. Pressures for survival and the adventuresome nature of the pioneers lent themselves to the development of new, pragmatic social institutions. Many later immigrants were from deprived and persecuted groups who specifically came in search of freedom from political, religious, and social constrictions. Freedom of choice became a major value in the creation of the new form of government with its ideology of individual participation and responsibility. Ethnic, cultural, religious, and economic diversity increasingly characterized the population. The utility of a pluralistic egalitarianism became self-evident in carving out homes and farms, and then commerce and industry. Thus, the recognition of others' rights to be different became a positive value. The frontier spirit, with its expansion into seemingly endless space, added a sense of limitless possibility. Successive waves of immigrants and generations acquired the ever stronger belief that change per se was good. It meant progress for themselves, and especially for their children. If only one had sufficient initiative, self-reliance, and determination, everything was possible. Anyone (at least any native born white male) could become president (Erikson, 1950). He could if he wanted to, that is, for success was valued in many forms, and it was up to the individual to decide for himself what he wanted.

Much of this is just the "American dream," a myth whose reality has been well exploded. But the fact that these beliefs often have turned out to be cruelly untrue, even for those who have most cherished them, is entirely beside the point. What counts is that they have been believed and, to some extent, are still, and that they have played a major part determining the American *Weltenshauung,* and do still.

Many of these same attitudes appear in the outlook of people throughout the other "advanced" Western nations. Basic to this is our common heritage of western cultural traditions. The Protestant emphasis on individual responsibility and the progressive spread of the political philosophy of democracy, modified by Marxist influences, has led to much of the same idealized emphasis on self-determination tempered by a spirit of group cooperation. A decisive influence has come recently from the direct importation of the American value system. The immense power and success of this nation in the twentieth century has led to its tremendous influence, so that the American version of the Protestant ethic and related values have been widely imbibed along with Coca Cola.

Until recent times, these energies of self-determinism and individual responsibility necessarily have been channeled into the struggle for sheer survival. In the burgeoning following World War II, however, new elements have been added to the mix: incredible technical and economic success. In the appropriate concern about those who have been denied the fruits of the success of the system, it is easy to forget how major a success has been achieved. Ours is now a predominantly middle-class society. Problems of production have been yielded to problems of distribution and (fairer) allocation (Galbraith, 1958).

With this affluence for the growing middle class has come a new freedom of time and energy once devoted to the struggle for survival. There is physical and psychological leisure to think about Self and its world. The current deep concern with correcting social and economic injustice, the very fact that notice is taken of them at all, is at least partly a product of that freedom. There has been so much success that people can now afford to examine the remaining areas of failure. This has led to a healthier public conscience and to its active expression in major programs of social change that began most prominently in this country with the New Deal social legislation of the 1930s, and which extend now to virtually every area of human welfare.

Expressions of alienation are nothing new. What has changed is their ubiquity. Medieval schoolmen were deeply troubled over man's alienation from God. Romantic scholars worried over man's alienation from nature. But for centuries there were only a few who were sufficiently rich and educated to have the genuine opportunity to turn their thoughts to such matters. The rise of a large, affluent, educated middle class, however, provides a predominant group who can have such concerns— and they do.

What also has changed is the content of the concern. It is no longer with God, but with who man is, and who his neighbors are, and how they are related. The concern is with identity itself. This particular form of alienation is, as I have suggested, understandable in terms of the historical evolution of the national character traits sketched above.

But history only provides the fertile soil. The decisive push comes from the nature of modern society. Among other features, we have created a level of technological development that has exponentially multiplied the array of choices open to each person.[33] There is a plethora of types and sizes and variations of models of products, services, occupations, organizations, avocations, groups, locations, etc. The advantages of greater possibility of choice as a source of increased personal freedom is obvious. Equally clear is the despotism of having to make choices needlessly. Less and less of life is simplified by being a given. Moreover, the basis for choice becomes ever more difficult as the possibilities multiply. There becomes

---

[33]I am not for a moment so naive as to believe that choice is quite so generally free or extensive as the text may seem to imply. For one thing, the vast variety of models, brands, colors, etc. of available products represent mere superficial modifications which serve to camoflage the fact that there may be as much or more standardization of their basic attributes. Yet even economically sophisticated middle-class consumers who "know" this, tend to get caught up in the need to make choices among these, and their decisions do have consequences for their identity both as they perceive it and as others do. Nor are there, in reality, many options open to Blacks and other socioeconomically deprived groups. But, again, people in these groups seem to feel, and act, as if there were. Their aspirations are heavily influenced by the conventional cultural values, including the mythology of freedom of choice. Moreover, in the area of product choice, their lack of consumer sophistication makes them especially vulnerable. For a virtuoso display of the array of "overchoice" presented by our culture, colored by a naive capitalist optimism, see Toffler (1971, pp. 261-322).

less time to note, evaluate, and compare more parameters of difference among more alternatives. At best, the process wastes time and energy. At its worst it stimulates confusion and serious self-doubts about the capacity to make the "right" decision.

This resonates directly with the sense of identity. Who one is depends on the conglomerate of past and present, active and passive choices—what one chooses to do, say, wear, avoid, feel, etc. If there are doubts about the capacity to choose, then there is doubt about who one is.

The problem is especially acute for the adolescent who is in the very process of trying to choose who to become. In past times, the adolescent had to decide who (who) he could be from a limited number of choices. Now he must decide what (who) he wants to be—and this choice includes not only his occupation, but such formerly choiceless areas as his religious, political, and moral value systems. Small wonder that he experiences greater difficulties in doing so, and requires more time and more opportunity to try out new things without permanent commitment. His freedom cuts both ways. It gives him this opportunity but threatens to engulf him in open options. This age group has profited most directly from the affluence of the society by a reduction in the immediate pressures to assume responsibility that inevitably limits choice. The middle-class adolescent, particularly, has been given maximum franchise and financial underwriting for the most complete, prolonged period of moratorium in history. The seeming paradox that it is the materially most comfortable who are the most alienated is no paradox at all.

Because of this, the identity crisis that characterizes adolescents, by developmental necessity, now has become markedly accentuated. Their task is made still more difficult by the partial inadequacy of existing adult identity models for coping with the demands of technocracy, and by the conflicts between these and the alternatives suggested by the counterculture. With the progressive isolation of the expanding adolescent subculture, this magnified self-concern has fed on itself to grow more. As a consequence, their concern with identity has become a pervasive, dominating force in their subculture. From there, it seeps outward to involve their elders, already all too vulnerable to this concern. The idealization of youth, so characteristic of the core culture, promotes this influence. The potent force of commercialization gives this process a further push: inevitably transmitted along with the material superficialities of the youth subculture are significant parts of its value system and its preoccupations—preoccupations about identity. Thus, throughout the society, individuals have become increasingly preoccupied with concerns about their identity in the same form that ordinarily only adolescents experience. In this sense there is a far more significant and generalized "adolescentization" of our society than the connotation of widespread adolescent influence and power.[34] In

[34] Practical limitations of space preclude more than a brief consideration of the factors involved in the "adolescentization" of society. For a more complete view of the process, see Roszak (1969, pp. 1-41).

fact, I would suggest that this term can be used to characterize the most central aspect of the current American (and western) identity. What I am saying is that the hallmark of our national character in the present age is a collective self-consciousness, characteristic of the adolescent, and understandable in terms both of our history and current sociocultural processes.

This characterization of our whole society is by no means some kind of outrageous "put-down": an accusation that we are "just a bunch of immature adolescents." Rather, it is a statement that, at a social level, our collective identity is homologous to the type of identity found at the individual psychological level in adolescence, that is, that it has homologous characteristics, including the same anxious preoccupation with the Self.

With this caveat, this interpretation provides a context in which one can view the alienation that pervades not only the adolescent and countercultures but our society as a whole. The term adolescentization was chosen also to express the fact that it is a change in process, and at the very earliest stage of that process. What now exists reflects this transitional quality of a new social organization in-the-making. Some of the confusion, self-doubt, and self-consciousness experienced by individuals and members of the society is an expectable product of this mixture of the old and new, and of increasing dissatisfaction, that is, alienation, with the old. But the evidence suggests that more of it is inherent in the nature of the early stage of this particular type of national "identity" formation. What is seen in the normal adolescent process, with its repetitive experiments with various transient identities, including rebellious forays into provocative negative ones, its flights into premature foreclosure, and its insistence on "hanging loose"; its grasping for ideologies; its awful self-consciousness and its sense of worthlessness, purposelessness, absence of reliable values and guidelines—in short the process of identity formation with its constant fears of identity diffusion and alienation—is analogous to what is being played out in the larger theater of society.

There is no telling just how the culture will evolve. Yet one might recall that adolescents have always managed not only to survive but, on the whole, to grow to adults who are a little better than their parents—despite the dire predictions of the latter. There are signs in the "new society" of much that is fresh and creative, and of possibilities for a higher morality, along with some wanton destructiveness, selfishness, and plain nonsense. One can only hope that the former qualities will develop further and the latter decrease, and work towards that end.

Man is an incredibly adaptive creature whose achievements are nothing short of magnificent when viewed against the passage of evolutionary time. He has managed to rise to every challenge and, over the long run, to do and be better. One does not have to believe that man is more than that to reject the current wave of pessimism which often purports to be philosophy when it is only loss of nerve. But neither can one meet a challenge without recognizing the need for change. Many of our "alienated" social critics are perceptive and accurate. Through their criticism they furnish us with the tools that allow a sapient man to adapt successfully to the new challenge and move on to still other achievements.

## REFERENCES

Benis, W. G., & Slater, P. E. *The temporary society.* New York: Harper, 1968.

Camus, A. *The stranger.* New York: Knopf, 1946.

Cohen, A. K. The sociology of the deviant act: Anomie theory and beyond. *American Sociological Review,* 1965, *30,* 5-14.

Eissler, K. Notes on problems of techniques in the psychoanalytic treatment of adolescents: With some remarks on perversions. *Psychoanalytic Study of the Child,* 1958, *13,* 223-254.

Ellul, J. *The technological society.* New York: Vintage Press, 1967.

Erikson, E. H. Identity and the life cycle. *Psychological Issues,* 1959, *1,* 18-171.

Erikson, E. *Childhood and society.* (2nd ed.) New York: Norton, 1963.

Fisher, S. *Body experience in fantasy and behavior.* New York: Appleton, 1970.

Freud, S. Group psychology and the analysis of the ego. In J. Strachey (Ed.), *Standard edition of the complete psychological works of Sigmund Freud.* Vol. XVIII. London: Hogarth Press, 1955. Pp. 69-143.

Freud, S. Formulations regarding the two principles in mental functioning (1911). In J. Strachey (Ed.), *Sigmund Freud: Collected papers.* New York: Basic Books, 1959.

Galbraith, J. K. *The affluent society.* Boston: Houghton, 1958.

Horney, K. *Neurosis and human growth.* New York: Norton, 1950.

Knoff, W. F. The psychiatrist reads Camus' "The Stranger." *Psychiatric Opinion,* 1969, *6,* 19-25.

Kris, E. *Psychoanalytic explorations in art.* New York: International Universities Press, 1952.

Lichtenstein, H. The effect of reality perception on psychic structure: A psychoanalytic contribution to the problem of the generation gap. 1972, in press.

Lifton, R. J. Protean man. *Archives of General Psychiatry,* 1971, *24,* 298-304.

McClosky, H., & Schaar, J. H. Psychological dimensions of anomy. *American Sociological Review,* 1965, *30,* 14-40.

Maslow, A. H. Peak experiences as acute identity experiences. *American Journal of Psychoanalysis,* 1961, *21,* 254-260.

Mead, M. Cultural change and character structure. In M. R. Stein, A. J. Vidich, & D. M. White (Eds.), *Identity and anxiety.* Glencoe, Ill.: Free Press, 1960. Pp. 88-98.

Mead, M. *Culture and commitment: A study of the generation gap.* New York: Doubleday, 1970.

Merton, R. K. *Social theory and social structure.* New York: Free Press, 1957. Pp. 131-160.

Mumford, L. W. *Technics and civilization.* New York: Harcourt, 1963.

Murchland, B. *The age of alienation.* New York: Random House, 1971.

Nettler, G. A measure of alienation. *American Sociological Review,* 1957, *22,* 670-677.

Reich, C. A. *The greening of America.* New York: Bantam Books, 1971.

Riesman, D. *The lonely crowd.* New Haven: Yale University Press, 1961.

Rogers, C. The necessary and sufficient conditions of therapeutic personality change. *Journal of Consulting Psychology,* 1957, *21,* 95-103.

Roszak, R, *The making of a counter culture.* Garden City, N. Y.: Anchor Books, 1969.

Russell, B. The superior virtue of the oppressed. *Unpopular essays.* New York: Simon & Schuster, 1950. Pp. 58-64.

Schachtel, E. On alienated concepts of identity. In E. Josephson & M. Josephson (Eds.), *Man alone: Alienation in modern society.* New York: Dell, 1962.

Spitz, R. A. Hospitalism: An inquiry into the genesis of psychiatric conditions in early infancy. *Psychoanalytic Study of the Child,* 1945, *1,* 53-74.

Sullivan, H. S. *The interpersonal theory of psychiatry.* New York: Norton, 1953.

Tietz, W., & Woods, S. M. Alienation: A clinical view from multidisciplinary vantage points. *American Journal of Psychotherapy,* 1970, *24,* 296-307.

Toffler, A. *Future shock.* New York: Bantam Books, 1971.

Weiss, F. A. (Ed.) Alienation and the search for identity. Symposium. *American Journal of Psychoanalysis,* 1961, *21,* 117-279.

# Chapter 4

# An Introduction to the Notion of Alienation[1]

## Ephraim H. Mizruchi

Maxwell School of Citizenship and Public Affairs

## INTRODUCTION AND HISTORICAL BACKGROUND

No term is more widely used to refer to the despair and malaise of contemporary men than the term alienation. Indeed, the rhetoric of alienation has become so widespread that few would have the audacity to describe the social and political movements of our time without reference to this presumed phenomenon. A major question for us is how can the behavior of so many diverse segments of so heterogeneous a society as ours be characterized by a single descriptive term? The answer to this question is, of course, that it cannot, and yet words have meanings which call out the response of real people to concrete situations. Our specific objective here is to attempt to throw some light on the origins of the idea of alienation and to suggest some of the ways that it has been, and is being used and abused.

Alienation has for a long time been a dominant idea in the writings of nineteenth and twentieth century men. The fundamental notion of alienation is at least as old as recorded time. Bell (1966) has traced some of these origins to their pre-Christian sources:

[1] Paper presented at the Institution on Alienation, TTT Project, Syracuse University (Maxwell School), and State University of New York, Upstate Medical Center (Department of Psychiatry), October 9, 1969. I thank Manfred Stanley and Frank Johnson for some helpful suggestions at various stages of the writing of this paper.

111

> The Greek idea of *ekstasis* (in Latin *superstitio*), the leaving of one's body
> in the mystery rites, or ecstacy, was regarded by the Romans as mental aliena-
> tion (*abalienation mentis*) and is socially reprehensible. To the early Christians,
> alienation meant the separation of man from God; and to Hegel, in his *Phenom-
> enology*, the *"unglickliches Bewusstsein,"* the unhappy Consciousness (or the
> Christian spirit) which follows the Skeptical (Greek) and Stoic (Roman) con-
> sciousness, is "the Alienated Soul which is the consciousness of self as a divided
> nature, a doubled and merely contradictory being [p. 699]."

Some of the most interesting precursors to the idea are to be found in Greek
literature and the Old Testament. As Schaar (1961) suggests:

> In some of its meanings, the idea of alienation is as old as literary history. . . .
> Homer had written of the "tribeless, lawless, heartless one," the one outside the
> fellowship, doomed to work his way through the desolate regions beyond the
> friendly fire of clan and kin. The motif of the eternal wanderer begins in the
> dawn of the Jewish tradition and weaves in and out of the whole subsequent
> history of Western religion. Abram is the prototype and universal symbol of ali-
> enated man. Separated from his family, his nation, and his national religion, he
> wanders, without a home, in soil, society or faith. He is the nomad, unable to
> love and belong. Unable to love, he subjects himself to a transcendent power and
> substitutes law for communion, subordination for love. Estranged from himself,
> Abram projects all that is good in him onto a strange absolute being, which is no
> longer *his* absolute being. In return for this, he gains a new identity, which is
> symbolized by the change of his name to Abraham.[2] All this was long before the
> modern Existentialist teaching that alienation is rooted in the human condition
> [p. 174].

Although Hegel may be recognized as the most influential source of ideas on
alienation before Karl Marx, it was Ludwig Feuerbach who provided the link between Hegel's idealistic conception of the problem of alienation and Marx's socioeconomic conception of alienation.

Contemporary with the emergence of Marx's ideas on the role of man in an
increasingly complex world was the growth of existentialism as a philosophical
movement. Among proponents of the latter, Kierkegaard stands out as the founder of "individual existentialism," focusing on traditional philosophy's failure to
place the individual in its systems while pointing out that Feuerbach's "social individualism" stressed that "man resides with others in a community (Mizruchi,
1964)."

The central concern of Marx and his followers, on one hand, and the existential philosophers, on the other, was with the apparently increasing process of fragmentation and depersonalization of the individual in complex society.

> Existential thought can be viewed as a reaction of protest against the nega-
> tion of integral man in dominant philosophical circles. It may also be viewed as
> a protest against the negation of integral man in the modern urban-industrial

---

[2] This idea of reward of a new identity for his subordination to a transcendent power
anticipates both the idea of Rousseau that one subject himself to the collective authority of
the community through alienation and Hegel's idea of the transcendent nature of alienation.

world. It is this felt negation which makes existential thought what may be
called a philosophy of the crisis of the relation between the individual and society in modern civilization. Existentialism represents an attempt to prescribe a
place to the individual in mass, technological society; its extraphilosophic problem, basically, is to give an authentic status to the person in an impersonal
world [Tiryakian, 1962, p. 76].

Regardless of the specific problems faced by other nineteenth century philosophers, it is to Marx that we must turn for the most influential analysis of the
various forms of alienation to which man is increasingly subject in an industrial age.

Marx elaborated these ideas in his oft-quoted *Economic and Philosophical
Manuscripts of 1844,* which is both a statement on alienation and a critique of political economy, particularly the views of Adam Smith and his followers.

Of the relationship between the production and its effect upon the laborer,
Marx wrote (as quoted by Fromm, 1961).

> The *devaluation* of the human world increases in direct relation with the *in-
> crease in value* of the world of things. Labor does not only create goods; it also
> produces itself and the worker as a *commodity* and indeed in the same propor-
> tion as it produces goods. The fact simply implies that the object produced by
> labor, its product, now stands opposed to it as an *alien being,* as a *power inde-
> pendent* of the producer.

This process, according to Marx, leads to the *objectification* of labor—the
worker is related to the product of his efforts as to an *alien object.*

Alienation is not only a consequence of the process of objectification but it
appears in the *process* of production: "within productive activity itself . . . the alienation of the object of labor merely summarizes the alienation in the work activity itself."

> What constitutes the alienation of labor? First, the work is external to the
> worker; it is not part of his nature, and, consequently, he does not fulfill him-
> self in his work but denies himself. He has a feeling of misery rather than well
> being, does not freely develop his mental and physical energies but is physically
> exhausted and mentally debased. This is self-alienation, as opposed to the above
> mentioned alienation of the thing [Fromm, 1961, pp. 99-100].

Human alienation, above all the relation of man to himself, is first recognized
and expressed in the relationship between each man and other men. Every man
views other men according to the standards and relationships in which he finds himself placed as a worker.

There are, then, four forms of alienation: alienation of the worker from the
process of his work; alienation of the worker from the product of his work; alienation of the worker from himself; and alienation of the workers from his fellows.

Marx viewed alienation as the result of activities in a specific institutional
context—the economic system—which leads to estrangement from one's self and
others in other spheres of life as well. Alienation is the final outcome of specific
institutional processes. To eliminate alienation, institutions must change.

In more recent years, Erich Fromm has been the most influential intellectual proponent of the classical or Marxian conception of alienation.

In *The Sane Society*, Fromm (1955) defines alienation as:

a mode of experience in which the person experiences himself as an alien. He has become, one might say, estranged from himself. He does not experience himself as the center of his world, as the creator of his own acts—but his acts and their consequences have become his masters, whom he obeys, or whom he may even worship. The alienated person is out of touch with himself as he is out of reach with any person. He, like the others, is experienced as things are experienced; with the senses and with common sense, but at the same time without being related to oneself and to the world outside productively [p. 120].

Fromm (1955) turns to the Old Testament for an interesting historical perspective. Focusing on idolatry, he argues that the essential distinction between monotheism and polytheism "is not one of the *number* of gods, but lies in the fact of self-alienation [p. 121]."

Associating idolatry with polytheism, Fromm (1955) points out that "Idolatrous man bows down to the work of his own hands. The *idol represents* his own life-forces in an alienated form."

These ideas are capsulized in his use of a familiar quotation from Psalm 135: "The idols of the heathen are silver and gold, the work of men's hands. They have mouths but they speak not; eyes have they but they see not; they have ears but they hear not; neither is there any breath in their mouths. They that make them are like unto them; so is everyone that trusteth in them."

In the present, the processes that characterize life in industrial societies ultimately lead to alienation in all spheres of life. "Life has no meaning, there is no joy, no faith, no reality. Everybody is 'happy'—except that he does not feel, does not reason, does not love."

Fromm (1955) is concerned with a problem unknown to Marx, which is expressed in our final quotation from his provocative study:

The danger of the past was that men became slaves. The danger of the future is that men may become robots. True enough, robots do not rebel. But given man's nature, robots cannot live and remain sane, they become "Golems," they will destroy their world and themselves because they cannot stand any longer the boredom of a meaningless life [p. 122].

Fromm (1955), like Marx, is nevertheless directly concerned with the complex problem of achieving a meaningful, productive experience for the individual in modern society. As with the existentialists, then, the concern is with the subjective sphere.

## MAN AND SOCIETY

Unlike most of existentialist philosophers of the nineteenth and twentieth centuries, however, Marx and Fromm (1955) have suggested changes in the objective circumstances in which the person finds himself, in the social structure, to bring about more meaningful subjective experience. The personal experience is viewed as an integral part of the social structure in operation, as the reflection of the actor's point of view.

Thus, the fundamental problem in alienation is not simply Man's internal mental life, but his relationships with others, that is, society.

Fromm's (1955) and Marx's conceptions of alienation, like those of most contemporary writers, emphasize the undesirable aspects of the process. Earlier, Rousseau and Hegel had held that alienation was necessary both for society and for the attainment of an integral self. Marx also felt that alienation would decline as social structures were altered.

For Rousseau, attempting to understand the connection between men's natural state and society, alienation was necessary in order to subordinate one's self to the needs and aspirations of the majority as they are embodied in the idea of a whole community. For Hegel, alienation was a transitional state which was necessary in order to attain a consciousness of an integral self (cf. Rotenstreich, 1965).

In all of these notions, the fundamental idea appears to be that there is something amiss when a person, through some external medium, usually a social structure, is denied a feeling of integrity including the possession of his own soul and the ultimate determination over his physical being. Thus, human slavery, for example, is the most extreme form of alienation since it exerts ultimate controls over the slave's body and soul. In a more subtle form, society alienates men from thier own bodies by denying them the opportunity to dispose of their bodies as they personally desire through laws against suicide, and customs requiring clothing. Even in contemporary society, then, where man is presumably free, he alone does not determine what he shall do with himself as a physical being. What he does as a social being, that is, his public behavior, is even more pervasively controlled by the community.

One cannot understand the delicate nature of the tie between men and society without appreciating the implications of Rousseau's idea. Thus, the idea of the subordination of the self and man's aspirations to the presumed needs of the community and society, as reflected in its norms and values, is a fundamental notion in contemporary sociology. The relationship between alienation and anomie, another concept which is now becoming more widely used, will be discussed later. For the present, it is well to realize that the concept of alienation has been with us since antiquity and will surely continue to be an idea which excites the social and political imaginations of men.

Of course, the most discrete connections between the use of the concept in sociology currently and in the past lead back to the middle of the nineteenth century. The young Marx, the idealistic youth who wrote the 1844 manuscripts, may be viewed sociologically as representative of a broad perspective which can be described as German sociological romanticism. This perspective influenced most of the nineteenth century sociologists, including Emile Durkheim, the founder of modern sociology and most influential proponent of positivism. Thus, even the man who wanted to establish sociology as a measuring, formal science was contaminated by a perspective which was basically normative. What was this perspective and how is it connected with the idea of alienation? Shils (1957) has conveniently described this.

> German sociological romanticism, which found its decisive expression in Ferdinand Tonnies' *Gemeinschaft und Gesselschaft* (1887), in Georg Simmel's numerous works . . . and in Werner Sombart's early, quasi-Marxist writings on capitalistic society had at the very center of its conception of the world, a picture of a pre-modern peasant society in which men lived in the harmonious mutual respect of authority and subordinate, in which all felt themselves integral parts of a community which in its turn lived in continuous and inspiring contact with its own past. Traditions were stable, the kinship group was bound together in unquestioned solidarity. No one was alienated from himself or isolated from his territorial community and his kin. Beliefs were firm and were universally shared. . . . This idyll was juxtaposed against a conception of modern urban society. . . where no man is bound by ties of sentimental affection or moral obligation or loyalty to any other man. Each man is concerned only with his own interest, which is power over others, their exploitation and manipulation. The family is dissolved, friendship dead, religious belief evaporated. Impersonality and anonymity have taken the place of closer ties [p. 599].

The idea of community as reflected in the concept of *Gemeinschaft* is clearly an idea which assumes that the proper state of man is one in which he is closely bound up with his fellows in intimate and meaningful relationships. More specifically, his fellows are not instruments to be used as means toward other ends, but are whole beings recognized as valuable because they are brothers and deserving of the respect and dignity reserved for one's self. The use of others as means toward other ends is, of course, reminiscent of our early statement about alienation and slavery. The denial of determination over one's own human qualities, that is, to use another, is to impose a condition of alienation upon him. But more profoundly in this context is the perception of the need for community and this theme has been an important one among philosophers, particularly the late Marin Buber. Buber's distinction between *I and Thou*, and his concern for seeing the other as subject rather than object, is a direct outcome of the *Gemeinschaft-Gesellschaft* dichotomy. This is one of the areas in which sociological and philosophical perspectives merge. The similarities between Buber and George Herbert Mead, most influential for the symbolic interactionists among contemporary sociologists, have been described by Pfeutze (1954).

A connection dealing with still another aspect of alienation is described by Tiryakian (1962) where the focus is on the convergence of a number of themes in Durkheim and those of Sartre, Marcel, and other existentialist philosophers.

Although it is beyond our purposes here, it is well to keep in mind that it is primarily in the study of alienation and its concomitants that the interests of contemporary philosophers and sociologists are joined. The contributions of all of these authors reflect concern on the part of sociologists and philosophers with a growing sense of alienation in a social world being rapidly transformed by institutional revolutions. Since it is concern which has motivated, and indeed, given rise to the emergence of the social and psychological sciences, it is not surprising that there are implicit normative conceptions of the nature of Man and Society inherent in their scientific perspectives. Although we sometimes lose sight of the philosophical and normative bases of scientific perspectives, it is nevertheless true that the way scientists go about developing more profound understanding of given phenomena displays the major characteristic of their science. Thus, methodology provides us with guide lines for how to clearly state an assumption, and how to formulate specific statements which can then be checked against some form of objective observaitons. It provides us with rules of procedure for exploring the implications of ideas. The ideas themselves may be connected up with broader world views which are not subject to direct scientific assessment. The idea of alienation has been connected to normative notions which have implicitly suggested that all is not well in modern societies. Given a normative position, can the idea of alienation help us to understand more profoundly the nature of our social world? Does it contribute to greater awareness of the crucial problems with which modern man is faced? Let us attempt to respond to these questions by turning to some aspects of alienation in contemporary American society.

Before describing some selected examples of alienation on the contemporary scene, however, it is well to define two specific types of alienation, intentionally simplified, and deal with some fundamental sociological assumptions.

The two types which will be most useful to us at this point are social-alienation and self-alienation (using the description of Taviss, 1969):

1. Social alienation in which individual selves may find the social system in which they live to be oppressive or incompatible with some of their own desires and feel estranged from it.
2. Self-alienation in which individual selves may lose contact with any inclinations or desires that are not in agreement with prevailing social patterns, manipulate their selves in accordance with apparent social demands, and/or feel incapable of controlling their own actions [pp. 46-47].

In one, the direction of the search for sources of alienation is in the social system, in the other the direction is toward the self. But what is the nature of the systems in relation to which social and self-alienation have reference? A few brief assumptions will aid in our efforts to describe some of these sources.

When we observe the activities of large collectivities, we find it useful to distinguish between what people are doing and what we feel they should be doing. The former we refer to, of course, as the factual order and the latter as the normative order. While these two conceptualized orders are not the same there is, under normal conditions, sufficient approximation between "real" behavior and the "shoulds" and "oughts" of the group to allow for some flexibility in evaluating one's own and others performance. Ordinarily then, the rules themselves are not subject to critical appraisal by the members of the group and the organized activities are permitted to proceed in uneventful fashion.

The normative rules of society grow out of traditions which are typically bound up with institutionalized processes in society. Thus, they may reflect older forms of society which are no longer meaningful to more contemporaneous groups. For example, the existence of separate clubs and bars for men today are understood to be meaningless in a society where the idea of sexual equality is taken seriously. In spite of the contradiction in spirit, between the idea that all men, and women, are equal before the law, and in public institutions, it was legitimate for women to play designated female roles and to avoid performing male roles. But such contradictions are normal in large heterogeneous societies.

More significant, however, is the process by which organized systems grow and persist which are clearly incompatible with the contemporary normative order. These structures, associated with the factual order, represent the world as it is, not as it should be. Systems of differential privilege, patterns of job discrimination, exclusively organized leisure activities, all of these—part of the daily lives of most Americans—have always existed, while at the same time our country was being described as a land of equal opportunity in all spheres: social, political and economic. Americans were enjoined to strive for success ("anyone can make it"), while in reality this was often not the case.

## WORLD WAR II AND THE AMERICAN DREAM

From time to time crises emerge in societies which lead to critical assessments of the state of a nation. World War II represented such a crisis. Millions of men uprooted from civilian jobs and family life for duty in the armed forces and millions of women whose lives were transformed by the effects of war on the home front now found themselves playing new roles in society, responding to previously unknown and unanticipated expectations. A general declassification had occurred, and this time the very massive numbers involved assured that some profound consequences were to be experienced by all of the members of American society.

An aspect of this declassification was the sudden realization that the old rationalizations which helped support the structures of differential privilege no longer made any sense. Weren't men who had, in civilian life, played quite ordinary roles, transformed into leaders and responsible officials? Shouldn't they now pursue those goals and share in the opportunities that they risked their lives to preserve? Many did, and the contributions they made to our society are evident around us. But some did not, Blacks and poor Whites particularly, and their plight represented a conspicuous divergence from the way things are supposed to be in America. The opportunity to rectify this situation, following World War II, was not perceived or realized by all, thus creating a phenomenon in which many (but not all) who had been held back, as it were, before the war, came to prosper, fulfilling the mandate of the American Dream. The beneficiaries of this prosperity were, however, caught in a paradox. Their war experience made it clear that America could mobilize tremendous resources, both human and material, to solve problems. It was equally clear that these capacities were not being used to deal with domestic problems. But because they were too busy enjoying the new prosperity, their criticism of the failure to implement social values remained abstract. Not so for their children. The offspring of those who did prosper, the youth of today, had no difficulty recognizing the injustices which characterized this phenomenon and, particularly, the apathy of their parents' generation in ignoring the plight of the disadvantaged.

Coupled with the declassification, mobility, and reclassification of vast segments of the population was the breakdown in the ideology of millenial peace. World War II, like other wars before, was the war to end all wars. The horrors associated with the extermination of some twelve million Europeans by what had always been characterized as a civilized nation, and the Nuremberg trials, symbolizing the World's intolerance of inhumanity even in time of war, raised the hopes of Americans that wars had reached their strategic limits, that they could and would be controlled and that, in any case, the United States was finished with war.

The Korean War provided the first shock wave to batter the ramparts of pacifism. Although only a small handful of Americans were touched by its realities, it became evident that pacifism was only a romantic dream. Relatively few opposed our involvement in Korea, but antiwar sentiment was intense enough to influence the election of a man who promised "to bring the boys back home." Even Eisenhower, supported by conservatives, could not keep us from the growth in international commitments which was symbolized by our involvement in Korea. These commitments, the fault of no one man or group, thrust us into the unfortunate set of circumstances which has become the rallying source of alienation in our time, the Viet Nam War.

Thus many of our rapidly increasing youth population of the late 1950s and 1960s began to probe into the discrepancies between normative and factual, dream and reality, and the more they probed, the more the system appeared wanting to them. What were the consequences of these probes? Let us focus on some applications of the concepts—social and self alienation—and see what has been happening.

## FOREGROUND: SOME CURRENT MANIFESTATIONS

Certainly the most dramatic kinds of situations to which the alienation concept refers are reflected in today's rebellious youth movements, Black and White relations, and the conflict over valued institutions. All of these phenomena are indicative of some underlying sociological forces which have unleashed a massive avalanche of rhetoric and emotion and which has drawn the attention of observers

among both social scientists and laymen alike. The phenomena described as alienation are specifically manifest in our literature, in our arts and in our expressive behavior patterns.

## Literature

That the alienation theme has manifested itself in literature since antiquity
has already been suggested in our earlier quotations from the Old Testament and
Greek sources. Shakespeare was also clearly concerned with this theme as reflected in his play, *Timon of Athens*. The fact that this theme had also made its way
into his other plays suggests that Shakespeare was projecting perceptions based on
observations in his own society and time (Zito, 1973).

More recently, there has been an attempt to systematically analyze alienation themes in popular American literature, particularly popular middle-class magazines published around 1900 and 1950. Taviss (1969) took samples from the *Sa-
turday Evening Post* and *Cosmopolitan* magazines for the periods 1900 through
1906 and compared them with the periods 1954 through 1956. Two types of alienation themes emerged from her study, suggesting shifts in the structure of American society. Taviss' results indicated an overall rise in the appearance of alienation
themes in the 1950s, a slight decrease in social alienation, and a large increase in
self alienation.[3]

The basic shift from individualism to collectivism is expressed in the decline
of the Protestant ethic, the success theme, the commitment-to-a-cause theme, and
family responsibilities theme. Society in the 1950s is no longer the culprit in America; it is the inflexible individual. A system requiring a great deal of movement
from one place to another and from one occupational position to another, requires
that one must be open and sociable, must be able to enjoy fun and games, and must
be able to beat the system, because it appears impenetrable. Thus, rather than strike
out against the system, the literary character of the 1950s is a person who, although
he does not withdraw from his associates, contents himself with his private sentiments of malaise.

Themes associated with the 1950s still persist. A 1950 theme may be noted
in a dramatic series shown on "prime time" television for several seasons entitled
"Then Came Bronson." The hero is a peripatetic wanderer who is always on the
move encountering brief adventure but principally devoted to staying free of connection with people. Each week the show began with a scene in which Bronson,
perched on his motorcycle, stops for a traffic signal alongside a man in a station
wagon who enviously looks him over. The attitude of the "square" is nostalgic; he
would gladly trade places with our happy wanderer: "Boy, I wish I were you!"

---

[3] The focus on the breakdown of the regulative norms in society is also an important
theme in Shakespeare and has been described by Sullivan (1969).

Bronson's patronizing response every Wednesday night was, "Hang in there."[4] This same "hanging in there" is also apparent in the current comic strips. In Charles Schulz's "Peanuts," Charlie Brown, the loveable juvenile misfit, continually finds himself out of step with things despite his dedication to conform and do good. His reaction to repeated failure (often not of his making) is to put the blame on himself and suffer the insults of his playmates, even his dog. He rarely distributes the blame where it belongs, nor does he attack the Establishment.

These examples suggest that a major source of alienation in the 1950s was the feeling that the system somehow stood in opposition to us, unyielding and unalterable, and if "you couldn't beat it, you had to join it." Thus, it took a hardy soul to see the source of his malaise in the system, to fold, mutilate, and spindle. The alienation themes in the literary spirit are compatible with the studies of *The Organization Man* and *The Lonely Crowd*, and clearly reflect very widespread sentiment of resignation in American Society ten or fifteen years ago (Reisman *et al.*, 1950; Whyte, 1957).

Something happened between the 1950s and 1960s to drastically alter the state of American society. The youthful Americans to whom we referred earier were aided by a substantial increase in numbers, by an even greater proliferation of affluence, and a shift of concern about the moral state of affairs in the United States. While the Beatniks in the 1950s were a relatively small group, the Hippies were a much larger segment of the population.[5]

**Youth Movements**

Contrary to what most people in our society think—and indeed, probably intentionally, this difference is difference obfuscated—Yippies and Hippies represent two very different kinds of movements. Certainly both represent alienation from many aspects of the prevailing society and display a number of similar characteristics in lifestyle. The Yippies, however, direct their efforts toward the political order, while the Hippies' focus on the spiritual. They seem caught up in the incongruities in conventional morality and, particularly, the widespread conspicuous deviation from the fundamental vaules of contemporary American society on the part of those in leadership positions at all levels.

It is probably much easier for us to understand the Yippies given the fact that alteration of political arrangements have always been problems for society since antiquity. A struggle for political power, oriented by political ideologies, represents not a turning away from society but an effort to bring about a change in the form and substance of government. It is easy for the laymen to know what "they" want.

---

[4] The significance of the road theme in modern American fiction and motion pictures is discussed by Gelfant (see this volume, Chapter 13). For themes in Shakespeare's plays, see Zito (1973) and Sullivan (1969).

[5] For two systematic, perceptive essays on youth movements, see Flacks (1969) and Greisman (1973).

The Hippies, however, remain an enigma to most of us. They seem to want only to drop out, and tune in (the latter with the aid of drugs): to retreat from the "plastic" society. They are not typically and discernibly a threat to our society. Yet their activities have had more profound effects on us than have the Yippies. When a political threat emerges, the response is in the form of organized, consolidated opposition. A Bohemian phenomenon, on the other hand, is more subtle and is perceived as involving some deviant behavior. Ultimately, however, we expect that those who have dropped out will, with more maturity, return to conventional roles. Bohemian movements provide temporary refuge from the excessive pressures of a "conveyor belt" society which, although it provides a wealth of career alternatives, also requires that premature decisions are made regarding preparation for careers which restrict both perspective and contact with alternative ways. Thus, the Hippie provides society with an abeyance structure which siphons off some of the strain associated with alienation, and which actually protects the system from potential cadres of politically rebellious youth (Mizruchi, 1969). Regardless of the differences among youth, it is clear that alienation is the theme.

### The Black Movement

With the case of the Black Revolution, we have two different kinds of phenomena and both represent two types of alienation. On the one hand, we have the black segregationist movement, or what is called the Black Power movement, in which the major source of alienation is perceived by the leaders of the movement to be self-alienation. Efforts are made in this context to try to alter the self-concept, to try to rectify this problem not only through integration with a movement of like people (other blacks) but also through the manipulation of certain types of symbols: "Black is beautiful;" the glorification of black history; efforts to create, let's say, mythical historical ties with Africa; efforts to try to instill images of the ideological ties between contemporary members and the past—all of these reflecting self-alienation as a prominent feature. Social alienation is reflected in the black integration movement, and this is reflected in a different self description: the above group call themselves blacks, and the other group, the integrationists, call themselves Negroes. The word Negro symbolizes the acceptance of the idea of integration in the larger society. The alienation in this case is a feeling of being apart from the larger society because the larger society imposes constraints, restrictions, segregation, and the like, all of these merely temporal aspects of a society in which minority groups have had to overcome barriers along the way to full acceptance. If one is going to alter the circumstance, one is going to have to accept the larger society in order to penetrate it.

One of the interesting things about this movement is that it is often necessary, in order to build political support, to create feelings of disaffection. In the case of the black movement and, to a great extent, in the case of the present youth political movements, it has been necessary for the leaders to try to stimulate a consciousness of one's powerlessness and the inequities associated with a subordinate position in American society, to accentuate the ignominy of the imposed constraint. In this context, if it has not in some cases created a conscious feeling of alienation, it has certainly played an important role in reinforcing it.

Thus, alienation is not simply a natural outgrowth of structural conditions. It can actually be created and manipulated by others in the social system in order to bring about desired results. The black movement required that a widespread and mobilizable feeling of deprivation was shared by a vast segment of the black population. Unlike the alienation of the Hippies who could afford to drop out of the "plastic society" because comfort and affluence could be taken for granted, the blacks have, by and large, directed their efforts to attaining a more legitimate share of the social and economic wealth of the American society.

## The Forgotten Man

A description of the various contexts to which the alienation theme applies would be incomplete without directing some attention to the Forgotten Man, the middle-class, adult American. Frustrated over high taxes, and incomprehensible war abroad, campus riots, and political indecision, he is becoming more and more alienated from the traditional institutions of American society. Although he seeks stability above all else, he is more and more willing to allow the use of force in controlling rebellion; he is more inclined to reject referenda on education and community health needs; he is more concerned with the possibility of property loss due to invasion of neighborhoods by blacks and other nonwhite populations; bewildered by mounting inflation yet confident (according to a report several years ago in *Newsweek*) that America is capable of solving all of its social problems. His alienation reflects itself, not in an attempt to alter the existing social structure, but in an effort to "turn the clock back," or to slow down the changes which are in process ("The Troubled American," 1969). He, incidentally, exemplifies in his responses the social alienation theme of the 1950s. From looking over a portrait of this man as reflected in reports from the popular press, it becomes evident that the "forgotten," middle-class American was a decade behind the conspicuous critical themes characteristic of the large, rebellious avant garde segments of our society. The emphasis on law and order, a concern with censorship of movies and literature, the revulsion to increasing sexuality and the resistance to sex education in the schools, all reflect alienation from a set of values expressed in the idea of progress which has always been equated with change. Since he provides a crucial segment of the voting population, the decision he makes in local and national elections have a strong influence in determining the direction in which American society proceeds. Should a decline in either the security or relative affluence of middle class Americans occur (in addition to the already critical strains of American society), then it is likely that his alienation will be intensified and that even more dramatic results might be experienced.

Regardless of the support of institutions by those we have called The Forgotten American, these institutions, themselves, are breaking down. The process by which institutions break down and regulative norms decline in effective control over man's ways of pursuing goals—and the goals themselves—is called anomie. And the outcome of the pursuit of meaningless goals—those which are not normatively regulated—constitutes alienation from the goals themselves. This more chronic form of alienation which expresses itself in our not knowning, as Americans, what we are or what we really want in life, is a most pervasive pattern in our contemporary society.

If meaninglessness and confusion have not yet alienated the multitude, the following incidents will certainly contribute to its growth: scandal in the Supreme Court, our symbol of the legal institution; scandal in the Army, the military institution; daily scandals in the economic institution; the Watergate trials; the deinstitutionalization of our national sport, baseball; the deinstitutionalization of religion; and the decline of national heroes, generally.

The system is facing onslaught from all sides and alienation has been the harbinger of the depth of the crisis.

REFERENCES

Bell, D. Sociodicy: A guide to modern usage. *American Scholar,* 1966, *35*(Autumn), 699.

Flacks, R. Social and cultural meanings of student revolt. *Social Problems,* 1970, *17,* 340-357. Reprinted in Mizruchi, 1973.

Fromm, E. *The Sane Society.* New York: Holt, 1955.

Fromm, E. (Ed.) *Marx's concept of man.* New York: Ungar, 1961.

Greisman, H. Social movement and mass society: Requiem for the counter culture. In E. H. Mizruchi (Ed.), *The substance of sociology: Codes, conduct and consequences,* 2nd ed. New York: Appleton, 1973.

Mizruchi, E. H. *Success and opportunity: A study of anomic.* New York: Free Press, 1964.

Mizruchi, E. H. Alienation and anomie: Theoretical and empirical perspectives. In I. L. Horowitz (Ed.), *The new sociology: Essays on social theory and social research in honor of C. Wright Mills.* Cambridge: Oxford Univ. Press, 1964.

Mizruchi, E. H. Bohemianism, deviant behavior and social structure. *Society for the Study of Social Problems.* San Francisco, September, 1969. Mimeo.

Mizruchi, E. H. (Ed.) *The substance of sociology: Codes, conduct and consequences,* 2nd ed. New York: Appleton, 1973.

Pfeutze, P. *The social self.* New York: Bookman Associates, 1954.

Reisman, D. *et al. The lonely crowd.* New Haven: Yale University Press, 1950.

Rotenstreich, N. *Basic problems of Marx's philosophy.* Indianapolis: Bobs-Merrill, 1965.

Schaar, J. *Escape from authority.* New York: Basic Books, 1961.

Shils, E. Daydreams and nightmares: Reflections on the criticism of mass culture. *Sewanee Review,* 1957, Autumn.

Sullivan, P. Timon of Athens: A study in alienation and anomie. Unpublished honor's thesis, Syracuse University, 1969.

Taviss, I. Changes in the form of alienation. *American Sociological Review,* 1969, *34,* (February)

Tiryakian, E. *Sociologism and existentialism.* Englewood, N. J.: Prentice-Hall, 1962.

The troubled American. *Newsweek,* 1969, October 6.

Whyte, W. H., Jr. *The organization man.* New York: Doubleday, Anchor, 1957.

Zito, G. On Shakespeare and the sociology of literature. In E. H. Mizruchi (Ed.), *The substance of sociology: Codes, conduct, and consequences,* 2nd ed. New York: Appleton, 1973.

# Chapter 5

# Alienation in Medieval Culture and Society[1]

## David Herlihy
### Harvard University

History, which seeks to study all aspects of human life, must also and perhaps especially consider the mentalities of the past, the character of mind, the state of spirit, which seem to have marked particular ages or particular civilizations. In this paper we wish to explore the phenomenon of alienation in medieval history. A few preliminary words are necessary to explain how exactly we understand this central term. As described in previous chapters and in our abundant literature elsewhere, alienation is capable of sustaining many meanings, but in social science is used in two principal ways.[2] In its sense of self-alienation, it depicts individuals who believe themselves lost and isolated from their society, its purposes, and its values, and are consequently incapable of controlling or directing their actions in socially acceptable ways. Unfortunately for historians, and especially for medievalists, highly individual and personal forms of alienation are nearly impossible to study before the eighteenth century. With the salient exception of the confessions of St. Augustine, the literature of the ancient, medieval, and early modern worlds is all but lacking in introspective autobiographies which might tell us what a man thought of himself and not merely what he wanted others to think of him. Before the Romantic era, it was considered bad taste to bare one's soul in public or in print. Those de-

[1] Adapted from a presentation to the "Institute on Alienation" at Maxwell School of Citizenship and Public Affairs, Syracuse University, December, 1969.

[2] For a brief history of the term, with bibliography, see Lichtheim (1968). For a more extended discussion of the problem of alienation, see Sykes (1964).

scribed as *alienati mente,* "alienated in mind," are, to be sure, easily found in the older sources. But the phrase, in both classical and medieval Latin, referred to madmen and to fools.[3] Neither madmen, nor fools, nor those considered as such, have left much mark on the documentary record.

In its second and now perhaps more common sense—social alienation—the term refers to the estrangement of entire groups within society from traditional and established values and norms of behavior. The works of Karl Marx have undoubtedly given the term its present currency. As Ephraim Mizruchi has also pointed out, alienation for Marx described the plight of the industrial worker under conditions of capitalistic exploitation. No longer the owner of the means of production, no longer able to find outlet for his creative instincts in his physically and psychologically killing labors, the worker inevitably became spiritually divorced from his surroundings. Work, Marx maintained, was essential for man, but work under capitalism only degraded and repelled him. As a comparatively new usage meant to connote a malady peculiar to industrial society, social alienation still can well describe the situation of similar groups in preindustrial Europe. We may take, for example, as a fairly accurate medieval equivalent of the term, the phrase used by a writer of the early fourteenth century, Bernard Gui, in a handbook intended for the guidance of inquisitors. He pointed to the presence in his society of those *a communi conversatione fidelium vita et moribus dissidentes,* "those deviating in life and morals from the usual manner of living of the faithful [see Dovais, 1886, p. 260]."

But what is the value in learning more about dissident and disaffected groups of another age? It may perhaps enable us to view estrangement in our own society from a new and neglected perspective.

In the literature on alienation, the Middle Ages and, indeed, preindustrial Europe are often presented as societies free from such tensions . In this supposedly idyllic world, the individual lived out his days surrounded by a large and loving family, supported by friendly neighbors, and comforted by a religious belief which explained all things in the cosmos. He was, or so we are often told, completely at home with his world, his society, and himself. What this nostalgic reconstruction neglects to acknowledge is that traditional Christianity itself did not really promise contentment even to the saved. Rather, it attached a positive value to alienation from, and dissatisfaction with, the contemporary arrangements of life. The believer was to view this world as a foreign land; he was on this earth only a stranger and a pilgrim.[4] His treasure and his hopes were to be placed in a life to come. "My heart is restless till it rest in Thee," wrote St. Augustine; in like manner, all good Christians were supposed to be discontented with this present life. There was, however, a danger here. The alienation which was a virtue for the orthodox could easily become the aliena-

---

[3] For the use of *alienation* in classical Latin literature in the sense of demented, see "Alieno" (*Thesaurus,* 1900, p. 1566). For a history of madness in the early modern age, see Foucault (1965).

[4] Cf. I *Peter* ii.11, "Dearly beloved, I beseech you as strangers and pilgrims." On the two notions of alienation in medieval Christian thought, see especially Ladner (1967).

tion of the rebellious, the heretic, the demoralized, or the disillusioned. It mattered only where one placed the borders between the work of God and the work of defective nature and sinful man. Any view of the culture and the social psychology of preindustrial Europe cannot neglect the tensions which Christianity itself engendered in instructing the faithful that his present world and the ideal Christian society were out of joint, and that men were created for something far, far better.

Moreover, the myth of a supremely contented preindustrial society—the "golden legend" of the Middle Ages as one historian has recently called it—corresponds less and less with what we are learning of the actual life of the epoch.[5] Historians have been pushing their research into levels of society and aspects of preindustrial life largely ignored in the past, and they are finding tension and estrangement as much as peace. Perhaps they are only discovering that men before the age of machines were, after all, truly men. We would suggest that analyses of alienation even in our own society should take stock of what we are discovering concerning traditional Europe. The faulty notion of the mental tranquility of the preindustrial world has led, perhaps, to an exaggerated emphasis on recent or present-day conditions as the nearly exclusive sources of alienation. The further result has been perhaps a relative neglect of those issues and problems which have often troubled human societies, and still trouble our own. A consideration of this historical experience may, in other words, help us to see better, and to judge better, what exactly it is that we are facing.

We wish, therefore, in this paper to visit what we may call the medieval underground. Admittedly, the dissident and the alienated in medieval society are hard to approach directly. For to "deviate in life and morals" in the Middle Ages was, rightly or wrongly, to incur suspicion of heresy. The heretics or those suspected of heterodox opinion have left little direct testimony of what they really believed, and why. But they did attract considerable attention, investigation, and comment from their orthodox oppressors. What their enemies said of them is understandably distorted but nonetheless precious. Moreover, if the dissidents of the Middle Ages were harrassed, they were not really silenced. Those who rejected the socially acceptable norms of thought and behavior had recourse to forms of expression familiar to many underground movements—to allegory, to satire, and to parody. Estrangement as reflected in medieval literature is a large subject, still only partially studied, but there seems little doubt that its influence was enormous.

In these remarks concerning the phenomenon of alienation in medieval culture, we must refer to movements and attitudes which are not well known beyond the small circle of medievalists. It therefore seems necessary initially to describe, of course in broad terms, some representative examples of medieval dissent. We shall then review the complaints and criticisms against society which appear to have been

[5] For an interpretation of the Middle Ages which strongly criticizes recent scholars for exaggerating the accomplishments and the supposed contentment of the epoch, see LeGoff (1965, esp. pp. 13-19).

widely characteristic of protest movements in the Middle Ages. Finally, we should like to examine one factor which seems to have contributed to the strength of dissent in the medieval world. Specifically, we want to glance into the interior life of the medieval family in serach of influences which may possibly have contributed to the estrangement of its children.

For the first five centuries of its history, medieval society remained overwhelmingly rural in character, nearly without cities or an urban class, and without a highly creative culture or vigorous dissent. From about the year 1000, medieval civilization changed fundamentally. The population, stagnant or declining since the days of the Roman empire, began at last substantially to grow. Historians can neither measure nor explain this rapid multiplication of the European peoples, but today most consider it a major force in the transformation of the medieval world. Pressed by their own enlarged numbers and apparently also encouraged by a new self-confidence, Europeans poured over the old frontiers. At home, trade quickened and artisan skills grew among the people. As a capstone to these changes, Europe from the eleventh century witnessed a rebirth of urban life. For the first time since the fall of Rome, cities became a prominent factor in medieval social and cultural history. Historians now speak of a kind of enlargement of the Western consciousness in the eleventh and twelfth centuries, a new awareness of the place of Latin Christendom in the world and in history (see esp. Bloch, 1968). This discovery of self certainly contributed to the high achievements of a young and vigorous Europe. But here we are interested in an opposite if still related phenomenon—the alienation from self, in the sense of a violent rejection on the part of many men of the West of the religious and social norms which their parents, and society, sought to impose upon them.

In 1007 at Orleans in France, two heretics were burned for their beliefs, apparently for the first time since the fall of the ancient world. This is only an early and especially brutal manifestation of the growing forces of dissent, and of repression too, in the West. To illustrate even briefly the varieties of dissent which appear in medieval society from the eleventh century requires that we impose upon them some sort of order and classification. We shall, accordingly, group our examples into three principal categories: religious alienation, or the rejection of norms of behavior (not necessarily religious in origin) defended by society at large, ethical alienation, or the rejection of standard moral conceptions about love, marriage, and emotional fulfillment, and intellectual alienation, or the rejection by groups within the ranks of scholars of received opinions concerning the nature of the cosmos. To be sure, none of the movements or ideas we shall consider is really pure, and the borders of our categories are necessarily fuzzy. But these divisions still may help us grasp better the broad characteristics of medieval dissent.

To consider religious dissent in medieval society is inevitably to encounter heresy, and here a word of caution is required.[6] In the literal sense of its Greek root,

[6] On heresy in medieval and early modern society, see most recently LeGoff (1968). The work contains a "Bibliographie des études récentes," pp. 407-467. The meaning of the term is discussed in the first communication by Chenu (1968).

the heretic is the person who "chooses" rather than rejects, in the sense of selecting a positive set of beliefs opposed to official teaching. He is not, by a strict interpretation of the word, isolated, distraught, or confused. Rather, he confidently believes that he has the truth, that the orthodox majority is wrong, and that his own views will ultimately prevail. Heresy, in its specific theological definition, is not therefore synonymous with personal or social alienation.

On the other hand, in the Middle Ages, the words heretics and heresy were used in a much looser sense. Bernard Gui and other authors who offered guidance to inquisitors repeatedly complained of the fluctuating beliefs of many heretics which made it difficult for the inquisitor to detect their poisonous presence. He attributed their pliable theology to crafty dissimulation, but it does appear that few of the major heretical groups possessed a developed theology. Several scholars have recently stressed how difficult it is to identify by classification of beliefs the numerous heretics who appear in the West from the eleventh century.[7] Bernard Gui (see Douais, 1886) maintained that many heretics consciously avoided a rational presentation of their theology.

> It should be noted [he warned inquisitors] that heretics sometimes pretend
> to be fools or to be alienated in mind, as David was in the presence of Achis.
> When they preach their falsehoods, they intersperse irrelevant or bantering words
> or those almost senseless, and by this they disguise their errors. They appear to
> say in jest what they speak, and I have often seen such people [p. 256].

Our author also noted that unusual styles of clothing were grounds for suspecting heresy, and here religious dissent overlaps with what we are calling ethical dissent.[8] One of the principal charges pressed against Joan of Arc was, of course, her use of masculine garments. A still stronger suspicion of heresy derived from unusual behavior, especially in regard to sexual practices. As shown by their surviving proceedings, the inquisitorial courts inquired with great diligence into the sexual habits of the suspected in search of clues concerning the strength and nature of their religious beliefs.[9] Joan of Arc was examined not only by theologians to establish her orthodoxy but by women to determine her past sexual deportment. The heretics, perhaps not without reason, were repeatedly accused of condoning sexual license or conducting sexual orgies. It is better to marry than to burn, wrote St. Paul. The heretics interpreted this text to mean, or so they were accused, that it was good not to burn, and that any base act which freed the spirit from the distractions of the flesh was justified. The result was that any one who lived in violation

---

[7] Russell (1968) has questioned, for example, the influence of the eastern Bogomils and Paulicians on the spread of heresy in the West and has stressed the importance of local factors in the growth of heterodox belief.

[8] Gui (see Douais, 1886) "cum vehementer sint suspecti, tamquam a communi conversatione fidelium vita et moribus dissidentes. . . quam ex habitu quem portant in aliquo specialem et distinctum quasi sit alicujus religionis habitus singularis. . . [p. 263]."

[9] Cf. the register of the inquisitor Jacques Fournier in southern France, which describes in often meticulous detail the confessions of sexual aberrations given by those under suspicion (Duvernoy, 1965).

of accepted moral standards was likely to be called a heretic, no matter what were his true beliefs.

Bernard Gui, in instructing inquisitors, compiled a list of the principal heresies of his day, and we may take from his list some representative examples of the varieties of religious alienation in medieval society. The only group mentioned by Bernard with a developed system of dogmatic beliefs, the only group which perhaps deserves to be called heretic in the full theological sense of the word, is the *Cathari,* meaning the "pure ones," or the Albigensians, named for the town of Albi in southern France, an early center of their cult (Nelli, 1953; Niel, 1967).[10] They were essentially Manichees, retaining beliefs which were in fact older than Christianity. Two deities, a god of light and a god of darkness, were contending for supremacy in the cosmos, and the realm of darkness was essentially equivalent with this material world. Those who lived fully up to the rigorous demands of their faith, the so-called *perfecti,* refrained from marriage and procreation; this enlisted additional subjects under the banners of the dark god. They abstained from all foods produced by sexual union and espoused a life of rigorous poverty. In spite of a rather bizarre ethical system, the Albigensians were the best organized of the heretical groups and from the twelfth century seemed likely to wrest entire provinces of Latin Christendom from allegiance to Catholicism.

Much in contrast to Albigensianism, the next heresy mentioned by Gui was based rather on the selection of a distinct way of life than a distinct set of dogmatic beliefs. Sometime about 1170, a rich merchant of Lyons named Peter Waldo abandoned all his possessions and adopted the life of apostolic poverty, life as the first Christians had supposedly lived it. A group of followers gathered about him and these were called Waldensians, after their leader, or the "Poor Men of Lyons," after their place of origin. Good men should own no property; rather, they should live from their own labor or by begging and freely share what they gained with their brethren. This exaltation of poverty, which was not a virtue much stressed in the earlier and poorer Middle Ages, seems itself to represent an alienation from the life of buying and selling, and from the comfortable living now possible for the rich urban classes. The Waldensians were heretics not for what they espoused—there was nothing heretical about Apostolic poverty—but for what they rejected, specifically, the authority of the hierarchy and the value of sacraments administered by corrupt priests. They are therefore good examples of heresy consisting not in positive choice but primarily in rejection.

If the Waldensians were founded on a kind of alienation from the new bourgeois affluence and morality, another sect mentioned by Bernard rather reflects the new conflict of classes. These were the Apostolic Brethren, and their appeal was clearly to the disaffected poor in both city and countryside. Their founder was an illiterate artisan of Parma in Italy, Gherardo Segalelli, who, in about 1260, announced the imminent coming of a new age and warned that men must prepare for the millen-

---

[10] Albi was, however, only one of many centers of the heresy, and it is still not known why this town gave its name to the entire movement.

ium. Segallelli was burnt at the stake and the leadership of the brethren was passed to the illegitimate son of a priest, Fra, or Brother, Dolcino (Anagnine, 1964).[11] With some 4000 followers he set up a perfect society in the Alpine valleys of northern Italy. It is not entirely certain how he understood social perfection, but he seems to have envisioned an end to private property and an end to marriage, or the private use of women. Settled in a mountain valley, Fra Dolcino and his followers awaited the call of trumpets which would announce the advent of the millenium and the extension of these new social norms to the entire earth. The trumpets he heard were only those of a crusading army which the pope had directed against him. In 1307 the fires of the stake gave him deliverance from this world of imperfections.

Still other groups of heretics seem to have organized to provide a social dimension which the orthodox Church was either failing to fill, or filling inadequately. This was evidence in the spontaneous appearance of indigenous religious communities formed by men or women who, for reason of poverty or some other impediment, could not gain admission into the recognized religious orders. The women were known as Beguines and their male counterparts the Beghards (McDonald, 1954). These unauthorized communities first appear in Flanders in the twelfth century. The Church was suspicious of them for reason of their loose discipline and the lack of an approved rule. The names Beguines and Beghards were thereafter loosely applied to many true heretics in the late Middle Ages, but most of the persons forming such societies were seeking to follow a religious vocation which they could not pursue through the officially sanctioned channels.

In regard to our second type of estrangement, ethical alienation, by far the most influential and remarkable example of deviation from orthodox norms of behavior in medieval history are the attitudes concerning love, marriage, and emotional fulfillment, collectively known as the cult of courtly love (de Rougemont, 1962; Pollman, 1966). From about 1100, troubadours closely associated with the noble classes of southern France were singing of love in extraordinary terms, and their literary conceits, of course, affected all the vernacular literatures of Europe. According to the chief contemporary theoreticism of the art of love, Andreas Capellanus, true love could not even exist within marriage.[12] Both partners in the exercise had to be free to retreat, advance, and parry. The lovers could not therefore contemplate marriage as the fruition of their relationship, and still less the procreation of children. Courtly love was, however, not a celebration of sexual license, as the lovers were obligated to be faithful one to the other, nor even of adultery, as it clearly stressed the ideal over the physical rewards of love. But this sexual ethos was nonetheless inalterably opposed to Christian conceptions of marriage and of

[11] For a stimulating interpretation of millenary movements, especially in the later Middle Ages, see Cohn (1962).

[12] A "court of love" (see Trojel, 1892) decided that the relationships between spouses and between lovers were so different that they could not even be compared. "Maritalis affectus et coamantium vera dilectio penitus iudicantur esse diversa et ex motibus omnino differentibus suam sumunt originem [pp. 280-281]."

the character and purposes of sexual attraction. It was no less opposed to the conventions which governed the selection of a mate among the nobles of southern France. Rather, it clearly parodied these official codes. The lover's fidelity and service to his lady closely resemble the feudal obligations of a vassal toward his lord. The lover, usually of a lower social station than his lady, spoke to her in terms appropriate for a lord, even to the use of a masculine title on occasion in addressing her. The love tie seems also a parody of Christian mysticism. Some scholars have claimed that this expression was a secularization of the mysticism of Bernard of Clairaux (cf. the remarks of Gilson, 1955). The successful lover, like the Christian mystic, was infused with joy—one of the gifts of the Holy Spirit—and came to inhabit a new heaven and a new earth, which St. Peter promised the faithful. The late Father Denomy (1947) rather traced the roots of this concept to the Albigensians who similarly separated sex from marriage and reproduction, although his ideas have not won much support from scholars. The Albigensians were, after all, convinced puritans; they were forbidden even to touch women, even when administering a sacrament. Their stern asceticism seems far removed from the troubadours' often sensuous celebration of female beauty. But there surely are, within courtly love, elements of dissent and alienation from the Christian ethic and social practice governing marriage.

Our third type of alienation—"philosophic heresy," or the rejection by members of the scholarly or intellectual community of received notions concerning the cosmos—takes us to the schools of the twelfth century and the universities of the thirteenth. Writers in the twelfth century such as Bernard Sylvester and Allan of Lille celebrated, in what seems extravagant terms, the autonomy and perfection of nature in a manner which left little room for the traditional emphasis upon the defects of the natural world and the need for grace to repair them. In the thirteenth century, intellectual dissent in the universities took the form of the espousal of the ideas of the Muslim philosopher Averroës who denied the possibility of reconciling faith and reason, and even questioned the personal immortality of the soul. One of the best examples of dissent within the intellectual classes is the long epic poem of the thirteenth century, the *Romance of the Rose.* [13] Jean de Meun, author of the second, longer, and more outspoken part of the work, was apparently influenced by Averroistic ideas. He castigated basic institutions of Church and society, reserving particular scorn for the mendicant orders and for women. He implied that the norms of Christian marriage were artificial and, consequently, ignored. According to him, a faithful wife was hardly to be found in the whole of France and the wise man should follow the dictates of nature and seek to perpetuate his kind at every available opportunity. It is hard to envision what kind of society Jean de Meun was advocating, but it is certainly clear what he hated. The *Romance of the Rose* is usually represented as a great classic of antifeminist literature, but its target was equally the institution of marriage.

[13] For the relationship between the *Romance of the Rose* and intellectual dissent at Paris, see Paré (1947).

We have no time here to consider other forms of departure from accepted norms. For example, the French *fabliau,* and, soon after, the Italian *novelle* present a thoroughly naturalistic view of society reminiscent of the *Romance of the Rose.* Parodies of the sacred liturgy offer another example. Many of Europe's churches celebrated feasts of the ass or feasts of fools in which the services moved on the borders between rough good fun and blasphemy (Moncelle, 1914). Witchcraft and sorcery, another concern of the inquisitors, maintained a powerful appeal, especially to the rural classes. Outbreaks of religious hysteria, particularly pronounced in the plague years of the late Middle Ages, present another fascinating topic for the social historian.[14] Bands of flagellants, beating themselves mercilessly, roamed from city to city calling upon the people to do penance. Our list is far from complete, but perhaps this brief review has at least illustrated that medieval culture offers abundant materials for those interested in studying psychological and social estrangement and dissent.

We have considered the varieties of dissent in medieval culture, and now we must review some points of agreement uniting them. One common trait is immediately apparent. All the movements were highly critical of the orthodox Church, its priesthood, and pretensions. The *Romance of the Rose,* the *fabliaux,* and the *novelle* represent the clergy, and especially the frairs, as greedy lechers, lazy and slovenly, who adjured their parishoners to work while they stole their bread and seduced their wives. Among the heretics, this anticlericalism spilled over into anti-sacerdotalism—into a denial that the orthodox priesthood could aid the believer to reach salvation. The heretics characteristically maintained that it was better to pray in a stable, amid cattle and horses, than with the hypocrites of Rome. The Albigensians manifested an especial contempt for the chief symbol of the Christian religion. Nearly from the first, a refusal to venerate the cross marks the heretical movements. If your father was killed upon a gallows, the Albigensians demanded, would you venerate the instrument of his torture? (Gui, see Douais, 1886, p. 242).

For one other major insitution of society, these movements manifested a hostility nearly the equal in consistency and vehemence to that directed against the Church. That hated institution was the family. In regard to authority and property, the dissident groups show no great consistency. Only the Apostolic Brethren seem to have envisioned a total reorganization of society in preparation for the coming millenium. The Albigensians and Waldensians denied certain powers to the prince. They refused, for example, to take oaths, and denied that the prince had any authority to coerce his subjects in matters of belief. The Albigensians were similarly opposed to killing, even of animals and still less of men. The nonviolence and pacifism of the *perfecti* thus would have prohibited wars not only among Christians, but also against the infidel. On the other hand, the Albigensians certainly cultivated the support of the princes of southern France and, by denying all authority to the orthodox hierarchy, favored an enlargement of the princely prerogatives. So

---

[14] For further comment on the character of these movements in Italy, see Herlihy (1967).

also, their attitudes toward property were inconsistent. Both the Waldensians and Albigensians urged a return to the Apostolic life in which all good Christians would share their belongings, though this was a counsel of perfection to be followed by their priests and leaders, not a formula for the overhaul of society. But the heretics and the other dissident groups seem remarkably unified in hostility against the family, marriage, and procreation. *In matrimonio non est salus,* "in matrimony there is no salvation." This tenet of Albigensian belief, taken, it must be admitted, from an orthodox source, still seems to represent a basic principle of the Albigensian social ethic.[15] "For the common opinion of all *Cathari,*" a former Albigensian wrote in the thirteenth century, "is that physical marriage has always been a mortal sin, and that in the future life no one will be punished more severely because of adultry or incest than for legitimate matrimony. So also among them no one is more gravely punished than for this . . . [Sacchoni, 1717, p. 1761].

To lie with a daughter or son, to commit sodomitic acts, were no worse than, and, indeed, preferable to lying with a wife. The Albigensians similarly entertained remarkably harsh attitudes toward children. Like the Anabaptists of another age, they maintained that there was no hope of salvation for those who died before the age of reason when at last faith and commitment were possible for them. The child who died in his tender years—and of course myriads did in this society—would be punished in the afterlife as cruelly as a thief and murderer (Sacchoni, 1717, p. 1761). There was no Limbo to receive them as a kind of eternal orphanage. Those who took the deplorable step of marrying and bearing children had to recognize the suffering they would almost inevitably cause.

Here, as in other beliefs, the Waldensians were less clear in their affirmations, and apparently less radical in their denunciation of marriage. But they too allegedly maintained, still according to the orthodox, that marriage was a "kind of sworn fornication, unless the husband and wife abstained from sexual relations; they say that other unclean acts are more licit than marital union."[16] They further held that a man who wished to join the ranks of the wandering *perfecti* was justified in abandoning wife and children. For he who preferred his relatives over Christ was not worthy of Christ.

Even within contemporary orthodox movements, most notably the new Franciscan and Dominican orders, there appears a hostility to the family. In one of the first acts of his religious career, St. Francis of Assisi, a man who much resembles Peter Waldo, broke publicly with his father. Standing in the marketplace before the bishop of the city, he threw to earth a purse containing his father's money and then removed all the clothes which his father had given him. Naked he had come to him and naked he would leave him. "From now on," he told the persons gathered on the square, "I shall call as father the One Father Who is in heaven, and

[15] Cited by Guiraud (1912, p. 1628) from an unpublished manuscript, "Albigeois."

[16] Sacchoni (1717), "Matrimonium dicunt fornicationem iuratam nisi continenter vivant; quaslibet alias immunditias magis licitas dicunt quam copulam conjugalem [p. 1779]."

not my father according to the flesh, Pietro Bernadone [Daniel-Rops, 1962, p. 20]."
The scene is the more remarkable as Francis, as all Christians, was obligated to honor
his father and mother. Another resident of Assisi, Clare Offreducci, still in her teens,
in imitation of Francis but in outright defiance of her family's wishes, fled her home
to found the order of Poor Clares. Her still younger sister followed her into the religious life and faced the even more violent prohibition of her parents (Daniel-Rops,
1962, pp. 28-29). To read the great body of hagiography and legends of the thirteenth century is frequently to encounter similar situations. Albert the Great faced
the opposition of his uncle in entering the Dominicans. Thomas Aquinas was kid-
napped and imprisoned by his brothers. The impression left by this literature is that
more often than not, family loyalties and the family itself was considered more likely to oppose the pursuit of a religious vocation and, indirectly at least, to interfere
with the service of God. Admittedly, in much stronger terms, the heretics held a similar position. Both groups were fond of quoting the words of Christ according to St.
Luke, that "he who would not abandon father and mother because of Him was not
worthy of Him."[17]

Even apart from properly religious movements, the other examples of dissident values we have mentioned took the family as a principal object of resentment.
Father Denomy was probably not right in considering courtly love an expression of
the Albigensian heresy, but he was certainly right in noting the extraordinary similarities of both movements in their ideas on marriage. The cult of courtly love carries, without question, a contempt of marriage. For the courtly lover as for the Albigensian heretic, human and emotional fulfillment could not be found in the married state. For the courtly lover as for the Albigensian heretic, *in matrimonio non
est salus.* Troubadour love poetry refuses to accept any connection at all among
sexual attraction, emotional fulfillment, marriage, and the procreation of children.
So, also, the strong current of naturalism in the medieval schools, the *Romance of
the Rose,* the *fabliaux,* and the *novelle* implicitly satirized the institutions of the
family and its ethical pretensions.

In these movements of dissent, this nearly ubiquitous hostility to marriage
offers, we would suggest, lies one clue to the social origins of estrangement and alienation in medieval society. Why was the family so hated? In prudence, of course,
we should affirm or reaffirm that these movements are of extraordinarily complex
origins. Before taking up the properly familial roots of alienation, we should mention some current opinions concerning the origins of dissent. Again, the heretics,
because of the openness of their views and the investigations which their orthodox
contemporaries made of them, are the most easily studied.

It is certain, for example, that class antagonism played a major role in sowing
the seeds of dissent. While the earliest heretics seem to have been peasants, the movement beyond doubt struck its deepest roots in the new and growing towns (see most

[17]*Matthew* x.37.

recently, Morghen, 1968, Russell, 1963; Violante, 1968). All the urban classes had reason for psychological dissatisfaction. Traditional Christian teachings forbade certain practices, such as the taking of any profit on a loan, which handicapped mercantile exchange and pushed many merchants into either sin or defiance. The Albigensians, on the other hand, denied that usury was a sin.[18] Moreover, traditional Christian belief had been highly suspicious of wealth. "It is as hard for a rich man to enter heaven as for a camel to pass through the eye of a needle."[19] To the rich merchant fearful of salvation, the heretics held out the hope of a deathbed conversion, of initiation into the ranks of the perfect, and of assured salvation.

The heresies seem to have exerted an even stronger appeal to the poorest urban classes, especially those weavers and cloth workers associated with the growing urban industries. In the twelfth-century sources, the word *tixerant*, weaver, is often used in north-French documents as a synonym for Albigensian. The weaver's quarter of Toulouse was the city's stronghold of heretical belief. The scant information which our sources give us about the principal heretical figures lays stress on their illiteracy, suggesting that they came in large numbers from the humblest levels of urban society. Living a life of poverty and desperation, poorly served by the orthodox Church, the weavers and artisans turned in large numbers to heresy which gave expression to the antagonisms they felt against both the wealthy and the official religion (Volpe, 1922, p. 28). But most scholars today would maintain that heresy cannot be interpreted exclusively as a middle-class or proletarian movement. Albigensianism, for example, enlisted many nobles of southern France, especially among the poorer knights. A recent interpretation has noted the strength of heresy among the more mobile groups of the population (Violante, 1968, p. 195). To those cut off by circumstances from their homes, heresies, and the heretical communities, offered a kind of physical and spiritual haven. Finally, the heresies had a remarkable appeal to women, which is hard to explain exclusively in terms of the conflict of classes. Many of the sects allowed them to preach, and some admitted them into the priesthood (Koch, 1962).

In southern France the heretics seem to have operated schools for young girls, supporting them and teaching them how to read when orthodox institutions and their own families left them in neglect. "They teach little girls," a tract of the thirteenth century says of the heretics, "the Bible and the epistles, so that from youth they may be accustomed to embrace error."[20] The same tract gives an example of the preaching of the heretics. Significantly, the bearers are addressed in words of the feminine gender, as if the preacher could expect to find his most receptive audience among women. St. Dominic founded the first Dominican convent for nuns at Prouille, specifically for the reason that the nobles had hitherto given their daugh-

---

[18] Sacchoni (1717), "ipsi tamen dicunt usuram nullum est peccatum [p. 1764]."

[19] *Mark* x.25.

[20] Tractus de haeresi pauperum de Lugduno (Sacchini, 1717). "Puellas parvulas docent evangelium et a pueritia consuescant errorem amplecti [p. 1782]."

ters to the heretics.[21] The Beguines and Beghards in the late Middle Ages constituted a movement always including more women than men. As a great medieval scholar has written: "Women now appear in the history of heresy as in no other phase of life."[22]

Numerous social factors, and numerous social situations, thus contributed to dissent in the Middle Ages. But the heretics, whether they were the knights in their castles, the merchants in their counting houses, or the weavers in their hovels, shared at least this common experience: They were all products of a family. The hostility to the family, manifested in all these movements, strongly argues that one root of dissent was a generational conflict, a revolt of the young against the parents who raised them. As the heretic viewed the world, the persons who gave him life were sinners and servants of Mammon, worse than adulterers and sodomites. Paradoxically, the principal evidence for his parents' sinful habits was his own existence, his very person. It would be hard to find a set of beliefs more suggestive of generational conflict than what the heretics affirmed concerning their own parents.

Why were parents apparently so condemned, and marriage so disparaged? The roots of generational conflict within the medieval family have never been satisfactorily explored, and we can here offer only a few comments. We must return to a point we have earlier made. Medieval society was growing rapidly from the eleventh century, and historians today are justifiably impressed by its accomplishments. But contemporaries themselves certainly did not think in terms of an ever changing, ever growing world—one of inexhaustible opportunities. Rather, the goal for them remained a stable society, with sons replacing fathers in smooth succession over the generations. But what should happen when there were more sons than fathers, more persons demanding places in society than there seemed places to be had? In other words, the medieval world faced, as every growing society must, a disequilibrium between the generations and an acute problem of finding a social and spiritual home for its children. This problem involved especially, but not exclusively, the younger children of a family—not exclusively, as numerous progeny affected the fortunes and prospects of all the siblings.

Medieval society, that is to say the elders who ruled it, responded in several ways to this problem of finding place and position for its numerous, even superfluous youth. For the sons of knights and for many others besides, there was the appeal of crusading. In speaking to the assembled knights at Clermont in 1905, Pope Urban II is reported to have told them that they were already too many for their narrow land pressed between the mountains and the sea. War against the infidel in Palestine promised them both material and spiritual rewards. The young nobleman, facing an uncertain future at home, thus was promised two things he needed: the prospect of economic support, and a spiritual and psychological commitment.

[21] According to Jordan of Saxony, Libellus de Principiis ordinis Praedicatorum, cited in Laureilhe (1956, p. 56).

[22] Volpe (1922). "Nella storia del' eresia appaiono, ora, come in nessun' altra manifestazione di vita [p. 17]."

But the exodus of young men to Europe's new frontiers aggravated the social position of their sisters and mistresses who remained at home. It is possible to argue, as we have elsewhere done, that the absence of men within the noble classes of Europe in the crusading period eventually added to the influence which women exercised over society (Herlihy, 1962), but it separated many others, young women especially, from their loved ones and condemned them to a life of loneliness. A French source tells of a lady who, when the death of her troubadour lover was reported to her, was so despondent that she gave herself to the heretics.[23] They alone, it seemed, offered an explanation for her plight.

Moreover, society, meaning again the elders who ruled it, frightened by its own numbers, sought to limit the opportunity to marry by insisting upon high dowries and by uniting ever more closely the ownership of wealth and the chance to marry and to reproduce. The biographer St. Dominic, as we have noted, related that because of poverty the nobles of southern France would not or could not care for their daughters and delivered them to the heretics who alone, before the advent of Dominic, were willing to educate and nourish them. The unmarriageable daughter remains a major social problem for the entire course of medieval history, for every social class.

The heretics of southern France, in founding schools and convents for these unwanted girls, were thus fulfilling a real social need. In the twelfth century, the old Benedictine monasteries for women seem to have offered no reasonable alternative to marriage for large segments of the population. They were too few, too small, and too closely tied with the highest levels of society. In supporting girls, the heretics further offered them an ideology which made sense of their plight. They learned that their fathers and mothers had sinned in bringing them into this unhappy world, that the marriage they could not have was anyway evil, that the Church which would not accept them was wicked and corrupt. For dislodged persons, for the superfluous young, the heretics thus offered a physical and cultural home which neither the family nor the Church was providing, Not until the foundations of the Dominican and Franciscan convents did the orthodox Church offer a comparable service, and then not completely. Loosely disciplined communities of unmarriageable women (the "Beguines") formed a common part of medieval society through all the epoch.

We wish we could say more about the poorest urban classes in this period, but they figure far less prominently than the knights in our available sources. It seems certain, however, that marriage and the support of a family were difficult for the urban poor and denied to many of them. So, also, before the coming of the mendicants, there was no religious order to which the humble could easily repair. The Benedictine monasteries, Cistercians and Cluniacs, seem to have remained aristocratic establishments par excellence. The humble faced an insecure present

---

[23] The source is the life of the troubadour Raimon Jordan, viscount of St. Antonin (Koch, 1962, p. 142).

and an uncertain future. Heresy offered them both spiritual fellowship and an explanation for their misery. These forces which placed them where they were—their own parents, the church, in some measure, the prince—were evil, but they still might serve the True God, Who had no responsibility for this sorry world.

This, then, was the situation in which medieval society found itself in this period of rapid growth. Inevitably, the younger generation was larger than the older. The family was prone to deal harshly with its children, its younger sons and daughters especially. These were often denied the chance of marrying, urged to leave their homes, or even abandoned to the heretics. Many seem to have reacted against this rejection, and alienation from parents easily became alienation from society.

Is there an insight to be gained into our own problems from this review of the Middle Ages? Perhaps only this: Any growing, changing society is likely to face the problem of maintaining a smooth succession of the generations, of offering both a social and a spiritual home to the enlarged numbers of its young. So, also, in any growing society, numbers of the young, facing the pressures of finding places in a shifting world, are apt to consider themselves lost and abandoned, and, rightly or wrongly, to accuse their parents of not responding to their needs. Generational conflict, then, in turn easily becomes social estrangement. This problem of generational disequilibrium, of a breakdown in the functions of socialization and acculturation required of the family—a failure, in other words, of the older generation to serve the needs of its children—seems to have been critical in the medieval world, and has not been entirely resolved even in our own advanced society.

One final point may be made: Every society is tempted to regard itself as unique, as something new under the sun, as facing problems never seen before. But every society, if it wishes for wisdom, should consult the experience of its ancestors. That is the function of history, and that ultimately is the justification for this present visit to the distant world of the Middle Ages.

## REFERENCES

Anagnine, E. *Dolcino e il movimento ereticale all'inizio del trecento.* 69. Florence: Biblioteca di Cultura, 1964.

Bloch, M. La prise de conscience. In *La société féodale.* Vol. 1. *La formation des liens de dépendance.* Paris: Evolution de l'Humanité, 1968. Pp. 161-164.

Chenu, M. D. Orthodoxie et hérésie. In J. LeGoff, (Ed.), *Hérésies et sociétés dans l'Eurpoe pré-industrielle, 11e-18e siècles. Communications et débats du colloque de Royaumont.* Vol. 10. Paris: Civilisations et Sociétés, 1968. Pp. 9-17.

Cohn, N. *The pursuit of the millenium.* New York: Harper and Row, 1962.

Daniel-Rops, *Claire dans la clarte.* 72; Paris:Biblioteque Ecclesia, 1962.

Denomy, A. *The heresy of courtly love.* Gloucester, Massachusetts: Peter Smith, 1947.

de Rougemont, D. *L'amour et l'occident.* Paris: Plon, 1962.

Douais, C. (Ed.) *Bernardus Guidonis: Practica inquisitionis heretice pravitatis.* Paris: A. Picard, 1886.

Duvernoy, J. (Ed.), *Le registre d'inquistion de Jacques Fournier évêque de Pamiers* (1318-1325). Toulouse: E. Privat, 1965. 3 vols.

Foucault, M. *Madness in civilization.* New York: Random House, 1965. (Originally published as *Historie de la folie à l'âge classique.* Paris: Plon, 1964.)

Gilson, E. Courtly love and Christian mysticism. Hypothesis of influence. *The mystical philosophy of St. Bernard.* London: Sheed and Ward, 1955. Pp. 186-197.

Guiraud, J. *Dictionnaire d'histoire et de géographie ecclésiastiques.* Vol. I. Paris: Letouzey et Ané, 1912.

Herlihy, D. "Land, family and women in continental Europe, 701-1200. *Traditio,* 1962, *18,* 89-120.

Herlihy, D. *Medieval and Renaissance Pistoia. The Social History of an Italian Town.* New Haven: Yale Univ. Press, 1967.

Koch, G. *Frauenfrage und Ketzertum im Mittelalter. Die Frauenbewegung im Rahmen des Katharismus und des Waldensertums und ihre sozialen Wurzeln (12.-14. Jahrhundert).* 9. Berlin: Forschungen zur Mittelalterlichen Geschichte, 1962.

Ladner, G. B. *Homo viator:* Mediaeval ideas on alienation and order. *Speculum,* 1967, *XLII,* 233-259.

Laureilhe, M. T. (Ed.), *Saint Dominique et ses fils, textes choisis, traduits et annotés.* (Textes pour l'histoire sacrée, choisis et présentés par Daniel-Rops.) Paris: A. Fayard, 1956.

LeGoff, J. *La civilisation de l'Occident médiéval.* Paris: Arthaud, 1965.

LeGoff, J. (Ed.), *Hérésies et sociétés dans l'Europe préindustrielle, 11e-18e siècles. Communications et débats du colloque de Royaumont.* Vol. 10. Paris: Civilisations et Sociétés, 1968.

Lichtheim, G. Alienation. In D. Sills (Ed.), *International encyclopedia of the social sciences.* Vol. 1. New York: Macmillan & Free Press, 1968. Pp. 264-268.

McDonald, E. W. *The Beguines and Beghards in mediaeval culture with special emphasis on the Belgian scens.* New Brunswick, N. J.: Rutgers University Press, 1954.

Moncelle, P. Ane (fete de l'). *Dictionnaire d'histoire et de géographie ecclésiastiques.* Vol. II. Paris: Letouzey et Ané, 1914. Pp. 1816-1826.

Morghen, R. Problèmes sur l'origine de l'heresie au moyen age. In J. LeGoff (Ed.), *Hérésies et sociétés.* Paris: Civilisations et Sociétés. 1968. Pp. 121-138.

Nelli, R. *Spiritualité de l'hérésie. Le catharisme.* (Toulouse: E. Privat, 1953.)

Niel, F. *Albieois et Cathares.* Paris: Collection "Que sais-je?," 1967.

Pare, G. *Les idées et les lettres au XIIIe siècle. Le roman de la rose.* Montreal: Centre de Psychologie et Pedagogie, 1947.

Pollman, L. *Die Liebe in der hochmittelalterlichen Literatur Frankreichs. Versuch einer historischen Phänomenologie.* Frankfurt am Main: V. Klosterman, 1966.

Russell, J. Interpretations of the origins of medieval heresy. *Mediaeval Studies,* 1963, *XXV,* 26-53.

Sacchoni. R. Summa de Catharis et Leonistis seu Pauperibus de Lugduno. 1717. In E. Martène & U. Durand (Eds.), *Thesaurus novus anecdotorum.* Vol. V. Paris: Montalant, 1717.

Sykes, G. *Alienation. The cultural climate of our times.* New York: G. Braziller, 1964.

*Thesaurus linguae Latinae.* Vol. 1. Leipzig: Teubner, 1900.

Trojel, E. (Ed.), *Andreae Capellani: De amore libri tres.* Hauniae: Gadiana, 1892.

Violante, C. Hérésies urbaines et hérésies rurales in Italie du 11e au 13e siècle. In J. LeGoff (Ed.), *Hérésies et sociétés.* Paris: Civilisations et Sociétés. 1968. Pp. 171-198.

Volpe, G. *Movimenti religiosi e sette ereticali nella società medievale italiana (secoli XI-XIV).* 6. Florence: Collana Storica, 1922.

# Chapter 6

# The Concept of Alienation:
# Some Critical Notices

*Theodore C. Denise*

Syracuse University

. . . [T] he original human nature was not like the present. . . primeval man was round, his back and sides forming a circle; and he had four hands and four feet, one head with two faces looking opposite ways. . . Terrible was their might and strength, and the thoughts of their hearts were great, and they made an attack upon the gods. . . .

Doubt reigned in the celestial councils. Should they kill them and annihilate the race with thunderbolts, as they had done the giants, then there would be an end of the sacrifices and worship which men offered to them; but. . . the gods could not suffer their insolence to be unrestrained. . . . Zeus discovered a way. He said: "Methinks I have a plan which will humble their pride and improve their manners. . . ." He spoke and cut men in two, like a sorb-apple which is halved for pickling. . . .

Each . . . [man] . . . when separated . . . is always looking for his other half. . . . And when one of them meets with . . . the actual half of himself, the pair are lost in amazement of love and friendship and intimacy. . . . [However,] the intense yearning . . . does not appear to be the desire of lover's intercourse, but of something else of which the soul . . . has only a dark and doubtful presentiment . . .; [namely, of] melting into one another, . . . [of] becoming one instead of two.

—Aristophanes' speech in Plato's *Symposium*
(The Jowett Translation)

141

## INTRODUCTION

Why is it that the physical sciences fail to avail themselves of the concept of God as omnipotent and responsible for all that transpires? Is it because all scientists happen to be agnostics or atheists or scientific humanists? The answer lies in another direction and it is simple: When employed, the traditional concept of God fails to provide us with accounts meeting those standards which are decisive for scientific explanations. We may agree, for example, that the statement "Sunspot activity is greater this month than last because all-powerful God has so willed" explains a given set of recent solar observations about which, as it happens, we are concerned, but we do not agree thereby that the set of observations has been explained scientifically. The explanation is not scientific because, among other things, it entails no statements which can be tested against future solar observations or even against those recorded in earlier times.

It can be argued with conviction that something comparable must be said about the concept of alienation and its correlative, the concept of dealienation. With the standards of modern science firmly in mind, it is difficult to believe that theories employing these concepts have enriched our scientific understanding in any field. Typically, a neo-Marxist accounts for revolutions in terms of man's alienation and social tranquility in terms man's dealienation, but neither he nor we are enabled by his theory to deduce predictive statements about the where and where not and the when and when not of specific revolutions. A new "critical" sociologist-anthropologist tells us that certain features of American advertising are in part explained by alienation of the self, but when we reflect we discover that the concept of self-alienation adds nothing to his account as otherwise stated (see Henry, 1963, pp. 95-96). Again, a sociologist who is fully aware of the requirements of science attempts to prepare the concept of alienation for work in scientific analyses and theories both by purging it of its nondescriptive meanings and by making it amenable to measure. Reducing the concept to a cluster of five operational definitions, he offers us the prospect of measuring personal "alienation" in any of its five forms, viz., powerlessness, meaninglessness, normlessness, social isolation, and self-estrangement. But, as it turns out, the concept resists being reduced and factored in this way: counter-cases are readily offered to show that "a multitude of alienated persons would be dissatisfied equally with—as he has set them forth—conditions of power-possession, meaningfulness, norm-orientedness, involvement, and self-acknowledgment [Feuer, 1963, p. 140]."

Virtually all of the present day thinkers who employ alienation and dealienation as technical terms are, I believe, willing to forego the claim for them that they stand ready for scientific use in the way, say, that the terms "supply of mechanical heat" and "curl of a vector field" stand ready for physicists. However, most of them would vigorously reject the suggestion that this difference between terms is essentially one of degree, immense degree. Indeed, the very point they invariably make—

the theme which unifies their efforts—is that man's fundamental inquiry, his effort to in some sense grasp concrete reality, cannot be carried through within the boundaries of science as narrowly conceived. In all strictness, alienation theorists are men apart from the social and behavioral scientists with whom they so frequently mingle: The latter think of themselves as working tentatively, but hopefully, with relatively primitive scientific concepts in notoriously resistant fields of inquiry; the former think of themselves as working resolutely with a pair of master concepts which can provide perspectives for comprehending and responding to the modes and ways of reality. Surely some alienation theorists are, as are social scientists, sustained in their endeavors by the thought that Newton came so soon after Galileo, but each of them is, whether or not he fully realizes it, animated by the history of metaphysics rather than by the history of science. His intellectual impetus comes directly from Hegel, or, as is more likely, from Hegel as followed by Marx.

The view that the standard method of science is suited solely for limited, static subject-matters obtained through finite abstractions from an infinite and dynamic reality is built into the philosophies which feature the concepts of alienation and dealienation. For those who share in the spreading fear that modern science has become a procrustean bed whereby issues of vital importance—most notably, normative issues—are cut off from effective and affective inquiry, this view can come to sound as though it is simply a striking reminder that scientific inquiry, properly, is no more than one type of cognitive endeavor within the far-ranging, but integrated whole of human activity. This fear-induced underestimation of the conceptual reorientation involved, accounts in part for the increased audience being afforded alienation theorists by trained social scientists (e.g., see Stein, 1963). But more is involved—much more. The following criticism, for instance, may sound like an invitation for social scientists to look with interest at alienation theories, but it does not at all carry the case for adopting any of them: ". . . [H] ard-nosed social scientists, in their zeal to be value free, eschew the use of concepts of what *ought* to be . . . in favor of concepts of *what is*. . . . [N] eutralism and indifference . . . align the scientist with values and social forces least compatible with the freedom without which science itself cannot survive [Odegard, 1963, p. 38] ."

I have been suggesting that it is a mistake to think of alienation theories as scientific ones, or even—whether the intent is to hold out hope or to be patronizing—as prescientific ones. It is not my design, however, to continue on with the approach wherein I say what alienation theories are not, even though some people may think them to be. With the nature of these theories so little understood in their own right, the technique of successively denying that they can be assimilated into this or into that well-known intellectual enterprise can scarcely satisfy our curiosity about them or our desire not to prejudge them. I am prepared to argue additionally, for example, that they fail to be ethical theories, but I am afraid that beyond having shown or alleged that they lack certain key features, for example, testability for science and a logical distinction drawn between human purposes and human actions for ethics,[1] the question of what they are, in and of themselves, will not have been sufficiently answered, or, at least, not convincingly so. It remains that I have sounded a warning from the back side of the coin, however. We shall not arrive at an adequate understanding of alienation theories if we begin by presuming that they are members in good standing of some preferred discipline, or that they must be made to be.

My hope for this paper is that it will contribute to a proper understanding of what is going on in alienation theories. I must emphasize that my effort is very limited in the face of the clarification which is presently needed, and that it is critical. There may be grounds for the charge that I hit and run on occasions, but I hope not. My criticisms are intended to be by-the-nature-of-the-case ones which, in large part anyway, the most convinced alienationist would want to take into account. In any event, I shall not attack from a counter-philosophical position. For example, while I believe that the extreme doctrine of internal relations (and I suspect that the concept of alienation is drastically weakened without it) lost much of its plausibility in philosophical wars that occurred some time back, I am not going to introduce that issue here. This is less politeness on my part than it is a determination to become clearer myself about what is actually involved in these proliferating theories that are so much a mark of our times.

## "ALIENATION" AS A TECHNICAL TERM

Alienation is widely regarded as a term which can, of itself, contribute to conceptual work in an extraordinary way. As evidenced by the variety of its uses in the literature of philosophers, theologians, ideologists, psychologists, literary critics, and social theorists, however, its agreed-to sense is limited to the condition of one thing being separated from another. This is more than a suspicion on my part and on the part of many others: Richard Schacht has recently completed an admirably detailed and scholarly study which confirms it.[2] As a technical term, alienation suffers from deep ambiguity.

Surface ambiguity is, perhaps, to be expected: it occurs when it is noted that the denotation of a term is insufficiently determined within various of the contexts in which the term either does or might occur. Such vagueness about application is typically responded to by slightly emending the term or by appending it with additional specifications. While ambiguity brought about by such corrections and re-

---

[1] For a criticism somewhat along these lines, see Kamenka (1969).
[2] See Schacht (1970). As an indication of how runaway the term alienation has become in contemporary serious thought, and how it is being read back into works of the past, I suggest checking out the items so indexed in such a standard textbook as Binkley (1969).

finements may indeed invite faulty reasoning and misunderstandings in communication, it does not greatly erode the original sense of a term. Put ideally, the point here is simply that since each meaning which results from a "precising definition" of a term depends, in fact, on its basic sense, the basic sense is thereby retained rather than abandoned.

Deep ambiguity carries no comparable guarantee of unity in difference. It results when emending gives way to amending, and appending gives way to eliminating. If, by ignorance, incompetence, or intent—or by a commingling of them— a sophisticated general term is freed for whatsoever redefinition and conscripted for whatsoever use, then, on the day of judgment when the meanings which the term has come to have are sorted out, we can expect to find that precious little of its original sense has survived to serve as a common denominator. In our time, alienation stands as a case of a term afflicted with deep ambiguity.

All of this is strange in one way, but not in another. It is strange because the two thinkers who most account for the term's capability, Hegel and Marx, are of the near rather than the remote past. Hegel is the source of alienation as a technical term (actually, two related terms), and Marx (who fuses Hegel's two terms into one) is the source of the present inspiration to put it to work; furthermore, their names, particularly the latter's, are regularly invoked by most alienation theorists. Thus, it would seem that we might anticipate that the term's modifications would be limited in number and modest in extent. On the other hand, it is not strange because in the past decade and a half the attitude toward the term has been more nearly "here is a readily available term with the power to resolve a wide array of our most profound and pressing problems" than it has been "here is a deceptively simple term which fairly begins the work of explicating a powerful explanatory concept." Concern for term-integrity can seem small-minded when opposed to a prospectus for unlimited term-accomplishment.

## The Term as Miraculous

The present preoccupation with alienation began in the 1940s when Herbert Marcuse and particularly George Lukacs drew attention to it by claiming nothing less than that it constituted a link of central importance between Hegelianism, early Marxism, and existentialism. By the 1950s and 1960s, the theoretical need—let us spare ourselves mention of the practical—for these schools to achieve accommodation was felt by a very considerable number of intellectuals. Hegelians were cautiously emerging from the shadow of banishment that Anglo-American philosophers and others had imposed; early Marxists were suddenly speaking in all languages and saying things that were different from the militantly official version of Marxian ideology; and the soil of subjectivism giving way beneath them, existentialists— most theologians and hordes of literati among them—were moving about in search of firmer ground. It was a time when a newly affirmed conception in common could serve partisan interests in several ways.

But this is only a foreground sketch. The background is equally important to the picture because it shows conditions which can help account for the phenomenal acceptance of the term alienation by nonpartisans. It contains the nearly simultaneous and measurable loss of confidence in many of the prolegomena, theories, and attitudes of the first half-century: John Dewey's vision for the social sciences was fading; Sigmund Freud's insights had become commonplace and were proving less and less fruitful for those who must frame and solve human personality problems; Lucien Levy-Bruhl type arguments to the effect that scientific progress assures social progress did not survive the 1940s; G. E. Moore's bold offensive under the banner of ethical realism ended in surrender to the loosely allied tribes of emotivists and relativists; the revolt against logical positivism occasioned by the later Wittgenstein was having the not wholly intended effect of weakening the resolution of anti-metaphysicians. We shall stop with the list barely begun. The background of the picture shows the intellectual world in a serious crisis, a crisis which invited, and still invites, over-reactions. At least the dramatic types and those not given to distinguishing the long of intellectual history from the short felt themselves faced with a choice between slow and fast intellectual and cultural death, between death by academic ritual and suicide by irretrievable irrationalism.

The positive feature of the foreground, the term alienation as promising, takes on added significance against this background. The effect of crisis on some, even in conceptual contexts, is a lowered threshold for belief in miracles; and, here, surely, was, and, as we shall say, is, a miraculous term.

Consider: It is the basis for demonstrations allegedly underway to show nothing less than that instances of the unbridgeable are, after all, bridgeable, viz., romanticism (early Marx and Engles) and communism (late Marx), idealism (Hegel) and materialism (Marx), and individualism (existentialism) and collectivism (Hegel, Marx). Consider: Removed from the complexities of deeply philosophical contexts, it seems capable of wide, direct, and uncomplicated applications. (Is not this portentous?) Consider: It seems to bespeak the primacy of the humanities. (Does not this match up with our sincerest need in an age wherein science has turned tyrant?) And, finally, consider: It seems to preempt the normative-descriptive distinction. (It is this distinction, is it not, which, beyond all else, renders us pathetic: assured about means but confused about ends?)

### The Term as Chameleon-like

Let me shift from the figure of alienation as a miraculous term to an appeal by here and now experiment. The phenomenon of the term's seemingly natural fit—its "obvious" suitability for diverse theoretical contexts—can, I believe, be witnessed in the two expositions which follow. Hopefully, responding for my reader as well as for myself, I shall insert the terms alienation and dealienation parenthetically as they suggest themselves.

The religious existentialist, Martin Buber, is famous for his elaboration of the distinction between what he terms "I-It" and "I-Thou" relations. An I-It relation obtains when, for example, I regard another merely as a means to my own ends (an instance of alienation), but an I-Thou relation obtains when—several other requirements also being met—both I and another seek to be, and are, directly related (an instance of dealienation). "No system of ideas, no foreknowledge, and no fancy intervene between I and Thou [Buber, 1958, p. 11]." As perhaps can be anticipated, a man is encouraged by his I-Thou relations, which are I-to-limited persons, to believe that he can enter into an I-Thou relationship, which is I-to-unlimited person (instances of man-to-man delaienation are one sign that a necessary condition for instances of man-to-God dealienation can be met). One of the ways in which this ultimate I-Thou relationship for human beings, this direct experience of God, manifests itself to an individual is by a newly won universal readiness to enter into I-Thou relations with every other limited person, and, indeed, with every object (those men who occur in instances of man-to-God dealienation satisfy a sufficient condition for instances of man-to-man dealienation among themselves). Furthermore, and here Buber appears to take the familiar theological road, God's nature is such that He cannot occur in an I-It relation (God never occurs in instances of alienation).

Now a question: Have we been told that God is available to man for an I-Thou relationship at all times? Buber moves to take advantage of what seems to be a logical opening. To say of God that He never occurs in an I-It relation is not to say that He forever seeks direct relationships with all men and continues His established I-Thou relationships uninterruptedly (God may, in effect, limit the instances of dealienation, that is, He chooses instances of nonalienation). This surprising turn onto a theological byway permits Buber his much discussed doctrine of God in Eclipse. "God desires that men should follow His revelation, yet at the same time He wishes to be accepted and loved in his deepest concealment. . . . Let us ask whether it may not be literally true that God formerly spoke to us and is now silent [Buber, 1952, p. 66]."

Our first exposition completed, notice how readily the correlative terms alienation and dealienation have been inserted, and how, once inserted, they can come to seem integral to the account.[3] Why is this? I submit that it comes about for a combination of reasons:

1. The terms are offered as candidates for use in a familiar and highly structured context which would traditionally be served by the standard terms "evil" and "good(ness)." The hidden effect of this structure is to reassure us throughout that the terms are, so to speak, themselves controlling the uses to which they are put.

[3] We are not here concerning ourselves with Buber's limited but actual use of the term alienation (*"Verfremdung"*).

2. For most members of the intelligentsia, neither alienation nor dealienation suggests a precise, technical sense with sufficient force to warn against the uses proposed; we do not, that is, have grave misgivings about our having misused this pair of terms.

3. Moreover, on the other side of the coin, the above reason frees us from the feeling that the terms are no more than synonyms for "evil" and "good(ness)," in whatever of the latter's senses may be intended. Thus, it can appear to us that we are no longer facing the exquisite problems of theology armed solely with terms which have failed time and again. Our belief in the power of the new terms seems more appropriate still when we realize that Buber (1952) is offering a novel theological twist, and, perhaps, since we know ourselves to be as we are, demandingly appropriate when we realize the full importance for humanity of Buber's doctrine of a self-concealing God, viz., to save traditional religion for people who must acknowledge that evil can, in our times (as with Hitler and Stalin) be organized so as to extend its power unprecedentedly.

Other engaging but quite different contexts for continuing the experiment are readily available. I select, for this purpose, the briefest possible account of the theory underlying most of Bertrand Russell's many books and articles on social and political matters (see esp. Russell, 1916, Ch. 1). Each man has a central principle of growth from which his various impulsive tendencies emanate (an instance of $alienation_1$). His environment, including the social and political institutions with which he either does not empathize (an instance of $alienation_2$) or does empathize (an instance of $dealienation_2$), is of decisive importance for his actual growth. If an individual's growth is restricted, then his impulsive tendencies are disharmonious (an instance of $alienation_3$); but if his growth is unrestricted, then his impulsive tendencies are harmonious (an instance of $dealienation_3$).

The insertions are again readily made. But notice: A little reflection shows that we have drawn on, or instituted, three different senses for alienation in this second exposition, and that none of them correspond well with the senses of the term as we used it in the Buber exposition. Without making the effort of analysis required to distinguish between the differences in meaning which trace to the applications of the term as variously used and those which trace as well to fundamental shifts in the sense of the term, let us list a sufficient number of relevant observations to show that we have deep as well as surface ambiguity on our hands: We are scarcely prepared to say about "$alienation_1$" that it has an opposite, "$dealienation_1$" which stands to it in a way comparable to the way that "$dealienation_2$" stands to "$dealienation_2$" or that "$dealienation_3$" stands to "$alienation_3$." (Whether unified or disunified, there is no alteration in the nature of the items being so assessed in the latter cases, although there would be in the first case.) "$Alienation_1$" does not seem to have the import bad, but both "$alienation_2$" and "$alienation_3$" do. The applications of "$alienation_2$" and "$dealienation_2$" depend on the presence or absence of a specific mental projection (or, perhaps, mental state), but, whatever else, the applications of "$alienation_3$" and "$dealienation_3$" do not so depend. A comparison between the first occurrence of "alienation" in Buber and "alienation$_3$" suggests that, at some level, it becomes imperative to distinguish between "alienation" and "self-alienation." Buber's God in Eclipse doctrine led us to distinguish nonalienation from both alienation and dealienation; this was not otherwise suggested in our expositions.

Let us break off. If any warning can be made by an experiment of this sort, it has by now been made.

## Difficulties in Maintaining the Integrity of the Term

It is well to remind ourselves that a term which is fundamental for a given theoretical explanation—whether that explanation is more accurately classified as philosophical or as scientific—contributes importantly to that complex whole of meaning. We have so far been pointing out that alienation as a miraculous term, a term that at once makes minimal demands on a context and chameleon-like accommodations to it, cannot be a fundamental term in any explanation. The end result for such a term in extensive use by one man or by many is deep ambiguity. Even if a man's motive for an alienation theory is the modest one of dealing with disparate problems in such a manner that they are drawn together for us to see as aspects of a more central one, he will fail if his term is less than fundamental. His seeming success will come to little more than successful equivocating.

### The Term as Reduced by Ambiguity

At the risk of being ungracious, it is instructive to point out that Erich Fromm a man who, as much as any other, is responsible for the present-day enthusiasm for alienation, has worked more against serious theoretical accomplishment by means of his favored term than for it. Admittedly, he is the source of numerous insights that connect psychologically with the term, and he should be thanked for these; but, despite this, he has beclouded matters thoroughly by allowing it to greatly shift its sense time and again. His program as announced in *The Sane Society* should have put him on guard: "I have chosen the concept of *alienation* as the central point from which I am going to develop the analysis of the contemporary social character [Fromm, 1955, p. 103]." This announces that the term is to be fundamental, that it is to bear weight, that it is to be a constant proceeding through a variety of contexts, that it is to be sufficiently complex to do work, that it is to be resistant to expedient mimicry of other terms, that, in short, it is to be a term sufficiently fixed as the surrogate of a distinctive concept to pit it (and not other unmentioned concepts) against the problems proposed. It is in this way only—indirect though it must remain—that the concept of alienation can be held up to our poor but independent measures of success and failure.

Consider, for example, what Fromm has to say in this book concerning the origin of man's alienation from nature. His term is here being outfitted with a portion of the critical minimum of theory which he feels it requires to be an instrument of analysis. At the outset we are assured that (1) such alienation is an automatic state of affairs upon the emergence of "self-awareness" within the individual, that is, it attends a man's recognition through reason, that he knows nature as an object distinct from himself (Fromm, 1955, pp. 30-35). But farther on he indicates that (2) the man who is unalienated or dealienated from nature is precisely the one who "uses his reason to grasp reality objectively [Fromm, 1955, p. 241]." Hence, in effect, he seems to assure us that (3) both alienation and dealienation of this form are brought about by one and the same thing. Furthermore, and this is the immediate point, we are left with no assurance whatsoever that we can know what alienation refers to, or, more radically, that it can have any application for us to know. It may well be objected that such a quickly cited difficulty will dissipate when seen in the full development of his thesis and the full range of his books. But this is simply not so in this case, nor typically. Without benefit of having fixed his term at a level where it can contribute significantly, the more frequently he addresses himself to a problem the greater our confusion grows. Thus, the illustration of the same point could equally well have been as follows: (1') The origin of man's alienation from nature is his "mastery" over it (Fromm, 1944, p. 49). But (2') man's dealienation from nature is achieved by mastery over it (through "productive work") (Fromm, 1955, p. 68). Hence, once again, (3) both alienation and dealienation of this form are brought about by one and the same thing.[4]

### The Vogue Term and its Fallacies

When this term is treated more by its spirit than by a fixed letter, it invites improper thinking on a grand scale. It is a commonplace to note that fallacious thought attends many technical terms that have suddenly become popular: We know this is so by consulting intellectual history and our own memories (Darwin's "evolution," Peirce's "pragmatism," the statisticians' "average man," Freud's "libido," Minkowski's "fourth dimension," Heisenberg's "principle of indeterminacy," Sartre's "freedom," etc.)

But it is less than a commonplace to note that, by an unspoken principle of caricature, technical terms in their typical theoretical contexts can sometimes partially determine the shape of the deformities of thought which mark their popular versions. This is clearly so in the case of alienation. With its emphasis on separation, alienation invites the fallacies of bifurcation, restrictive classification, and even hypostatization. With its normative import and relativising of morality to cultural stages, it invites elevating personal preferences into moral judgments and dismissal of the approved moral order upon convenience. With its ideological orientation, it invites endless politicizing carried through without fairminded concern for appropriate categories. With its integral relationship to conceptions of historical process and human development, it invites prophesy-fulfilling actions, distortions of his-

---

[4] I have drawn rather directly on Schacht in this paragraph, see his careful analysis of Fromm's terminological difficulties (Schacht, 1970, pp. 116-140).

torical and personal facts, over-applications, and various forms of the fallacy of false cause. An examination of some of the popular writings and speeches of the day will serve to verify this list, to show that it is incomplete, and to leave one saddened.

I do not mention "alienation" as a vogue term in order to divert attention away from it as a technical term, however. I do so, rather, to suggest that, as the latter, it is particularly vulnerable to becoming no more than the former. At best, it is a term perched precariously on a slippery slope, a slope which descends into the term's own caricature. In "The Inevitability of Alienation," for example, the distinguished Hegelian scholar, Walter Kaufmann, draws attention to the fact that some serious neo-Marxian alienation theorists have developed an immunity to the historical record (replete with details and straightforward interpretation) in their dedication to their own assumptions and conclusions (in Schacht, 1970, pp. xiii-lvi). One of the propositions they are most given to protect against the possibility of historical disconfirmation (and so, of course, of genuine historical confirmation) is, not surprisingly, the following: The alienation of man is essentially a phenomenon of modern capitalistic society. Again, Kaufmann prosecutes the case against them that they disregard and/or distort what we know about the psychology of, as well as the biographies of, outstandingly creative people. Defensive mechanisms are brought to play here in order to protect the happy-day vision of a world wherein all men are dealienated against the charge that in such a world a necessary condition for extraordinary human accomplishment would be missing.

The methodological approach that dogmatic alienation theorists come to adopt is this: If one's theory fails to fit the data as independently assayed, then he is free to disallow the data, or, better, to make its examination and assessment ("relevance") depend decisively on his own theory. The history of thought abounds with abandoned technical terms which could have remained successful under this "heads I win, tails you lose" methodological directive. The resulting fallacy is appropriately named "poisoning the well" (shades of the reasoning that pervaded the Salem witch trials).

### Some Requirements for the Term's Clarity

It is a standing enterprise of contemporary alienation theorists to distinguish between different forms of alienation. There are, however, standards to be met if, as is usually intended, these forms are to be conceived of in such a way that they fall under the master concept of alienation attributed to Hegel or Marx. Thus, each form of alienation must be conceived of, and terminologically dealt with, in such a way that the questions "What, exactly, is alienated from what?" and "What is the source of the alienating activity?" are answered.[5] But there is more; I am afraid that there is considerably more.

---

[5] Petrovic (1967, pp. 78-79) develops an approach of this sort. His treatment is not, however, sufficiently accurate to serve more than general purposes.

*Hegel's Two Senses of the Term.* It is time, perhaps past time, to speak directly about the term alienation as it occurs in Hegel.[6]

The term has two major, but nevertheless related, senses. In the first sense, it pertains to an awareness on the part of an individual that he has become separated from something from which he is not essentially different and with which he was formerly unified. It is in this sense that the term shows an affinity with the ordinary term "alien" in certain of its uses. In the second sense, "alienation" pertains to an individual's deliberate surrender or renunciation of himself as separated from something from which he is not essentially different and with which he was formerly unified, that is, the sacrifice of himself as he occurs in a situation of alienation (the first sense) in order to eliminate the grounds of that separation. It is in this sense that the term shows an affinity with such notions in political philosophy as Rousseau's social contract theory and with one of the conspicuous themes of Christianity. We may, for our purposes, regard the distinction between "self-alienation" and "alienation" as a matter of application rather than of sense.[7]

In order to induce a feeling for, and, more importantly, to expose the force of these senses, we must briefly inspect that case in Hegelian metaphysics from which they are primarily gleaned. Hegel actually uses the term under investigation in only his first major work, *Phenomenology of Spirit,* a work in which he is concerned to portray the continuous development of the human spirit throughout all stages in its ceaseless effort to realize itself. Hegel's objective is to do this in a systematic, principled way.

It will not surprise the uninitiated to learn that Hegel insists that the world of social, political, and cultural institutions, the "social substance" (Hegel's term), is created and sustained by human activity. But it will no doubt surprise them to learn of what, according to Hegel, the full conception of the social substance consists: For one thing, the social substance must be thought of as an objectified expression of the human spirit, an embodiment which, by the degree of its perfectness as a coherent and universal arrangement, marks the various stages in the latter's development. (It may be helpful in understanding "the degree of its perfectedness" to reflect on progressions in comprehensiveness which are quite obvious; thus, for example, family, community, state, and magic, primitive religion, religion.) For another thing, the social substance must be thought of as a product of the human spirit which is integral to the latter's process of development. (Although somewhat crude, the following captures some of the point: If the social substance were not produced, then the human spirit would be arrested in a stage of its development

---

[6] We will be speaking throughout of "alienation" from *"Entfremdung"* and not from *"Verausserung"*; Hegel uses the latter term in connection with the transfer of property in the *Philosophy of Right.* It is not "alienation" in this second sense that directly informs present-day alienation theory.

[7] I have here drawn almost directly from Schacht's results; his discussion includes a careful sifting of the evidence and supportive analyses (Schacht, 1970, pp. 30-65). If Schacht is to be faulted, it is that he overly liberalizes Hegel's senses of the term. My definitions are less liberal.

wherein individuals are no more than dissociated particulars, that is, no more than centers of subjective experience.) But to be conceived fully, the social substance must be thought of as an aspect of the human spirit, a mode of its being, and not as something which is substantially independent from it: This amounts to realizing that the social substance is identical in essence with the human spirit.

It should not be inferred from what we have so far said, however, that the distinction between a person in his individuality and the social substance has, in effect, been obviated. The recognition by individuals of themselves as particulars, as independently existing persons with distinctive characters, is also integral to the development of the human spirit. The very phase of the developmental process which eventuates in the divorce of the social substance from the individual has a constructive prior moment. As an individual's tie to the social substance through identifying himself with it weakens (as firmly tied, he is sufficiently characterized by his various social roles), the condition is achieved for his ego to emerge. (Another somewhat crude statement: If the ego, the individual in his conscious self-awareness, were not produced, then the human spirit would be arrested in a stage of its development wherein individuals are no more than automatons.) Just as the social substance is an expression of the human spirit, so too, is the ego. It is an expression of it as conscious self-awareness, and a mark of its developmental advance. And, finally, individuals, no less than the social substance, are identical in essence with the human spirit; they, too, constitute an aspect of it, another mode of its being. There is, of course, an immediate corollary: There is no essential difference between the individual and the social substance.

The development of the human spirit is toward unification, yes; but it is always toward the unification that identity-in-difference constitutes, a unification in which the differences in its modes of being, its aspects, are maintained rather than collapsed. As can be sensed, however, Hegel is convinced that no genuine unification, no identity-in-difference reconciliation, can be achieved at one and the same level where an outright divorce between an individual and the social substance occurs. He would argue that, as with any historical event, a divorce in being cannot, in any strict sense, be annulled; and, again, that there is no abstractive principle of development which, as in the formal reasoning we employ in coming to understand things, eliminates differences in favor of abstract commonality. No, according to Hegel, the only unity possible for individuals and the social substance grown apart is that of combination, of synthesis. They, like the pieces of a puzzle, must come into that arrangement where they fit together, where, as it were, they fall into place. Now when, in the process of the human spirit's development, the individuals and the social substance are so associated, they form a novel whole, that is, a whole which is such that if the process of development is not yet completed and the distinction between individuals and the social substance again becomes acute, neither those individuals nor the social substance will be as they were previously.

When given intricate detail about the developmental process of the human spirit which includes the individual's awareness of certain stages and his deliberate

participation in others, an account of this sort stands as the source of the senses of
"alienation" we offered. Let us now attempt to summarize much of the account,
as we have suggested it to be, by applying the term in both of its senses in a single
statement: When the individual is alienated (in the first sense) from the social substance, that is, when he is thus self-alienated (first sense), he may act to resolve
the circumstance of arrested development through alienation (in the second sense),
that is, through self-alienation (second sense). Notice how much has been packed
into these two senses of the term, the work they do. These are technical senses designed to help characterize the principled development of a substance made known
to us through its aspects, and to refer to stages and acts in this development. The
term in its senses is representative of a bold explanatory and normative conception.

*Marx's Sense of the Term.* There is a continuing debate about whether or
not the Marxian term "alienation," with its sense as established in *The Philosophical Fragments of 1844,* could have been used appropriately by him in the presentation of his later thought, and, relatedly, what we are to understand Marx's philosophical position, all things considered, really to be. As interesting as this debate
is when pursued by those who are neither propagandists nor apologists (in the desperate sense), it goes well beyond our immediate purpose to comment on it.[8] Let
us content ourselves with a statement of the term's sense, a lengthy parenthetical
remark, a minimal comment to assure that we understand the relation of this sense
to Hegel's two senses, and an indication of the term's typical applications.

The Marxian sense pertains to an awareness on the part of an individual that
he has become separated from something with which he is not essentially different
and with which he was formerly unified, and that this separation has been (1) brought
about by someone and/or something (them) which is essentially different from himself and (2) consumated through their making him surrender to them that from
which he has become separated.[9]

Parenthetically, it is scarcely necessary to point out that when alienation in
this sense is regarded primarily as a term which is to function evocatively in literary
contexts or provocatively in political action contexts, it must be seen as having the
potential to compete equally with any other term which one might select for this
purpose from traditional religion, politics, or morality. Examples of this potential
realized abound among the young people of our period. Many of them live at that
level of feeling and action where alienation rhetoric has become a primary and automatic source of their stimulation. This being so, they are so revolted by named instances of exploitation, whether real or imagined, that they reject all counsel of
caution; thus, for example, the suggestion that they have not sufficiently analyzed
a given circumstance to determine whether or not the criteria of term-application

---

[8] See, for example, Feuer (1963, p. 140) and Hook (1962) on one side, and Tucker (1964)
on the other.

[9] Once again I have drawn almost directly from Schacht (1970, pp. 65-111).

have been met, or the suggestion that the extrinsic good be measured against the intrinsic bad of an instance of exploitation, or the like, are regarded by them as evasions. Furthermore, they are convinced that those who speak from different "conceptual" traditions cannot be comparably concerned, cannot be comparable to them in moral sensitivity. They are secular John Browns. But this neorevisionist rhetoric of alienation is not without apparent irony. Although the Marxian term "alienation" plays a key role in popular case-making from stringent forms of possessionlessness, the term itself entails the notion of possession, the absolute possession of something's being a part of, or an embodiment of, someone or some group. Thus, it can seem to those who are not themselves thoroughly tied to that rhetoric that, the more indiscriminately the term is applied in the advocacy of possessionlessness, the greater the variety of kinds of possessiveness they stand obligated to acknowledge.

But at a more sophisticated level still, one where the Marxian conception of synthesis is available to those who reflect, there is genuine irony. The outside agent or system, the alienator or the exploiter, if you will, must be regarded as a necessary means to the benign stage of unity which is to come; he is, therefore (less even than Milton's Satan) from the unrestricted point of view, not worse (and, of course, not better) than the party exploited. Those for whom morality is largely a language of reflex but who feel themselves to be fighting the intrinsically bad on all fronts out of conscience are thus, in reality, tacit subscribers by language to a grand metaphysical view that altogether reduces their categorical morality to mere prudence.

Returning to Marx, we may say that his use of the term combines Hegel's two senses of alienation into one. Both separation and surrender are involved in the new sense of the term. But the role that surrender plays for Hegel is not at all comparable to the role that it plays for Marx: The former is an act initiated by an already alienated party and imposed on himself; the latter is an act initiated by an outside agent and/or agency and imposed on an as yet not fully alienated party. The former is necessarily a deliberated act; the latter is not. The former serves to effectuate dealienation; the latter serves to effectuate alienation. In terms of the dialectical process which so permeates the philosophies of both men, Marx's sense of alienation and Hegel's first sense of the term connect with the thesis-to-antithesis, antithesis-to-thesis stage of development, while Hegel's second sense of the term connects with the thesis-antithesis-to-synthesis stage.

According to Marx, there are two major corrections to be made in Hegel's *Phenomenology*. As against our layout of things, the first of these has to do with the sense of the term, alienation, and the second has to do with the nature of the things to which the term applies. About the first: Marx rejects Hegel's insistence that the emergent ego (conscious awareness of oneself and one's pertinent circumstance) constitutes a sufficient condition as well as a necessary condition for dealienation, that is, for synthesis. About the second: Marx rejects Hegel's notion of the self as spirit; it is material. (We elect not to divert into a discussion of what, exactly, this means; suffice it to observe that in using "material" he at least means that the self is nonspiritual.) His concern here is to focus on the real man (material) and not on just an abstraction derived from him (spiritual). But Marx is not suggesting by this that man does not have essential characteristics; indeed, he would argue that, in abstracting from flesh and blood man to man *qua* thinker of thoughts, Hegel allowed man's essential sensuality to drop out of consideration. Beyond this, he is in agreement with Hegel about man's essential individuality and universality, albeit he would insist that Hegel speaks of them in their abstract or idealized form; thus, for example, Hegel's "universality" becomes "sociality" for Marx. The difference between Marxian and Hegelian ontology is radical with respect to the self, but it is not so with respect, say, to the social substance (terminology aside). This is readily anticipated: Hegel is here speaking of an embodiment.

With this second correction before us, let us reexamine the first. An individual as referred to in Marx's sense of alienation is a real man, a man with a range of feelings, drives, and material needs which remain as effective after the emergence of the ego as before. It is this man who is subject to alienation, and not, as it were, just his top layer. If he is alienated from his society, the product of his labor, or his labor as such, it is because of the material arrangement of things which determine the forces that impinge upon him. And, contrariwise, if he, and others like him, are to do anything about eliminating the alienation from which they suffer, then it can only be done through concerted actions which can alter that material configuration which sustains the alienating force.

With his corrections seen to, Marx remains within the Hegelian framework. We shall not here concern ourselves about whether or not this is philosophically possible.

*A Dilemma.* Both the Hegelian and the Marxian conceptions of alienation entail the notion that an individual can, in spatio-temporal actuality, become separated from that with which he is essentially identical. The power of their alienation theories to explain "from what," "to what," and "why" resides precisely in this: Although the description and analysis of such entities in their divided existence fails to disclose that they are essentially indistinguishable, this ultimate fact about them is disclosed by that distinctive sort of reasoning (dialectical) through which we can know the developmental process of the human spirit (Hegel) or of nature (Marx). As thus disclosed, their separation is a necessary but passing stage in the process whereby their essence is being fully actualized. The foregoing review suggests that, at the very least, numerous would-be alienation theorists are confronted with the following dilemma: If a thinker has followed contemporary philosophy, theology, psychology, and the social and physical sciences in their drift away from the essentialists' view of man, then he cannot adopt the "with which he is not essentially different" portion of the Hegelian and Marxian senses of alienation. But no sense of the term which is in this way lacking retains the power of explanation which otherwise characterizes the term. If, on the other hand, a thinker does adopt a genuinely Hegelian-like or Marxian-like sense of the term, one which retains the explanatory power as noted, then it is no longer open to him to maintain a typical position with respect to contemporary thought.

*The Response of Essentialism.* If one is solidly in the essentialists' tradition, there is no dilemma since he has already renounced the majority's view. (This does not mean, of course, that an essentialist may not have grounds for rejecting both the Hegelian and Marxian philosophies or any other process philosophy which may come along to embrace a fulsome concept of alienation.) Such a person is free to enrich alienation theory by, say, introducing a precising definition which applies quite specifically to some aspect or form of deprivation of the essential self which has been neglected or gone unrecognized. He would, admittedly, be making the already bothersome surface ambiguity of the term worse, and it might be better for him to decide on a different terminological solution. But, be this as it may, he would not be introducing a disparate sense of the term, a sense without the characteristic explanatory power.

We have the premier example of just how far one essentialist may effectively alter the alienation theory of another in the early Marx. As we have seen, he radically changes the application of the Hegelian term (in the talk of this paper, he imposes novel precising definitions and thereby increases the surface ambiguity of the term viewed generally). But he also insists that Hegel is in error at the level of detail about the inner workings of the dialectical process (thus, he does indeed contribute to the deep ambiguity of the term viewed generally). He does not, however, so alter the term that he sacrifices its characteristic explanatory power (at least the basis for saying that he has is not apparent at the level of analysis to which this paper is confined).

It would seem that Marcuse, Fromm, and, more interestingly, Karen Horney are examples of present-day essentialists concerned with bringing alienation theory in its Hegel-Marx tradition to bear on contemporary problems (see esp. Horney, 1950).

*The Response of Existentialism.* There is likewise no dilemma if one is a thoroughgoing existentialist. Entry into existentialism depends on the flat denial that man has an essential nature or anything which can, in some understandable way, be mistaken for one. In effect, this amounts to rejecting the entire motif of a dynamic losing-seeking-gaining of that which is, by the nature of the case, properly myself. Those religious existentialists who want to remain Kierkegaardian and those atheistic ones who want to be represented in at least a general way by Jean-Paul Sartre's *Being and Nothingness* cannot join ranks with either neo-Hegelians or neo-Marxians. The term alienation ("estrangement" is the favored term in the existentialists' tradition) in connection with oneself does occur in the writings of existentialist purists. But it typically does no more than can be done by the common words "alien" or "strange"; it simply depicts or describes a manner in which things are seen or reacted to. If we were to substitute the classical "alienation" in its appropriate sense for the existential "estrangement" in a given circumstance, we would not only be depicting a manner of seeing, or of responding to, things, but also the process for which coming to see, or coming to respond to, things in such a manner is integral.

*The Middle Response.* As one might expect, attempts by alienation theorists to go between the horns of the dilemma, that is, to preserve the concept of alienation to the extent that it retains its explanatory power while maintaining something less than an essentialist's view of man and nature, are the order of the day. Some might think that the late Christian "existentialist" Paul Tillich could be cited, but this is not the case. While there are components of existentialism in his theology, and he certainly does set an existentialist's tone, he openly embraces an essentialist's view of man. In his uses of the term "estrangement," he is a loyal Hegelian.

Sartre, in his later period, is the conspicuous example. In recent years (*Critique de la Raison Dialectique,* 1960), he has been at work modifying his own earlier position and the positions of both the earlier and the later Marx. Although his intellectual "conversion"—his passional conversion is of long standing—is regarded as a major event by partisan neo-Marxists, thorough assessments of his intricate work are still underway. The issue centers on his altered account of the emergence of the ego (both existentialists and neo-Marxists may be thought of as working within an Hegelian framework on this and many other matters). Loosely speaking, in his earliest work, Sartre conceives of consciousness as a theoretical agency, an agency in quest of knowledge; but he finds by analysis that there can be no guarantee against subjectivism (this is reminiscent of Descartes doubting the existence of an external world). He moves progressively toward richer views of consciousness until, in his latest work, he conceives of it not only as a theoretical agency, but also as an agency of practical response; so conceived, he finds by analysis both a guarantee against subjectivism and a basis for claiming that there is a dialectical process of such a sort that the term alienation retains explanatory power without the presumptions of essentialism.[10]

***The Term and the Social Sciences.*** Despite the declarations which now dot the scene wherein we are told that the social sciences need to embrace full, bold, and non-value-free concepts such as alienation, there seems to be no careful suggestion as yet about how this can be accomplished within those sciences. This is not, of course, to challenge the right, say, of certain sociologists to abandon their field entirely in favor of social commentary or advocacy. May they recognize that their circumstance is rather like that of Russell (1916) who, despairing of his own and others' ability to do strict social philosophy, frequently distinguished between his work *qua* technical philosopher and his work as a social critic who was otherwise a philosopher.

[10] See Cumming (1966, esp. pp. 38-44) for a very able—but not critical—tracing of Sartre's entire philosophical development.

It would be unfair to apply the foregoing comment impatiently or categorically however. It is still an open issue among social scientists as to what, exactly, the nature of their endeavor is, and this is particularly the case among sociologists. While the latter have been strongly attracted by the successes of the physical sciences, they cannot forget that in their brief heritage of heroes some were deeply influenced by the process philosophies of Hegel and Marx. Thus, it is to be expected that sociologists will continue to be very much alerted to the concept of alienation and that many of them will hope that it can be accommodated. There can be a considerable distance between intent and deed however. And in this instance there clearly is. It is worth mentioning that the kind of features drawn from Hegel and Marx which still survive for many sociologists—features, for example, such as Karl Manneheim's notion that the concepts for properly interpreting and assessing human affairs in a given society are necessarily relative to the historical stage and place of that society—are the very features from these philosophers which, as treated by earlier sociologists, did not import the assumption of man's having an essential nature into their subject-matter and its methods of inquiry.

The vast majority of social scientists are determined to proceed as empirical scientists charged with investigating a roughly specifiable subject-matter. Thus, whether enthusiastically or despairingly, they place themselves under the restraint of finding data which are sufficiently measurable in some public manner to confirm or disconfirm the theories they propose. This constitutes a formidable problem for them since these data must be drawn from a quantitatively-resistant, qualitatively-rich array of phenomena. Their difficulty in, as it were, collecting data on order has the effect of restricting them to simple theories, precisely those theories for which they have a well-grounded suspicion that they can produce evidence. It is not remarkable, therefore, that social scientists have come to adopt the practice of introducing new concepts into their theories through operational definitions. But it is also not remarkable, to come to the case at hand, that the concept of alienation when so dealt with is completely stripped of its explanatory power. For example, it is typical of the sociologists who have sought to introduce the concept into their theories to do so through what amounts to a statement-form, "The alienation of a person X from something of the sort Y," restricted in explication to the set of attitudes or feelings measured by such a device as a specific questionnaire. It may well turn out, of course, that we can advance by theory into the generalization that those people who are greatly alienated in this way, say, concentrate less well on mathematical problems than those who are only slightly alienated. But, there is neither logical connection between alienation as thus defined and the classical term in any of its senses, nor comparability of explanation between this theory and any instance of a classical alienation theory.

The foregoing line of criticism is so readily extended that we can perhaps leave it with things unsaid. But it sould be remarked that nothing about it places the heuristic use of the concept of alienation by social scientists under attack. Indeed, the empirical sciences have been well served throughout their history by making such use of, as we shall say very loosely, *a priori* conceptions.

There is, however, a fundamental point to be noted, one which returns us to the dilemma. It is suggested by the final phrase of the preceding paragraph: Alienation and dealienation as conceived of by Hegel and Marx and by neo-Hegelians and neo-Marxians is part and parcel of a necessary process of development. It is not for them just a contingent fact that the human spirit or nature so develops. Furthermore, at the level of more detail, it is not just a contingent fact that men have essential characteristics nor that society is properly regarded as essentially indestinguishable from men. The counters in public experience to which the empirical scientist is tied do count toward our finding our place in the story which must be told, but they do not count in confirming or disconfirming that story. Neither classical alienation theories nor their modern progeny, *qua* what they are, await a decision to be rendered by scientists. Science is as speechless in fundamental arguments about the concept of alienation as it is in arguments about the concept of God. It is well to know when one shifts his domain of discourse from physics to metaphysics. As to the quality of Hegelian and Marxian metaphysics, that is not a matter we have set out to discuss in this paper.

## REFERENCES

Binkley, L. *Conflict of ideals.* Princeton, N. J.: Van Nostrand-Reinhold, 1969.

Buber, M. *The eclipse of God.* New York: Harper, 1952.

Buber, M. *I and thou.* (2nd ed.) New York: Scribner's, 1958.

Cumming, R. D. Introduction. In R. D. Cumming (Ed.), *The philosophy of Jean-Paul Sartre.* New York: Random House, 1966.

Feuer, L. What is alienation? The career of a concept. In M. Stein & A. Vidich (Eds.), *Sociology on trial.* Englewood Cliffs, N. J.: Prentice-Hall, 1963.

Fromm, E. *Escape from freedom.* New York: Avon Books, 1941.

Fromm, E. *The sane society.* New York: Fawcett Premier Books, 1955.

Henry, J. *Culture against man.* New York: Random House, 1963.

Hook, S. *From Hegel to Marx.* Ann Arbor: University of Michigan Press, 1962.

Horney, K. *Neurosis and human growth.* New York: Norton, 1950.

Kamenka, E. *Marx and ethics.* New York: St. Martin's Press, 1969.

Odegard, P. The social sciences in the twentieth century. In G. W. Sowards (Ed.), *The social studies: Curriculum proposals for the future.* Chicago: Scott, Foresman, 1963.

Petrovic, G. Alienation. In P. Edwards (Ed.), *The encyclopaedia of philosophy.* Vol. 1. New York: Macmillan and Free Press, 1967.

Russell, B. *Principles of social reconstruction.* London: Allen & Unwin, 1916.

Schacht, R. *Alienation.* New York: Doubleday, 1970.

Stein, M. The poetic metaphors of sociology. In M. Stein & A. Vidich (Eds.), *Sociology on trial.* Englewood Cliffs, N. J.: Prentice-Hall, 1963. Pp. 173-181.

Tucker, R. C. *Philosophy and myth in Karl Marx.* London & New York: Cambridge University Press, 1964.

# Part II

# CONTEMPORARY PERSPECTIVES

# Chapter 7

# Alienation: Contemporary Sociological Approaches

Eric Josephson
Columbia University School of Public Health
Mary Redmer Josephson

## THE PROBLEM

This volume is evidence, if any were needed, that the problem of alienation—a major cultural issue for more than a century—continues to seize our interest. Ten years ago, C. Wright Mills said:

> The advent of the alienated man and all the themes which lie behind his advent now affect the whole of our serious intellectual life and cause our immediate intellectual malaise. It is a major theme of the human condition in the contemporary epoch and of all studies worthy of the name. I know of . . . no problem . . . that is . . . so much involved in the possible default of contemporary social science [Mills, 1969, p. 171].

Other chapters have traced the development of the concept of alienation in our culture and have dealt with a number of its contemporary aspects. Our task here is to review critically some of the ways in which contemporary American social scientists have attempted to define and empirically measure alienation. In discussing their work, Mills's statement about the "default" of social science will be examined and tested.

163

Alienation is a term with many meanings. In general, the idea is that something—ties or bonds—connecting man to himself, to others, to the community and to the technologies and social institutions he has created, is lost, missing, or severed, and that this state of affairs leads to various "pathologies." This is just a start at defining it.

As we noted in our introduction to a collection of writings on the subject (Josephson & Josephson, 1962), alienation has been used

> to refer to an extraordinary variety of psycho-social disorders, including loss of self, anxiety states, anomie, despair, depersonalization, rootlessness, apathy, social disorganization, loneliness, atomization, powerlessness, meaninglessness, isolation, pessimism, and the loss of beliefs or values. Among the social groups who have been described as alienated in varying degree . . . are women, industrial workers, white-collar workers, migrant workers, artists, suicides, the mentally disturbed, addicts, the aged, the young generation as a whole, juvenile delinquents in particular, voters, non-voters, consumers, the audiences of mass media, sex deviants, victims of prejudice and discrimination, the prejudiced, bureaucrats, political radicals, the physically handicapped, immigrants, exiles, vagabonds and recluses [pp. 12-13].

To which we added: "This is by no means a complete listing, yet even allowing for duplication it includes a sizeable majority of persons living in any advanced industrial society such as ours."

If anything, this tendency to use alienation in global terms is even greater today. Thus, in 1967 *Life* magazine published a series on the "crisis of the individual" and his "uneasy sense of emptiness and anonymity." In 1968, Louis Harris, the pollster, reported that 30% of all Americans were alienated—or 6% more than in 1966! (We shall refer again to this survey.) In his 1968 presidential election campaign, Richard Nixon made a special appeal to what he called "forgotten Americans," that is, the presumably alienated lower-middle class, and in October, 1969, *Newsweek* devoted a whole issue to the mood of this group.

At another level, Christopher Lasch and Eugene Genovese have written recently that "a peculiar feature of neocapitalism in America is the presence of large groups which are excluded from production and which, because they are economically superfluous, must be kept in places of detention. The most important of these groups are the blacks and others of the new poor, young people, and women." Paul Goodman said that "contemporary conditions of life have certainly deprived people, and especially young people, of a meaningful world in which they can act to find themselves."

Even government reports have begun to recognize alienation—a phenomenon in itself. Thus the Kerner Commission report on the so-called civil disorders notes: "There is a widening gulf in communications between local government and the residents of the erupting ghettos of the city. As a result, ghetto residents develop a profound sense of isolation and alienation from the processes and programs of government." A recent report on technology by the National Academy of Sciences begins by saying that,

> whether rightly or wrongly, the belief is now widely held that the continuation of
> certain technological trends would pose grave dangers for the future of man, and, in-
> deed, that the ill-considered exploitation of technology has already contributed to
> some of the most urgent of our contemporary problems: the specter of thermonuclear
> destruction; the tensions of congested cities; the hazards of a polluted and despoiled
> biosphere; the expanding arsenal of techniques for the surveillance and manipulation
> of private thoughts and behavior; the alienation of those who feel excluded from
> power in an increasingly technical civilization (1969) [p. 1].

Many other such examples could be given, but we think this is sufficient to
show how much the idea of alienation animates popular and scholarly thought and
has entered into our social discourse.

What accounts for this great interest? The reasons are not hard to find. First
we can cite the social and technological trends so well summarized by the National
Academy of Sciences. Moreover, we confront a number of major intellectual influences which have already been dealt with in preceding chapters, but which will
briefly be listed here. Any such list must of course include Karl Marx, who, in his
early work, described the industrial worker as having lost control over both the
product of his labor and the means of production, and thereby becoming alienated
or estranged from himself and from others. (As we shall see, this powerful
insight which has stimulated much of the subsequent discussion of alienation has
also led to very serious methodological difficulties, particularly with regard to defining and measuring self-alienation.)

Another major figure in this list is the German sociologist, Max Weber, who,
in revising and extending Marx, suggested that it was not just industrial workers
who were alienated from the means of production, but bureaucrats, engineers, soldiers, and many others. We should also like to mention the philosopher, Nietzsche,
and his pronouncements about man alienated from his gods. We must also note the
French sociologist, Emile Durkheim, and his conception of anomie, or normlessness,
that is, the collapse of rules of conduct—to which he attributed such behavior as
suicide. (An important cause of alienation, anomie, is often confused with it; we
shall have more to say about this later.) Finally, although representing a totally different tradition, we should not fail to mention Freud and his theory of the repressed
or hidden self. In the hands of his revisionists, who attempt to relate intrapsychic
phenomena to social structure, this has also had a major influence on modern thinking about alienation.

These are only a few of the thinkers of the past who have contributed to
theories and studies of alienation in modern industrial society. Their influence has
made itself felt in the works of our most penetrating social critics and commentators: Hannah Arendt, Jacques Ellul, Erich Fromm, Jules Henry, Paul Goodman,
Herbert Marcuse, C. Wright Mills, David Riesman—these and others have, in many
diverse ways, described alienating features of our society and the alienated in it. Here,

for example, is Erich Fromm (1955) who has tried to combine Marxist and Freudian perspectives:

> In the nineteenth century the problem was that *God is dead;* in the twentieth century the problem is that *man is dead.* . . . The danger of the past was that men became slaves. The danger of the future is that men may become robots. True enough, robots do not rebel. But given man's nature, robots cannot live and remain sane, . . . they will destroy their world and themselves because they cannot stand . . . a meaningless life [p. 360].

While most contemporary American social scientists are not social critics, many of them have in various ways dealt with alienation—its sources, its correlates, and its consequences. One of the most recent to do so is the sociological theorist, Amitai Etzioni (1968). For him an alienating society is one which is unresponsive to basic human needs, by which he means particularly the need for control or power. While recognizing that there is no evidence to prove that preindustrial societies were less alienating that modern ones, Etzioni claims: "large segments of the citizens of contemporary industrial societies feel powerless and excluded, and are uninformed about the societal and political processes which govern their lives."

Having mentioned very briefly only a few of the influences on our thinking about alienation, we must now come more closely to grips with the problem of defining the term. As we have indicated, alienation is a concept which has lent itself to many definitions and this of course complicates the effort to measure it. However, we think it is important to distinguish between alienating *conditions* on the one hand, and estranged *states,* on the other. This distinction is not always easy to preserve. By alienating conditions, we mean those objective circumstances such as conditions of work or social interaction, or the distribution and exercise of political power. It seems appropriate, therefore, to limit the term alienation to mean an individual feeling or state of dissociation from self, from others, and from the world at large.

Such states, although functions of the conditions that produce them, should not be confused with the conditions themselves. For example, Durkheim's notion of anomie or normlessness (to which we referred earlier) can be regarded as an important *cause* of alienation but should not be confused with alienation as a state of mind. Similar considerations apply to other concepts which are often confused with alienation. To take another example, social isolation may lead to a state of estrangement, but not all isolates are alienated. Indeed, alienation may result from the social pressures of group, crowd, or mass, as David Riesman and others have suggested. By the same token, alienation should not be confused with "social disorganization," since estrangement may be found in highly organized bureaucracies. Alienation is often associated with loneliness, but, again, not all lonely people are estranged. Neither should alienation be confused with disenchantment or rage, although these states may at times be connected. In many ways it is easier to say what alienation is not than what it *is.*

Helpful in bringing some order out of chaos here is the conceptual scheme of the sociologist, Melvin Seeman. In an influential paper which appeared some ten years ago, Seeman distinguished five alternative meanings of alienation as sub-jectively felt states of mind. (Seeman, 1959.) The first is *powerlessness,* and Seeman suggests that this aspect of alienation can be conceived as "the expectancy or probability held by the individual that his own behavior cannot determine the occurrence of the outcomes, or reinforcements, he seeks." (For example, people may feel powerless about their ability to affect political events.) A second mean-ing of alienation, according to Seeman, is *meaninglessness,* characterized by "low expectancy that satisfactory predictions about future outcomes of behavior can be made." A third meaning is *normlessness,* that is, anomie, a situation in which rules or norms regulating individual conduct have broken down. A fourth type is the feeling of *isolation,* as, presumably, in the case of certain intellectuals. (More about this later.) The alienated in this sense are those who assign low values to goals or beliefs that are typically highly valued in the society. The fifth and last meaning of alienation in Seeman's scheme is *self-estrangement;* the idea is illus-trated by the person who (as described by Mills and Fromm) makes an instrument of himself and is therefore estranged from himself. While there has been some argument over Seeman's definitions, his formulation nevertheless has stimulated a number of efforts to measure alienation in many of the empirical studies to which we shall refer.

Defining alienation—no easy task—is one thing; but it is something else again to measure it, even after arriving at a definition that makes some sense. Here, there are two major approaches. One consists of the search for social or behavioral *indica-tors* which presumably reflect alienated states; the other involves the measurement of those states of mind themselves and falls into the category of *attitude* research. The first approach is exemplified by writers such as Fromm who attribute high rates of suicide, homicide, alcoholism, drug addiciton, mental illness, and other disorders to the alienation of those groups, communities, or nations which produce these rates.

To take another example, some observers have attributed nonvoting to alien-ation; others have attributed political activism (e.g., participating in anti-war demon-strations or opposition to fluoridation) to alienation. Still others have tried to show that alienation and violence are linked. The problem of course is not just a semantic one, but also a logical one. That is, can the behavior in question be attributed chief-ly or exclusively to alienation? If not, what does the theory contribute? Thus, do all alienated people become violent; are all violent people alienated? In raising such questions, we do not wish to underestimate the importance of research on alien-ation which seeks to make predictive statements about its behavioral consequences. After all, what people do is more important than what they say.

But precisely because social science is still limited in its ability to predict be-havior—let alone explain such behavior in terms of concepts which lack clear defi-nition—many investigators have tended to concentrate their efforts on the attitudi-

nal dimensions and correlates of alienation. This is the second major approach to
the problem and it is usually descriptive rather than explanatory or predictive. There
are many problems here too. Attitude research, still more an art than a science, can
tell us within fairly reasonable limits whether people will vote for Tweedledum or
Tweedledee, or whether they prefer Product X to Product Y; but it is not so simple
to obtain reliable measures of deep-seated attitudes, feelings, states of mind, or mood.
This is complicated in the case at hand just because of the underlying assumption
that alienation, however defined, involves the "self" and techniques for probing
the self are fairly primitive, particularly in social science. The crucial question is
whether available techniques of attitude measurement permit us to say anything
significant about behavior.

Such, very briefly, are just some of the conceptual and methodological problems which have confronted social scientists applying their tools to the study of
alienation. We hope these issues will be clarified as we review studies which address
the question of who in our society are the alienated, how they are alienated, and
with what effects.


## SOME CASE STUDIES


Let us begin with a review of some recent surveys that deal with the status
and attitudes of blacks in our society. Many observers, black and white, suggest that
because of the many manifestations of racism in our society, blacks are particularly alienated and that it is their alienation which explains their protest movement
and the so-called civil disorders of recent years. Thus, Gary Marx, the director of
an important national survey of black attitudes conducted in 1964 (more of this
in a moment) has very recently been quoted as saying that a significant minority
of blacks in the United States "holds attitudes indicating a depth of estrangement
and bitterness unique in American history." Marx also said that the "relative proportion [of alienated blacks] is growing and increasing noticeably among the young
and those in the North." But he added that "much of the anger which exists remains
directed toward inclusion in the system" (*New York Times,* October 25, 1969). Now,
right here, we believe, is a good example of ambiguity regarding the concept of alienation. Should black rage at injustice be regarded as alienation or estrangement—
particularly if, as Gary Marx himself says, that anger is aimed at *inclusion* in the system? We think not. But of course that does not means that some blacks are not
alienated, and with good reason. What then do the surveys show?

Here we are concerned not with the whole range of black attitudes toward
life in the United States, but only with the evidence of black alienation. Defining
and measuring it chiefly in terms of morale and feelings of powerlessness, a number
of national attitude surveys show fairly significant differences between whites and
blacks. Thus, Louis Harris, to whom we referred earlier, has asked respondents
whether or not they agree with the following statements:

> Few people understand how it is to live like I live.
> What I personally think doesn't count very much.
> The rich get richer, the poor get poorer.
> People running the country don't really care what happens to people like me.
> Almost nobody understands the problems facing me.
> Important things in the world don't affect my life.
> I feel left out of things.

(Respondents agreeing with a given number of these items were scored as alienated.) By such a measure, 24% of a national sample of American adults were scored as alienated in 1966; among black respondents the proportion was 34%. Two years later, Harris repeated this series of questions and the proportion of Americans as a whole who scored as alienated had risen to 30%; but among blacks, the corresponding figure was up to 54%. However, at least in 1966, low-income whites in the Harris survey were much more alienated than were blacks (Erskine, 1969). We think it is important to recognize that these measures of alienation are very limited conceptually; but, given these limitations, the results are about what we would expect. It is scarcely necessary to say that those who are deprived economically and socially are most likely to feel out of things.

In this connection we want to mention also James Coleman's widely reported finding in *Equality of Educational Opportunity:* that children with some sense of power or mastery over their future are likely to be higher achievers in school. To quote the Coleman *et al.* (1966) report,

> a pupil attitude factor which appears to have a stronger relationship to achievement than do all the "school" factors together is the extent to which an individual feels that he has some control over his own destiny.  . . . The responses of pupils to questions in the survey show that minority pupils, except for Orientals, have far less conviction than whites that they can affect their own environments and futures. When they do, however, their achievement is higher than that of whites who lack that conviction [p. 23].

The Harris surveys are purely descriptive. The Coleman report, however, suggests a relationship between feelings of powerlessness, a major variant of alienation, and behavior or achievement in school.

The nationwide study of black attitudes which Gary Marx (1967, Ch. 2) himself conducted in 1964 also looked into the matter of morale, or normlessness— as we saw earlier, one of the variant meanings of alienation. As might be expected, he found that the higher the morale, or, put conversely, the less alienated by this measure, the greater the expressed militancy. (Marx also found that blacks who regarded themselves as in good health were also more likely to be militant than those who rated their health as poor.) Both these findings confirm the old axiom about revolutions being started, not by the weak, the demoralized, the despairing, or the alienated, but by the strong and the hopeful—those who have a sense of relatedness to their fellow men.

Further confirmation of this simple truth is provided by the study of participants in the 1967 riots conducted by Robert Fogelson and Robert Hill (1968) for the Kerner Commission. This study successfully demolished the so-called "riff-raff theory" of riot participation. Their conclusion: "the rioters were a small but significant minority of the Negro population, fairly representative of the ghetto resident and especially of the young adult males, and tacitly supported by at least a large minority of the black community."

To be sure, the "riffraff" theory wasn't a very good one to begin with; for, certainly, alienation per se should not be equated with militancy. This does not mean, however, that certain alienated individuals are not at times drawn into violent encounters. Evidence that this can be the case is provided by H. Edward Ransford (1968) in a study of Los Angeles Negroes interviewed shortly after the Watts riot. Ransford found that isolated blacks, who feel powerless and who voice strong disaffection at discrimination, appear to be an extremely volatile group—two thirds of them being willing to use violence. But, again, expressed willingness to use violence does not mean necessarily that violence will be used.

Here, it is useful to note, as suggested by Angus Campbell and Howard Schuman in the conclusion to their survey of 5000 Negroes in 15 cities, also conducted for the Kerner Commission, that the way in which many whites perceive so-called riots is not necessarily how most blacks regard them. (We say "so-called" riots because of the negative connotation in which the term is held. For many blacks, the word "protest" seems more appropriate.) Put otherwise, with one set of words we can say that alienated blacks, willing to use violence, are likely to participate in riots; with another set of words we can say that militant blacks are engaged in protest or revolt—which, of course, is the language used to describe the founding of our nation.

To quote further from the conclusions which Campbell and Schuman (1968) drew from their study:

> While there is no doubt that Negroes want change and some of them are prepared to do desperate things to bring it about, the changes they have in mind are essentially conservative in nature. The great majority do not propose to withdraw from America; they want equal status in it. They do not talk of tearing down the economic and political institutions of the nation; they seek to share equally in the benefits [p. 61].

In short, the evidence with regard to the attitudes of blacks, which we have only cursorily and selectively reviewed here, suggests that while substantial numbers may be alienated, alienation alone does not explain either the militancy which some have expressed or the forms which that militancy may take. Nor do these data say much about those blacks, as yet a small minority, who consciously and deliberately reject the very values of American society which others are militantly striving to make their own. This distinction between those who want "in" and those who want "out" is crucial—and not only in the case of blacks.

To illustrate this point further, let us turn now to another group in our society which is presumably "high" in alienation—youth. Let us suggest at the outset, however, that we not confuse opposition to the Viet Nam war with alienation; some of the students participating in the antiwar movement may be alienated in particular senses of the term, but not all. Indeed, to the extent that the student peace movement has been able to influence national policy with regard to the war, it has shown power, not powerlessness. To be sure, if students begin to feel that their efforts are to no avail, some may fall into alienated states, but there is no evidence that this is yet the case. It would be more appropriate, if not completely accurate, to refer to those who are completely indifferent to the war as being alienated. As with certain blacks, we must be careful in applying the alienated label to those whom the French call the *enragés*.

Leaving the war and its opponents aside, there are other, possibly more useful ways in which we can consider the alienation of youth. Here we owe a considerable debt to Kenneth Kenniston and his studies of middle class college youth. To many such youth, Kenniston suggests, "the psychological imperatives, social institutions and cultural values of the industrial ethic seem largely outdated and irrelevant to their own lives." Rejecting adult values, alienated youth postpone adulthood and search for a new ethic of their own. (Paul Goodman, another interpreter of alienated youth, has described this search as essentially a kind of religious crisis.)

How representative are such alienated states among youth? One of the few surveys to deal with this question was conducted among eighteen- to twenty-four-year-olds, both in and out of college, by Daniel Yankelovich (1969) for *Fortune*. The purpose of the survey was to measure youthful opinion regarding basic values, parents, career plans, and current political issues. One of the most interesting findings in this study was that college students could be divided between those for whom higher education was essentially a practical matter (i.e., to promote self-advancement) and those for whom college meant "something more intangible, perhaps the opportunity to change things rather than make out well within the existing system." Approximately three out of five fell into the first category, and they were of little concern to *Fortune*. But the two-fifths in the minority were of concern to *Fortune* since they were typified "mainly by their *lack of concern* about making money." As might be expected, this minority was more likely to express radical opinion on such issues as war and racism; about half of them believed that the United States is a "sick" society.

What do these findings mean? From one point of view, it can be argued that a significant, and, in *Fortune's* opinion, a growing minority of American youth is alienated from and therefore rejects, the prevailing values of our society. From another (e.g., the traditional Marxist) point of view, it could be argued that those who are chiefly concerned with making money are the alienated. As in the case of the black protest, much depends on the point of view of the observer.

We have already suggested that youthful radicalism or protest cannot be explained in terms of alienated states alone; indeed, such states may be more descriptive of silent or indifferent rather than of vocal youth. Let us now take up another aspect of youthful behavior about which there is much concern and which many adult observers attribute to some form of alienation: the use of drugs. As in the cases of black and youthful protest, it is risky to generalize about behavior which may range from true addiction to hard drugs at one extreme to occasional use of soft drugs at the other. There is no single explanation—psychological or sociological—which describes, let alone explains, such a range of behavior. Thus, in the rapidly growing literature which deals with student drug use, there is quite conflicting evidence as to whether such behavior is associated with political militancy. There are, for example, some studies which suggest that youthful drug users are politically indifferent, apathetic, or alienated. A number of investigations, however, show the opposite, that is, that there is a positive relationship between drug use and political activism.

One study which sheds some light on this controversial and murky field is that by Edward Suchman on the so-called "hang-loose ethic" and the spirit of drug use. By the hang-loose ethic, Suchman means the repudiation of "such cornerstones of conventional society as Christianity, 'my country right or wrong,' the sanctity of marriage and premarital chastity, civil disobedience, the accumulation of wealth, the right and even competence of parents, the schools, and the government to head and make decisions for everyone—in sum, the Establishment." To test the hypothesis that adherence to this "ethic" is highly associated with drug use, and chiefly marijuana, Suchman conducted interviews with a representative sample of some 600 students at a West Coast University. As might be expected, Suchman found that the more the student embraced the antiestablishment hang-loose ethic, the more likely he was to use marijuana. Were such students alienated? Here is how Suchman (1968) answered the question:

> A series of four questions designed to index "alienation" . . . showed no statistically significant relationships to smoking marijuana, despite the claim . . . that "smoking marijuana has become almost an emblem of alienation." . . . The "hang-loose" ethic, while it may represent antagonism to the conventional world, does not appear to create apathy and withdrawal. Subscribers to this ethic are not so much alienated in regard to society in general as critical of the "Establishment [p. 151]."

If marijuana-smokers are not necessarily alienated, what about those who are more deeply involved in and committed to the subculture of drugs, that is, the Hippies Here the label is perhaps somewhat more appropriate. But there are many questions about the Hippies that remain to be answered. For example, is their alienation (a term which we use here in the sense of detachment from prevailing norms) more a consequence of their drug behavior, or is it a cause of such behavior? In our opinion, we don't know enough about the so-called Hippies (and hippie is as imprecise a term as alienation itself) to give any definitive answer. We suspect a strong element of faddism in the youth culture and that most who adopt the hippie posture will eventually outgrow and repudiate it; but in all fairness we must recognize the possibility that what we are witnessing is not a Bohemianism in new dress or form, but, rather, a far more radical break with conventions.

From the question of youthful deviance, let us now turn to the problem of alienation from work. As you will recall, the idea here is that the conditions of modern work, and particularly those in industry, are alienating in the sense that through deprivation of control over the means and the product of his labor the worker loses something in and of himself. Although, presumably, this is linked with job dissatisfaction, something more than that is meant. However, no other aspect of alienation has received as much attention as this, and, therefore, we shall have to be very selective in discussing some relevant research findings.

Let us begin by reviewing a number of studies which are cross-sectional in their scope, that is, which attempt to compare the degree to which men in different social classes or different occupational groups are alienated by their jobs. One such nationwide interview survey was conducted in 1957 by Gerald Gurin and his collaborators for the joint Commission on Mental Illness and Health; it is reported in the volume, *Americans View Their Mental Health.* For our purposes, perhaps the most important reported finding has to do with class and occupational differences in the relative importance or salience of "ego" and "extrinsic factors in men's attitudes toward their work." By the ego factor, Gurin and his associates meant personal involvement—some expression of the self—in the job; by extrinsic factors they meant such things as money, job security, and working conditions. They wrote, "In making this distinction, there is no attempt to minimize the importance of these latter reasons; the crucial consideration is not whether a person is concerned with such things as money and security, but whether his concern with such matters excludes consideration of the ego factors." Only in considering ego factors did they speak of alienation from the job. There should not be much argument with this formulation.

As one might expect, when questioned about their jobs, men in higher educational and occupational groups expressed greater ego involvement in their work, greater satisfaction, and also more work problems; on the other hand, men in lower occupational groups were less likely to indicate ego involvement in their jobs and more likely to express grievances in terms of the extrinsic factors. From this the authors of the study conclude that:

> Although higher status jobs offer more opportunity for self-fulfillment, and people
> in these jobs much more often mention ego satisfactions on the job, they also express
> a greater degree of frustration of ego needs. . . . Conversely, people in lower status
> jobs less often experience the lack of ego gratification on the job as a frustration

> either because they [have] lower expectations . . . or because they become adjusted
> to the lack of opportunities for such fulfillment [Gurin *et al.,* 1960, p. 173].

In other words, according to this interpretation, men at the lower end of the
job hierarchy, concerned chiefly with extrinsic factors in the job, are thereby more
alienated; nevertheless, they expect less from their jobs, and since they are less ego-
involved in their jobs they are less likely to suffer damage to their ego—which could
be interpreted as lack of alienation. The confusion here is due to the fact that the
authors of this study fall back on what is essentially a psychological explanation
of the class differences in attitudes which they report; that is, the alienation of
those in lower status jobs is attributed chiefly to lower expectations of self-fulfillment on the job.

That other interpretations of such findings are equally plausible is suggested
by another major survey by Melvin Kohn. His study of class and occupational
differences in orientations and values was described in the October 1969 issue of
the *American Sociological Review.* Based on interviews conducted in 1964 with
a national cross section of men, Kohn's study also found significant class and
occupational differences with regard to the importance of extrinsic and intrinsic
values in work. However, his conclusion as to what determines such differences
is somewhat different:

> Conditions of occupational life at higher social class levels facilitate interest in the
> intrinsic qualities of the job, foster a view of self and society that is conducive to
> believing in the possibilities of rational action toward purposive goals, and promote
> self-direction. The conditions of occupational life at lower social class levels limit
> men's view of the job primarily to the extrinsic benefits it provides [and] foster a
> narrowly circumscribed conception of self and society [Kohn and Schooler,
> 1969, p. 677].

Here of course the stress is on social structural factors rather than merely on the
expectations and demands which men bring to their jobs; indeed, the inference is
that it is social structure which determines what men's general outlook and expectations will be; in our opinion, this is a far more satisfactory explanation of
class differences about work and its psychological consequences.

The two studies just mentioned deal with broad interclass differences in work
and work-related orientations; they support the hypothesis that men at the bot-
tom of the job hierarchy are in general most likely to be alienated from work and,
consequently, in other ways as well. But it is not just sociological quibbling to suggest that the picture is somewhat more complicated.

Thus Harold Wilensky, who defines alienation in terms of the violence
which the work role does to a man's self-image, suggests on the basis of his own
studies in the Detroit area that the specific details of the work role, occupational
group, and organizational context, are more important causes of work alienation
than is social class alone. And he finds that differences between occupational

groups within the same occupational stratum may be greater than the difference between groups two strata apart. He concludes that the vast majority of Americans are "playing it cool," neither strongly wedded to the job nor feeling it to be an intense threat to their identity. In other words, he says, most men are indifferent to their work in the sense that their jobs neither support nor violate their prized self-image. To quote him:

> [If we relate] measures of alienation, attachment, and indifference, that top prized self-image, to specific attributes of work role and workplace, and to the careers and occupational groups that cut across them, we find that a work milieu that provides little freedom, a career that has been blocked and chaotic, and a stage of life where consumption pressures outrun income, [all] foster work alienation. Control over the workplace, opportunity for sociable talk on the job, and an orderly career foster work attachment [Wilensky, 1967, p. 165].

The hypothesis that intraoccupational differences in work alienation are greater than interoccupational differences is supported by a number of studies. One such study is by Robert Blauner, reported in his book, *Alienation and Freedom* (1964), and based on the analysis of data from a survey conducted by Elmo Roper for *Fortune* magazine in 1947 of workers in four industries—printing, textiles, an automobile factory, and an automated chemical plant. Taking four major dimensions of alienation—powerlessness, meaninglessness, isolation, and self-estrangement—Blauner found considerable variation between the four industries. As he says, they varied widely in the degree of mechanization of technology, rationalization of division of labor, concentration of economic structure, and bureaucratization of social organization. What Blauner found was that workers in automobiles and textiles were most alienated, and workers in the printing and chemical industries enjoyed the most freedom and integration. Interpreting his findings historically, Blauner suggests that in the preindustrial period of craft industry (still reflected to some extent in printing), alienation is at its lowest level; alienation increases in modern assembly-line industries, for example, automobile production, where "a depersonalized worker, estranged from himself and larger collectives, goes through the motions of work in the regimented milieu of the conveyer belt for the sole purpose of earning his bread"; but, then, and, perhaps, most striking, according to Blauner, alienation may decline under certain conditions of automated work, as in the continuous-process chemical industry, where the worker gains control over his work process and where the result is "meaningful work in a more cohesive, integrated industrial climate." Many social critics would disagree violently with Blauner on automated labor; yet his data are suggestive not only as regards differences between industries but also as regards possible future trends in the conditions of work. The main point is that however work alienation is measured, it is not just a function of mechanization but rather a function of the social controls under which mechanized labor is performed.

In this context we can look at many other examples of work alienation. Thus, we have Arthur Kornhauser's (1965) study of the mental health of automobile workers in Detroit and his finding that there is a relationship between optimum mental health (clinically validated) and the amount of skill required in the job; that is, the more skill required and the greater the opportunities for its exercise, the "better" the health of the workers. On the other hand, there is the report by Melvin Seeman (1967) that manual workers in a Swedish city are not alienated in the sense of powerlessness, and that this may have something to do with the conditions of life apart from the job in such a society.

We have by no means exhausted the very considerable literature on work alienation; however, we hope that we have been able to convey the idea that whether or not a man is alienated from and by the work he does is dependent on precisely what kind of work he does, where, and when, and not only on that. But it seems fairly clear that whatever he does, the chances are slight in our society that he can escape some degree of alienation from his job and, if we accept the Marxist formulation, from himself as well.

Marxist or not, the fact that many men and women in our society cannot find, fulfill, or achieve themselves in work remains a problem. Consequently, a number of social scientists have speculated as to whether alienated workers somehow fulfill themselves more in their leisure activities than in work. David Riesman once thought that this was the case, although he has since reversed himself and repudiated the notion. Many problems present themselves here. For one thing, it is necessary to distinguish between leisure and free time; they are not synonymous. Time off the regular or main job is not necessarily leisure time; it is often spent moonlighting or traveling to and from work. Sebastian de Grazia has calculated that while the average workweek in the United States has been reduced by approximately thirty hours in the last century, the actual gain in free time has been only a few hours. In other words, the oft-proclaimed milennium of leisure has yet to arrive.

What then do most Americans do with whatever leisure they have? On a day-to-day basis, most, of course, collapse in front of the television set. Here, let us explore a study which sets out to determine whether highly alienated persons are more likely to use the mass media as an escape from the realities of life, and its finding that alienated adults spend no more time with the mass media than the nonalienated (McLeod *et al.*, 1965-1966). Does this mean that such use of leisure is not alienating? There seem to be no reliable answers, but there are many strongly expressed opinions. For example, Wilensky, in a paper on mass culture, says, "To be socially integrated in America is to accept propaganda, advertising, and speedy obsolescence in consumption." (By this token, the alienated are those who would reject such values.) And Robert MacIver once wrote that if some

of us achieve freedom for an hour or a day, others find only a "great emptiness."
Escaping from work, they also try to escape from themselves.

So far we have tried to show how the concept and measurement of alienation
contributes to our understanding of the status of blacks, youth, and workers in
our society. We have not been able to do justice to the many empirical studies which
bear on any one of these groups. Nor can we do justice to many other studies which
treat other aspects of alienation, or deal with other groups altogether. Before concluding, however, we should like very briefly to mention a number of other approaches
to the problem.

One has to do with what is sometimes called a "sense of purpose" (national
and personal); presumably those who lack this sense are alienated. One example
often cited concerns the behavior of American prisoners-of-war in North Korean
and Chinese camps during the war in Korea (Mack, 1967, pp. 25-29). Many of them
apparently became apathetic and demoralized; indeed, one in three died in captivity
and a few were persuaded to turn against their own country. This behavior has been
interpreted by many as evidence of alienation. But it is interesting to note that during World War II the death rate among Americans in Japanese prisoner-of-war camps
was just as high as in Korea, while among those captured by the Germans only 1%
died. Why the great difference? Unless it can be demonstrated that the soldiers who
fought in Japan or Korea were more alienated to begin with than those who fought
in Europe, we do not see that any theory of alienation is particularly helpful in explaining their behavior after capture. How the Germans, Japanese, and Koreans differed in their treatment of war prisoners may be more significant in explaining such
behavior. In our opinion, considering that it was a popular conflict, the World War
II differences are of greater interest than what happened in Korea, where we fought
an "unappreciated" war, like the war in Vietnam.

Let us turn now from international conflict to the fear of crime or violence
and the impact of such fear on social life. Here we are concerned not with crime
rates but, rather, with the public's perception of the threat that crime poses.
There is plentiful evidence that many Americans fear most the crimes that are
actually least likely to affect them, that is, crimes of violence, which are actually
most prevalent among people who know each other (husbands and wives, or
friends) and not among strangers. Now while there is no hard evidence that
the fear of criminal violence has significantly affected traditional patterns of
social life, it is a possibility worth considering. Just how much of a possibility
it is is suggested by the recent President's Commission on Law Enforcement
(1967).

> Fear of strangers has greatly impoverished the lives of many Americans. . . .
> The general level of social interaction in the society is reduced. When fear of
> crime becomes fear of the stranger the social order is further damaged. As the

level of sociability and mutual trust is reduced, streets and public places can indeed become more dangerous. Not only will there be fewer people abroad but those who are abroad will manifest a fear or a lack of concern for each other. . . . However, the most dangerous aspect of a fear of strangers is its implication that the moral and social order of society are of doubtful trustworthiness and stability. . . . The tendency of many people to think of crime in terms of increasing moral deterioration is an indication that they are losing their faith in their society. And so the costs of the fear of crime to the social order may ultimately be even greater than its psychological costs to individuals [p. 52].

Is this not alienation?

How people behave under the stressful circumstances of war or the fear of violence displays something about the relative strength of bonds between them; presumably, when those bonds are weak, men are more likely to betray each other and themselves. The slogans of "law and order," cynically exploited by politicians, can probably be interpreted as addressing themselves to this question, even though the end result of law and order at the expense of sociability may be to alienate people still further from each other.

Two other aspects of alienation remain to be mentioned. One concerns those who are physically or psychologically unable or unwilling to perform the functions and carry out the roles which our highly productive society demands of its citizens. Although they are not usually listed in treatises on the alienated, we suggest that the term may also apply to many among the "unwanted" or "surplus" populations, such as the visibly impaired or handicapped, in homes for the aged, sheltered workshops, mental hospitals, and so forth—in other words, people who are kept out of sight as much as possible, and without whom the rest of the society could survive (as Farber says with regard to the mentally retarded). Insofar as they can be described as being in alienated states, we daresay this has as much to do with their rejection and stigmatization by "normals" as it does with some intrinsic deviant characteristics; we know more about the former process than the latter.

It is in this context that some writers, such as Thomas Scheff (1966) and R. D. Laing (1967), have focussed attention on the labeling process by which some among us are certified and treated as "mad," with various degrading and alienating consequences for them and for us. Our view is that this labeling and stigmatization does not "explain" madness, but does describe the alienating conditions which may result from this particular effort to maintain civic order. Or, as Laing says about the schizophrenic, "More completely, more radically than anywhere else in our society, he is invalidated as a human being." Is this not alienation?

Last, but by no means least, we should like to say a few words about a group which has long been regarded as quintessentially alienated: the intellectuals. Who are they, and what is the nature of their alienation? Until recently, it has been fashionable for some self-appointed spokesmen for intellectuals to proclaim their acceptance and integration into American society. Several things can be said about this claim. First, not all scholars or academics are intellectuals; the converse is also true. Second, according to an interpretation that we find congenial, an intellectual can be described as one who is alienated by definition, that is, alienation is *necessary* for him wherever he is. Put otherwise, he may dissent from the silent or vocal majority; he may also dissent from the dissenters. This idea of alienation as necessary —more opinion than fact and mentioned elsewhere in this volume by Mizruchi in another context—distinguishes intellectuals from many of the other groups discussed earlier; presumably, intellectuals would not escape their alienated states even if they could.

## CONCLUSIONS

We have tried in this brief inquiry into contemporary social scientific thinking about alienation to provide some idea of both the contributions and the limitations of this approach. It should be evident that the conceptual as well as the methodological obstacles are formidable. As a catchword, alienation lends itself to many interpretations. Lack of conceptual clarity therefore only further complicates the task for those who would study it. Since there is as yet little agreement on how to define the term, there is even less agreement on how to measure it. Considering its ancestry (described elsewhere in this volume), this is hardly surprising.

Yet precisely because these unresolved conceptual and methodological problems exist, the studies we have described are often inconclusive and even misleading. Thus, as we have suggested, it seems inappropriate to describe as alienated those blacks and youths who are engaged in various forms of social and political protest. Indeed, we think that this kind of labeling is merely another way of stigmatizing rebels as "deviant" or "pathological." Here, the concept of alienation becomes a polemical weapon in the hands of those bent on rationalizing social repression.

Similar considerations apply to studies which attempt to show that other kinds of deviants, such as drug users, are alienated. Some may very well be, but whether an alienated state is more cause than effect of such behavior remains to be determined. And if this question is still open, how does the concept help us to understand that behavior?

More appropriate, and more conclusive, it seems to us, are studies dealing with some of the psychological consequences of work in modern society. It is no easy task to determine what these consequences are, and the data available suggest that we cannot generalize about work alienation, that is, not all those employed in a factory are alienated. But it is also fairly clear from the studies we have cited that most people receive little personal or intrinsic gain from the work they do, which, of course, is what Karl Marx first saw. As noted earlier, Marx created difficulties for the social scientists following his lead by casting the problem in psychological as well as sociological and economic terms. Perhaps, however, too much stress has recently been given to studies of the inner satisfactions and dissatisfactions of work and not enough, following Marx's lead, to the social structures in which work is performed. This bias is illustrated by the tremendous effort exerted by management to make men "happier" on jobs which are inherently alienating. As Marx himself said, "the philosophers have only *interpreted* the world differently, the point is to *change* it."

However, the fact that social scientists interested in alienation have so far been uneven in their contributions does not necessarily imply that the term has little or no utility. On the contrary, we believe that, when used judiciously, it is an important tool of social criticism. The trouble is that it is often used recklessly by those who contribute more heat than light to our understanding of the conditions of our lives. The challenge for social scientists, which has yet to be met, is to refine the analytical approaches required for a deeper understanding of this phenomenon. Only then can they assist in movements toward a less alienating society.


## REFERENCES

Blauner, R. *Alienation and freedom: The factory worker and his industry.* Chicago: University of Chicago Press, 1964.

Campbell, A. & Schuman, H. Racial attitudes in fifteen American cities. *Supplemental studies for the National Advisory Commission on Civil Disorders.* Washington, D.C., United States Government Printing Office, 1968.

Coleman, J. S. *et al. Equality of educational opportunity.* Washington, D.C., United States Government Printing Office, 1966.

Erskine, H. The Polls: Negro philosophies of life. *Public Opinion Quarterly,* 1969, *33,* 147–158.

Etzioni, A. Basic human needs: alienation and inauthenticity. *American Sociological Review,* 1968, 33, 870–885.

Fogelson, R. M. & Hiss, R. B. Who riots? A study of participation in the 1967 riots. *Supplemental studies for the National Advisory Commission on Civil Disorders.* Washington, D.C., United States Government Printing Office, 1968.

Fromm, E. *The sane society.* New York, Rinehart, 1955.

Gurin, G., Veroff, J., & Feld, S. *Americans view their mental health.* New York, Basic Books, 1960.

Josephson, E. & Josephson, M. *Man alone: alienation in modern society.* New York: Dell, 1962.

Kohn, M. & Schooler, C. Class, occupation, and orientation. *American Sociological Review,* 1969, *34,* 659–678.

Kornhauser, A. *Mental health of the industrial worker.* New York: Wiley, 1965.

Laing, R. D. *The politics of experience.* New York: Pantheon, 1967.

Mack, R. *Transforming America: patterns of social change.* New York: Random House, 1967.

Marx, G. *Protest and prejudice: A study of belief in the black community.* New York: Harper & Row, 1967.

McLeod, J., Ward, S., & Tancill, K. Alienation and uses of the mass media. *Public Opinion Quarterly,* 1965–1966, *29,* 583–594.

Mills, C. W. *The sociological imagination.* New York: Oxford University Press, 1959.

National Academy of Sciences. *Technology: processes of assessment and choice.* (Report to the Committee on Science and Astronautics, U.S. House of Representatives). Washington, D.C., United States Government Printing Office, 1969.

*New York Times,* October 25, 1969.

President's Commission on Law Enforcement and Administration of Justice. *The Challenge of crime in a free society.* Washington, D.C., U.S. Government Printing Office, 1967.

Ransford, H. E. Isolation, powerlessness, and violence: a study of attitudes and participation in the Watts riot. *American Journal of Sociology,* 1968, *73,* 581–591.

Scheff, T. *Being mentally ill.* Chicago, Aldine, 1966.

Seeman, M. On the meaning of alienation. *American Sociological Review,* 1959, *24,* 783–791.

Seeman, M. On the personal consequences of alienation in work. *American Sociological Review,* 1967, *32,* 273–285.

Suchman, E. The "hang-loose" ethic and the spirit of drug use. *Journal of Health and Social Behavior,* 1968, *9,* 146–155.

Wilensky, H. Work as a social problem. In H. Becker (Ed.), *Social problems: a modern approach.* New York, Wiley, 1967.

Yankelovich, D. What they believe. *Fortune,* 1969, *79(1),* 70–71, 179–181.

# Chapter 8

# Alternatives to Alienation:
# A Japanese-American Example

*Colleen Leahy Johnson*
Syracuse University

Among the many pieces of contemporary literature on alienation, one must look long for direct contributions from anthropologists. Indirectly, however, the study of primitive society provides the groundwork for recent theorizing on certain antithetical features of life in contemporary urban settings. Why anthropologists have rarely used the concept operationally, particularly in their studies of developing nations, provides an interesting subject in itself, but is beside the point here. What is of concern is the study of contrasting modes of social organization, presented by anthropologists, which have generated theories of cultural change that readily lend themselves to the understanding of processes and states of alienation. In this chapter, these theories will be examined in the light of empirical data on the Japanese-Americans residing in Honolulu.

In reading descriptions of primitive society, one comes away with a highly positive impression of cultural integration and adaptation that has been supposedly irretrievably lost in more complex societies through the processes of industrialization and urbanization. In contrast to modern society, the primitive lives in a small, homogeneous society, enveloped in an all-embracing kinship system, with a strong sense of group solidarity, where sex, age, and family are the major status determinants. Such a structure creates a highly direct system of social relationships. Political, legal, and economic behaviors are transacted within a system of direct acquaintance and personal knowledge. Robert Redfield (1953) eloquently describes the quality of simpler cultures:

In this condition of humanity, the essential order of society, the nexus which held people was moral. Humanity attained its characteristic, long enduring nature as a multitude of different but equivalent systems of relationships and institutions each expressive of a view of the good. Each precivilized society was held together by largely undeclared but continually realized ethical conceptions [p. 15].

Stanley Diamond (1963) defines the major task of anthropology today as the definition of primary human nature through the analysis of primitive society, with the aim of better understanding our "contemporary pathology and possibilities." He sees the search for the primitive arising out of a feeling of remorse and loneliness due to the inability of contemporary man to incorporate the organic ties present in simple cultures into modern society. He sees modern man living in a "rationalized, mechanized and secularized civilization [which] tends to produce standard and modal rather than natural varieties of persons. The individual is always in danger of dissolving into the functions of the status [Diamond, 1963, p. 104]." There is, then, a tendency to picture primitive society as a lost Paradise, idealized as a direct antithesis to confusions and alienation present in modern society. The suggestion has been made that Man has lost integral parts of himself in the process of his social evolution.

Anthropology has provided descriptive accounts of diverse simple cultures, displaying great variation among them, but showing patterns of stability and cohesion rarely seen in complex, technological civilization. Macroscopic theories of social change have arisen out of these ethnographies which stress the polarity between man's primeval past and his present condition. For example, Redfield's (1953) folk-urban continuum traces the changes in world view from the moral order of the primitive society to the technical order of civilization. Henry Maine deals with primitive society as a status society where the family was the basic unit bound together by sentiment. This is contrasted to the contractual nature of social relationships in modern society where the individual must either mediate for himself or seek technical assistance. Toennies' ideal types of relationships distinguish between *Gesellschaft* (contractual) mechanistic ties, where each individual follows his own rational pursuit of self-interest, and the *Gemeinschaft* (kin-like) organic relationship, bound by an immediate, personal, and moral element. These theories and others have provided a stimulus to students of contemporary society as models of explanation of the current social malaise. However, contradictions have arisen in the form of recent empirical data which have challenged the notion of the existence of a simple continuum between these various polarities. As might be expected, macroscopic theories of social change employing polarities run the risk of oversimplifying complex changes as well as invidiously scaling the value of phenomena (where the simplest are suggested to be "better").

For example, it has been a common assumption among sociologists that the isolated nuclear family is the basic social unit in the United States. As a corollary to this, the nuclear family has been linked to stress-producing socialization practices and segmented extra-familial relationships (Parsons, 1949). Although the nuclear family has been viewed as functional in terms of producing members capable of thriving in a mobile, individualistic society, it has at the same time been held responsible for accentuating the emotional conflicts in the young and intensifying the loneliness of adults. The attenuation of the extended kin relationships is considered to be a serious casualty that has occurred in the process of industrialization and urbanization. Furthermore, Wirth (1964) cites urbanization as causing a mode of life where depersonalization is a common occurrence. It is as if survival in complex urban environments requires the proliferation of fragmented, secondary relationships at the expense of the intimate bonds of family and kinship. "Populations in large numbers suggests individual variability, relative absense of intimate personal acquaintanceship, segmentalization of human relations and their anonymous, superficial, impersonal transitory and utilitarian character [Wirth, 1964, p. 225]."

Such conceptions as these, rather than being used as ideal models on which to base testable hypotheses, have been used by some observers as the reality itself. This use of these concepts has added to the feeling of the inevitability of despair regarding the supposed loneliness and depersonalization of posttechnological, urban existance. Fortunately, however, there are some studies of modern urban kinship systems which are stimulating a rethinking and reformulation of these assumptions. Interpretation of these studies has indicated that even in the highly mobile United States, most groups maintain extensive kinship relationships. Although these relationships do not assume the form of corporate groups, functioning extensively in both instrumental and expressive areas (as in simple societies), they nevertheless preserve an emphasis on sentiment and sociability, as well as mutual aid (Winch, 1968). Although one cannot completely agree with the statement that the isolated nuclear family is a "myth" [Rosow, 1965, p. 341], one must take note of Goode's (1970) extensive data which indicates that "Studies seem to show that no matter what index is used, the family in most industrial nations has not taken on the supposed character of the nuclear family system. The extended kin networks continue to function and to include a wide range of kin who share with one another, see one another frequently, and know each other [p. 75]."

Granted, then, that in studies of the social organization of the city one can detect certain processes which might lead to alienation, perhaps it would be more specific to state that one may also observe various processes of reintegration going on in urban life, some of which operate to alleviate states of alienation. Anthropologists, in their focus on the small group, whether family, neighborhood, or networks of social relationships, have been studying these processes of reintegration in urban areas in Africa. In providing descriptive accounts based on face-to-face relationship rather than the quantitative attitude surveys, anthropologists have shown that although the structure of society changes rather drastically in urban areas and new functions replace the old in the family and tribe, African migrants to the city are by no means cast adrift and without identification (Southall, 1961).

The point here is not to deny the vast qualitative and quantitative changes in modern life which can have disadvantageous effects on the quality of human existence; rather, my thesis is that although the structure of modern urban society has produced notable fractionation of economic, political, and legal institutions, the same fractionation of concrete social relationship does not necessarily follow. At the organizational level of day-to-day interaction, functional adaptations can take place among some groups in response to the pressure for disintegration. In other words, there are parallel processes, which, for convenience, can be termed *Gesellschaft* and *Gemeinschaft,* operating in a selective and relevant way to guide behavior in various sectors of activity. Therefore, options are open for some whose subculture provides them with supporting modes of organization, reaffirmed by traditional norms and values. For them, alienation is not an inevitable by-product of urbanization, since sources of integration and group solidarity can be found in their cultural backgrounds. The purpose of this chapter is to identify some of these sources of integration in one particular group: Japanese-Americans in Honolulu.

The various meanings attached to the concept of alienation have been reviewed elsewhere in this volume, so its usage here will be only briefly explained. When I say alienation is virtually absent, I am referring to those forms of social alienation usually considered by sociologists, that is, alienation in terms of separation from other people and in terms of disassociation from cultural norms and values. In other words, rather than experiencing meaninglessness, loneliness and normlessness, the Japanese-Americans avoid being alienated through having a high degree of mutual interrelatedness, a regularized system of mutual expectations, and a stability of role functions over time. The average individual conforms to the social system as his most comfortable alternative, even in a multicultural setting which offers other prescriptions. This is strictly in a sociological sense, however, and refers to social alienation. It must be distinguished from the personal or psychological alienation which can exist among the Japanese, as it does everywhere, for the more marginal individuals.

One explanation given for the relative absence of social alienation among the Japanese-Americans concerns their precedence given to collective value orientation over an individualistic or ego-centered value orientation. The individualistic orientation implies the individual's relative freedom to put his ego-centered interests ahead of the interests of the group. Gratification of personal needs takes priority over one's responsibilities to others. A collective orientation, on the other hand, implies a greater conformity to group demands at the sacrifice of one's personal desires. This is, of course, not an "either-or" situation, but, rather, a direction of emphasis which varies cross-culturally.

The important point is that the collective orientation displayed by the Japanese-Americans in Honolulu facilitates the operation of a solidary, supportive system of social relationships; this makes loneliness quite foreign in the experiential world of a large majority of the population. It is my contention that this high degree of social relatedness, operating in conjunction with a compatible system of norms and values, is derivative from the culture of Japan. This is complementary to, but quite distinct from American culture.

BACKGROUND OF THE JAPANESE-AMERICANS IN HAWAII

The Japanese immigrated to Hawaii in large numbers between 1890 and 1910 for the purpose of working as unskilled laborers in the sugar and pineapple plantations. Coming principally from rural regions of Southern Honshu and Kyushu, the explicit goal of virtually all of these laborers was to accumulate sufficient money in a few years to return to their ancestral villages in a state of relative affluence. For a number of reasons, such goals did not materialize. After a few years, many men sent home for brides, usually chosen by their parents, and, consequently, the Japanese family was transplanted to Hawaii. By 1920, the Japanese constituted 42.7% of the total territorial population. With the 1924 Oriental Exclusion Act, immigration stopped, and some movement back to Japan and mainland United States occurred. Since that time the in-migration of Caucasians and non-Oriental migrant workers has diminished their relative percentage of the population. The numbers of Japanese declined to 32.2% in 1960, and slightly less than 30% in 1970. Nonetheless, from 1900 until the last decade, the Japanese have been the dominant group numerically in Hawaii (Lind, 1967).

Such large numbers plus the geographical insularity of Hawaii facilitated the retention of traditional institutions, norms, and values. Although the immigrants had little education themselves, they were highly motivated to provide the best possible opportunity for their children. By 1960, they had the third highest median education, 12.5 years, lagging behind only the Caucasians and the Chinese (Lind, 1967). The more educated nisei (second generation) no longer were content in the rural occupations of their parents and migrated with the assistance and approval of their parents to Honolulu to continue their education or seek commercial or laboring opportunities. By 1960, 53.5% of all Japanese in Hawaii were living in metropolitan Honolulu, increasing from 9.8% in 1896 and 22.4% in 1920 (Lind, 1967).

Despite this high degree of urbanization, the indices of social disorganization have not risen commensurately. In fact, in comparison to the other ethnic categories in Hawaii, the Japanese portray impressive signs of social and emotional stability. In 1968, the Japanese-Americans made up only 7.4% of all admissions to the Honolulu Jail (Honolulu Police Department, 1968). They had the lowest rate of illegitimate births (Department of Health, 1968). In 1960, they ranked lowest in numbers receiving public welfare assistance (3.4%) (Department of Social Services, 1964). Correspondingly, in the area of mental illness they have the lowest admission rate to public and private mental hospitals (Kimmich, 1960). In terms of general health disability, they have the fewest numbers of days away from work for reasons of illness (Bennett, Tokuyama, & Bruyere, 1963). Finally, they have the lowest out-group marriage rate (17 per 100 marriages). Of the in-group marriages, they have the lowest divorce rate, 14 per 100 marriages (Lind, 1964).

The Japanese immigration to Hawaii took place during the Meiji Period, a time when Japan was undergoing rapid modernization and social change. Because these emigrants mainly originated from rural areas outside the centers of industrialization, they brought conservative traditions with them. Even today, however, the degree and quality of social change in Japan is the subject of a great deal of scholarly debate. One point of general agreement relates to the continuance of a distinctive system of social relationships which stands in marked contrast to Western cultures at corresponding levels of industrial development. While the United States has institutionalized individualism as a dominant trait, Japan has continued to stress collectivity as an organizational factor (Bellah, 1962).

In Japan, each individual is closely bound to a series of specific groups throughout his life. The family is the first of these. In a way that makes other child rearing techniques appear quite casual, filial piety, social sensitivity, and vertical loyalties are taught and developed to a very high level of conscious conformity. Other institutions adopt these same familistic norms, incorporating patterns of paternal responsibilities to those below the individual, and filial obligations to those above. These relationships are replicated and reinforced by public education as well as through norms involving relationships to peers, friends, and acquaintances. Even the occupational sphere is within the framework of the simulated kinship organization. For those in positions of permanent employment, these same themes of loyalty, interdependence, and mutual trust typify the qualities of industrial, commercial, and professional life. Only in a few areas is individualism allowed to develop and flourish. Instead, the Japanese tend to move in a limited social nexus where mutual assistance and interdependent cooperation can be carefully employed. These circumscribed relationships demand that the individual be highly sensitive to his relationship with specific others—the prime requirement being adeptness in reading the cues and responding in appropriate ways (Nakamura, 1964). Other important directives patterning behavior *(on, giri* and *ninjo)* are pertinent here and will be discussed later in the chapter. These modes of organization derived from Japan have been singled out here as being significant determinants of the positive integration and stability of the Japanese descendents in Hawaii.

## SYSTEMS OF SOCIAL RELATIONSHIPS[1]

The information reported here was collected in 1970-1971 as a collaborative research project with my husband, Frank A. Johnson. As much as possible, subjects were chosen to match the characteristics of the general Japanese-American population in Honolulu. Open-ended interviews were used, ranging in time from two to

[1] Since this report is concerned with relating alienation to certain sociocultural variables, it is necessarily descriptive in nature. As such, it cannot pause to account for each finding presented. A more detailed presentation of our methodology and findings plus reports on others' research will be published at a later date.

five hours. In addition, specific questions were asked concerning the relationships within the subject's family and kinship units as well as in his working and friendship associations. Quantitative and qualitative aspects of these relations were specifically sought. The sample included 104 families. Some of their characteristics are shown in Table 8-1.

TABLE 8-1

*Subject Population (104 Families)*

| Generation[a] | Nisei | 47% |
|---|---|---|
| | Nihan | 28% |
| | Sansei | 25% |
| Age | 45-55 years | 27% |
| | 35-45 years | 47% |
| | 25-35 years | 26% |
| Education (husband's) | College | 47% |
| | Some college | 10% |
| | High school or less | 43% |
| Occupation | Large business or professional | 25% |
| | White collar or small business | 50% |
| | Blue collar | 25% |

[a]The Japanese-Americans calculate generation level by labeling the original immigrants, the *Issei,* as the first generation. The *Nisei* are the "second generation," that is, the first generation born in the United States. *Nihan* (a contraction meaning 2½) refers to those subjects who had one parent from the first generation and one from the second. These individuals are either more like second or third generation rather than transitional between these generations. *Sansei* refers to the third generation.

The description and analysis of the social organization of the Japanese-Americans is based on the observation that a high degree of social integration operates in the small group of the individual's day-to-day relationships. The institutionalization of roles for family, kinship, and friendship relations call upon traditional values which stress the collective over self-orientation. The sacrifice of personal interests, in order to fulfill the role expectations of one's closest friends and relatives, is motivated by the internalization of traditional Japanese values. Socialization practices which stress dependency, respect for elders, consideration for others, and compassion promote the acquisition and internalization of these values at an early age. They define one's adult roles in terms of a moral commitment which transcends personal desires and gratifications. Therefore, at the level of primary relationships, a high degree of social solidarity exists. In these interactions, personal interests and those of the group closely coincide.

As one moves from primary relationships to the more impersonal secondary ones, it becomes increasingly difficult to apply collectively oriented behavior to one's social relationships. For one thing, the system of mutual expectations is less applicable, particularly if one is outside the Japanese-American group. Persons from outside the ethnic community simply do not respond to the cues in a positive or predictable manner. There is less fit between one's role definitions and performance, customarily found in close relationships, and what one faces in secondary, instrumentally-oriented relationships.

Most individuals of second and third generation have a range of acceptable behaviors to call upon, selected from both cultural systems and defined by varying degrees of mutual expectations, affectivity, and moral commitment. There is a gradient in the intensity of response beginning with the nuclear family and progressing outward to the kinship group, the peer group, and the ethnic community. This proceeds with a gradually diminishing use of traditional role behaviors along with less expectation of acceptable responses from others. When one moves outside the ethnic group into the community at large, the individual must draw upon the knowledge and experience he has gained from his partial assimilation to the middle-class American culture (in its particular Hawaiian version). These relationships outside the ethnic group lie largely in instrumental associations: occupational for adults and educational for the young. Here the individual chooses between parallel systems of behavior, one for the *Gesellschaft* or secondary relationships of his work day, another for the *Gemeinschaft* or primary relationships of his leisure time. If given a choice, the great majority of Japanese-Americans in Honolulu opt for the small ethnic-centered group where social alienation in interpersonal relationships or discontinuities from cultural norms and values are rarely experienced.

## SOCIAL NETWORKS: WHO SEES WHOM

The term network is used here as a means of describing a map of social interaction. The individual can be conceptually depicted in the center of a collection of friends and relatives. Relationships can be represented by lines radiating from the center. The social field itself is flexible, in the sense that new ties are formed while old ties can be modified or broken. In contrast to the concept of a social group, which has common aims, interdependent roles, and cohesiveness, the network has no external boundaries or, conceptually, no internal divisions (Barnes, 1954; Bott, 1957). In actuality, most Japanese-Americans make a clear distinction between close relationships, where the ties are cohesive and long-enduring, and other relationships where less solidarity exists. I have called the former the central core of the network, labeled so by the individual's diffuse allegiance to the other members of the network. However, each one in the central core is not necessarily bound to the others with the same degree of allegiance. Hence, the overall unit does not necessarily form a social group in the sociological sense. Within this social network, the quality of the relationship changes as interaction moves from the center to the periphery, as ego's commitment becomes more narrowly circumscribed and more rationalistic.

This theoretical network is concretely observable in daily life. As one observes social groupings on the street, on school campuses, in restaurants, or on the beach, the predominant impression is that the Oriental groups are homogenous. The occurrence of a mixed group of perhaps Caucasians and Orientals outside of structured situations, while not rare, is less common than observing Orientals clustered by themselves. Even in businessmen's lunch groups where one might expect to find more ethnic mixing, groups are generally ethnically homogenous. Furthermore, newcomers to the Islands find that they may form few close associations with Japanese-Americans outside the context of public or instrumental situations. Interestingly, this difficulty is encountered by some Japanese from Japan, as well as by Japanese-Americans from mainland United States.

TABLE 8-2

*Composition of the Social Network with Whom One Spends Most of His Time*

|  | Percentage |
|---|---|
| Ethnic determinant: | |
| Within the Japanese-American community | 78% |
| Outside the Japanese-American community | 22% |
| Kinship or friendship: | |
| See mostly relatives | 47% |
| Divide time equally between relatives and friends | 27% |
| See mostly friends | 20% |
| See mostly occupation or organizational associates | 5% |
| See few people outside occupation | 1% |
| Other characteristics: geographical and economic determinants: | |
| Three-generation households | 14% |
| Relatives living in the immediate neighborhood | 18% |
| Economic cooperation in family business | 11% |
| Values emphasized in socialization: | |
| Collective-centered values | 65% |
| Ego-centered values | 16% |
| Other | 19% |

The data in this study overwhelmingly support the more impressionistic judgments—namely that approximately 78% of the respondents describe their friendships as being predominately with other Japanese-Americans. Those who define their friends as being from mixed groups still show a marked preference for other Orientals. (These in-group preferences are compounded by a long tradition of Caucasian exclusiveness which exists despite the widespread myth of the Hawaiian melting pot.) However, most respondents state that they have few alternatives because of the time-consuming system of social obligations within their own group, or because of the lack of opportunity to meet others. Permeating most of these discussions is the more subtle theme that the close-knit ethnic network, although confining at times, offers the most predictable and secure environment.

High in-group preferences are a natural product of a number of social forces: demographic and historical factors, intergenerational continuity in the family system, and well defined ethnic boundaries. Historically, the plantation system clearly delineated ethnic categories into separate residential and organizational units. The transposition of elements of Meiji Japan to rural Hawaii reaffirmed in-group cohesiveness. Buddhist temples, Japanese newspapers, prefectural organizations, language schools, and aesthetic and recreational associations flourished. The resistance of the *issei* to learning English or countenancing the out-marriage of their children reinforced this segregation. Prior to the war, almost all *nisei* children attended Japanese language schools where the inculcation of traditional moral training was encouraged through their texts as well as through the demeanor of the teachers.[2] In pre-war Honolulu, some residential concentration took place, paralleling the conditions on plantations. Although the Japanese-American population is today residentially dispersed, their large numbers and presence throughout the city precludes the necessity of seeking relationships outside their own group for most institutional functions.

In Japan, the psychological focus on a limited social nexus has been described in detail by Nakamura and corroborated by nearly all scholars who survey Japanese culture. This same focus is evident in Japanese-American life in Honolulu. The family supersedes all other relationships; its central significance to the average Japanese-American is indicated by the results of this current study. Excluding their occupational relationship, 47% state that they associate predominately with relatives, while 27% divide their time approximately evenly between relatives and friends. Twenty percent see friends more than relatives, but, of these, one-half have few relatives in Honolulu and are hence not really exercising any option. Five percent limit most of their relationship to occupational or other instrumental associations. Only 1% can be termed isolated in that they see few people outside the nuclear family. In summary, it can be concluded that there is a striking tendency for the Japanese-Americans in Honolulu to associate mainly within their own ethnic group and to prefer relationships with kin.

## FAMILY, KIN, AND FRIENDS

From a structural point of view, the Japanese-American family is of an isolated nuclear type, if that is defined as being economically independent and residing in its own residential unit (Parsons, 1949). The average household size is 4.1 persons (United States Census, 1960). In the sample of 104 families reported here, only 14% live in a three-generation household, while an additional 18% have rela-

[2] See Sociology Club (1935-1963). These annual publications of student papers provide useful descriptive accounts of family life and social organization which have supplemented other historical accounts.

tives living in the immediate neighborhood. Economic cooperation in family businesses takes place in only 11% of the families. Since this is well below the 74% who spend from half to all of their free time with relatives, it can be concluded that the importance of the kinship unit is not simply a consequence of geographical propinquity or shared business concerns; rather, it is connected to cultural patterns which identify the modified extended family as an important locus for primary emotional interaction.[3]

In defining who constitutes the family, most respondents state that their immediate family is composed of spouse and children, their own parents and siblings, and their families of procreation. In other words, the central core of the kinship unit is not merely the nuclear family of procreation, but is extended to include each spouse's family of orientation. This recognition changes as the children in the nuclear family reach adulthood and marry. At that time, the immediate family is usually redefined as the spouse, their parents (if still alive) and one's children and their families of procreation. Siblings and their families of procreation usually decline in importance as the descending generation expands. However, certain relationships with favored siblings, aunts, uncles, and cousins may continue on the basis of compatibility and shared interests. Nevertheless, a principle of economy operates in these primary relationships. Because the emotional investment developed in these primary relationships is intense (by comparison with most Caucasian patterns), the numbers held in these relationships is necessarily limited.

At the central core of the network, *Gemeinschaft* relationships find their strongest expression. Bound together by strong feelings of group solidarity, the family, kin, and most intimate friends are seen frequently, almost daily, by many. Mutual aid and sympathy are given unstintingly, in terms of emotional support, advice, child care, homemaking assistance, and financial support on a noncontractual basis. A strong sense of obligation to these selected kin and friends extends over large and unspecified areas. Ideally, conflict must be avoided by each member in upholding mutual respect and consideration. Adherence to these obligations is an expression of a moral commitment of an involuntary, often unconscious nature. Conflicts and controversy, of course, occur in these relationships. Interestingly, such differences are often dealt with through silence, changes in vocal nuance, or through kinesic expression rather than by verbal arguments. Bargains are made implicitly whereby each one agrees to give a little in order to avoid open ruptures and to insure the other's cooperation in the future. (These cultural modes for

---

[3] Although statistical verification has not been used to determine the relationship between social class and the ethnic and familial networks, it is apparent from the data and from my personal acquaintance with many respondents that social class is not the most significant variable in assimilation. However, those respondents who remained independent of the kinship unit or ethnic community usually lived on the mainland for an extended period. They could be the professionals with long years of training away from the extended family, but also included are those from other occupational groups who found it necessary to spend some time away.

handling conflict are quite distinctive, but are too complex to be fully discussed here.)

As one moves from this central core to the larger kinship unit, this commitment diminishes in intensity and is supplanted by more formal mechanisms devised to maintain group solidarity. Kin at a more distant level are not considered family; they are relatives. They are seen less frequently and, ordinarily, are not relied upon for frequent mutual aid. Unless one chooses otherwise, obligations to these relatives are narrowed to attendance at large, periodic gatherings on holidays, funerals and memorial services, and other ritualized events of the life cycle.[4]

At this level of relationship, mutual obligation is formalized into a system of *kosai,* where more formally specified rules apply. Such relationships are similar to close friendships in that obligations are fulfilled in the same reciprocal manner. The amount of contact one has with friends, however, is initially purely voluntary. Also, one can choose his own friends, although there is pressure (not necessarily verbalized) from the family to seek one's friends within the ethnic community. However, once a friendship becomes established, it assumes many of the nonvoluntary characteristics of the kinship relationships. Close friendships, like kinship relationships, are characterized by periodic meeting and a methodical system of gift-giving. (Friendships can develop an intimacy and intensity that characterize those relationships in the central core of the network. In these cases, the same *Gemeinschaft* principle of nonvoluntary obligatedness and diffuse commitment operates.)

The system of mutual obligations to more distant relatives and nonintimate friends is subsumed under the *kosai.* This is defined by most respondents as their "circle of social obligations." In including relatives and friends, the *kosai* requires that one give gifts of money at funerals, weddings, graduations, births, trips, special birthdays, and illnesses. At marriage, the *kosai* is initially formed by all those who donated at the wedding and continues to expand throughout life to include new relationships. Very careful records are kept of these reciprocal obligations so that one can in the future discharge his obligation through an equivalent gift of money. The most compelling requirement is in the reciprocity of funeral obligations. These obligations are incurred toward all those in his own circle and are even extended to their close family members who often may be outside the range

---

[4] Japanese-Americans of Okinawan ancestry are grouped with those from Japan proper by the census and by all those outside the ethnic group. They are estimated to make up approximately 15% of the Japanese-American population in Hawaii. Although their proportion in my study, 15%, is too small for precise comparisons with the other Japanese-Americans, my data and the predominate opinion of the ethnic community indicate that the Okinawans have some distinctive characteristics. For one thing, primary relationships, mutual aid, and economic cooperation more frequently extend over a wider circle of collateral relatives. Second, their ethnic identity as Okinawans is probably characterized by a higher degree of commitment to the entire ethnic group, not just the central core. If this proves to be the case, the definition of the social network would have to be somewhat revised when applied to the Okinawans.

of the giver's actual acquaintanceship. An eldest son, for example, has responsibility in honoring the *kosai* of his deceased parents, particularly in regard to funeral obligations. Hence, throughout adult life, the *kosai* functions as a concrete, formal representation of a family's system of social relationships. This is maintained conscientiously, except in cases of the most serious financial reverses. Although it may consume a relatively large proportion of the family's resources, very few individuals would consider breaking this chain of reciprocities. To do so would symbolize withdrawal from one's social network and, by implication, rejection of his Japanese identity. At the very least it would imply the person's failure to meet his expected obligations and also would directly impugn the reputation of his family.

Lest the *kosai* appear superficially similar to American gift-giving customs, two distinctions should be made. First, the *kosai* is compulsory, in the respect that the individual feels that he is compelled to give in order to maintain his social identity. (Some retired individuals with reduced incomes may reluctantly choose living with a child on the mainland if they cannot afford to keep up their obligations.) Second, the value of the gift of money given on specific occasions is established by relatively inflexible rules, even to the point of allowing for inflation.

At this point, some clarification is needed. Those relationships within the central core of the network are characterized by gift-giving and some formal reciprocity. In this sense, they are part of the *kosai,* but there are far broader implications for primary relationships. These reciprocities are more flexible and spontaneous because they are based on the immediate needs of the receiver and the circumstances of the donor at the time. A high degree of obligatedness and expectation of future reciprocities are established which assume considerable psychological significance. Here one becomes emotionally indebted in his relatedness to the other; this transcends tangible reciprocity. A common example would be an individual who has been sent through college by his older brother. This would generally not be repaid monetarily, but would, rather, generate a perpetual, diffuse obligation that cannot be discharged. In contrast, the *kosai* outside the central core defines the degree of obligatedness more exactly and contractually. This may be repaid in full at the appropriate time, so that the emotional counterparts to social indebtedness do not weigh so heavily upon the individual.

Reciprocal obligation is a highly important element in Japanese culture. However complex it be for the Westerner to grasp, it is essential to understanding the diluted forms in Hawaii, not only in regard to the *kosai* but also in regard to the solidarity of the family.

Japan has been noted as being one of the few cultures which has made a clear-cut distinction between contractual behavior and behavior "undertaken as a result of individual interest or spontaneous feelings [Sugi, 1963, p. 268]." In all his vertical relationships throughout life, an individual passively incurs obligations through the benevolence of others (called, *on*). Repayment must be made contractually according to the ethic of scrupulously measured equivalence (called, *giri*) (Befu, 1958). At the same time, a noninstitutionalized system for horizontal relationships is present which allows for human desires and feelings (called, *ninjo*). This is concerned with a mutual awareness of others' emotional needs, and a noncontractual desire to satisfy and indulge the other person. In feudal Japan, *ninjo* was subordinated to *giri* in order to reduce conflict between personal desires and the demands of the social system. Hence, relationships were formalized to an astonishing degree (by Western standards) and demanded an acute awareness of loyalties and reciprocities in a hierarchical scheme governing potential action.

In Hawaii, the communication of these social demands is largely inexplicit, and the compelling, direct nature of these demands has been somewhat diluted by the acculturation process. Few Japanese-Americans can distinguish between the compulsory demands of *giri* relationships and the personal, emotional nature of *ninjo* relations. At the same time, there is a diminishing accentuation of vertical relationships at the expense of horizontal ones. Nevertheless, the concept of obligation constitutes the strongest expression of solidarity found in the operation of the social network. The *kosai* represents this reciprocal obligation, but obligations to friends and kin, however arduous at times, can be discharged with *giri*-like components. The element of human feelings receives more emphasis. The proposition that parents should be seen often, loved, and respected is unquestioningly endorsed, but it is no longer a one-way street. Mutual esteem and consideration, plus an awareness of others' needs, bilaterally permeate the parent-child relationship as well as all other primary relationships. The indebtedness is perpetual and diffuse, but has been colored with considerable affective attachment.

Obligation then, rather than being seen as a feudalistic, old-fashioned dictum, has been so permeated with the *ninjo* element that the solidarity of the family and the central core of the network has an internal perpetuation of its own, adhered to voluntarily by its members. The *on-giri* system alone would be nonaccommodative to the demands from the prevailing culture. But through the emphasis on the affectional element, *ninjo,* the mutual awareness of others, pleasing them, and avoiding hurting them, facilitates the nonconflictual functioning of a social network of primary relationships. Furthermore, the obligatory nature of *giri,* as displayed in the *kosai,* is a boundary-maintaining mechanism for one's other relationships. The Japanese-Americans thus have a readily adaptive and modifiable system which has functioned in an integrative capacity in acculturation.

Therefore, the individual may be seen to be surrounded, first, by his immediate families of procreation and orientation, which, along with a few intimate friends, constitute the central core of his social network and the source of his basic security and emotional support. Outside of this central core, he is surrounded by an expanding circle of relatives and friends, usually Japanese, which remain stable throughout life. These latter constitute obligatory relationships in terms of *kosai,* but are voluntary in terms of informal social contact. The central relationships are characterized by a *Gemeinshaft* quality (moral, organic, intimate), while the peripheral relationships are more contractual, although still formalized structurally as "personal relationships." Both types are imbued with a heavy sense of obligation and with a compelling quality resembling *giri*. However, sentiments derived from *ninjo,* particularly at the central core, color these relationships with warmth and security.

In relationships outside the ethnic group, friendships may be formed. Occasionally, such a friend might be incorporated into the central core of the network; more frequently, however, they are not. Those who are met outside the Japanese community, who are seen frequently, are generally met at work, school, or in the neighborhood. Ordinarily, such friends remain on the periphery in terms of some specific mutual area of interest, and are only loosely connected to others within the network. Also, they are not formally included in the *kosai*. Few members from other ethnic groups are included, for they usually cannot understand the inexorable, scrupulous implications of gift-giving and are unlikely to respond appropriately. (With blithe good intentions, Caucasians may easily upset their Japanese-American friends either through failure to reciprocate when given something, or, worse yet, in a rush of impulsive generosity, by giving a friend an expensive or unexpected gift that places the recipient in an impossible dilemma about how to reciprocate.)

One can see clearly that with these systems of social relationships, the individual is never alone, bereft of social support, or dependent only on the scant resources of his nuclear family. Whatever he faces in his occupation or in the impersonal, indifferent world outside, he returns to be enveloped in a close-knit, supporting world at the end of the work day.

## MECHANISMS FOR MAINTENANCE OF THE NETWORKS

One might well ask how such a world is maintained in the face of urbanization, the pressures for assimilation, and the urgency of the contemporary generation gap. Although changes are taking place between generations, and Americanization is increasing, there is a continuity in values underlying the mechanisms of socialization and social control which continue to apply at the level of primary relationships.

In the area of child rearing, a very prominent feature is that individualism, assertiveness, and independence are not singled out as desirable social traits. Instead, the values of conformity to the small group and sensitivity to the feelings of others are traits regarded as desirable and are directly instilled in the child. When asked what they considered the most ideal personality characteristics they wanted in their children, 65% of the mothers mentioned traits which can be classified under a collective orientation. Examples are: "To be considerate or compassionate of others," "To think of others before yourself," "To be respectful." Only 16% mentioned individualistic or ego-centered traits such as: "To be independent," "To find a life he is most comfortable in," or "All of my children are so different, I can't say." (Other responses from this group fell into categories not directly applicable here, such as "To be happy," "To be serious," or "To study hard.")

This collective orientation clearly incorporates the concept of *ninjo,* discussed above, where one must strive to satisfy another's emotional needs. Another behavioral characteristic, which is complementary to *ninjo,* is that of *enryo.* Although some third-generation Japanese-Americans might not recognize the term, they readily recognize its meaning. Most respondents translate it as "to hold back." More literally, as delivered in admonitions to children, it means "Don't act like a pig" or "Don't be pushy." As a formal category, it includes those traits which Westerners associate with modesty, reserve, and hesitancy to impose on others. As a normative standard, the behavioral correlate to *enryo* is a commonly encountered trait guiding the quality of the Japanese-Americans' mode of interaction.

The emphasis on collective values is not merely ideological, but is concrete and practical in everyday life. The child moves in the *Gemeinschaft* world of his parents. He is included in most of their social activities and is rarely left at home. If he must be left, a babysitter, who comes from outside the central core of the family's network, is quite rare. Most commonly, a grandmother or an aunt is brought in. Except for those who go to college on the mainland or enter the armed services, young people rarely live away from their families until marriage. This collective orientation is reinforced throughout the ethnic community. The child also has the examples of his own parents' behaviors, which exemplify this same ethic. Forces from outside the subculture have yet to interfere significantly with this basically Japanese model.

As with most parents, a serious dilemma centers around the mechanisms of social control in the disciplining of their children. The desire to underplay individualistic gratification of personal desires through stressing respect and consideration for others is coupled with the emphasis on achievement in the broader society. This gives rise to ambivalence, since the parents want their children to compete with the more verbally-assertive Caucasians. Hence, talking back or being disrespectful to parents or elders in general must be negatively sanctioned at home, but most parents realize that this discourages "speaking up" and expressing oneself in school. Therefore, an uneasy compromise is made between essentially contradictory expectations. Nevertheless, such contradictions are not dissimilar to those which the parents faced in their own maturation and from which, presumably, their own parallel systems of social relationships, norms, and values are derived. Such contradictions can be conceptualized as biculturism and testify to the tensions encumbent on the incorporation of two conflictual systems governing certain actions. As in most emigrant groups, the second and third generation display a significant degree of acculturation to the predominant culture, particularly in linguistic and motivational areas for instrumental activities. This in no way (at least in the case of Hawaiian Japanese-Americans) precludes the retention of traditional features of cultural directives which define primary relationships and intraethnic interaction.

There is a "fit," then, between certain of the norms and values learned in the home and the realistic world faced in day-to-day relationships. Hence, a high degree of social solidarity exists at this level. As one moves from these primary relationships, with their unconscious moral commitments, to the Japanese community at large, the uniformity in expectations of reciprocating behaviors continues, but it must be more formally and consciously enforced. The *kosai* is one mechanism illustrating this, but it does not apply to new or casual acquaintances. In its place, a system of etiquette stressing politeness and *enryo* is formalized, where being "pushy," assertive, or too openly competitive is criticized. Such behavior implies that an individual is exhibiting behavior outside the range acceptable to the ethnic group's normative standards.

Furthermore, these more distant relationsips cannot always be transformed into sincere and spontaneous systems of reciprocities, however high the sense of ethnic identity may be. For example, Japanese-American politicians complain that they cannot always rely on the "block-vote" of their own people. Others active in Japanese organizations criticize the presence of excessive factionalism and lack of cooperation. Essentially, more ego-centered interests begin to take precedence as one's orientation becomes affectively neutral.


## COMPROMISE BETWEEN CONFLICTING LOYALTIES

In contrast to primitive societies, where instrumental activities are integrated into the kinship system, industrial society is characterized as producing a series of conflicting loyalties between individualistic tendencies, occupational involvement, and family responsibilities. Parsons defines the nuclear family as a compromise between the familial and occupational structures, in that the head of the family, being responsible for only one small, encapsulated unit, is freed to pursue his ego-centered interests, which require social and geographical mobility. In contrast, Japan's bureaucratic system is noted for its paternalistic functions which, rather than undermining the features of loyalty and security in the family, incorporate these into its structure (Abegglen, 1958).

In Hawaii, however, Japanese-Americans move in two worlds: the competitive occupational system of the American capitalistic economy (derived from Christian, Occidental cultures) and the closeknit social network of primary relationships (derived from Confucian, Oriental patterns). How then can they compromise ego-centered occupational demands, on one hand, and the highly developed, collective-centered system of loyalties on the other? For one thing, it should be remembered that the *Gemeinschaft* relationships are limited to the central core of the network involving only a relatively limited number of people.

Also, although Orientals are now represented at all levels of Hawaii's occupational structure, such was not always the case. Because of restrictive hiring practices, Japanese-Americans traditionally sought opportunities in the professions, civil service, small business enterprises, and public education, and in many ways were not exposed in their work lives to the pressure for wholesale assimilation to Western culture. In these particular jobs, they became the dominant group; this simplified personal role performance and created little strain in loyalties toward family and subculture. Additionally, with the presence of a sizable ethnic community, the opportunity for establishing and conducting business essentially within their own ethnic community were, and still are, extensive. For all these reasons, then, relatively few Japanese-Americans have been exposed to the "dynamic" and competitive American corporate settings which do in fact demand extraordinary commitment and expect conformity of personal style toward the image of the organization. Furthermore, although this has not been studied systematically, one hears the general assumption that there may be a selective migration of those individuals with stronger ego-centered interests to greater economic opportunities on the mainland. If true, this factor would act to diminish the problem of divided loyalties in the Hawaiian, Japanese culture.

The great majority, however, remain in Honolulu and show little evidence of conflict in regard to exposure to the outside culture. Like the American nuclear family, the Japanese-Americans have considerable conjugal role segregation, with the husband's occupational role being largely divorced from family activities. Although many wives work, their occupation is almost always considered to be secondary and less important, irrespective of the nature of their jobs. The wife is required to be responsible not only for the care of the children and the performance of household tasks, but also for maintenance of the primary and secondary social obligations of the family. She is the instigator and *major domo* of the family's social network, while the husband functions as a participant. It is her responsibility to see that no one is neglected or dropped from the *kosai* because of other demands.

The social network of the average Japanese-American family is maintained on the level of highest priority by the wife and supported by the husband and children in conjunction with their instrumental activities. The fact that conflicting and divisive loyalties do not generally develop results from the only partial assimilation into the American culture and the continuous transmission of Japanese culture to the second and third generation descendents in Hawaii. Rather than being marginal (the plight of many descendents of other emigrant groups) or lost between two worlds with only a fractionated identity with either, the Japanese-Americans in Honolulu possess a very cohesive subcultural identification. They constitute the largest plurality and live in an environment manifesting considerable tolerance of ethnic differences.[5] Maintenance of traditional norms and values in the individual's private life receives considerable social support, and the effectiveness of the family in the continued transmission of their culture reconfirms the allegiance and attachment. In addition, the precedence given to a collective orientation at home, and the necessity for learning the ego-centered orientation in school gives each individual long training in the facility of switching from one behavioral world to another.

Given the high degree of integration found in Japanese-American society, which is attributed to compatibility between normative orientations and the system of ethnic interaction, the possibility comes to mind as to whether they might be alienated from the broader American society. This does not seem to be the case. For one thing, their achievement orientation corresponds closely with the middle-class American pattern (Caudill, 1952). Second, the Japanese-Americans are bicultural, living in a pluralistic society where Far Eastern people dominate in numbers, and Caucasians of Northern European origin make up far less than a majority.[6] As mentioned above, relative harmony and tolerance between groups is the rule of the day. Finally, the lieutenant governor, three of the four congressmen, and 54% of the state legislators are Japanese-Americans, by no means an indication of political alienation.

## CONCLUSIONS

This chapter has been concerned with reporting certain characteristics of Japanese-American cultural life in metropolitan Honolulu in an attempt to display the way in which social alienation may not affect this group. Information abbreviated from a larger study of a hundred and four families residing in the community has been analyzed in terms of their social relationships, their system of obligation, and their dominant values. The experience of personal alienation has been left unexamined; data on experience of this sort are available, but, in interest of economy, are not presented here. Social alienation is defined here as a series of discontinui-

[5] The Japanese attack on Pearl Harbor had a great impact on the Japanese-Americans in Honolulu. For one thing, prejudice against them was blatantly intensified. All Japanese cultural organizations were closed: language schools, clubs, newspapers, and Buddhist temples. However, they never were subject to wholesale evacuation as were their counterparts on the mainland. Furthermore, the success of the *nisei* soldiers in the European campaigns later in the war considerably modified anti-Japanese prejudice. Wholesale rejection by the *nisei* of their Japanese heritage proved to be a temporary phenomenon. Then too, many returning veterans used the G. I. Bill to move into secure middle-class positions from which they occupy leadership positions today (see Murphy, 1954).

[6] Although the Caucasians of Northern European ancestry (haoles) are a minority group, they nevertheless provide a point of reference signifying the American culture. Whether their life style is accepted or rejected by the individual Japanese-American, the Caucasians represent the "moderns" in a continuum where the polar position belongs to the *issei*.

ties in primary and secondary relationships and incompatibility with the prevailing norms and values.

These conclusions have been based on the large majority who choose a mode of interaction which is seen as derivative of their Japanese heritage. Hawaii is a particularly favorable environment for the preservation of such continuities. Since the emphasis has been placed on systems of social relationships and supporting norms and values rather than on psychological adaptation, no attention has been given to the confining or, possibly, conflicting demands such a system makes on some individuals. As would be expected, the nonconformist has difficulties with the social restraints inherent in such group solidarity. (The fact that few of these individualistic types were encountered in the sample is probably due to eliminating mixed marriages—assuming that the nonconformist is more likely to marry outside the group.) By limiting the sample to families where both parents were Japanese and by choosing "normal" families without social or emotional deviance, an optimal or "rosy" view has been presented. However, much of the research of urban American life is problem-oriented or deriving from social or psychological deviance. These approaches should be counter-balanced with studies relating to integration and positive adaptation to urban life by a modal population. In any case, population statistics on social deviance attest to a low incidence of social alienation in terms of crime and divorce rates, need for public assistance, or mental hospitalization.

The Japanese-Americans have generally been able to preserve the collectively-oriented Japanese values and norms concerned with the regulation of family life. The preservation of a highly integrated central core of relationships is evident in most of the families surveyed in this study. Relationships which are peripheral to this central core are also endowed with an extremely carefully administered series of reciprocal interactions guaranteeing continuity of relationships *(kosai)*. The sense of obligatedness to one's family, friends, and relatives is exceedingly explicit and operates to promote security, mutual aid, and reciprocity in social relationships. The affectional characteristic of *ninjo* has also been discussed as cementing relationships within the central core. They have maintained well-defined ethnic boundaries in their social relationships and have been able to create a close-knit social network where mutual expectations and emotional support are complementary. A system of mutual obligations reaffirms these allegiances to a limited social nexus. Furthermore, socialization practices instill a collective orientation in contrast to an ego-centered pursuit of self-interest. For these reasons, most Japanese-Americans have been able to avoid socially alienating experiences characteristic of modern urban society.

## ACKNOWLEDGMENT

I am indebted to my husband, Frank A. Johnson, for his careful readings, suggestions, and invaluable assistance in the preparation of this chapter. Gordon Bowles, Michael Freedman, and Glynn Cohcrane also were of assistance in commenting on the work. The responsibility for the content, however, is entirely my own.

REFERENCES

Abegglen, J. *The Japanese factory: Aspects of its social organization.* Glencoe, Ill.: Free Press, 1958.

Barnes, J. A. Class and committees in a Norwegian island parish. *Human Relations,* 1954, *7,* 39-58.

Befu, H. Gift-giving in a modernizing Japan. *Monumento Nipponica,* 1958, *23,* 445-456.

Bellah, R. Values and social change in modern Japan. *Asian Cultural Studies,* 1962, No. 3 (Oct.), 13-56.

Bennett, C., Tokuyama, G., & Bruyere, P. Health of Japanese Americans in Hawaii. *Public Health Reports,* 1963, *78,* 753-762.

Bott, E. *Family and social network.* London: Tavistock, 1957.

Caudill, W. Japanese-American personality and acculturation. *Genetic Psychology Monographs,* 1952, *45,* 3-102.

Department of Health. *Annual reports.* 1968.

Department of Social Services. Characteristic of recipients receiving general assistance, 1964.

Diamond, S. The search for the primitive. In I. Galdston (Ed.), *Man's image in medicine and anthropology.* New York: International Universities Press, 1963.

Goode, W. *World revolution and family patterns.* New York: Free Press, 1970.

Honolulu Police Department. *Annual reports,* 1968.

Kimmich, R. Ethnic aspects of schizophrenia in Hawaii. *Psychiatry,* 1960, *23,* 97-102.

Lind, A. Interracial marriage as affecting divorce in Hawaii. *Sociology and Social Research,* 1964, *49,* 17-26.

Lind, A. *Hawaii's people.* (3rd ed.) Honolulu: University of Hawaii Press, 1967.

Murphy, T. *Ambassadors in arms.* Honolulu: University of Hawaii Press, 1954.

Nakamura, H. *Ways of thinking of eastern people.* Honolulu: East-West Center Press, 1964.

Parsons, T. The social structure of the American family. In R. Anshen (Ed.), *The family: Its function and destiny.* New York: Harper, 1949. Pp. 173-201.

Redfield, R. *The primitive world and its transformation.* Ithaca, N. Y.: Cornell University Press, 1953.

Rosow, I. Intergenerational relationships: Problems and proposals. In E. Shanas & G. Streib (Eds.), *Social structure and the family: Generation relations.* Englewood Cliffs, N. J.: Prentice-Hall, 1965.

Sociology Club of the University of Hawaii. *Social process in Hawaii.* 1935-1963.

Southall, A. *Social change in modern Africa.* New York: International African Institute, 1961.

Sugi, M. The concept of ninjo. In. J. W. Bennett & I. Ishino (Eds.), *Paternalism in the Japanese economy.* Minneapolis: University of Minnesota Press, 1963. Pp. 267-272.

United States Census of Populations. 1960.

Winch, R. Some observations on extended familism in the United States. In R. Winch & L. Goodman (Eds.), *Selected studies in marriage and the family.* New York: Holt, 1968. Pp. 127-138.

Wirth, L. Rural-urban differences. *On cities and social life.* Chicago: University of Chicago Press, 1964. Pp. 221-225.

# Chapter 9

# Freedom, Order, and Alienation

## Paul Meadows
### State University of New York

*We are not very reliably at home in the interpreted world.*
—Rilke

## THE ALIEN AND THE NATIVE: TOWARD A NEW VIEW OF THE SOCIAL

Almost without exception, the voluminous literature on alienation presents a clinical view: alienation as a symptomatic, disturbed, wasteful, inappropriate, thoroughly (and often nostalgically) unhappy human condition, destructive of established values but somehow lastingly linked to human values. Historically, it is clear that what began as an emancipating metaphor has become an imprisoning symbol, thus, once again bearing witness to the unfortunate career pattern of metaphors generally in social thought and practice. As captive symbol, it has become the stomping ground of stratigraphical semanticists, the wailing wall of the disenchanted intellectuals of literary and social criticism, the rallying slogan of the professional problem-solvers rushing like volunteer firemen to put out the blaze.

In this brief discussion I propose to return the discussion of alienation to its original home—to the fresh, metaphoric condition of its original conception. In so doing I shall seek to turn the usual discussion of the concept on its head, to reverse the customary in favor of the initial meaning, to seek in such incongruity the

social insight of the native version: in sum, to restore alienation by means of etymological and philosophical primitivism to its rightful place as one of the major
revolutionary concepts of the last two centuries.

Such a large-scale effort must, in so short a space as this, necessarily be sketchy.
It must also be unduly assertive, even formalistic; and it must, to begin with,
be philosophically simplistic. It must start with the underlying theoretical concerns,
premises, issues, and implications which form the essential context of so ambitious
an enterprise. In so doing, however, I hope that this discussion, which must appear
as naive intellectual conceit, may be able to take on the revolutionary cogency of
the alienation concept itself.

## BACKGROUND CONSTRUCTS OF THE ALIENATION THEME

The literature of social theory conventionally centers on certain fundamental concerns. These may, with obvious limitation and omissions, be identified as
(1) concern with the nature of "the social" and "the self," (2) concern with the
nature of social origins, and (3) concern with the nature of social structure.

In the first concern, there has been preoccupation, on the one hand, with
the nature of the social bond, that is, with the problems raised by its reenforce-
ment and its weakening (the nomic and the anomic problems) and on the other
hand, with the identity and integrity of the self, that is, with the problems raised
by its freedom and its control; in the language of anthropologist W. I. Thomas, the
temperamental as against the characterological problems of the self.

In the second concern, there has been preoccupation, on the one hand, with
the source of the social bond, that is, with the problems raised by its presumed
givenness as against its presumed creation (the datum versus the contract views of
the source of "the social," and, on the other hand, with the source of the social
act, that is, with the problems raised by presumed originative direction (the view
of "the social" as imposed by divinity, nature, history, force, and so on) as against
the view of "the social" as immanent and emergent.

In the third concern, there has been preoccupation, on the one hand, with
the status of social forms, that is, with the problems raised by the place, operations,
and sanctions of authority (the view which opts for heteronomy of and conformism
with "the social" as against the view which accents the autonomy and privatism of
the self), and, on the other hand, with the change of social forms, that is, with the
problems raised by their dynamics (the appeal to collective tradition as against the
appeal to personal experience).

These three paramount concerns of social theory generally start with certain
philosophical premises. In the first case, the focus on the ontological status of "the
social" and of the self entails either a sociologistic or a solipsistic premise: the primitive conception of man as *"socius"* or as "man alone"–*solus ipse esse.* In the second

case, the focus on the nature of social origins stipulates a position as to the historical status of "the social," either as a given world-ground of existence (as in the concept of social being) or as historical product of social transaction (as in the concept of social becoming). In the third case, the focus on the nature of social structure predicates a position as to the normative status of "the social": a first position which accepts the primacy and priority of either the organizational or the personalistic aspects of human experience.

Each set of premises formulates separate intellectual issues. The first set, with its value orientation to the nature of "the social" and of the self, raises the issue of the primacy of either one or the other. The second, with its value orientation as to the nature of social origins, raises the intellectual issue of the directionality of "the social." The third, with its value orientation as to the nature of social structure, raises the intellectual issue of the authority of "the social."

These three sets of major concerns of social theory are characterized by obvious and serious implications not only for human thought but also for human action. (1) Each set propounds a major value choice for the social theorist and human actor. (2) Each set is rooted in the ancient theorem of human nature: the *homo duplex* theorem—*homo internus* and *homo externus*. (3) Each set involves a major philosophical orientation: the social thesis bound to some variety of philosophical orientation: the social thesis bound to some variety of philosophical idealism (i.e., the whole is greater than, better than, different from the sum of its parts, which it also shapes if not indeed determines); the self thesis bound to some variety of philosophical empiricism (i.e., the parts as primary data which by contrivance or convention may be seen as forming or constituting a whole, or, as in contemporary argot, a system). (4) Each set involves for the social theorist or the human actor a major ideological commitment: in the case of the social thesis, to sociological romanticism (viz., the esthetic or religious or political primacy of "the social" in all of its dimensions and all of its forms); in the case of the self thesis, to sociological individualism (viz., the creative energy of the autonomous, transacting human being). (5) All three sets formulate a dialogical situation in which advocates become adversaries, a dialogical situation whose pattern of interaction spiraling toward irreconcilable conflict can be transcended only by conversion into a dialectical situation with its search for synthesis.

This last comment forms the basis for the present proposal: to seek transcendence of the duality and inevitable polarity of the dialogical discussion of our major concerns by a reversal of a concept crucial to all three sets of concerns: to reverse the definition and conception of alienation which see it as a residuum of social interaction: instead, to see it as the proto-process of all things social, as the world-ground not only of "the social," but also of the social self. I am proposing, in other words, to set the discussion of our common concerns about the nature of the human condition in the context of alienation as the voluntaristic action of the self.

## ALIENATION AS A PRIMITIVE CONSTRUCTION OF SOCIAL REALITY[1]

What I am proposing is to situate the idea of alienation in another context of consideration, partly historical, partly sociological, a context which holds that alienation is indeed the world-ground of our social being, that the very achievement of a social existence cannot occur without it, that it is the proto-process of all social experience at any level of abstraction and personalization, that it is the source and background of all our social forms. This contextual view sees alienation as a primary not residual social process. Alienation is viewed thus as a primitive construction of social reality, a construction which has both personal and collective dimensions.

*Alienate,* we are told, means "to transfer the ownership of something to another person." This occurs, we are advised by the etymologists, only "by the act of the owner." The intentional, voluntary act is central to the understanding of alienation.

Durkheim (1953), in a famous lecture on Rousseau, found in Rousseau an important guideline which expresses this human, this very primitive act, creating the very possibility of social existence. Said Rousseau: "Find a form of association which will defend and protect with the whole common force the person and goods of each associate and in which each, while uniting with all, may still obey himself alone, and remain as free as before." Commenting on this injunction, Durkheim (1933) observed: "Such an association can result only from a contract by which each member *alienates* himself with all his rights to the community [p. 98]." Here, Durkheim asserts, "is the true foundation of society." He adds: "By this contract, each individual will vanishes into a common general will [p. 98]." In markedly Rousseauan terms, Durkheim proceeds to point out: "Since the alienation was effected unreservedly, no member has a right to complain. Thus the anti-social tendency inherent in each individual simply because he has an individual will is nullified [p. 98]."

This compensation for this voluntary act of surrender and attachment—this "alienation of my person"—is "the assurance that we shall be protected by the full force of the social organization against the individual encroachments of others [Durkheim, 1933, pp. 99-100]." This process of "abdication"—Durkheim (1933) uses the word synonymously with "alienation [p. 103]"—is an objective process,

---

[1] I should like to acknowledge with great gratitude my indebtedness for many of the insights and the Durkheim references in this section of the chapter to an unpublished manuscript, "Alienation, the Objective Process," by my friend and colleague, Professor Robert E. Morrison, Empire State College.

generative of all "objectification" of social experience. Indeed, failure to engage
in abdication is, in fact, anti-alienation; primary deviance is nonsurrender to the
common will. It is also a reclaiming of the individual right from the collective.

The crux of the matter is the paradox that the individual, as Durkheim (1933)
said, "is the sole organ of society since he is the sole creator. However, it is necessary to submerge him in the mass, in order to modify his nature as much as possible and prevent him from acting as an individual. Anything of a nature to facilitate
individual action must be regarded as a danger [p. 108]."

At the heart of "the social," indeed, of the creation of "the social," certainly integral to its continuity, is the proto-process of the alienating action of the individual human being. Asserts Durkheim (1933): "Social solidarity, in short, results from the laws that attach the individuals to the group and not to each other.
They are linked to each other because they are linked to the community, that is,
alienated within it [p. 112]." In other words, to alienate, to engage in the acts of
alienation, is the proto-process of becoming, and to have become, social. The individual human being is, in this action of primary alienation, not alienated from "the
social"; he is in fact alienated to it. It is a social act, creates social action, and thus
fuses the individual with the thus-created collective.

It is withal a moral act. "Everything," observed Durkheim (1933), "which
forces man to take account of other men is moral, anything which forces him to
regulate his conduct through something other than the striving of his ego is moral,
and the morality is as solid as those ties are numerous and strong [p. 398]." To
act socially, to act morally is to engage in alienating action, and can occur only if
and as we thus engage. Alienation is a process of objectifying and rendering "present in the objective world that which is individually contained [Durkheim, 1953,
pp. 25-26]." The alienating act is an act of obligation to the thus-created collective. "Following the collectivity, the individual forgets himself for the common
end and his conduct is oriented in terms of a standard outside himself." It is to such
standards, says Durkheim, "that the individual alienates himself." To use our contemporary term, "socialization" is the process of voluntaristic alienating of the self,
of the ego becoming external to itself. "Man alone" creates "social man," "species
man," other-than-individual man.

Herein lies the dangerous and the eternal paradox: that the credentialing, the
validating, the ground of existence are to be found in the objective social reality
created by individual human beings thus alienating themselves. The social, the cultural, the collective—these are only some of the names—are the behavioral products
of the alienating ability of man from which he does not (and, then, only with severe
hazards) divorce himself. The private existence becomes pervasively social. Dialec-
tically speaking, personality as an entity, like society, becomes the fusion product
and process of self-alienation.

## POSTALIENATION: SOME CAREER PATTERNS OF A PROCESS

Following Durkheim, thus, we view the social reality of man as deriving from the irony of man's voluntary self surrender issuing in social bondedness: the alienating action of man makes possible his social action. The autonomous self creates the heteronomous society.

There are, however, lastingly important legacies of this two-valued orientation of human beings. The alienating self establishes the reciprocating "other." "The social" originates in a transaction; it is an exchange process: there is a *quid pro quo,* —liberty for security, freedom for order, self-sufficiency for services, autonomy for utility. "The social" begins in exchange; it continues in exchange, but with a significant limitation: the inherent necessity of a balanced exchange: ego gratifications and realization, on the one hand, collective normations, on the other. The pattern is utopian: the achievement of a just social existence in which the bond to the collective is formed and strengthened at the same time that the bond to the self is safeguarded and maintained. From this continuous and essential transaction comes the enormous and intricate structuralization of stable human existence: the emergence, elaboration, and development of institutional patterns of social existence: culture. But also from it comes the primary socialization of the human being: the formation and articulation of personal patterns of social existence: personality.

This unceasing process is one of uneasy equilibrium, continuously threatened by emerging imbalances of the exchange process: the never-ending thrust toward greater and greater collective normation, demanding conformism and the equally demanding pressure for ego gratification and realization: conformism and privatism: the externalities of collective expectations, the internalities of autonomous identity and integrity: nomic collectivism, nomic privatism. The first, because it is social, requires and acquires authority and power; the second, because it is personal, insists

### TABLE 9-1

*Patterns of Primary Alienation*

| Self-orientation | Collective orientation | |
| --- | --- | --- |
| | Privatistic | Conformistic |
| Privatistic | 1. for example,<br>self-identity mechanisms,<br>self-integrity mechanisms | 3. for example,<br>personal motivations,<br>moral normations |
| Conformistic | 2. for example,<br>belief systems,<br>primary group loyalties | 4. for example,<br>social controls,<br>primary group expectations,<br>ethical normations |

on liberty and freedom, literally, on the removal of restraints and on the capacities to act. The transactional arts of self-alienation create a continuously variable arrangement of conformistic and privatistic patterns of human social adjustment, illustrated in Table 9-1.

These patterns of primary alienation enable the development of public patterns of social existence which bind, in a community of will and sentiment, the orientations of the self and the collective, and which do so in terms of those integrants of social existence, "order," and "freedom." The variable patterns of order in primary alienation are illustrated in Tables 9-2 and 9-3, in which the patterning possibilities are stated ideologically in terms of authority and power.

TABLE 9-2

*Ideological Patterns of Order in Primary Alienation*

|  | Power | |
| --- | --- | --- |
| Authority | Bond to the self | Bond to the collective |
| Bond to the self | 1. for example, individualism, anarchism, decentralism, personalism | 3. for example, traditionalism, constitutionalism, contractualism, professional ethics |
| Bond to the collective | 2. for example, pluralism, conservatism due process of law, of power, of administration | 4. for example, monism, corporatism, elitism, totalism |

In the same manner, the variable patterns of freedom in primary alienation are stated ideologically in Table 9-3.

TABLE 9-3

*Ideological Patterns of Freedom*

|  | Collective orientation | |
| --- | --- | --- |
| Self-orientation | Liberty | Freedom |
| Liberty | 1. for example, anarchism, classic individualism | 3. for example, welfare stateism, socialism |
| Freedom | 2. for example, classic liberalism | 4. for example, totalitarianism |

Earlier it was stressed that primary alienation is a process of uneasy equilibrium, involving a constant searching and adjusting movement between self-orientation and collective normation. The cybernetic metaphor can be exploited to portray the mobile equilibrium maintained by this process, as in Diagrams I and II.

**DIAGRAM I**

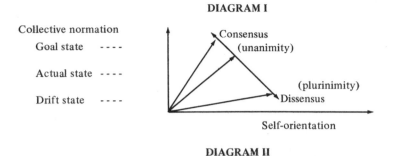

**DIAGRAM II**

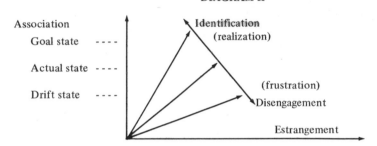

Perhaps because "the social"—the "external" reality created by the action of primary alienation—is indeed externalistic, as Durkheim insisted, it has been both the object of multidisciplinary reporting and analysis by the sciences and the target of multidimensional engineering and technology: we not only know more

**TABLE 9-4**

*Institutional Patterns of Primary Alienation*

| Self-orientation | Collective orientation | |
| --- | --- | --- |
| | Bond to the self | Bond to the collective |
| Bond to the self | 1. for example, role selection and identification, personal life style, situated self perception | 3. for example, social values, social beliefs and sentiments, social interaction patterns |
| Bond to the collective | 2. for example, social attitudes, consensual processes, social control mechanisms | 4. for example, social norms, culture complexes and patterns, authority patterns, power structure |

about this reality, but it establishes its suzerainty over ourselves through a huge variety of institutional demands and claims, as suggested in Table 9-4.

## POSTALIENATION: THE REJECTION OF PRIMARY ALIENATION

I have repeatedly stressed the salient fact of primary alienation, the uneasy equilibrium created and maintained by the transactional character of the alienating action. This is the elliptical swing between self-orientation and collective normation.[2] Systems of ethics, grounding their source of claim and canon in one or the other of these polarities, reflect the constant tension inherent in primary alienation. Thus, the stress of collective ethics, as, for example, in Rousseau, Kant, Marx, Durkheim, is laid on the obligatory nature of the bond to the collective. The stress of ego-oriented ethics, as, for instance, in hedonisms of various sorts: Benthamite utilitarianism no less than contemporary ecstatics (East or West), accent the pleasure-rewardfulness of the bond to the self. In between are varieties of interactional ethics, as, for example, in neo-Freudianisms, designed to find in compromise formations elements of both pleasure and obligation which shape cogent acceptance of bondedness. The evaluating self and the normative collective, however, meet in all of the systems of ethical thought in continuous uneasy equilibrium: the first, judging and being judged in terms of effectiveness; the second, judging and being judged in terms of efficiency; the ethics of "emotion" and the ethics of "reason." The "tipping point," to use an inadequate but telling metaphor, remains the state of gratification and realization of the alienating self. In primary alienation, the action of alienation is tentative and evaluative: the transaction must yield a con-

**TABLE 9-5**

*Patterns of Withdrawal from Primary Alienation*

| Self-orientation | Collective orientation | |
|---|---|---|
| | Bond to the self | Bond to the collective |
| Bond to the self | 1. for example, varieties of neurosis, varieties of psychosis, despair, despondency, indifference | 3. for example, utopian hope, ethnicistic or class identifications, millenialism |
| Bond to the collective | 2. for example, anxiety, guilt, anger, hostility, extropunitiveness | 4. for example, culticism, sectarianism, situated intimacy, primary sensitivity systems |

[2] I am using the word "normation" in place of a word perhaps more familiar but more awkward, "normatization." It is used as an inclusive generic term for all forms of normative action.

dition and process of basic acceptance. Basic acceptance remains as the "beginning" and the "end," both in a chronological and teleological sense, of the transactions of primary alienation. In other words, basic and authentic acceptance is both the beginning of primary alienation and the source of its termination.

For, if the alienating self finds that the transactions of alienation have brought a condition and process of unacceptable, unbearable, unrewarding social existence, one direction of response is the development of patterns of withdrawal, their destinies to be determined. The possible patterns of withdrawal from alienation are suggested, and only suggested, in Table 9-5. Note that the typology stipulates the continuing presence of both the bond to the self and the bond to the collective in some condition of strength and/or negativity.

The preceding typological schema makes it clear that withdrawal from primary alienation generates an extensive range of options of adjustment: from (1) complete withdrawal from "the social" (as in schizophrenia, an involutional alienation, so to speak, thoroughly and often irretrievably privatistic), to (2) emotional (and often irrational) reaction-formations which acknowledge, at one extreme, and which attack, at another, sources of hurt and damage that may prove, indeed, to be the self (as in guilt) or "the social" (as in violence), to (3) undefined, future-bound, and collective-oriented objects of hope and expectation, and, finally, to (4) the adoption of group situations as objects and occasions of withdrawal from the endangering wider worlds of "the social." The main theme running throughout is indeed withdrawal from the larger society of the empirical world: whether to the *Gemeinschaften* of psychotic illusion or to the *Gemeinschaften* of microsocial reality. In between these two extremes, the future, capable of rich endowment of personalized hopes and faith, orients the withdrawing self, generating an abundant yield of gratifications. In all cases, protest is the passion that spins the various plots of withdrawal from primary alienation.

TABLE 9-6

*Patterns of Surrogate Alienation*

| Self-orientation | Collective orientation | |
| --- | --- | --- |
| | Bond to the self | Bond to the collective |
| Bond to the self | 1. for example, detachment, compartmentalization, creative leisure | 3. for example, bureaucratic ritualism, false personalization, masked role performance |
| Bond to the collective | 2. for example, over-socialization, split-level role behavior, masked deviance, dramatistic forms: farce, satire, etc., escapist leisure | 4. for example, penal confinement, involuntary hospitalization, imprisonment, total institutionalism, ideological authoritarianism |

But withdrawal is only one direction which the rejection of primary alienation may take. Another direction is determined by the weight of "the social" in the behavioral adjustment of the alienating self. Just as privatistic protest underlies and indeed drives the withdrawal patterns, so conformistic coercion underlies and drives the development of what may be called surrogate alienation, with all of its varieties of coerced conformity. The possible patterns of surrogate alienation are suggested, and suggested only, in Table 9-6.

This typological schema of surrogate alienation stipulates the presence of involuntariness in the action of the alienating self. Coercive conformism to "the social" and by "the social" and, indeed, as much as possible for "the social" is the passion that spins these various plots. Strategies for the inducement of such inauthentic acceptance range from (1) retreatism "elected" by the self, to (2) separatism, which overtly accepts the social form, as in oversocialization, or which covertly engages in suppressed or tabooed deviances, or which pretensefully employs a double language of expression, as in satire, to (3) acquiescence, which identifies at some level of rationalization with ritualism or which manipulates role styles in terms of some sort of private rationale, and, finally, to (4) submissiveness, which tentatively or resignedly accepts the imposition of coercive conformism in either its withdrawal or ideological forms (as in involuntary confinement to hospital or prison or in racistic authoritarianism).

Surrogate alienation insists upon some amalgam of authority and power. It ranges from brainwashing to naked force, with intermediate stops at privatized protest, as in split-level role behavior or concealed deviancies, and includes public ceremonialism which imposes a legitimate model of "due process" or "appropriate" form in the name of efficiency or some irreducible minimum of order, as in bureaucratic ritualism. Social control processes pervade the entire grid of surrogate alienations. Their tenure hinges not so much on merit as on transcendent or, in any case, on overriding public interest or welfare. Inauthentic freedom is purchased in the name of legitimized power. In Marxian terminology, surrogate alienation presents classic instances of "false consciousness."

However, withdrawal from alienation and from surrogate alienation, it must be emphasized, represent basic rejection of primary alienation, that is, of the voluntary alienating action of the self which creates a much-desired, bargained-for "social." The first may be thought of as privatistic rejection because the direction and the variable forms of withdrawal both stem from and find their ultimate sanctions in the protestive self, seeking their inspiration and their canons of acceptance in the maintenance of freedom in some form and at some level of the alienating self. The second may be thought of as conformistic rejection because the alienating self, by virtue of a rationale of hopelessness, or helplessness, or even an untouched core of private values unrealizable in the freer forms of apparent public acceptance, inauthentically "accepts" the conditions and processes of coercive conformity.

These forms of rejective alienation, however, do not tell the whole story of the alienating self. They constitute only some of the aftermath of primary alienation. Other aspects of the sequentiae of primary alienation were detailed earlier in these pages as part of the portrayal of "postalienation." There, the enormous ingenuity of the alienating process was highlighted, just as in the discussion of patterns of withdrawal from alienation attention was called to the protestive theme that runs throughout the variable forms of response to the thus-created conditions and processes of social existence.

Here, then, are the two dimensions of the alienating self that need to be looked at again, this time in the context of what I am calling "derivative alienation." For here the inventive and the protestive self returns, after the wastelands of inauthentic alienation, to the possibilities of a new level and of new forms of creative alienation: a new search and seizure of the mythology of the eternal return which seeks, in the chaos of rejection and the fertility of surrender—to paraphrase Nietzsche—the creation of dancing stars of social reality, the enactment of man's fate.

## DERIVATIVE ALIENATION: SOME CAREER PATTERNS OF A PROCESS

"To alienate is to transfer the ownership of something to another person"—"by the act of owner." Like primary alienation, derivative alienation starts with the voluntary transfer of something owned, something of the self, by the self. But there is, this time, a difference: the difference that the past makes: the past of cultural experience, of institutional forms, of private meanings, of the full range of human existence generated by the polymorphic encounter with the thus-created social reality. It is also the difference the future makes: those edges of experience which lie along the "not yet," but which also lie along the "no longer." Derivative alienation is present experience interpenetrated both by the protestive past and the inventive future.

In derivative alienation, the alienating self discovers that he is not a captive of his past as were primitive, archaic, and classical men, not caught in the encirclements of eternal return tightly drawn with no exits. He is free because of the essential character of his existence as an alienating human being. He is free to create ever-new orders of social reality from the raw materials of his socialization experience, just as in primary alienation he was free to create ever-new orders of social reality personality and culture—from the raw materials of original nature. It is not an infinite freedom, whether primary or derivative, for finite being does not create infinite becoming. The pattern of creation is both one of push and pull: the push of unsatisfying, intolerable, incomplete, protestive alienation and the pull of gratifying, fulfilling inventive alienation. It is the essentially revolutionary discovery that alienating man is himself "the new creation."

The finiteness of derivative alienation is defined in the parameters of the earlier alienation: the dimensions of privatism and conformism, of freedom and order. But, following Mannheim, to these we must now add the powerful parameters of utopia and ideology, literally of the substance of things hoped for, the evidence of things not yet seen. These parameters echo the protest experiences of the past just as they reflect the inventive possibilities of the future. The alienating self gives up to "the social" his memories of the impossible past and his dreams of the possible future. It is a surrender as informed as it is hopeful, as wise with what has been as it is passionate about what might be. The burden of the past is lightened, and continuously lightened, with the dreams of the future. Knowledge and skill combine with imagination to transfer to "the social" a new imagery of existence, a counter-existential dream.

Change, because of the large role played by involvement and commitment, dominates the landscape of derivative alienation. Reflecting the utopian and ideological dimensions of intentional change, protest and invention enter into and shape the various possible patterns of change action, as illustrated in Table 9-7.

TABLE 9-7

*Patterns of Social Change in Derivative Alienation*

| | Collective orientation | |
|---|---|---|
| Self-orientation | Utopian | Ideological |
| Utopian | 1. for example, futurism | 3. for example, reformism |
| Ideological | 2. for example, developmentalism | 4. for example, revolutionism |

As in primary alienation, here the dimensions of privatism and conformism remain as determining directional variables in the contouring of social existence. As the following typological schema (Table 9-8) of social patterns of derivative alien-

TABLE 9-8

*Social Patterns of Derivative Alienation*

| | Collective orientation | |
|---|---|---|
| Self-orientation | Privatistic | Conformistic |
| Privatistic | 1. for example, art, deviance, primary group experiences culticism, sectarianism | 3. for example, cultural invention, institutional innovation, social movements |
| Conformistic | 2. For example, familism, professionalism, social services systems, subcultures | 4. for example, collective ethics, elitism, social planning systems, counterculture |

ation suggests, there is a sizable shift to the social sectors of existence: the Durkheimian orientation is markedly manifest but, perhaps, with less coercive constraint, for internalization of collective expectations plays a more decisive role, and the pathogenic "fall-out" is thus greatly reduced. The movement is toward structuralizations of stability-in-change.

The preceding typological schema suggests that derivative alienation generates a developmental continuum of adjustment behaviors, ranging from (1) internally oriented options of social behavior, to (2) group identifications and involvement, to (3) collective efforts at collective problem-solving, and to (4) the adoption of collective systems of change agency and advocacy. Levels and intensities of commitment to change characterize the social climate of derivative alienation.

The orientation ultimately to change agency and advocacy is mediated by the personal patterns of derivative alienation; the alienating self becomes the active center of change facilitation, as illustrated in Table 9-9.

### TABLE 9-9

*Personal Patterns of Derivative Alienation*

| Self-orientation | Collective orientation | |
| --- | --- | --- |
| | Bond to the self | Bond to the collective |
| Bond to the self | 1. for example, patterns of self esteem, nuclear role definitions | 3. for example, organizational role behaviors, civic participation, pattern of social commitment |
| Bond to the collective | 2. for example, social attitude-value systems, normative decision making patterns | 4. for example, group identification and commitment, totalistic collective acceptance frames |

Clearly, the continuum swings from (1) the adoption and development of self and role patterns, to (2) the adoption of social normations in attitudes and decisions, to (3) commitment to organizational and community participations, and (4) complete identification with collective ideologies and collective social situations. "man alone," in primary alienation, creates "social man"; but "social man," in derivative alienation, creates "collective man."

The collective accent becomes sharper and louder in the ongoing derivative alienation, so much so that it sometimes echoes the unhappiness of the older and nostalgic complaints sounded in the conventional literature on alienation. Obviously, there is always, in derivative as in primary alienation, the possibility of sociological romanticism prodding and precipitating some kind of sociological individualism. Be that as it may, there is no escaping the clearly collective dimensions of social existence at the level of derivative alienation: the alienating self becomes, for better or worse, "sociological man." The manner in which derivative alienation assists and promotes this development is suggested in Table 9-10.

TABLE 9-10

*Institutional Patterns of Derivative Alienation*

| Self-orientation | Collective orientation | |
|---|---|---|
| | Bond to the self | Bond to the collective |
| Bond to the self | 1. for example, role stabilization, institutional identification and involvement | 3. for example, institutional value systems, institutional interaction systems, organizational ethos |
| Bond to the collective | 2. for example, institutional commitment, participating involvements, professionalisms, science | 4. for example, institutional norms, institutional authority and power systems |

Here again is the familiar spectrum shift from (1) role and institutional definition, to (2) participating involvement and commitment, to (3) crystallization of institutional valuations and interactions, and to (4) institutional normative and power structuralization. These sociologistic modes describe an orbit of alienating man into a social world which he may, indeed, not want in time to claim but which, in time, completely claims him.

For once in this alienating orbit, the self remains in orbit, perhaps at times responding to its own autonomous guidance system, perhaps relying at times on inertial momentum, but more likely, most of the time, responsive to master guidance systems of the collective which monitor, direct, and correct the flight pattern of his existence. The metaphor is used to emphasize the belief that modern alienating man is outward bound in a fashion and at a tempo undreamed of in the tentative and hopeful explorations of primary alienation. If, as I believe, alienating man is indeed "the new creation," his triumphs at the derivative level may, in time, assuage the memories of the tragedies and traumas at the primary level. However, to this end somehow he must come to terms with the fact, haunting and disturbing but ever insistent, that, as Rilke observed, he is not and perhaps never will be "very reliably at home in the interpreted world."

## REFERENCES

Durkheim, E. *Montesquieu and Rousseau. Forerunners of Sociology.* Ann Arbor: University of Michigan Press, 1960.
Durkheim, E. *The division of labor in society.* New York: Macmillan, 1933.
Durkheim, E. *Sociology and philosophy.* Glencoe, Illinois: Free Press, 1953.

# Chapter 10

# Prometheus and the Policy Sciences: Alienation as the Decline of Personal Agency[1]

## Manfred Stanley
### Syracuse University

## INTRODUCTION

It has become customary in many quarters to assume that the proper way to take account of the "human factor" in public policy analysis is to give equal weight, along with the physical sciences, to the social sciences. This view has become as important in the struggle by social scientists for a larger share of the federal budget as it has in the efforts to use social science in societal policy planning and problem solving.

This strategy obviously has a certain surface plausibility. Is not social science the repository of organized human intelligence with respect to the disciplined study of human behavior? Does not social science represent a concern for specifically human affairs as against physical gadgetry? Do social scientists not share in the long scientific tradition, celebrated by C. P. Snow, of selfless, disinterested, investigation of phenomena which compares so favorably as an ideal with the avarice and greed so often shown by politicians?

[1] This paper is based on research being conducted by the writer on the conceptual foundations of pessimism regarding the role of technics in modern society. I would like to acknowledge the support of the Harvard Program on Technology and Society where I was research associate from 1970 to 1972. Special thanks are due to Robert Daly and Emmanuel Mesthene for helpful comments.

221

This argument, in one way or another an explicit theme in some sectors of classical social thought from Saint-Simon to Karl Mannheim, has now become central to the all-out effort to create a bridge between social science and public affairs. A salient example is the policy sciences movement.[2]

It is a striking fact, however, that in the same historical moment during which this is taking place, one also witnesses a renewed vitality and sophistication in the stream of critical literature directed against the culture and social organization of modern technological societies. I refer not to that literature which is simply a naive diatribe against science, technology, reason, and the intellect. There is, rather, a literature, much of it produced by persons in or conversant with the social sciences, that criticizes modern societies for alienative tendencies which can collectively be called technicism.

In brief, authors of such literature claim that modern societies are converging in the direction of a social order dominated wholly by "techniques." Their thesis is that the sole reason for existence of contemporary forms of organization is the development of some particular techniques, physical or social, and to advance the interests of those persons who have tied their energy, faith, and hopes for personal advancement to the marketability of techniques. The common assumption of those who hold this view is that the goals of techniques get lost in the shuffle, and that all that counts in modern society is the perpetuation of organizations and patterns of action which were originally designed to solve a particular problem or provide a specified service. Thus, for example, bureaucracies typically end up existing only for themselves rather than for the fulfillment of the purposes for which they were set up. In this technicist model, then, society is viewed as a structure of means—an assemblage of human activities not under the control of any human agent capable of setting authoritative goals in whose name physical and social techniques are definable as means. The maintenance of an alienated world of techniques thus becomes an end in itself, unrelated to the ongoing evolution of men's moral consciousness and purposes.

---

[2] This term will be referred to repeatedly in the course of the essay. Therefore, certain reservations about my use of it should be made now. I do not wish to be interpreted as opposing the concept of a policy science per se. Policy sciences cover a wide range of efforts to analyze information relevant to a variety of persons who have to make decisions applying to large numbers of people. This essay is cast into a critical mold not because of opposition on my part to such rationality. But when any particular idea becomes the center of a social movement (as the idea of policy science may again come to be among social scientists seeking to be "relevant"), the enthusiasm of true believers becomes a danger. The scientistic and technological rhetoric endemic in much of policy science literature has triggered concern among many people, including some identified with the policy science idea, who are worried about technicist trends. This essay attempts to set this concern into its appropriate theoretical context. It should be construed not as an attack upon policy rationality but only as an invitation to practitioners to help clarify their operations in light of the issues raised here. This assumes, of course, that they share the values underlying the invitation.

This theme has been associated with some of the most profound thinkers of this or any age. They represent all points of the ideological compass, religious and secular, and are scattered throughout many disciplines and nations. This galaxy includes, among others, Martin Heidegger, Max Weber, Friedrich Hayek, Ludwig von Mises, Jacques Ellul, Hannah Arendt, Herbert Marcuse, and Lewis Mumford. The issue is not unknown among Communist intellectuals either, as the travails of Leazek Kolakowski and Adam Schaff, among others, would seem to suggest. Finally, the critical themes of such authors have been lent a near-demonological cast by a distinct tradition of anti-utopian pessimistic fiction stretching from H. G. Wells through Orwell to Kurt Vonnegut. These men of letters have helped to popularize the sense of anxiety about the direction which modern societies are taking.

Our task in this essay cannot be to give an account of technicism as a theory of social development.[3] Rather, I intend more specifically to examine the basis for anxiety about technicist potentialities in the policy science rhetoric. This rhetoric chiefly reflects the ambitions of those who seek to apply the social sciences to the great problems of our time in the most systematic possible manner.

In the deepest sense, perhaps, the founding myth of policy science is expressed in Genesis.

> And God said: "Let us make man in our image, after our likeness and let them have dominion over the fish of the sea, and over the fowl of the air, and over the cattle, and over all the earth, and over every creeping thing that creepeth on the earth."

Several classical questions have followed from this. Who is it that shall have this dominion? How shall it be attained and exercised? In the name of what shall it be exercised, and at what cost? Conflicting answers to such questions have created many a civil war within the ranks of Western civilization. It was once thought that the advent of modernism had resolved such issues. The modern world was born amidst the rusting fetters of manor, church, and crown, in an aura of celebration about what promised to be a new era of human dominion over nature. The inexorable advance of democratic aspirations seemed to herald the triumph of personal volition and of participation in civil society. Paradoxically, however, the old Biblical problem of the meaning of dominion took on some of its most complex and morally puzzling forms with the development of the modern age.

The present cultural situation in the West is characterized by forms of the tension between two philosophical perspectives on human consciousness. One of these is the quest for objective (i.e., precise, predictable, consistent) knowledge, including knowledge of the "laws" of human action itself. This objectification of the human being is exemplified in the thrust toward a comprehensive sociobehavioral science. The other perspective is that of the human self as the agent of his chosen projects—the tradition of self-determination and personal responsibility. This

---

[3] This is attempted elsewhere (see Stanley, 1972).

perspective, repeatedly denied and repeatedly affirmed, is found in the depths of the Christian drama of sin and redemption vis-à-vis a personal God and in the secular preoccupation with authenticity so characteristic of contemporary atheistic existentialists.[4]

In the work of Karl Marx, the ideal of human agency is expressed in a radical critique of alienation rooted in a secular eschatology of *praxis*.[5] Part of this critique stressed the manner in which social theorists who see as their mission the positing of objective laws in the social realm, reify into illusory "objects" the dynamic process of men making their world. For Marx, the result of this was that the works of men—in the forms of the "economy," the "state," "property," and even the atomistic "individual" himself—became as icons in a temple of icons created by some unseen alien hand to be worshipped and obeyed by men. The present state of the world is such that Marxist notions, like humans repossessing an alienated world of labor, suggest possibilities so remote as to be plausible only in the mind of some secular Augustine positing a city beyond history.

But our concern here is not with the impossible task of recapitulating the interplay of these two traditions of epistemology. Rather, the focus here is on the tension between these two traditions of epistemology as they are expressed in the so-called policy sciences' thrust toward policy relevance. Let us turn directly to this topic.

## THE METAPHORS OF OBJECTIVITY

The effort to encompass the social world as a determinate set of objects is very old. As is well known, the two great metaphors for representing the social (and sometimes cosmic) order have been that of the machine and the organism. Our purpose here is not to review the history of these metaphors but to comment upon the significance of their use relative to the topic of technicism. It is important that this be done in view of the renewed prominence of cybernetics, a symbol system which seeks to fuse elements of both mechanical and organic modes of thought into a vocabulary that many thinkers hope to use as a vehicle for the wholesale application of the social sciences to social engineering. Before turning to this new vocabulary, three general comments on the influence of such metaphors are in order.

The metaphors of mechanism and organism share an important property. They have reference to phenomena at a subpersonal level: machines and living biological organisms. That is, while these metaphors have proven highly useful for

---

[4] Cf. Niebuhr (1963). For an excellent general treatment in the context of sociological theory of the relationships between literacy, democratization, and images of selfhood, see Karl Mannheim (1956).

[5] For a detailed analysis of Bruno Bauer's influence upon Marx's use of "alienation," see Rosen (1970).

some purposes of scientific conceptualization, the price for this usefulness was reductionism, that is, their lack of philosophical adequacy for conceiving the person as a human agent. These metaphors encourage the sacrifice of an adequate formulation of the self-as-agent in favor of a seemingly more objective view which appears to result when one reduces discourse about human action to the simpler conceptual frameworks of mechanical or organic systems.[6] The vocabulary of force, vector, functions, reflexes, and behavior, exudes a comforting sense of the knowableness of human actions as determinate objects of scientific investigation. The price has been the gradual loss of a vocabulary which pertains to personal responsibility (intention, purpose, reasonableness, conscientiousness, conviction, etc.).

It is an item of conventional wisdom that there has been a progressive refinement of objective scientific language about human behavior. What has not been noted is the regressiveness of an increasing popular illiteracy relative to languages appropriate to moral deliberation, emotional and aesthetic refinement, and translation of the abstractions of civility into situational contexts.[7] The situation now is such that the study of statistical manipulations is the main focus of many social science methodology courses. But the heritage of whole vocabularies deriving from other forms of participation, observation, and experience in human affairs are collectively dubbed "the humanities" and are transferred out of the purview of the "scientific disciplines."[8]

For example, how many graduate students in the social sciences are actually encouraged to ask themselves what the uncritical reduction of human acts to the notion of "forces" or "behavior" does to our sense of what constitutes an expla-

---

[6] One of the most useful short discussions of the role of metaphors in sociological theory is still Pitirin Sorokin (1928). The Scottish philosopher John Macmurray (1936) wrote: "We do not know how to represent our knowledge of the personal as idea. I have indicated my belief that this is the emergent problem of philosophy in our own day [p. 142]." Macmarray's Gifford Lectures entitled "The Forms of the Personal" are the fruits of many years of effort to rectify this situation in philosophy. The results should be part of the education of all social scientists (cf. Macmurray, 1957, 1961; see also Black, 1962; Meadows, 1967; Turbayne, 1970). For a philosophically informed attempt to apply the cybernetic metaphor to the analysis of the human person, see Karl W. Deutsch (1966). This is perhaps one of the most ambitious attempts to translate the concept of human agency into cybernetic form.

[7] It is instructive to compare today's level of political discourse with that of the *Federalist Papers*. One has but to read of the techniques of casuistry, the logic of moral analysis applied to the demands of conscience, to recognize the crudeness with which contemporary discourse proceeds regarding justification of action (see, for instance, Kirk, 1927). Hannah Arendt is one of a handful of authors who has written extensively on problems of responsible action in the full glare of the lessons of contemporary totalitarianism. See also the interesting confrontation of conflicting doctrines of action in Peter Berger and Richard Neuhaus (1970). For a sophisticated attempt, by now almost a minor classic, to explicate the operational meaning of the democratic "public," see C. W. Mills (1962).

[8] This is probably least applicable to the discipline of Anthropology which has always retained a strongly humanistic strain. On this general issue as a philosophical problem of methodology in political science, see Sheldon Wolin (1969). For a fine example of humanistic sensibility in the technical study of sociological theories of suicide, see Jack D. Douglas (1967).

nation of human activities? Under such conditions, statistical pyrotechnics for their own sake often become the criterion of methodological sophistication. Of course, when it is assumed that human feelings, purposes, and actions have no logic of their own but are only reflections of organic drives within human animals, or else simply functions of impersonal forces, the uncritical use of statistics then necessarily follows quite readily upon this initial reductionism. Such moral philistinism is usually explained away as the price of "parsimony," as if societies, cultures, and human passions were organized parsimoniously for the convenience of observing scientists!

To take another overdrawn, but hardly invalid example: what are the consequences for a civilization in which experts on human activity can accept the platitudes of a love-sick adolescent besodden with pop-culture as a datum for the sociology of emotions along with the testimony of an undiscovered Kierkegaard, and count both as one check-mark on a questionnaire in a statistical sample? A common response to such a comment is: "Well, such differences are in the province of literature." It is difficult to imagine an orientation more likely to produce illiteracy about the subtleties of human behavior.

It is valid to argue that the arts have a different function from the sciences. It is quite another matter to use the arts as a dumping ground for all those data of experience the existing stock of "operational definitions" cannot handle and then encourage students deliberately to impoverish themselves by studying only those phenomena within the ambience of convenient techniques—all in the name of science. This impoverishment, when it is not overcome by the individual's common sense, is often concealed by a fact which spares the incipient expert some of the consequences of his own technical orientations. Via training in the tools of his trade, the student is at least permitted entrance into an almost mystical neo-Pythagorean elite by virtue of his mastery of the very numerical techniques with which he reduces others to faceless laws of ciphers. Since the tools of this elite are increasingly relevant to the social and linguistic interests of the megapersons (states and corporations) that inhabit our world—interests which include their desire to mystify the public about their operations—such tools are obviously of political significance.

Apart from this commentary about the reductionism inherent in both metaphors, and some of the implications of this reductionism, two more general points may be briefly made.

Despite the tenor of the foregoing remarks, it would be a mistake to assume that the mechanical and organic metaphors were always or even predominately experienced as being at the service of a rigidly deterministic definition of human action. The notion of organism in medieval times was not seen as necessarily incompatible with the theological argument for personal responsibility. The metaphor of mechanism served well as a foundation for the social liberation of individual energy and aspiration associated with the rise of market liberalism. It is rather that the idea of personal agency, once instituted as a cultural value, seems periodically to break through the social routines which constrain its expression. Thus, just as the theological version of free will proved pale and wanting in the light of later secular doctrines of freedom, so the moral credibility of liberalism is now threatened by humanistic Marxism with its critique of wage-slavery and other forms of involuntary dependence.

Finally, the deterministic objectivity implied in the two metaphors did not and does not now remain unchallenged on the level of social science theory. It is sufficient to remind ourselves of the great methodological debate in Germany early in the century about the problem of objectivity in the physical as against the social sciences. In the United States, the tradition of "symbolic interactionism" has kept such issues alive in sociology and psychology. In more recent years we have seen the vigorous reemergence of discourse and research strategies stressing the need for an account of men as creators and maintainers of shared meanings and of the consensus underlying social institutions (for references, see Berger & Luckman, 1966; Blau, 1964; Boler, 1968; Bourke, 1964; Brand, 1970; Churchill, 1971; Cicourel, 1964; Douglas, 1970a, 1970b, 1967; Gouldner, 1970; Klausner, 1965; Manis & Meltzer, 1967; McGowan & Gochnauer, 1971; Nelson, 1965; Schutz, 1967).

This, then, is the situation in the social sciences in the context of a heralded and increasingly well-financed effort towards the translation of social theory into practical policy. What form does the response to this demand for "relevance" appear to be taking? Where does this response stand with regard to the tension between objective knowledge and personal agency we have been reviewing? And can answers to these questions help us understand the dark strain of pessimism evoked from some of the most distinguished minds of the twentieth century regarding the promise of relevance of the social sciences for public policy?

## CYBERNETICS AND SALVATION: SOME ISSUES

Cybernetics is a metaphor of order based upon an image of society as a servo-mechanism capable of constant adaptation to the vicissitudes of social and physical environments. Cybernetics subsumes the mechanical and organic metaphors by reducing all processes and transactions to the notion of information flows. Implicit in its application to policy science is a program for reorganizing society in such a way as to allow for the translation into operational procedures of three values widely but abstractly shared in democracies. These values are relevance, accountability, and reduction of the undesirable, unanticipated consequences of purposive social actions.

Relevance and accountability are implied by the strong emphasis on input-output and cost-benefit analysis which are features of cybernetic procedures.

Reduction of unanticipated consequences of action is implied in the notion, central to cybernetic thought, of feedback loops for system self-correction. Presupposed here, of course, is a large volume of accurate information about what goes on in "a system." For would-be policy scientists this implies an argument in favor of massive data gathering and storage procedures. In the light of such a benign program, why does cybernetic thought exemplify the type of thinking which has led to pessimistic attacks upon technicism?

## The Problem of Goal Definitions

The goals of cyberneticians presumably are societal survival and efficiency. But efficiency and even survival have no meaning without reference to real life. Concrete referents are needed: specifications, conditions, priorities. Yet the relativism of modern culture does not facilitate the formation of a large-scale consensus on substantive collective goals (substantive as against abstract slogans like "free enterprise," "getting ahead," and "national security").

Unlike what was true in premodern times, the modern definition of freedom includes the view that defining "ultimate concerns" or end-values is a private matter. What is public is the process of exchanging utilities. The logic of this exchange under conditions of scarce resources (i.e., when people cannot have everything they want and must choose) is the subject matter of economics. It must be remembered in this connection that despite their constant use of the word "value," economists have never claimed actually to be studying values as such. In economics, real value is presumed to be an almost unexaminable phenomenon "interior" to the hearts and minds of individuals. What economists really want to study is what people do once they have attached some kind of utility criterion to what they value—utility in the sense of a publicly understood and established medium of exchange. This medium is money.

In pluralistic and relativistic cultures, money—because it is a criterion that reduces everything to a quantitative difference—became the final arbiter of public validation with respect to the objective meaning of most social values. This is the ontic significance of economics as the language of public life in modern societies, as Marx so clearly recognized.[9]

[9] Indeed, money's general significance had been understood much earlier, as is evident in this quotation by Jeremy Bentham: ". . . if we would understand one another we must make use of some common measure. The only common measure the nature of things affords is money. . . . Those who are not satisfied with the accuracy of this instrument must find out some other that shall be more accurate, or bid adieu to Politics and Morals [quoted in Commons, 1961, p. 233 (original 1934)]." For Marx, see David McLellan (1971). For some striking examples of quantification in American work life, see Daniel Bell (1961). For an account of Simmel's important contribution to the sociology of money, see Nicholas J. Spykman (1966).

In this light, the juxtaposition of modern democracy and the quantification of values in the public domain is no historical accident. The cultivation and refinement of aristocratic nonquantitative criteria of public discourse on values has normally been the province of upper social classes who hold exclusive access to the educational and other resources necessary for such activities. Nonquantifiable criteria of evaluation have both been developed by upper classes and been used to legitimate their power (it is not usually the down-and-out who define themselves as carriers of "civilization").

Thus, money is connected with democracy in pluralistic cultures because it has two properties of great significance. When institutionalized as a medium of exchange, money is a quantitative arbiter between conflicting vocabularies of evaluation. To say that, economically, money is a universal medium of exchange is to say that, culturally, it is a potential arbiter between competing vocabularies of evaluation. Money's second significant property is that, in principle, it can be "understood" and "made" by anyone capable of market rationality in the sense of providing utilities to someone else able to pay money for them. This means that in a money economy, social mobility is no longer necessarily dependent upon exposure to aristocratic criteria of value, nor upon fortunate birth, nor intense education, nor leisure. One does not need to agree with or even to understand in any deep sense why it is that someone is willing to pay money for something.

Money proved to be a democratic leveler not because anyone could, in fact, make it. Obviously the rich continue to get richer as always. Rather, money is a leveler because it establishes one easily understandable criterion of evaluation—quantifiable differences—as the public one, and neutralizes all other criteria by defining them as within the realm of private opinion. Once social class is redefined in terms of life chances in the market, symbolized by access to money-making opportunities, the parvenu can make his way to power even if the contempt of the well-born causes him to cry all the way to the bank.

The point of this brief digression on the significance of money is that it enables us to see how the general reduction of values and concepts to quantitative expression is virtually the key to stability in modern pluralistic democracies. Stability is preserved through the steady transformation of "aristocratic" conflict-producing subtleties of moral deliberation, logics of the heart, standards of craft and aesthetics, into "democratic" objective knowledge. That is, quantity is democratic, so to speak, because "everyman" can count. Bit by bit quantities —be they money, or numbers in a statistical table, or forced choices on a questionnaire—become the language of objective knowledge about values. As this process in the social realm intersects in the public mind with the mystique of mathematical science, the victory of the quantitative criterion of objective knowledge is virtually complete. All else becomes "opinion" at best, "mysticism" at worst.

We may now return to the problem of defining concrete referents for collective goals like efficiency, adaptation, and progress. What are the implications of what we have just said for the general problem of goal determination?

In the context of the social, political, and technological problems of modern industrial society, people are predisposed to speak of collective goals in quantitative terms: progress as gross national product, happiness as the mass provision of commonly desired utilities, leisure as clock-time away from work. Life becomes a vast scorecard. Indeed, simple humanitarianism induces the general feeling that it is somehow snobbish, romantically (or callously) elitist, to question the equation of progress with the stability and prosperity of a consumer society. Given the present state of a suffering world, fancy questions about the possible untoward consequences of quantitative, technological vocabularies of problem-solving can all too easily appear as the arid scholasticism of the well-fed. First comes the eating, said Bertolt Brecht, then comes the morality. It seems somehow irrelevant, if not faintly inhuman, to point out that strictly speaking this is at least as often false as true.

The issue, then, is goals. And it is an issue in at least two senses. One, of course, is the substantive question of what societal goals are to be. Here the attractiveness of cybernetic imagery clearly reflects the desire to coordinate solutions to social problems resulting from presently uncontrolled social processes that are beginning to be widely perceived as threats to the survival of the human species or at least to organized civilization. But the other sense of the problem of goals is how goals are set, and what the implications are of how goals are set for the evolution of that particular notion of human agency which is identified with terms like personal responsibility and self-determination.

In the minds of the pessimists, what is at stake in issues like technicism and alienation is the ideal of the person as a self-conscious and responsible agent. Two features of this general orientation should be noted. First, whatever its concrete meanings, personal authenticity is itself a goal, not a state into which one is born by nature. Traditions of authentic personhood always included programs for defining and achieving it. Second, the ideal requires a vocabulary appropriate to itself, and use of this vocabulary must be accompanied by some degree of faith that it reflects something more than sheer illusion.

The determinisms implied by the notion of objective knowledge in science did not necessarily challenge the integrity of that vocabulary so long as the analogy between physical and social science was not carried too far. As we have pointed out, various trends in social thought, from aspects of Marx's criticism of "theory" in the name of "praxis," through the long *verstehen* controversy, to contemporary movements in sociology like ethnomethodology, have kept alive the notion that social science must study not only abstractly defined products of human behavior, but the ways in which individuals mobilize themselves through social action to create and sustain (or destroy) these products.

For the pessimistic critics, the technicist tendency is part of the history of alienation (although not all critics use this term by any means). Technicism is seen as an ideology of social control in which the focus of human agency is shifted from the person, and his moral or rational evolution, to something called the "cybernetic society." For the critics this means the identification of human agency with the sociobiological operations of the human species itself. This is because the notion of society is reconceptualized in this ideology as an adaptive mechanism of macro-biological proportions.

In this pessimistic scenario of technicism, the language of human agency (volition, purpose, consciousness, etc.) is supplanted by a language of nonpurposive objective processes. This epistemological shift is facilitated by the explanatory power of scientific accounts like natural selection and operant conditioning.[10] Technicism is not advanced by way of the actual disappearance of words like purpose, intention, and will. Rather, it is visible in the emergence of a technicist meta-vocabulary of gyroscopic controls which, through its reduction of everything to the ambiguous status of "information," appears to be referring to a level of reality more "real" than that of human agency. Against the protestations of cyberneticians that "information" includes human acts and decisions, pessimists would hold that the overwhelming impact of such an ideology of gyroscopic controls has to be the effective obsolescence, through condemnation to a hopeless abstraction, of the whole vocabulary of values, personal agency, and responsibility. One brings to mind in this connection B. F. Skinner's (1948) famous novel *Walden Two,* considered by many to be a major technicist document.

In the book the narrator (representing the author) asks his friend Castle, a philosopher, if he thinks Frazier, the founder and social engineer of Walden Two, is a Fascist. In reply Castle, while stating that he does not know the answer, criticizes Frazier for overlooking all sorts of questions in his social engineering doctrines. Among these are "What about the dignity and integrity of the individual? Where does that come in? What about democracy? . . . And what about personal freedom? And responsibility?" Skinner has his narrator comment to himself on this, "So far as I was concerned, questions of that sort were valuable mainly because they kept the metaphysicians out of more important fields." While this remark could plausibly be read as an attack upon philosophers spinning abstractions, it is notions of engineering and social "experimentation" such as appear in Skinner's book that cause questions like Castle's to come up in the first place.

[10] For an extensive documentation of the depth and scope of this generalization in the social sciences, see Floyd W. Matson (1966).

## The Rhetoric of Pseudo-Objectivity: An Example

Let me illustrate what has been said with an example of how human goals appear in the cybernetic vocabulary.

> Social organization is man's adaptive tool; and the behavioral templates that are aggregated into a social system may after all coordinate their planned and goal-seeking behaviors. Adaptation in this form gives division of labor (with intra-species niches, and specialized behavioral templates, so plasticity becomes vital as men shift roles), and the derivation of which behavioral templates are appropriate to action becomes critical. Self-regulation in the social system gives efficiency as in the organism, suggesting that cybernetic elements in the social system are natural evolutionary developments toward greater adaptability. Behavioral templates are now stored in libraries, in giant organizations, and in technical apparatus, as well as in brains, all uncoordinated; and the critical problem is how to take lower-level adaptations in organizations as models for societal cybernetics. This is goal-seeking and planning, the ultimate extension of adaptive capabilities and social rationality.
>
> The failure of societies is in the realm of *control,* over the environment and over the mutually inconsistent behaviors within society. Energy resources do not give control, as any design engineer can tell us, for uncertainties will still exist at the energetics level; the need is always to resolve uncertainties as to the precise application of energetics to have controls. Information-poor *use* of energetics is what destabilizes systems, not the science and technology which produces energetics. . . .
>
> Social systems have biological and technical systems as components with their own cybernetics. Since "control" means bringing the degrees of freedom of a system's behavior within predictable tolerance limits, the complexity of the problem mushrooms if we have also to control for lower-level systems with their own internal degrees of freedom [Ray, 1968, p. 18 (italics his)] .[11]

The abstract nature of this terminology obscures some rather interesting assertions and assumptions. For example, we have here what sounds like a return to a Spencerian vocabulary in which societies are evolving social organisms. Unlike Spencer, though, the author does not invite us to have faith in the principles of development which Spencer thought pointed in such benign directions if only left alone, that is, "survival of the fittest." But like Spencer, the sense of salvation seems to lie for this writer in the realization that, no matter what you think you are doing, you are really a functional part of a much grander process of evolution and adaptation. Of course, Spencer invited us to continue what we were doing provided we did it as rational utilitarian individuals and recognized the evolutionary significance of it all. The cyberneticians, however, seem to place more emphasis on convincing us that some very serious restrictions might have to be placed on what we do.

This organic ambience seems to imply for the author some anxiety about information usage in society. We see this both in the very definition of "behavioral

[11] I wish to thank Sage Publications, Inc., for permission to quote from this essay.

templates" and in the attitudes toward these. Behavioral templates are defined as:

> ... information-processing, decision-making, image-forming, action-patterning,
> set(s) of information structures in the cellular structure . . . , and in the neural
> structure, and, in higher organisms (especially man), in the social structure [Ray,
> 1968, p. 18].

Given this approach to the notion of information and decision-making, it is not
surprising that the author feels some concern over the fact that "behavioral templates" are so uncoordinated on the level of societies. Now, in raising the point for
criticism, I do not mean to argue that, abstractly speaking, the author's generalization is wrong. Certainly it is not wrong. It would even be fair to concede that
most knowledgeable people agree that the degree of duplication and malcoordina-
tion of information in modern societies is generally unacceptable. But that is really
not the question any longer. What we really want to know are things like: what
sorts of information should be coordinated, how much so, by whom, for whom, in
what forms, and for what purposes? Simple emphasis on coordination without reference to such questions induces simply a spectre of some vast *Gleichschaltung* in
the mind's eye.[12]

Still a third comment is in order about this example. Questions come to mind
about an ideology which takes as its critical problem the "ultimate expansion of
adaptive capabilities and social rationality." Has Max Weber's deep moral ambivalence
over the rationalization process been for nought, that one can still so easily use a
word like "ultimate" in this connection? Are we really so certain that we will not
or have not already produced, as the price of such expansion, what Max Weber (1958)
so memorably called "Specialists without spirit, sensualists without heart; [a] nulli-
ty [that] imagines . . . it has attained a level of civilization never before achieved
[p. 182]."? Should not we be requiring of the proseletyzers of technical rationalization some awareness of such problems by now?

Finally, the orientation of hostility that appears in such writings toward the
very principle of "uncertainties" and "mutually inconsistent behaviors in society" is

---

[12] The same point is applicable to the proposal by Nicholas Golovin (1969) for an "evaluative branch of government" whose function it would be to: ". . . develop and coordinate
(but not necessarily to operate) national, state, and local information collection and processing systems aimed at providing the main agencies of government at all levels and the public
with objective and timely information concerning status, changes, and trends in the key characteristics of our society [p. 182]." The trouble with such proposals is that in the absence of
any analysis of problems in the sociology of information on a level raised, say, by Harold Wilenski (1967), the ideas come across as rather banal. This is a characteristic problem of thinking on such abstract levels as cybernetic systems engineering, and invites premature sneering
from social critics. The issue of public information is obviously a serious one, and Golovin's
proposal should be used to stimulate a generation of empirical studies in the sociology of
information-usage now being pioneered by Wilenski (1967), Douglas (1967), Tamotzu Shibutani
(1966), Aaron Wildavsky (1964), and Aaron V. Cicourel (1968).

quite striking. The abstract vocabulary of limiting degrees of freedom on so many system levels to predictable tolerance limits hides some important specific questions, to say the least.

The point of these critical observations is not to make light of the main thrust of the argument reflected in such writings. Briefly put, the point underlying such rhetoric is essentially this: control certain things or die! Indeed, the author of the example we have just reviewed does not seem unaware of the complexities of the problems he raises. For example, he argues strongly for "a major marketplace of ideas, especially of imagery of the future." And he recognizes, at the conclusion of the article, "that the 'us' of that era in the future will have been radically transformed in the process."

But it is precisely the apparent subordinate importance of the direction of transformation, the sense that almost whatever direction it takes may have to be the price of species survival, that goes to the heart of the main theme of my essay. In the article under review, the most crucial philosophical issues from the standpoint of those interested in the question of alienation are referred to in a footnote. It is worth examining how these issues are handled.

> A critical point for those who worry that a new realm of technical disasters and/or standardization will come . . . is that cybernetic technologies require criterion values, or "goals," and also indicators of effects, or performance criteria. In this context, precision and quantification are not identical, so the fear that only quantifiable social goods can be considered, and that only machine-talking specialists can monitor successes, is quite unfounded. The next generation of computer programs will be very close to ordinary language, and our development of social indicators *can* be done with humanity. Knowing what we are doing will probably be the critical problem—for planned change of institutions is the ultimate payoff. Planning will therefore require precise models of society [Ray, 1968, p. 19, footnote 6].

The point that quantification and precision should not be confused is a very important one. (Some examples of its relevance for cybernetic planning would have been helpful.) Equally important is the assertion that the next generation of computer programs will be very close to ordinary language. This notion raises some fascinating questions because the striking characteristic of ordinary language is its openness to spontaneity, its capacities for sustaining multiple levels of meaning: innuendos, subtle implications, myths, metaphors, and so on. Ordinary language is not a thing but, simultaneously, a highly dynamic instrument for and process of meaning-creation, accountability, aggression, persuasion, and many other symbolizing tasks. One of the points raised by some of the pessimist critics of technicism is, precisely, that an important requisite of technicist controls over society is the circumscribing of ordinary language to prevent its use for undermining the foundations of conviction about the validity, credibility, and reasonableness of the existing social order. The field of public relations is but the conscious technicization of the process of manipulating ordinary language for such purposes. It would therefore be rather interesting to know just how computer programs "will be very close to ordinary language."

Furthermore, after the reassurance that creating social indicators "can be done with humanity," we are told that planning, whose "ultimate payoff" is "planned change of institutions," will "require precise models of society." Now, this phrase can be taken either as meaning nothing on the ground that the word "precise" is used so generally as to signify anything short of total spontaneity, or else one must see it as implying the necessity of a deterministic theory of society as a prerequisite for social planning.

Unless one wishes the term "society" to be understood as a reified object, the term means the field of organization within which persons carry out projects, react at least in part spontaneously to new stimuli, or find new interpretations of what already exists. This all means that society has about it a flavor of contingency and, hence, a high degree of unpredictability.

Now, to argue that there are kinds of unpredictability which do threaten our species' survival, or the continued existence of certain humane ideals, is to remain within the world-view of human voluntarism, reason, and persuasion. But to say that solving such problems will require "precise models of society" is to move into a vocabulary incompatible with personal agency. For the only way in which one is going to get "precise models of society" is to eliminate the element of contingency. It is one thing to do this as an analytical exercise, that is, as part of the scientific search for organization, pattern, and meaning behind the flux. It is quite another type of act to take a precise model (simulation) of a society and attempt its concrete imposition upon whole populations through forms of planning which rest on putative predictions of what cannot really be predicted. It is this sort of ambition that results in the deliberate manipulation of human beings into modes of consciousness and behavior congenial to planners' categories.

If it be objected here that "precise," in this context, is not meant literally but only in some partial sense, that too is beside the point. The issue is the theoretical status for social science of the concept of contingency. Thus, the question the applied social scientist must answer is this: What are the concrete relationships between any theoretical model of "society" he adopts for purposes of policy analysis on the one hand, and the contingent, creative, active element of human agency on the other?

The vocabulary we have just reviewed reflects an increasingly common way of referring to social control. There are persisting reasons for the conceptual and philosophical ambiguities such as we have discovered in this example, The pseudo-objectivity of this rhetoric conceals the fact that concrete collective goals are not present in liberal modernism, either its world-view or its institutions. Freedom for liberals was defined as freedom from such collective goals. Yet current material circumstances and social problems have led to a widely felt need for making collectively binding decisions—and making them quickly. The pessimist position is that these decisions will be made at the price of surrendering the Western under-standing of personal agency. Such a cost would most clearly show up in the alter-ations of meanings, opportunities, and structures for individual participation in the making of society.

It may be objected that such fears are needless exercises in demonology be-cause real people do not willingly give up control over their own affairs in such a manner. I wish now to deal at some length with this objection.


## PATHWAYS TO ALIENATION


Major mutations in men's images of themselves and the world occur as vari-ations on familiar themes or as resolutions of strains in the fabric of the existing social order.

In a sense, technicism can be defined as the institutional fulfillment of the persisting cultural logic of a materialist, relativist, and technologically oriented world-view. The theoretical themes for this world-view have been at the core of modern culture since Galileo and Descartes transformed Western science and phil-osophy in the seventeenth century. These themes include: (1) the separation of self from a materialist definition of the objective world inherent in the Cartesian distinction between subject and object; (2) the notion of purposeless movement inherent in Galileo's theory of motion; and (3) the technological ego incipient in Descartes' famous utterance, "Give me matter and motion and I shall make the world once more."[13]

The disappearance of an ontology of human volition would be but the final step in this logic, the removal of an anachronism. Many modern scientists consider this anachronism (notions of personal agency) to be a vestige of premodern world-views. There were, too, some major technical problems holding up the formulation of a fully materialistic and deterministic account of man-in-nature. Such problems are resolvable now, these scientists argue, by the advent of modern biology and behavioral science. Therefore, we should all now look to our scientific models for survival even as our forbears turned to the scriptures for salvation.

Aside from the fact that technicist society would represent one form of in-tensification of modern culture rather than a radical break with it, contemporary history suggests a second reason why the victory of technicism might not be clear-ly recognizable for a while. That reason is anxiety. It is surely the case that a sense of things-out-of-control is spreading throughout our civilization. At such times the popular response to events is to intensify the quest for stability, order, predicta-

---

[13] Quoted in Hans Jonas (1963, p. 135). This essay is necessary reading for anyone in-terested in the details of the argument that modern scientific theory is technological in its essential orientation.

bility: in short, control. The emphasis on control shows up in some interesting features of how the cybernetic vocabulary is being used.

Two such features in particular are worth citing. First, the vocabulary is being applied to just about every imaginable social unit, no matter how far-fetched the occasion. Second, the rhetoric induces a mode of thought which lumps all sorts of intentions and actions of human agents together with all sorts of classes of physical events into a common category of "disturbances" which "impact" upon the servomechanistic, cybernetic system.

> Disturbances can be classified as social, economic, political, or natural. As an
> example of a social disturbance, one can cite the revolution of rising expecta-
> tions that is affecting not only our cities but the entire world. Recessions, wars,
> inflation, and high interest rates, which have a cataclysmic effect on the econ-
> omy of the city, are economic disturbances which are beyond the control of a
> mayor. Political disturbances affect the city when changes in administration at
> the state or national level have a profound impact on urban programs. . . .

> For examples of government-induced disturbances originating at other levels of
> government, one has only to consider the highway construction and mortgage
> policies of the federal government, which "developed" the countryside surround-
> ing the cities and peopled it with the cities' middle class. Also it is evident that
> the nation's welfare policies, particularly as implemented in certain states, have
> influenced the rate of migration from southern rural shacks to northern urban
> slums [Savas, 1970, p. 1070].[14]

The example seems harmless enough, almost trivial, when applied to a city mayor. And, on the surface, we seem invited only to think in terms of standard functional relationships between social events. But what is the point of the cybernetic imagery then? Why is it added on to the catalogue of events we already know about any American city? The answer is that it occurs as part of an argument designed to persuade us to adopt this imagery as that of a technology of social control.

If we take this invitation literally, we find ourselves imagining a city mayor with immense resources of power in his hands, who continues to look upon his city as a would-be stable servomechanism and feels overwhelmed by all these external "disturbances" of his system dream. There takes shape an image of a man fully capable in good conscience of using his power to control or suppress these "disturbances" whose noncybernetic meanings and significances he is no longer able to comprehend.

By a simple step of analogical reasoning we arrive along this road at a model of cybernetic imperialism in which the strongest nation-states, in a Hobbesian world, use their power to control realities internal and external to themselves according precisely to these motivations. "Feedback" becomes internal surveillance

---

[14] I wish to thank the American Association for the Advancement of Science under whose copyright this journal is issued for permission to quote from this essay.

and external espionage, and, to quote the words of the same author, in the name of "Feedforward control" which "involves planning to accommodate predictable, externally caused changes that would otherwise impact the system," governments are made to fall, the armies of counter-insurgency are on the march in alien countries, trade is manipulated, and whole societies are reduced to pieces in a vast international cybernetic domino game. Such are the ways of euphemism!

The skeptical reader would do well to read a surprisingly candid interview given by Eugene V. Rostov, Under-Secretary of State for Political Affairs in the Johnson administration ("A Reporter at Large," 1970). It gives remarkable insight into what can only be called the kind of megapersonal view of the world which gives rise to cybernetic imperialism. Likewise enlightening in this connection is Robert Gilpin's (1970) sobering review of the probable directions of the international and domestic technological policies of selected national governments under conditions of an Hobbesian world political situation. Also of relevance, finally, is David Halberstam's (1971) portrait of Robert McNamara's mentality; it is overpowering in its brilliance, and apparently almost totally technicist in its orientation.

There is a third reason worth reviewing why the possible transition to technicism might not be widely recognized for what it is. The technicist tradition in Western social thought does contain a moral justification of its own. From Saint-Simon to Thorstein Veblen, the argument has been made that the stable point of collective moral reference for modern society should be the marvelous engine of production and craft that is modern technological society itself. In 1817 Saint-Simon (republished 1964) asked himself in print where one could find the "organic social bond" to replace that which had been exploded by "the passion for equality." His answer was:

> In the idea of industry; only there shall we find our safety and the end of revolution . . . the sole aim of our thoughts and our exertions must be the kind of organization most favorable to industry . . . including every kind of useful activity, theoretical as well as practical, intellectual as well as manual [pp. 69-70].

The technologized world, its institutions and dynamics, is here the criterion of stability according to which society should be organized. Production of useful things is the moral reference point because without it all is chaos, but if enough can be produced eventually all men's goals will be satisfied. This is clearly not an inhumane vision because technology here is viewed as the humanization of an indifferent nature which can be molded to human will. As in the Platonic Republic, Saint-Simonism allocates people structurally in terms of their capacities to relate to a stable point of moral reference. In current language, people's attitudes, aspirations, and skills are collectively defined as their merits according to which people will be functionally stratified in what has come to be called a "meritocracy." The modern schools, like the Platonic dormitories, have indeed become institutions which exist to reorient the person from his parochial loyalties and provincial angles of vision to the great societal functions decreed "necessary" to perform. Like the original, the new Platonic Republic has its elite, now not the philosopher-king but the cybernetic systems engineer. For many today, as for Saint-Simon, the solution to the problems created by irresponsible liberalism is for everyone to have a function to perform in a productive engine which benefits everyone.

This vision has received new relevance now that automation and electronics increasingly take the place of human energy, opening the way for greater degrees of free time for large masses of people. Zbigniew Brzezinski (1968) has written of a society destined to be split into two levels: a knowledge-possessing technocratic elite working full time to maintain the system, and a mass population freed from labor functions by technetronics for the leisured pursuit of everything from humanistic play to hedonistic gratifications. Like the Platonic elite, the modern elite is theoretically open to penetration by those with the requisite aspirations and skills, the modern version of the myth of the metals being Brzezinski's "meritocratic democracy."

In another picture of such a society, Donald Michael (1962) reveals the mystic element of neo-Platonic elitehood when, in discussing the man-machine relationship experienced by his "cyberneticians," he says that they

> . . . will be a small, almost separate, society of people in rapport with the advanced computers. These cyberneticians will have established a relationship with their machines that can not be shared with the average man any more than the average man today can understand the problems of molecular biology, nuclear physics or neuro-psychiatry. Indeed, many scholars will not have the capacity to share their knowledge or feeling about the new man-machine relationship. Those with the talent for the work will probably have to develop it from childhood and will be trained as intensively as the classical ballerina [p. 123].

Thus, what is most seductive about the cybernetic model of society is that it appears to complete the technological rationalization of society inherent in Saint-Simonism without seeming to share in his attack upon the principle of individualism (a word he held up to scorn). This fusion of Saint-Simonian technocracy and liberal individualism is accomplished in the cybernetic model because of the existence of automation technology. The individual is provided with predefined functions to perform in an objectively defined world. But because the main weight of production has been thrown on automated machinery, that same individual is also provided with free time for private experimentation in what are officially defined as nonproductive activities. It is this private (cybernetically irrelevant) area of free time that is the appropriate domain for "subjectively" motivated initiatives.

It is probably this logic which renders the cybernetic model of society so compelling in the imaginations of many thinkers. However, those who see this approach as a solution to the anxieties expressed about technicism and alienation characteristically fail to appreciate the manner in which the argument simply does not address the problem of individualism as viewed from the standpoint of a social philosophy stressing personal agency. Let us take a moment to see why.

It is useful at this point to recall two important generalizations about the common distinction between public and private life. One is its historical relativism in the sense of the evaluations applied to the words public and private through historical time. For instance, the evaluative emphasis seems to have reversed itself since Greco-Roman times, with the private life now connoting the more desirable, while the opposite appears to have been the case in ancient times.[15] The second generalization is that the contemporary approach to the distinction between public and private is profoundly rooted in the radically relativist emphasis of modern culture. Ideologically, public life in liberal societies is supposed to be organized by market-dominated exchange processes reflecting a structure of supply and demand based on valuation decisions made in the private realm. More specifically, apart from the desire for commonly valued utilities, liberalism assumes that the content of what is being pursued in the "pursuit of happiness" is a matter for private determination.

However, this relativism was never accepted as absolute. Many liberals looked for harmonies of interests that could reconcile to some degree the worlds of the public and the private, while Marxism urged the transvaluation of the whole distinction. Thus the demand, in liberal societies, for freedom from state interference and collective goals was partially offset by demands for representation and other opportunities for civic participation in the running of society (Mills, 1962). Marx himself frowned on these notions precisely because of his feeling that bourgeois civil rights concealed and thus exacerbated, rather than resolved, the entrapment of men in what he regarded as the alienating abstractions of such dualisms as theory versus practice and individual versus society. Therefore, both the notions of bourgeois citizenship and of Marxist communism (however otherwise different from each other), take off from a common concern that the logic of dualism and relativism not sunder completely the realms of the public and the private in personal consciousness and action.

In this light, cybernetic technicism appears to imply an all-out intensification of the rift between public and private. Why is this so?

In the cybernetic model of society the "public" realm seems to be equated with statistically analyzable mass phenomena requiring cybernetic controls, while the "private" is seen as opportunities for withdrawal into cybernetically irrelevant zones of refuge from administrative attention.[16] That is, privacy would thus mainly come to mean the right not to participate in society as a cybernetic system. This, of course, is a negative freedom. It is tied in with the technicist possibility that the delicate equilibration of a cybernetic society may also render

---

[15] For the implications of this, see Hannah Arendt (1958).

[16] For a related argument which should be consulted by all interested in the issues raised in this essay, see Allen Schick (1970).

obsolete all morally positive definitions of participation apart from functional roles defined by criteria of social systems engineering.

To put it a little differently, pessimists think that in a cybernetic society the public sphere is destined to become the realm of collective (cybernetic) necessity. Equality of opportunity would be reduced, once and for all, to an ideal in the service of the freedom to integrate oneself into a social structure which the average individual will have had little if anything to do with defining or constructing. Conversely, the "private" must then become the realm of pure freedom-from, that is, the liberty to participate freely as a personal agent in anything but the direction of man's greatest collective achievement—society itself. As high as one might rise in the public realm, or as much leisure time for privacy as there may be made available by automation, these newly rigidified meanings of public and private would still remain valid in this pessimistic interpretation. As Frazier says about his own "experimental" program in an unforgettable passage in *Walden Two*, "I deny freedom exists at all. I must deny it—or my program would be absurd. You can't have a science about a subject matter which hops capriciously about."

Despite these considerations, cybernetic technicism appears as eminently "practical" in that it seems to be the most likely outcome of present trends, if despair about existing institutions continues to deepen. It promises the millenium of subjective freedoms without revolution. It may be only to a few that all this appears achievable at an unacceptable cost.

Finally, I should like to cite a fourth reason why the transition to a technicist order might be accomplished without public awareness. That reason is that the present loud preoccupation of the affluent intelligentsias and economically disadvantaged populations alike with decentralist, participatory, experimental, and anti-technological social movements may lead to ineffective efforts to check the technicist drift of modern society. It needs to be said that there is all the difference in the world, despite occasional overlapping rhetoric, between abstract ideologies (and rites) of participationism, and the call for a social theory and a social structure capable of taking into deliberate account the possibilities of human agency and personal responsibility. Abstract ideologies, in this case participatory democracy, are almost by definition not theoretically adequate to the problems they address. In the present instance, participatory rhetoric is really a cry of anguish. It is an affirmation of deep mistrust and disappointment with the types of leaders typically generated by contemporary political and economic institutions. It expresses a desire for a revival of personal dignity. And it is a demand to be freed from social controls which increasingly appear as arbitrary prejudices. At its extreme, abstract participatory ideology reflects a nihilistic breakdown of the capacity simply to trust somebody. And, in general, participatory ideologues hardly bother to address themselves to the crisis of theory in the received notion of "self-interest." This is so despite the fact that this crisis has been of rather evident concern to serious thinkers of all persuasions except those blinded by the crudest kind of utilitarianism. Unwillingness to face up to this is probably one cause of the violent fluctuations in the ranks of the New Left between antinomianism and elitism.

Indeed, it can be argued that technicism and abstract ideologies of participation, far from being opposites, are really complementary styles of response to the exigencies of social change and moral conflict. The inevitable deceptions and mystifications of technicism do inspire the mistrust and frenetic activism which characterize participatory movements. But it is also the case that the inefficiencies and confusions of fruitless participatory rituals can in their turn result in exhausted dependence upon those who can convincingly claim the mantle of expertise. Part of the more sinister view of technicism is the thought that a really efficient form of social control would be one that could contain the drive toward participation by effective manipulation not only of selected information, but of mass ignorance as a social force in its own right.[17] The now routine use of public relations agencies in political campaigns is, to say the least, a marked step in that direction.

I cannot hope to do justice to the technicalities of personal agency and alienation in the allotted space. However, the points made in this essay are subject to some misunderstandings which it will be helpful to address directly.

## PERSONAL AGENCY AND SOCIAL DECISIONS

My strategy here has been simply to examine one particular rhetoric of social control (cybernetics) in order to determine the extent to which it is or is not concerned with the problem of personal agency. At least three misleading interpretations of this analysis are possible. They are as follows. First: by contrasting cybernetically oriented policy analysis with the concept of personal agency, it might be thought that I am implying conscious authoritarianism on the part of would-be social engineers who are oblivious to the pluralistic nature of liberal societies. Second: stress on the concept of personal agency could be interpreted as equating the dignity of personal agency with an argument for the equal validity of all opinions to be found in a given population. Third: the particular example of cybernetic rhetoric utilized for critical analysis could be interpreted as an allegation that systems engineers view everything in terms of hard-core determinism. Against this it would be appropriate to object that cybernetically oriented analysts

[17] The social functions of ignorance have received remarkably little explicit theoretical and research attention in sociology. Two important exceptions are W. E. Moore and M. Tumin (1949) and Schneider (1962). This lack of attention is remarkable in view of the existence for years of data such as utilized by Philip Converse (1964). Participationism as a panacea solution to all these considerations has not gone unopposed (see Kaufmann, 1969; Wilcox, 1969).

think in terms of probability calculations applied to the behavior of masses of people, not individual persons. Thus it would follow that cybernetic analysis leaves ample room for personal variations and decisions. Let us address these questions one at a time.

1. It is possible to argue that cybernetically oriented social engineering rhetoric has totalitarian potentialities without denying that its exemplars recognize the existence and abstract legitimacy of social pluralism. This is because there are ways of handling pluralism that are consistent with a totalitarian approach to decision-making.

One way to facilitate totalitarian decision-making is to pay lip service to pluralism while encouraging the steady reduction of meanings to the status of quantifiable operational indicators, thereby creating an easily manageable public and machine analyzable criterion of meaning. Money is the paradigm here. To the extent that such indicators replace other criteria of meaning, such a solution can be called decision by reduction.

A second approach to decision-making that can reconcile the rhetoric of pluralism with the drift to cybernetic totalitarianism is to redefine the principles that legitimize constraints on pluralistic variety. There is, after all, no such thing as a fully or purely pluralistic society. There are always constraints. Though difficult to define exactly, these constraints are rooted in certain broadly shared but abstract principles such as definitions of reality, norms of propriety, the alleged importance of certain institutions and values, and some conception of national purpose. At a time, such as today, when these shared patterns of meaning are breaking down and when pluralism appears to border on anarchy, there comes a point when people begin to worry about what the new constraints should be that could arrest the pluralistic drive before it does indeed lapse into anarchy. Such anxiety could facilitate an uncritical acceptance by the public of new constraints. Among these new constraints could be the somewhat arbitrary interests and values of social engineers—these interests and values being disguised by abstract talk of system equilibrium, disturbance, feedback, computer languages, and cybernetic controls. Since the public is unprepared to evaluate the credibility of such technical language, this tendency could be called decision by technocratic mystification.

Finally, there is a third approach to pluralism that is not inconsistent with totalitarian drift. Pluralism, as has been noted, is something of an abstract term. It does not carry with it its own referent, that is, the unit of analysis referred to. Thus, one can point to pluralism in social practice, social interest, values and norms, and styles of life. Perhaps the most firmly established unit of analysis in liberal culture is the pluralism of opinions. Whatever other disagreements there are, almost everyone would insist on the right of anyone to "their own" opinion.

There are two dangers in grounding pluralism in the markets of opinion. Consider the distinction between "opinion" and "judgment." Phenomenologically, the term opinion refers to the expression of untutored logic, compartmentalized levels of abstraction, extreme subjectiveness, and "ready-at-hand" justifications. What people mean by "judgment," on the other hand, makes judgment definable as an orientation resulting from a thoughtful application of certain procedural rules to experience. These rules are designed to validate an opinion according to principles considered justifiable by the judger, not by reference merely to his "own" opinions but by higher-order notions he believes to be legitimate and rational in some more lasting historical sense. In short, people appear more casuistically careful with their judgments than with their opinions. Opinion is unstable and therefore easily manipulated. It is moreover a potent force when it is managed because of its intimate association with emotionally charged symbols. To define pluralism simply as the right of untutored opinion to exist, therefore, is to invite subversion of personal agency by state managers through selective utilization of information. This may be called decision by propaganda.

2. This review of three approaches to decision-making that seem to reconcile the rhetoric of pluralism with the totalitarian potentialities of social engineering enables us to address a second misunderstanding which could result from the preceding discussion. That is, it will be recalled, the equation of an emphasis on personal agency with the equal validity of all opinions.

As the distinction between opinion and judgment implies, there are valid and invalid, tutored and untutored approaches to human values, emotions, and norms, however difficult such determinations might be in particular cases. The relativities of experience are not rooted in the realm of mere opinions, but in the much more finite range of variation in fundamental values of the sort that underlie cohesive "life-styles." Something as deep as a "style" of valuing and acting has a certain internal logic and cohesion of its own. This has been taken for granted by serious thinkers through the ages. In our times, men as diverse as Soren Kierkegaard and Max Weber wrote extensively on this point, Weber in his work on the sociology of religion, and Kierkegaard in his delineation of the inner contours of the ethical, aesthetic, and religious ways of life.

As a criterion for action, intensity of opinion is entirely unrelated to wisdom of judgment. Wisdom (as distinguishable from "horse sense") results from the cultivation of clues and insights concerning human action and its consequences which have been accumulated in the heritage of reflection about the spiritual itineraries of the human race. This heritage includes myths, religions, arts, sciences, and biography. It is this heritage of insight into the qualitative dimensions of the human "life world" which should provide the standard of judgment to be applied to all particular ambitions to quantify discourse about human aspirations and actions. All this is obviously not to be taken as an argument against quantification in appropriate circumstances. It is only a warning about its use as a substitute for the cultivation, and application to the decision-making process, of refined human sensibilities.

3. Finally, we may turn to a third possible misunderstanding of this presentation. This is the view that our whole argument is based on a misconception of the

cybernetic orientation as one of hard determinism instead of what it really is, a probabilistic approach to social processes.

The issue here is not hard determinism versus probabilism. Rather, the issues are these. First, what is the locus of human agency? Second, what are the criteria for distinguishing rational from irrational human agency in different social contexts? Third, what is the place of answers to these two questions in the structure of social science theory?

This essay should not in any way be interpreted as categorically rejecting cybernetics, simulation, or any other form of systems analysis. That would be a form of Ludditism. We are concerned with maintaining the status of these things as tools, as instruments of human agency. Perhaps few people have expressed this agenda better than the founder of modern cybernetic analysis himself, Norbert Wiener (1954).

> For the man . . . to throw the problem of his responsibility on the machine, whether it can learn or not, is to cast his responsibility to the winds, and to find it coming back seated on the whirlwind.

> I have spoken of machines, but not only of machines having brains of brass and thews of iron. When human atoms are knit into organization in which they are used, not in their full right as responsible human beings, but as cogs and levers and rods, it matters little that their raw material is flesh and blood. *What is used as an element in a machine, is in fact an element in the machine* [p. 185 (italics his)].

The essence of my argument, then, is that, while the scientific test of systems analysis is its contribution to the efficient operation of actual social processes, from the standpoint of Western humanism the ultimate moral test must be the degree to which such analyses function as a tool for the refinement of insight as regards rational human agency and its constraints. The ultimate danger of systems analysis is that it might provide the most seductive of all opportunities yet conceived for what Sartre (1966) has called "bad faith." He means by this a form of alienation: the nonconscious projection of responsibility onto socially created symbols (roles, systems, nations) by reifying these into falsely concrete objects whose agent we then become. These points bear some modest elaboration.

Whatever the ambiguities, the basic notion of the person implied in our essay is that of an organizer of meaningful acts; that is, of social events which are patterned according to meanings called reasons and intentions.[18] Clearly, not all human behav-

---

[18] The phrase personal agency hides numerous problems of great philosophical complexity under a single label. For a general introduction to the various traditions of voluntarism in the West, see Vernon J. Bourke (1964). A good source for ongoing discussions of the concept of agency generally is the journal *Philosophy and Phenomenological Research* (see, e.g., Boler, 1968). A kind of conceptual table of contents of the issues involved as the philosophers now see them can be had by perusing the reader edited by Myles Brand (1970; see also McGowan & Gochnauer, 1971). Analysis of voluntarism has proceeded along somewhat independent lines in philosophy

ior is comprised of acts in this sense. Nor does the locus of personhood in the jurisprudential sense have necessarily to be understood as residing in the human ego-self. Kin groups, corporations, and states have been legal persons at various times throughout history. However, in this analysis we are concerned with the generic sense of a person as the socially patterned self functioning as an agent in his environment. An assumption that is central to contemporary Western liberal humanism is that the person so defined is the legitimate final source for the defining of his interests. Assuming he is "responsible," it is in this sense that the person is today thought of as a "free agent," however unwise his acts may be regarded by others. Western culture today understands by responsibility basically two things: the absence of totalistic external constraint upon the agent's ability to organize meaningful acts, and the agent's internal capacity to organize such acts. This capacity, or, if one will, rationality, may be thought of as an agent's insight into the relationships between acts and their consequences in the context of a human environment. A human environment means a setting constituted by interpersonal expectations, cultural values, social norms, institutions, and material objects. Let us explore for a moment the ideal humanistic meaning of rationality.

In this general tradition—influenced variously by Enlightenment rationalism, by romanticism, and by Marxism—the relationship between an agent, an act, and its consequences, is characterized by the integration in the agent of three types of awareness about the nature of a consequence. These dimensions of awareness may

---

and social science. While social scientists have normally been quite uncritical about the metaphysical problems involved in using the concepts of self and action, philosophers have, by and large, not been very attentive to the problem of integrating their work into the technical agenda of social science theory.

Until recently, American social scientists have largely restricted their awareness of the issues of agency to variations on the themes laid down by George Herbert Mead, John Dewey, and related thinkers. These themes have been developed generally under the term "symbolic interactionism." A useful introduction to the styles and variations in this tradition of social psychology is the collective work edited by J. G. Manis and B. N. Meltzer (1967). There has been little effort to take account of the analyses of action to be found in the works of European philosophers like Heidegger, Sartre, Maurice Blondel, and Paul Ricoer. However, in recent years the influence of European phenomenology (notably Husserl's) has made itself felt in American sociology, notably via the essays and books of Alfred Schutz. A convenient place to begin examining the works of this seminal mediator between European and American social thought is Schutz (1967). This study, first published in 1932, is a critical examination—in the light of Husserl's phenomenology—of Max Weber's uses of the terms "meaning" and "subjective."

These influences are spreading somewhat in American social thought because of what the sociologist Dennis Wrong has called "the oversocialized conception of man," in part associated with the theoretical dominance of structural-functionalism. One example of the concern felt by some about the status of voluntarism as a concept in social theory was the publication of a symposium edited by Samuel Z. Klausner (1965). An especially useful contribution to this volume by Benjamin Nelson (1965) should be noted. This essay contains a massive bibliography on the topic.

Two other theoretical traditions have been at least indirectly responsible for keeping open a view of society as flexible enough for effective personal agency. One is the sociology

be set forth by means of questions that a hypothetically thoughtful agent would ask, prior to acting if he could.

1. Regarding a given consequence of my action, what is its probability of occurrence? (A demand for full predictability would constitute a denial of contingency, including the action of other agents.)

2. What is the nature of the consequence as a physical state? That is, what does the consequence do, in its manifestation as a physical object or complex of objects, to me or to other people, or to my situation?

3. What is the nature of the consequence as a value state? That is, what does the consequence do in its manifestation as a force for good or evil as I and my environment define these terms? (The notion of value relativism can be misleading here. The value dimensions of a consequence are no less "objective" than its physical dimensions. What is relative to particular cultures are the rules for evaluating consequences as good or evil. But once such a standard is set, it imposes an objective logic on such matters.)

## CONCLUSION

These characteristics of rational agency point up an important generalization. The rational person does not displace his agency onto a reified conception of the social system. Neither does he place himself solipsistically at the center of

---

of conflict, recently stressed again in Alvin Gouldner (1970). The other tradition is the social-psychological "exchange" theories of interpersonal relations. This approach, which involves application of the "economic man" paradigm to the study of social relations generally, is best exemplified by Peter Blau (1964).

However, the most systematic contemporary attempts to incorporate notions of human agency into sociological theory occur in the following works. Although they seldom use the term directly, a comprehensive treatment of the dialectical relationships between agency and objectification occurs in Peter Berger and Thomas Luckman (1966). From a body of work collectively called ethnomethodology, inspired by some of Schutz's works, there is coming forth an increasingly sophisticated line of empirical research on the processes of constructing, sustaining, and manipulating the social world and its roles. Names associated with this intellectual movement include Harold Garfinkel, Aaron Cicourel, and Jack D. Douglas. Three books, two collective works edited by Douglas (1970a, 1970b) and another written by him (Douglas (1967) should be closely consulted by those who desire a rich introduction to this promising line of work on human agency in social theory. Perhaps the most important text in social science for those interested in the methodological problems pertaining to the effective scientific study of personal agency is Aaron Cicourel (1964; see also Churchill, 1971). It should be understood that the researchers we have mentioned here are not concerned simply with reproducing the subjective reports of respondents uttered in common-sense terms. That would be nothing but crude ethnography. Their goal, rather, is to incorporate models of common-sense experience into the models that the scientific observer generates from a more comparative data base. In this way the categories of the scientist will have something to do with the way in which a given society is lived and "intended" by its members.

As of now, however, with a few exceptions, the literature of the philosophy of action and of the sociology of action have evolved independently of each other. The work of integrating the moralist's concern for personal dignity, the scientist's interest in explanation, and the engineer's desire to solve problems remains a task for a new generation.

the world. The rational person thinks in terms of projects and constraints inter-twining with each other to form patterns of action through time.

The chief characteristic of the alienated form of thought that has been the topic of this essay, however, is a severance between doing and knowing that is so total as to sometimes eventuate in two different social types of people. Let us draw them as unflattering moral extremes, insofar as they apply to policy prob-lems.

One type is a walking calculator, abstractly concerned with solving a prob-lem, but really fascinated with the convolutions of the technique systems he uses to do so.

The other type is a participatory ideologue, unable to trust anyone to the point of delegating any authority. He also is abstractly concerned with solving a problem, but is really fascinated with the process of feeling himself in action.

It does not take too much insight to see, first, that these are complemen-tary types and, second, that they symbolize in their severance from each other a fragmented culture. One type is the human being as pure intellectual knower, in a frenzy to reduce the whole world to a determinate object so he can understand it. The other type is the human being as pure subject, in a frenzy to reduce the whole world to action. Between them, properly joined, they would comprise one authentic human being. It is not clear how this can be accomplished, but the sus-picion grows that if it is not, they may kill each other.


## REFERENCES

Arendt, H. *The human condition.* Garden City, N. Y.: Doubleday, 1958. Pp. 45-65.
Bell, D. Work and its discontents: The cult of efficiency in America. *The end of ideology.* New York: Collier Books, 1961. Pp. 227-272.
Berger, P., & Luckmann, T. *The social construction of reality.* Garden City, N. Y.: Doubleday, 1966.
Berger, P., & Neuhaus, R. *Movement and revolution.* Garden City, N. Y.: Doubleday, 1970.
Black, M. *Models and metaphors.* Ithaca, N. Y.: Cornell University Press, 1962.
Blau, P. *Exchange and power in social life.* New York, Wiley, 1964.
Boler, J. F. Agency. *Philosophy and Phenomenological Research,* 1968, *29(2),* 165-182.
Bourke, V. J. *The will in western thought.* New York: Sheed & Ward, 1964.
Brand, M. (Ed.), *The nature of human action.* Atlanta: Scott, Foresman, 1970.
Brzezinski, Z. America in the technetronic age. *Encounter,* 1968, *XXX*(1).
Churchill, L. Ethnomethodology and measurement. *Social Forces,* 1971, *50*(2), 182-190.
Cicourel, A. V. *Method and measurement in sociology.* New York: Free Press, 1964.
Cicourel, A. V. *The social organization of juvenile justice.* New York: Wiley, 1968.
Commons, J. *Institutional economics.* Vol. 2. Madison: University of Wisconsin Press, 1961.
Converse, P. The nature of belief systems in mass publics. In D. E. Apter (Ed.), *Ideology and discontent.* New York: Macmillan, 1964. Pp. 205-262.
Deutsch, K. W. *The nerves of government.* New York: Free Press, 1966.
Douglas, J. D. *The social meanings of suicide.* Princeton: Princeton University Press, 1967.
Douglas, J. D. (Ed.), *Deviance and respectability: The social construction of moral meanings.* New York: Basic Books, 1970. (a)

Douglas, J. D. (Ed.), *Understanding everyday life.* Chicago: Aldine, 1970. (b)

Gilpin, R. Technological strategies and national purpose. *Science,* 1970, *169,* 441-448.

Golovin, N. The evaluative function in government. In E. M. Dewan (Ed.), *Cybernetics and the management of large systems.* New York: Macmillan (Spartan Books), 1969.

Gouldner, A. *The coming crisis of western sociology.* New York: Basic Books, 1970.

Halberstam, D. The programming of Robert McNamara. *Harper's Magazine,* 1971, February, 37-71.

Jonas, H. The practical uses of theory. Reprinted in M. Natanson (Ed.), *Philosophy of the social sciences: A reader.* New York: Random House, 1963.

Kaufmann, H. Administrative decentralization and political power. *Public Administration Review,* 1969, *29*(1), 3-15.

Kirk, K. *Conscience and its problems.* London: Longmans, Green, 1927.

Klausner, S. Z. (Ed.), *The quest for self-control: Classical philosophies and scientific research.* New York: Free Press, 1965.

Macmurray, J. *Interpreting the universe.* London: Faber & Faber, 1936.

Macmurray, J. *The self as agent.* London: Faber & Faber, 1957.

Macmurray, J. *Persons on relation.* London: Faber & Faber, 1961.

Manis, J. G., & Meltzer, B. N. (Eds.), *Symbolic interaction: A reader in social psychology.* Boston: Allyn & Bacon, 1967.

Mannheim, K. The democratization of culture. *Essays on the sociology of culture.* London: Routledge & Kegan Paul, 1956. Pp. 171-246.

Matson, F. W. *The broken image.* Garden City, N. Y.: Doubleday, 1966.

McGowan, R., & Gochnauer, M. A bibliography of the philosophy of action. In R. Binkley *et al.* (Eds.), *Agent, action and reason.* Toronto: Toronto University Press, 1971. Pp. 167-199.

McLellan, D. (Ed. & Transl.), *The grundrisse.* New York: Harper, 1971. Pp. 59-69.

Meadows, P. The metaphors of order: Toward a taxonomy of organization theory. In L. Gross (Ed.), *Sociological theory: Inquiries and paradigms.* New York: Harper, 1967. Pp. 77-103.

Michael, D. Cybernation: The silent conquest. In M. Philipson (Ed.), *Automation.* New York: Vintage, 1962.

Mills, C. W. The mass society. Reprinted in E. Josephson & M. Josephson (Eds.), *Man alone: Alienation in modern society.* New York: Dell Publ., 1962. Pp. 201-227.

Moore, W. E., & Tumin, M. Some social functions of ignorance. *American Sociological Review,* 1949, *14,* 492-508.

Nelson, B. Self-images and systems of spiritual direction in the history of European civilization. In S. Z. Klausner (Ed.), *The quest for self-control: Classical philosophies and scientific research.* New York: Free Press, 1965. Pp. 40-103.

Niebuhr, H. R. *The responsible self.* New York: Harper, 1963.

Ray, P. H. Human technology, ecology, and the need for social planning. *American Behavioral Scientist,* 1968, *11*(6), 18-19.

A reporter at large. *New Yorker,* 1970, July 4, by-line William Whitworth, Pp. 30-56.

Rosen, Z. The influence of Bruno Bauer on Marx's concept of alienation. *Social Theory and Practice,* 1970, *1*(2), 50-69.

Saint-Simon, H. *Social organization, the science of man, and other writings.* 1817. (Republished: New York, Harper, 1964.)

Sartre, J.-P. *Being and nothingness.* New York: Washington Square Press, 1966. Pp. 86-116.

Savas, E. S. Cybernetics in city hall. *Science,* 1970, *169,* 1070.

Schick, A. The cybernetic state. *Trans-Action,* 1970, *7*(4).

Schneider, Louis. The role of the category of ignorance. *American Sociological Review,* 1962, *27,* 492-508.

Schutz, A. *The phenomenology of the social world.* (Transl. by G. Walsh & F. Lehnert) Evanston, Ill.: Northwestern University Press, 1967.

Shibutani, T. *Improvised news.* Indianapolis: Bobbs-Merrill, 1966.
Skinner, B. F. *Walden two.* New York: Macmillan, 1948.
Sorokin, P. *Contemporary sociological theories.* New York : Harper, 1928. Pp. 3-62, 195-218.
Spykman, N. J. *The social theory of Georg Simmel.* New York: Atherton Press. Pp. 219-253.
Stanley, M. Technicism, liberalism and development: A study in irony as social theory. In
    M. Stanley (Ed.), *Social development: Critical perspectives.* New York: Basic Books,
    1972. Pp. 276-325.
Turbayne, C. *The myth of metaphor.* (Rev. ed.) Columbia, S. C.: University of South Carolina
    Press, 1970.
Weber, M. *The Protestant ethic and the spirit of capitalism.* New York: Scribners, 1958.
Wiener, N. *The human use of human beings.* Garden City, N. Y.: Doubleday, 1954.
Wilcox, H. G. Hierarchy, human nature, and the participative panacea. *Public Administration
    Review,* 1969, *29*(1), 53-63.
Wildavsky, A. *The politics of the budgetary process.* Boston: Little, Brown, 1964.
Wilenski, H. *Organizational intelligence.* New York: Basic Books, 1967.
Wolin, S. Political theory as a vocation. *American Political Science Review,* 1969, *63*(4).

# Chapter 11

# Alienation and the U.S. Economic Future

## A. Dale Tussing

Economics Department, Syracuse University
and
Educational Policy Research Center, Syracuse

Anglo-American economics has, with few exceptions, avoided the subject of pathology. Instead, the emphasis has been on the proper functioning of an economy as a system. There is one prominent exception—aggregate demand instability—where economics concerns itself with cyclical unemployment and with inflation, both of which are pathological cases. But even here, while the economy is not viewed as an inherently harmonious and stable system, it is nonetheless viewed as a predictable and not inherently dysfunctional one, whose tendencies for instability are easily corrected. Moreover, an understanding of modern fiscal and monetary policy permits a "neoclassical synthesis" where the fundamentally harmonious underlying system continues to perform as an equilibrating and ameliorative order.

It might be added that for decades, until the publication of Keynes' (1936) *General Theory,* economic theory persisted either to misunderstand or, in effect, to deny the possibility of recessions and depressions because of a commitment to the market-equilibrium, exchange system of the economy whose logic precluded involuntary unemployment. There is little room in such a system of thought for the concept of alienation. Consequently, while the functioning of the economy may produce alienation, and while economists generally understand such functioning of the economy, an economist addressing the subject of alienation in the U. S. economy has little in modern economics literature upon which he can draw. There may be "economic alienation" in the real world, but no "alienation economics" in the lit-

251

erature. This is unfortunate, because a number of sources and dimensions of modern alienation are economic in origin; moreover, the early literature of economics, especially the writings of Karl Marx (1844), but even of Adam Smith (1776), made valuable contributions to the subject.

The purpose of the present essay, then, is not to survey the state of the professional literature in this area, but, rather, to catalog a number of economic sources and types of social and personal alienation. An attempt will be made to anticipate the progress of such alienation through the remainder of the century, basing such anticipations on some plausible and probable economic developments.

## THE RELATIONSHIP OF THE INDIVIDUAL TO THE ECONOMIC SYSTEM

The relationship of the individual to any economic system is either implicitly or explicitly one of reciprocal exchange: he performs some function, usually of labor, and in exchange he is entitled to the product of the function and efforts of others, and to a variety of other economic benefits. The exchange, which may or may not be a *quid pro quo* transaction of like values, is that he does something, and consequently gets something. From working (or from performing other accepted economic functions, such as initiating a new firm or organization, or investing and taking risks), the individual derives survival, significance, and legitimacy. That is, his performance provides him with what he needs to live and survive; it traditionally helps provide purpose to his life, particularly so in a secular society, and it makes him, his survival, comfort, and even affluence legitimate in his own eyes and in the eyes of others, and justifies his "membership" in society.

To simplify our nomenclature, let us call "job" any economic function or performance of the individual, not only what is called "work" or "labor" in modern industrial societies, but also all other functions for which people are paid and, therefore, all which are formally recognized as "productive" and which are in that way defined as socially legitimate.

### Work and Purpose

There are four types of purpose or meaning which individuals derive from their job, two of which derive from the work itself or its product, and two of which derive from job-holding, the formal economic and social relationship between the person and society. The first of these is a situation in which the individual's job is to produce his own goods for his (and his family's) own consumption—such as in a primitive, self-sufficient, or Robinson Crusoe-type economic arrangement (one cannot call this an economic system, since there are no economic relationships among its members, all self-sufficient families). In this primitive arrangement, even though there are no economic relationships, there is no economic alienation, since we take alienation to imply some kind of rupture of bonds that had once existed between the individual and society, or at least the failure of anticipated bonds to come into existence. In the self-sufficient case, no such bonds are presumed to have existed.

On the other hand, the self-sufficient economic arrangement provides the individual with the clearest sense of the worth and meaning of his own efforts. What he produces has clear and immediate value to him; it provides for his own survival and comfort. And there is no mystery about what precisely his role is in the production process; everything he produces, he produces from beginning to end. Compare his situation with that of the assembly-line or routine clerical employee in a large, modern corporate organization, who may not understand what he is helping to produce, or, if he does, may not understand the significance of that product, and may not understand how his own efforts fit in with others' to produce whatever it is. If the self-sufficient producer stops work for a period of time, his own well-being is affected; he may even freeze or starve. His efforts are demonstrably significant. If almost anyone in the present-day U. S. economy takes a few days off, his organization's output and his own income and consumption continue without change; the virtual interchangeability of each individual with hundreds of others is daily proof of his lack of essentiality. Indeed, one reason for organizing a business along modern corporate lines is to make the individual expendable.

While a self-sufficient way of life rarely existed in pure form, and even in approximations has all but died out, there is still a large component of each individual's efforts which he performs for himself rather than for others. These have more intrinsic meaning than those performed for and/or by others, and the more of one's day that is devoted to work for others, the more alienated an individual can be from his own efforts. Oddly, many of those "self-sufficient" efforts—gardening, hobby craftsmanship, hunting and fishing, etc.—are thought of as "leisure activities," especially among men, though in an earlier day they would have been regarded as part of the day's routine work. Presumably this is so because of a modern tendency to define as "leisure time" any for which one is not paid, as well as because such activities are intrinsically meaningful. For women, however, housework and childrearing are less universally regarded as inherently meaningful (women not having escaped such self-sufficient work as much as men), and women are less likely to regard work at home for which they are not paid as "leisure activity," though even here "scratch" cooking, breastfeeding of babies, and making one's clothes are regarded somewhat romantically as more basic and meaningful, and "feminine" in the same sense that shopcraft or deer hunting are "masculine."[1]

[1] There is a particularly strong reverance for nonexchange, self-sufficient activities among the neoprimitive and communal "subcultures" whose members recognize acutely the need to inject purpose into post-scarcity, twentieth century, American life.

When an individual produces goods for someone else's consumption and gets paid, and uses his money income to buy goods which someone else has produced, as is the case in a modern, money economy, then his job has lost some of its intrinsic meaning. To be precise, he becomes alienated from his work, though for a variety of reasons (to be discussed momentarily), he is not alienated from his job. As noted, we distinguish the meaning a person derives from the activity or the output of his work from the meaning a person derives from job-holding, and the former weakens as the product of the work becomes more remote from the worker.

The work may gain another kind of meaning in place of that lost, however (Morse & Weiss, 1955). It may satisfy a pride of craft or creativity, not only for artists or craftsmen, but for any worker who takes pride in doing good work, whether it be carpentry, stonemasonry, gardening, or driving a bus. This source of meaning is in danger, however, where the worker is used, in effect, as a machine, that is, doing standard, predefined, routine jobs which cannot be done well or poorly, but only right or wrong. The job may help produce a product in which the worker takes pride, even though his own role may be restricted, as, for example, where a person has a routine job in a factory where everyone nonetheless believes that their brand is best, and they identify with it. This kind of meaning through pride and loyalty is threatened in a variety of ways: by multi-product factories whose workers don't know what they're producing, by today's emphasis on the guilt from participating in the military-industrial complex, or in destroying ecological systems, or in having profited from racism, etc., by the decline of tradition in firms, and their marketing, as opposed to production orientation, and by the failure of most firms to produce products in which their employees can take any pride. Most of the same apply to government agencies as well as private firms. American institutions are more on the defensive in the 1970s than at any time since the late 1930s.

A job may be interesting, or provide recreational and/or aesthetic bonuses. It may provide companions, or even an entire system of friends, acquaintances, and leisure-time activities. And, increasingly, jobs are called on to provide, or to appear to provide, activities that are meaningful and relevant in terms of solving problems, answering challenges, and helping others. Of this last type, the Peace Corps and VISTA, as originally conceived and as presented to American society, are the paradigm cases, but corporate personnel departments have taken over this kind of rhetoric in their advertising and urge young graduates to make a difference in the world through corporate employment.

The work associated with most jobs in America today does not satisfy well this second need for meaning. Most have little creative component, and, in some, creativity is even rewarded by dismissal. In a complex economic system, creativity has its places—in the top ranks, or in the research and development department, or

in the universities—and elsewhere it is treated as disruption. Most jobs do not give
the worker a sense of pride either in his employer or in the product. Most jobs are
not inherently interesting or beautiful and few seem directly relevant to society's
needs, though in this area the ability to rationalize and exaggerate the significance
of one's job is surprisingly great.

There is, then, a tendency for Americans to become alienated from their work.
There is one countertrend. The kind of job which seems, through the next several
decades, most likely to disappear on account of automation, is precisely the kind of
job which is the most routine and devoid of meaning, where (as we have said above)
the worker is used as a kind of machine. Many of the most meaningless jobs will disappear. But, on balance, meaningful jobs become fewer, and the meaningful work
in individual jobs will decline. Small business, which a person can own or manage
himself, or where at least even as a clerk he can visualize the entire production process from beginning to end and understand his own role in it, continues to decline
in significance in favor of the giant corporation. Technology in America is so powerful and has been for so long that its ability to solve technical problems is increasingly taken for granted and much of the pleasure is thereby taken out of technical
jobs which would have been seen as exciting and challenging a few years ago. One
ironic consequence of the moon landing has been to make much technological
change of the foreseeable future seem anticlimactic and, hence, more routine and
apparently mechanical.

## Jobs and Purpose

What we face, then, is increasing alienation from work. As a consequence of
the decline of these first two types of meaning, the attention of Americans is increasingly focused on the job rather than on the work; that is, their concern is more
and more exclusively with (1) material survival and success (i.e., "the money"), and
(2) with the social legitimacy a job provides. One important implication is that the
rewards from work come primarily off the job and away from one's place of work.

Few people in America, or in the whole Western world, accept the definition
of the purpose of their lives provided by organized religion, and even where the
Church prospers, a successful person tends to be one who has prospered materially,
and a failure is one who is not only poor but dependent upon others. Even where
the product itself is not meaningful, where the activities involved are not pleasant
or inherently rewarding, and where there is no reason to take pride in what one ac-
complishes, a job is nonetheless meaningful, and, indeed, often the most meaningful thing in life, because it provides for survival and for success. Closely connected
with the powerful survival-and-success, measure-of-one's-life meaning people find
in their jobs is the legitimacy a job provides, not only to one's level of living, but

to one's participation in society. This legitimacy exists only through contrast with dependent populations whose incomes and whose total roles are deemed illegitimate.[2]

The search for legitimacy of income is a major preoccupation in the United States today (Tussing, 1969). Much time, effort, and ingenuity is spent by a large part of the population in seeking to justify either their absolute income level, or their relative position, or both. Some of the reasons for this preoccupation are the increasing affluence of many Americans, despite their declining hours of work and declining intensity of effort, with resulting guilt, the increasingly apparent inequities in the distribution of American income, and the conflict between an ideology which precludes a welfare state and the rise of such programs as Social Security.

The ultimate justification of income is from one's job, and "job" is defined earlier. In the views of many people, job-holders are members of and contributors to society; nonjob-holders aren't. Job-holding also legitimates one's political role, as well, usually under the label of "taxpayer."[3]

For women, income legitimacy has some curious features. A nonjob-holding married woman, a "housewife" that is, does not necessarily derive her income legitimacy (justification for her level of living, rather than a cash income) from housework or childcare. She derives it from being married to a man with a legitimate income. Women who have families but, for a variety of reasons, no husband, are generally expected to live off their former husbands' jobs through life insurance, alimony, etc., or to have jobs of their own. Those who live on welfare allowances live illegitimately; child-care centers are regarded as an obvious and necessary partial solution to the "welfare problem." Many affluent, middle-class, or even work-

---

[2] It might at first seem that legitimacy comes from work rather than a job; indeed, one hears much about a "work ethic" but little about a "job ethic." The reason for this is the confusion which exists between work and jobs (Green, 1968). But it is clearly possible for the job-holder, whether in the private or public sector, and whether "management" or "labor," to spend much of his day trying to avoid work, or through his union trying to bargain for less work, and, moreover, complaining about welfare recipients and other unemployed. And it is possible for railroads to demand "full-crew laws" or for printers to demand "bogus" typesetting, and to regard such patently unproductive efforts as nonetheless a source of legitimate income.

[3] A job is not the only source of income legitimacy, but the others relate in some way to job-legitimated income. For instance, one can, from one's just earnings, save for one's own retirement, either through a bank account or some formal pension scheme; and, similarly, one can provide through savings or insurance for an income while sick or for one's family when one is, as the life insurance advertisements put it, "no longer there."

Most public (government) social insurance schemes are constructed so as to resemble private pensions, insurance, and the like (Tussing, 1969). Social security, medicare, railroad retirement, unemployment compensation, and others are financed out of payroll taxes which resemble insurance premiums and obviously relate to employment. Only the system of programs for the poor, especially "welfare" or public assistance, are noncontributory and financed out of the general fund. And no one mistakes the highly legitimate social security check whose ultimate source is (or seems to be) one's own employment with the obviously illegitimate welfare check, which is (or seems to be) public charity to a dependent population.

ing-class housewives peform the same tasks in life as the husbandless welfare mothers—that is, bearing and raising children, cleaning, mending, cooking, etc.—and yet the latter are not deemed by society as "earning their way," and the former are. Clearly, the ultimate justification of the suburban woman's standard of living is her husband's job, not her own efforts. One conclusion is, again, that legitimacy derives from the job, not the work.

Can these two job-related sources of individual meaning ever decline in importance? And can one truly be alienated from his job as well as from his work? We are beginning to see the decline of this kind of meaning and the rise of this kind of alienation, and the disaffection of a fraction of our more sensitive youth may be only the beginning.

The reason is that both job-related sources of meaning—survival-and-success as a measure of one's life, and a job as the source of social legitimacy and personal adequacy—are imposed by society only in a scarcity-and-insecurity economy. Thus far, the world has known no other type, and every people has had if not poverty then at least insufficiency, and, moreover, have been troubled by the threat of periodic economic collapse—pestilence and flood and agriculture failure, or unemployment and depression from industrial failure, or both. And even those who were lucky enough not to share the poverty of the mass of people have shared in their insecurity; indeed, economic collapse always poses special threats to the wealthy.

Attitudes toward jobs, income, and economic legitimacy are strikingly different among generations, as between the older generation which has known real poverty, or real insecurity, or both, and which has lived through the most catastrophic industrial collapse that modern capitalism has to offer, and the younger generation which has experienced not only affluence but uninterrupted affluence. Rejection of traditional economic definitions of life's purposes is most common, moreover, among precisely those youths whose own family backgrounds have been the most comfortable and secure.

This is not to say that it is coming to be common among young people to reject material well-being. It is, rather, that material well-being is increasingly taken for granted, and that the quest for economic security has ceased to be a central task of life. Moreover, from a plateau of economic sufficiency, many young people who have not experienced want place less emphasis on earning still more and more, than do a depression-scarred older generation who sometimes appear to be trying to earn more than, even with great ingenuity, they can figure out how to need to spend. The postscarcity attitudes of a youthful fraction of the population are undoubtedly reinforced by a number of features of modern economic life. An important one is the "disposable" quality of many goods, not only our willingness to throw away everything from empty bottles to five-year old automobiles, but our willingness to sacrifice historic or architecturally important buildings, open countryside, and even clean air and water, to still further production. Young people, who have not known real insecurity, find it difficult to justify these costs by reference to added gross national product (GNP). Indeed, the business sector has come to be viewed as inherently illegitimate to the most disaffected of the younger generation.

Assuming continued affluence and prosperity, if the fraction of the population sharing these attitudes rises to its limit, 100%, the generational difference (on at least this important count) will subside, but the implied alienation from the economy and the absence of purpose in life will become more widespread.

Before turning to other concerns, one powerful implication must be noted. Where survival itself is no longer an issue, and where economic insecurity is really unknown, then one's "job" ceases to be the centerpiece of his life, or, if it does retain its meaning, it is because the job offers some special, noneconomic sense of achievement, presumably a kind of meaning which arises out of the work rather than the job. Since the schools, both in their educating and in their certifying functions, have so closely keyed their own purposes to "jobs" and "success," as the meaning of these declines in importance so must the meaning of the schools, unless they come up with new definitions of their purposes. When one examines the future of education in America through the year 2000, this is probably the single most important question: What are the schools to be for? (See Gerald Reagen, this volume, Ch. 15.)

It follows that alienation from the economy, and rejection of economic success as the central purpose in life, is associated with the disaffection of young people—once again, especially the affluent—from their schools.

## Consuming and Purpose

Individuals relate to the economy not only through their job roles but through their roles as consumers. A decade and a half ago, commentators were noting the rise of consumerism, where modern families, and especially housewives, gained stature and a sense of adequacy from knowing what to buy and where to buy it. Today the future of consumerism is in doubt. One wonders whether it can survive in a postscarcity economy. What does it matter whether one gets the best buy, if the savings are small compared with one's income, especially considering the effort involved in comparing products?

Another source of consumer alienation arises out of the American's loss of identity as a consumer of products produced for a mass market and not individually meant for him, of products identical with those bought by thousands or millions of others. It is for this reason that, in merchandising products, efforts are made to effect superficial differences between otherwise identical products; for reasons of economy and efficiency, most such differences are trivial. Whether an initial on his "personalized" monogrammed shirt makes the buyer feel that it really was made for him, or the purchase of a mass-produced coat-of-arms gives him a personal connection with history, is dubious. This loss of identity in mass-produced housing, clothing, leisure, and culture provides still another reason for the American to try to produce things for himself. Ironically, it creates a mass market for shop tools and similar do-it-yourself paraphernalia.

When a buyer deals with a small, independent business, he is typically made to feel important by those who serve him because, in fact, he is important to them. But when he deals with a massive modern corporation—an automobile manufacturer, a retail and mail-order chain, or the like—he is, in fact, unimportant, except in a statistical sense as a "representative sample" of an important-sized group. Of course, the large corporation is more efficient, and, for most purchases, economy and promptness are more immediately important than individual treatment. But the cumulative loss is great and of considerable importance.

Small proprietary and partnership forms of business still survive in some of the professions, particularly medicine, dental care, and law. But the time of these professionals is so valuable that their treatment of clients has come to be, if anything, more impersonal than that of the large corporation. Doctors, for example, not only do not make house calls, but instead expect their patients to wait for long periods in waiting rooms, and when most doctors see their patients, they do so for extremely brief periods. Rarely are patients, whether in a doctor's office or in a hospital, made to feel individually important. That this impersonal treatment is the product of institutional changes and technological and medical improvements which have also improved the quality of medical care is adequate explanation but small comfort.

For individual treatment and recognition of his fundamental humanity, in short, the average American does not turn to those from whom he buys.

## THE SPECIAL CASE OF THE POOR[4]

It is hardly surprising that, in some sense, the poor in a generally nonpoor society can be said to be alienated. If it is not generally accepted, it is at least not novel to say that the poverty of most American poor is powerlessness, of which moneylessness is an important part, a symptom, a symbol, and the most easily quantifiable index. That the pathology of poverty involves, or can involve, profound alienation from the rest of society, requires mention but perhaps not elaboration. We should note that (1) many poor are essentially nonparticipants in the economy—not unemployed, but rather not in the labor force; (2) many poor are dependent on welfare and other charity-like programs which, as mentioned earlier, are seen as socially illegitimate; and (3) many poor are those who have failed in the noneconomic institutional structure, particularly the schools and the legal system.

There are elements in the economic alienation of the poor which are equally important and equally difficult, but which are less known; they relate to what this

[4] This section is adapted from Tussing (1970).

author has called the "dual economy" (Tussing, 1970). A dual economy is one in which the large, dominant majority consists of nonpoor, and a minority are chronically poor. There is no precise dividing line between the two, but in the discussion that follows, the two groups are treated as if there were. And those with inadequate educations are not, in all respects, those with inadequate incomes, though in what follows the two will be treated as identical. Little violence is done to reality in either of these assumptions. The most salient characteristic of the dual economy is that it adjusts to and accommodates the state of development of the larger, dominant, nonpoor element, to the absolute as well as relative economic disadvantage of the poor, with the effect, moreover, of enhancing the isolation and alienation of the poor.

Three important implications of this proposition can be discussed, under "Consumption Technology," "The Advantages of an Education," and "Price Structure."

## Consumption Technology

The concept of "technology," which most people conceive of as applying only to production, will be recognized as applying also to consumption. Like production technology, consumption technology changes over time. Techniques employed by families in feeding, housing, transporting, amusing, and otherwise satisfying and gratifying themselves change in response to changed relative price (reflecting changes in production technology), to higher incomes, and to the introduction of new and/or changed products.

Poor families are, in many instances, forced to adopt consumption technologies appropriate to the nonpoor. And, as a consequence, they are made even poorer. To illustrate, consider the oft-heard proposition that American poor are really quite well-off, either from a world-wide standpoint or, within America, from a historical perspective. The evidence cited that American poverty is "only relative" is either that their money incomes are high or, more commonly, that they often have available to them consumer goods which none but the elite in truly poor nations have— telephones, automobiles, television sets, and even a basic education.[5]

[5] The four products mentioned are chosen deliberately as those most frequently cited. In fact, some school districts have apparently limited free-lunch distribution to those truly poor without telephones, automobiles, or television sets (Sherrill, 1970).And Clair Wilcox (1969), in a poverty-and-social-welfare college textbook, offers a similar set of poverty-indicator products:

> The American poor enjoy many things that would have been regarded as luxuries by their forebearers and that would mark them as belonging to the middle class in Europe or to the upper class in much of Latin America, in Asia, or in Africa. Among the fifth of the people who fell below the CEA poverty line in 1962, 14 per cent had bought an automobile within the previous year, 19 percent had a home freezer, 73 per cent had a washing machine, and 79 per cent owned a television set.

Of the four products cited, education is not principally a matter of consumption technology and will be dealt with separately; the other three, however, are.

For most people, to have a telephone in a generally poor country, an underdeveloped country, would be pointless. Most personal communications are conducted on a face-to-face basis, and since no one whom you might call is likely to have a telephone, there is no real value in having one. In a society which has not adjusted to the telephone, the lack of one does not constitute poverty. But in the United States, where much of the important daily business of production and consumption, and the major way of dealing with all kinds of emergencies requires the telephone, not to have one is deprivation. To a person so deprived, there are two ingredients in his deprivation: his lack of a telephone, and society's adjustment to that communications medium. When we ignore the latter, we misunderstand the former.

The same point can be made about the automobile. As most Americans have gotten richer, as they have acquired more, larger, and more luxurious automobiles, and as public transportation has accordingly declined in quantity and deteriorated in quality, those who have suffered have been those people too poor to have cars. The example of Watts, California, not only poor but remote from jobs and ill-served by public transportation, suggests itself. Throughout America, the development of suburban shopping centers and even large city supermarkets, remote from most poor, have depended on and assumed widespread ownership of automobiles, and those without them have suffered. Before World War II there was hardly a household need which was not available from either delivery men or some kind of mobile store. The vegetable wagon, the egg man, the bread man, and the like represented an extremely inefficient product-distribution system, and it is probably economic that it has been replaced, now that almost everyone has an automobile. But for those who today have only a pre-World War II income, the pre-World War II consumption technology is more appropriate.[6]

One virtually certain indicator of a poor neighborhood is the shopping carts, borrowed from supermarkets, parked near the homes of the car-less poor. And in America, only the poor ride taxicabs to buy groceries.

Incidentally, the chronically poor in our society are not alone in bearing the costs as society adjusts to the automobile. In new suburban tracts, sidewalks are frequently omitted on the safe assumption that no one who matters walks. That leaves children and old people, by and large, to walk in the streets. Even they, however, cannot expect to walk on the fenced-off, sometimes elevated, limited-access freeways and highways that have become the main links connecting these tracts with each other and with the city.

[6] As a consequence, the urban slum dweller is far more reliant on small "ma-and-pa"-type neighborhood stores than is his nonpoor neighbor, and even if slum chain stores have the same prices as nonslum chain stores, and if slum neighborhood stores have the same price as nonslum neighborhood stores (both arguable propositions), the slum dweller must pay more for his groceries.

Even the television set, symbol of affluence of the critic of public assistance, represents dominant consumption technology, in this case in the area of amusement. Is there a society so poor that there is no popular entertainment? In some, it will be television; in some others, it will be the movies, local "opera houses," or singing and dancing (live) on the nearest streetcorner, depending on the state of amusement technology in society. Whether we Americans are richer or poorer for having substituted television for less polished but more intimate forms of live entertainment is beside the point; television has taken over, and other forms of popular entertainment do not exist as alternatives for the poor. Where live entertainment still exists, in the form of plays and concerts, it is beyond the reach of the poor and is beginning to be beyond the reach of all but a wealthy elite. Even motion pictures, the dominant mass entertainment medium of only a few years ago, are becoming too costly for the poor.

Take away the telephone, the car, and the television set from Americans and they are cut off from participation in the economy and from interaction with their friends and with the nation. They are not merely poor, they are isolated.

One conclusion is that, in many ways, it is better to be poor in a poor society than in a rich one. Another is that the significance of individual products—whether they be automobiles or horses—cannot be assumed to be constant across societies. A third is that we underestimate the poverty of the American poor.

## The Advantages of an Education

The society also adjusts to the level of educational attainment of the dominant, nonpoor element. The results are similar to those of consumption technology.

It is widely believed that an education confers advantages on its recipient, but that as more and more others are educated, the advantages of an education become less. For instance, it is often said that the widespread attainment of high school graduation in the United States has lowered the value of a high school diploma, and that the value of a college (bachelor's) degree is declining because so many are receiving degrees. Sometimes it is added that a master's degree is needed to obtain the position once provided by a bachelor's degree.

These propositions contain elements both of truth and falsity. The reason is that they can be interpreted in either a relative or an absolute sense. Clearly, to an educated person, the education of others weakens his relative educational position in society, but does it make him worse off in an absolute sense, as the statement appears to imply?

It is instructive to look at the extreme case. If one is among only a handful of educated persons in an otherwise uneducated society, he will almost certainly have an important position—government official, lawyer, doctor, etc. His income and manner of living will probably be well above those of the rest of the community. But there will also be disadvantages. There will probably be no bookstores, newspapers, or magazines, except possibly from foreign sources. There are not likely even to be signposts, or if there are their message will be in pictures, conferring no advantage on the literate person. Another problem is that he will, as they say, have "no one to talk to." He runs the risk that he may not be believed. As a doctor, he may lose out to folk medicine; as a lawyer, he may find the law ignored; as a scientist, he may find that myth and superstition are too powerful for him. At worst, the educated person in an uneducated community runs the risk of being executed for his knowledge and the threat it poses.

As more people are educated, and as the society adjusts to a higher level of education, the advantages of an education increase. There are more books and periodicals, and some choice among them. If production techniques are reorganized on the assumption of some human expertise, then those having that expertise can exploit it. In a thousand ways, the accommodation of society to a high level of education—not only literacy and the ability to manipulate numbers, but such basic things as the idea of cause and effect, the ability to deal with new situations without fear, and the ability to tolerate ambiguity—confers advantages on those already educated. Having an education in an uneducated society is almost the same as having a telephone in a society without a telephone system; it only creates potential benefit, which does not become an actual benefit until a significant part of society shares it.

The conclusion is that in most cases and for most people, the widely held proposition cited earlier, that the value of a high school diploma or a college degree is declining since so many are attaining them, is incorrect. The more people who have these, the more valuable they are.

In a dual economy, however, where (as we assume) the poor are also the uneducated, those who don't have diploma or degree suffer in an absolute sense as more people attain them. As the society increasingly adapts to a high educational level, the uneducated person becomes less and less able to function. Even unskilled jobs require attitudes shared by the educated but not by him; he is bewildered by access codes, area codes, and direct dialing, afraid to fly, distrustful of banks, lost a few blocks from home, and generally left behind and set adrift by the educational progress of his society. He is the most alienated person imaginable.

## Price Structure

The price structure of an economy is of immense importance. It consists of the relations among all prices, wage rates, interest rates, and like measures, and reflects society's priorities and preferences as well as product and resource, scarcity or abundance. The price structure is a powerful determinant of what people buy and how things are produced (see, among others, Samuelson, 1970).

To understand price structure problems of the dual economy, let us, for just a moment, imagine that the two components of the economy, the poor and the nonpoor, are separate economies, each with its own currency and with an exchange rate between them, and—more important—each with its own price structure. The price structure in the poor economy will differ from that in the nonpoor in a variety of ways.

For one thing, there will be a severe capital shortage among the poor, reflecting their weak net worth position. Consequently, interest rates will be higher than in the nonpoor economy. And if the poor have (as often alleged) a higher time preference, the forces for higher interest rates will be further enhanced. Just as capital is (relatively) scarce, so labor will be (relatively) abundant and presumably cheap. With cheap (and, it should be added, generally unskilled) labor and scarce and expensive capital, the poor economy will have a comparative advantage and, presumably, will specialize in production of different products from those produced in the nonpoor economy—small handicrafts, possibly, which require large amounts of labor relative to capital.[7]

Of course, in the real world, there are not two separate economies, each with its own price structure. Instead, there is a dual economy; and the price structure is the one appropriate to the dominant, nonpoor element. That economy's comparative advantage and, presumably, specialization will be in those techniques which economize on labor, which use skills and talents which do not exist or are dormant in the poor economy, and which are relatively capital-intensive. The price structure is inconsistent, then, with the state of development of the poor economy. The poor are forced to live in an economic world of relative prices, wages, and interest rates that is appropriate to a more advanced state of economic development.

It would be far easier, for instance, for indigenous "black capitalism" to develop in central cities if the price structure of 50 years ago, rather than of today, were to prevail. Poor people may even be handicapped by high wages: if the socially determined minimum wage (which may or may not be the legal minimum) exceeds the marginal contribution of the unskilled poor person, he will not be employed at all. A person with low-wage skills in a high-wage economy suffers from the advanced state of economic development around him.

Of course, the would-be poverty-sector entrepreneur, investor, or laborer does not understand that the price structure is stacked against him, any more than does the corporate executive or labor union official. Instead, they all tend to share the unconscious assumption that it is just as easy to "make it" in America today as it was fifty or hundred years ago, when immigrants faced circumstances in many ways

---

[7] "Comparative advantage" is a concept commonly applied in the theory of international trade (Samuelson, 1970). It argues that an economy should (and in free trade will) specialize in the production of those goods which it can produce at lower cost than other countries, where "cost" is defined in terms of lost opportunities to produce other goods, rather than in terms of resource use or money cost. By this theorem, economies with abundant labor relative to capital should specialize in production of goods which require large amounts of labor relative to capital, even if to do so would mean using more units of labor per unit of output than in relatively labor-scarce economies.

similar to those faced by a majority of today's working-age poor. Indeed, in a variety of ways it looks easier today. Thus, poor and nonpoor alike often share the conclusion that both have played the same game, with the same rules, and the former have lost and the latter won, reflecting on the skill and merit of both players.

What takes place in a dual economy can be described, then, as economic alienation of a fairly pure form: members of a society are led to feel that they are, in an important sense, not its members, but, rather, aliens, much like visitors in a foreign land who do not understand the language or the customs of their hosts, and keep doing things wrong, except that the poor, unlike foreign visitors, tend to see their inability to comprehend and thrive in that alien environment as a reflection upon themselves and as an incurable condition, rather than as an understandable and temporary situation.

The dominant, educated, nonpoor majority continues, then, to reconstruct American society for its own convenience. It does so, by and large, unconsciously and unmaliciously; in fact, whether it could avoid doing so if it tried is not clear.

Unlike a great many problems economic in origin, but like those discussed earlier (The Relationship of the Individual to the Economic System), these problems are not easily solved through general economic progress. Indeed, the implication of the analysis is that any progress in which the underclass does not share aggravates and polarizes the situation. For that reason, it is impossible to anticipate the future development of the dual economy, except for one fairly clear and very gloomy implication discussed in the following section.

## CONFLICT AMONG THE ALIENATED

The discussion thus far indicates that the most economically alienated groups in American society ought to be, first, the most affluent, and among them, in particular, those young enough not to have known the fear of economic insecurity, and, second, the poorest. Both groups are influenced by subtle and complex though powerful economic forces, which, presumably, few in either group understand. For both, alienation may or may not be associated with focused anger, political militancy, and the like—more often it is not; but where it is, we might expect the anger to be directed somewhere other than at those ill-understood economic forces which are, at least in large part, responsible.

Curiously, both groups are, to a considerable extent, alienated by the same phenomenon, the increasing extent of affluence and security in the nonpoor sectors of American society. The effect of that phenomenon is markedly different for the two groups, but the result in both cases is a form of alienation.

The articulate among both groups, and especially among the youth movement and among young black militants, have developed similar critiques of American society, and have considerable sympathy for one another. It is easy to forget or to ignore how profoundly different the two alienated groups are.

In spite of the contrary rhetoric, especially from the politically sophisticated and articulate elements just mentioned, most minority poor really want economic success in the American tradition. They want better jobs, and they want the education system to unlock the door to those better jobs, as they seem to have done for others. Black parents in particular, but poor parents in general, seem to have a significantly more traditionalist, fundamentalist, and authoritarian approach to education than do nonpoor whites. The poor are less concerned with the ecology and more concerned with extracting more output from the economy. Their agenda is different from that of the alienated element of affluent white society.

The implication is that things will get worse.

We have already discussed most of the reasons. The sources of affluent, white society's alienation from the economy—primarily growing out of prosperity and security—will grow in importance, rather than decline, as time goes by. More and more young people, and, in fact, older and older people too, will share the sense of purposelessness that only an advance guard of young people and intellectuals now feel. As a consequence, there is liable to be a deepening and widening of the disaffection which exists today. That is the most pessimistic scenario available.

When one attempts to write an optimistic scenario, he is inclined to argue that, somehow, a new sense of purpose will be found, not only to make the schools and universities both free and relevant, but to effect the same changes in the larger economy, and in the whole society. But should the schools, the economy, and the society make these kinds of adjustments (and it is hard to believe that they won't, at least to an extent, even though it is all but impossible to predict what that will mean), then once again society will have adjusted to the needs of the dominant, nonpoor element, to the disadvantage of the minority of poor.

This conflict among the alienated is easiest to discern in the schools, particularly the secondary schools. There is pressure on the systems to provide a freer more open learning situation, to reorient schools around some notion of personal self-realization rather than skill-learning for economic success, and to make education more relevant for the solution of social problems. These changes may be the opposite of what is needed for the disadvantaged, for whom the old, training-for-economic-success model of the school is still relevant. The more the schools cater to the needs of the one group, the more ill-served will be the other. If the "free schools" growing up in every metropolitan area are windows of the schools of the future, then we can be sure they will not be of much value to those who are trying to make it economically.

To comprehend the magnitude of difficulties that will face us in the years to come, all that is necessary is that we extend this conflict from the schools, where we can understand it and perceive the shape and form it takes, to the economy and society at large, where its implications are decidedly unclear.

## REFERENCES

Green, T. F. *Work, leisure and the American school.* New York: Random House, 1968.

Keynes, J. M. *The general theory of employment, interest and money.* New York: Harcourt, 1936.

Marx, K. *Economic and philosophical manuscripts.* 1844.

Morse, N. C., & Weiss, R. C. The function and meaning of work and the job. *American Sociological Review,* 1955, *20,* 191-198.

Samuelson, P. A. *Economics.* (8th ed.) New York: McGraw-Hill, 1970.

Sherrill, R. Why can't we just give them food? *New York Times Magazine,* 1970, March 22.

Smith, A. *An inquiry into the nature and causes of the wealth of nations.* 1776. [Republished: New York, Random House (Modern Library).]

Tussing, A. D. *A social model of poverty and the progress of the welfare state,* a working draft. Educational Policy Research Center, Syracuse, N. Y., 1969.

Tussing, A. D. Poverty, education, and the dual economy. *Journal of Consumer Affairs,* 1970, *4,* 93-102.

Wilcox, C. *Toward social welfare.* Homewood, Ill.: Richard D. Irwin, 1969.

# Chapter 12

# The Political Use of the Concept of Alienation

*Stephen Koff*

Syracuse University

It is not surprising that the political uses of the concept of alienation are extensive and confused. The concept of alienation, as few others utilized in the behavioral sciences, the humanities, and related disciplines, has generated much conflict about its meaning. In spite of this confusion it has continued to receive extensive use. It is this extensive use which, to a great degree, is at the basis of the wide variety of meanings of the concept. A number of scholars from various disciplines have given overt and/or tacit recognition to alienation as one of the central features of human existence. This, too, has contributed to the confusion. The scholars, not to mention the journalists, bring to bear different emphases and methodologies—in many cases unique to their particular disciplines—to the study of alienation. Hence, it can be concluded that the gulfs that separate these disciplines, even though often artificial, contribute to the confusion about the concept. For example, although the philosopher, the sociologist, and the psychologist may be interested in the political ramifications of alienation, their interests are often subsidiary to other major concerns within their own disciplines. On the other hand, the political scientist, in some cases, has an exclusive interest in the political uses of alienation and adapts his methodologies to his own, narrowly defined, goals. That is not to say that the political scientist who studies alienation is not concerned with the philosophic, psychological, or the economic uses of the concept. (It is obvious that a clear-cut separation of the various applications of alienation

269

cannot be made.) Still, while recognizing that the pure abstraction of the political use of alienation is not possible, the concern of the political scientist is with political behavior. Hence, when dealing with political man and his behavior, a unique area related to the political uses of alienation can be identified. More cynically, a quotation from a recent textbook makes the point in a different fashion. "Most scholars will try to define or perceive a field of inquiry in such a way that their own training achieves maximum importance, and the importance of the kind of training they do not possess is minimized. . . [Galtung, 1969, p. 359]."

One approach lies in first distinguishing the different uses of alienation. This involves identifying those things or persons from which an individual or group is alienated. While it is generally acknowledged that alienation involves estrangement, it often is not clear from what, or from whom a person or group may be estranged. One can be estranged from family, friends, church, an economic organization, a government, or even from oneself. The interrelationships of all these possible forms of estrangement must be recognized. However, while not losing sight of these, special emphasis can be given to the study of alienation from more specific human and organizational forms. The student of political uses of alienation recognizes that a man's political behavior may be predicated on his alienation from his wife, his mistress, his work, his church, or his sports club—in spite of the fact that in traditional terms all of these may be considered apolitical. Still, the political uses of alienation can be more profitably defined if the major focus and attention of the student of the concept is given to things directly considered political. In other words, the concern of the political scientist should, to the largest degree possible, be with alienation from political institutions, groups, leaders, and processes. In the same way, students in other disciplines should give primary emphasis to alienation from organizations, groups, and people in those specific roles most related to the interest of their discipline.

It has been noted above that the individual can be alienated from himself. Marx, Horney, Fromm, Erikson, and other commentators used have made extensive use of the notion of self-alienation. For some, however, this is fundamentally an innate psychological condition. For others, it primarily involves societal conditioning. For still others, it consists of various combinations of the two. It is evident that alienation must be considered a sociopsychic phenomenon, since a rigid separation between the psychological and the social cannot be made. Furthermore, one can agree with Gould (1969) when he writes that there is an interactional reinforcement of social conditions and personal proclivities in the formation of an alienation syndrome. While recognizing the importance of the primarily psychodynamic approaches to political alienation, the basic concern in this chapter will be with a psychosocial model. It will be assumed that certain social (including political) conditions will produce alienation in almost all persons, regardless of their individual personality traits.

The emphasis on compartmentalization of approaches to a concept like alienation can be overdone and counter-productive. Clearly, such endeavors at interdisciplinary approaches, and the borrowing of research methods and techniques across disciplines is expanding significantly. Political scientists have themselves participated extensively in this expansion. In fact, according to some persons, the study of political science has undergone a behavioral revolution, involving a considerable amount of borrowing from the other behavioral sciences. Admittedly, there is some dispute whether the disciplines have, as a result of such borrowing, experienced anything approaching a revolutionary change. However, there can be no disagreement about the fact that there have been major changes in the study of politics since World War II. In part, these changes are the result of dissatisfaction with the emphasis on legal phenomena and institutional structures which marked the field of political science for the first two decades of this century. The difficulty of understanding authoritarian and totalitarian governments gave stimulus to a dissatisfaction with narrow studies of legal and institutional questions. Equally important has been the need to comprehend politics in the non-Western world, where culture-bound approaches to law and government provide insufficient tools of learning and interpreting political phenomena. Basically, the new approach has involved the study of human behavior in the political field, or, stated more simply, political behavior. There has been a clear shift of emphasis from institutions and constitutions, to individual and group behavior. Also, the endeavor to utilize more rigorous methodology has been evident. The earliest works of consequence incorporating these various changes has been the study of voting behavior.

Robert Dahl (1961), one of the foremost advocates of the behavioral approach, has discussed what he calls the "behavioral mood." He states:

> A . . . topic on which the scientific outlook has, in my view, produced some
> useful and reliable results of great importance to the understanding of politics
> is in the general domain of political participation [p. 769].

In this area he is concerned with the intensity of participation, nonparticipation, and apathy. It will be noted later in this chapter how closely related these subjects are to the political application of alienation. In the same article, Dahl (1961) goes on to discuss another subject on which he felt, ". . . the behavioral mood has clearly made itself felt. This is the understanding of the psychological characteristics of homo politicus: attitudes, beliefs, predispositions and personality factors."[1] These characteristics are receiving a great deal of attention in an area of increasing concern to political scientists called political socialization. This subfield is obviously and recognizedly, shared with sociologists, anthropologists, psychologists, and

---

[1] Dahl (1961) acknowledges that some of the most prominent work in this area has been done by scholars who were not known as political scientists but, rather, as sociologists and psychologists.

others. This is another area in which the study of alienation is prominent. It, too, will be discussed later in this chapter.

At the outset of this chapter it was suggested that there was a great deal of confusion and conflict about the meaning of concept and term "alienation." In fact, many works—particularly those that purport to establish a limited theoretical meaning of empirical proofs of alienation—begin with a statement bemoaning the misuse of the phrase in almost everything else ever written on the subject. Some of those authors who disclaim use of the term by others might excuse Hegel and Marx, because of their pioneer efforts. They might also exonerate a few other authors, finding their position close to the one supported by the writers involved. In most cases, however, particularly in the sociological literature, alienation is defined in terms of a set of specific referents (modes, themes, states, etc.). As empirical research efforts have developed, the breadth of the specific referents cited have tended to become more limited (while the overall capacity of the general term has expanded).

After acknowledging the confusion concerning a definition of alienation, I do not claim either uniqueness or definitiveness. As used here, alienation is a syndrome of related feelings. These include a range of attitudes from extreme pessimism to hopelessness, from cynicism to despair. While recognizing that these, in turn, need definition (especially if they are going to be utilized for empirical studies), this will not be undertaken here. Instead it will be noted that the feelings identified by Melvin Seeman clarifying the uses of alienation will be substituted for the above-mentioned feelings. Seeman (1959) identifies alienation with powerlessness, meaninglessness, normlessness, isolation, and self-estrangement.[2] As used here, the first four of these attitudes will be employed to exhibit the political use of the concept of alienation.

However, at this point it must be noted that the feelings or attitudes noted above are related to alienation in a general sense. Prior to applying this discussion to the political use of alienation, politics itself must be defined. This task, of course, is no easier than defining alienation. The boundaries of what is political have long been a source of intellectual dispute.[3] This dispute makes difficult the clear identification of the political organizations, roles, norms, processes, etc. from which man can be alienated. Traditionally, political scientists have taken two general approaches to defining politics. The first focuses on the state. In dealing with con-

---

[2] This will be discussed in terms of political use of alienation later in this chapter.
[3] David Easton (1971) makes an interesting point related to this dispute. "Although there is often uncertainty about the unity of political science as a discipline, most students of political life do feel quite instinctively that research into political aspects of life does differ from inquiry into any other, sufficiently so to constitute a separate intellectual enterprise. These students have been acting on the unexpressed premise that the phenomena of politics tend to cohere and to be mutually related. Such phenomena form, in other words, a system which is part of the total social system and yet which, for purposes of analysis and research, is temporarily set apart [pp. 96-97]."

ceptions of political science, Maurice Duverger (1964) wrote "on the one hand political science is thought of as the science of the State. This definition is closest to normal current usage of the word 'political' [p. 46]." Obviously, alienation from the state is both too legal and ill-defined to be very useful.

The second definition of politics focuses on power—in a general approach to the acquisition, distribution, and uses of power. Duverger (1964), in dealing with the subject, quotes Raymond Aron who wrote: " 'Politics is the study of the authority relations between individuals and groups and the hierarchy of power which establishes itself within all numerous and complex communities.' [pp. 46-47]." Although more useful in dealing with alienation, the power approach to politics is somewhat too broad, in one direction, for limited research. David Easton (1965) opts for a very broad definition of "political" ("those interactions through which values are authoritatively allocated for a society [p. 21]").[4] He proceeds to explain this definition in great detail. He sees his definition as combining the strengths of both the state and the power approaches. This definition is predicated on a systems approach to politics and, as such, is useful for studying the political uses of alienation. The following discussion points up some of the reasons for this utility:

> The concept of "political system" has acquired wide currency because it directs attention to the entire scope of political activities within a society, regardless of where in the society such activities may be located. What is the political system? How do we define its boundaries? What gives the political system its special identity? Many political scientists have dealt with these questions; while the precise language of their definitions varies considerably, there is some consensus. Common to most of these definitions is the association of the political system with the use of legitimate physical coercion in societies. . . . The political system includes not only the governmental institutions such as legislatures, courts, and administrative agencies, but all structures in their political aspects [Almond & Powell, 1966, pp. 17-18].

It is the legitimate use and potential use of force which is at the foundation of alienation of political man. It is now possible to state that alienation of a political nature involves the conscious rejection of the political system. This rejection involves the system and its components—the institutions, the processes, the leaders, the groups, the organizations, and, finally, the formal and informal "rules of the game." Individuals feel estranged from political forces that they conceive as affecting their lives. An analytical framework set forth by Kenneth Keniston (1970, p. 392) is germane to this political alienation. He raises four questions about alienation—three of which apply here. These questions are:

1. Focus: Alienated from what?
2. Replacement: What replaces the old relationship?
3. Mode: How is the alienation manifest?
4. Agent: What is the agent of alienation?

[4] See also Easton (1971). Especially pertinent to the above discussion are Chapters IV and V.

Noting the limitless number of varieties of alienation, and the fact that several possibilities appear in most of the literature on the subject, Keniston (1970) continues:

> For purposes of clarity, I will reserve the term "alienation" for only one of these possibilities—for an explicit rejection, "freely" chosen by the individual of what he perceives as the dominant values or norms of his society—and will use other terms to characterize other types of alienation [p. 393].

If the word "political" is added in front of values and norms, and it is recognized that institutions, processes, and leaders reflect these values and norms, Keniston's (1970) argument is useful for the understanding of the political uses of alienation. Many writers hold, unlike Keniston, that a man can be unaware of his alienation. This notion is rejected here, at least in regard to the political use of alienation.

In terms of political alienation, what kind of answers might be constructed to the questions Keniston has raised? The answers set forth here are not exactly the same as those Keniston gives because they are more narrowly directed at the political use of alienation. It has already been established that the focus on "alienation from what?" consists of the norms, values, institutions, groups, processes, and leaders involved in politics. The question of "what replaces the old relationship?" is a principal attribute of every variation of alienation. Keniston (1970) says that "the concept implies that something desirable, natural, or normal has been lost—that is a positive relationship has ceased to exist [p. 391]." This has to be applied with some care where the political use of alienation is concerned. For example, a difficulty is raised in answering this question when an oppressive government spans several generations and certain citizens, although clearly alienated, have never personally experienced another system of governance.

As for the question involving the mode "How is alienation manifest?" the answer in this discussion is, of course, in terms of political behavior. (It is interesting that in his own answer to this question, Keniston (1970) uses as an example of revolutionary activity that in which the alienated attempt to transform society. Clearly, revolution, above all, is a political act.)

Keniston's last question concerning the agent, "What is the agent of alienation?" also causes some difficulties in the political realm. Keniston (1970) correctly states that "Merely to note that an individual is 'alienated from society' does not tell us whether he deliberately rejects his society or whether it excludes him [p. 392]." While recognizing that there is a duality here, this chapter has chosen to examine only those political conditions where the individual is aware of his alienated condition. Conceivably, elements within the political system could exclude an individual from the system, or define his role in such a way that, according to some external observers, he would be alienated. While this occurs, I have chosen not to deal with unconscious states of alienation here. It should be evident that the very nature of political behavior presumes a degree of consciousness on the part of the individual or group concerning a relationship to others and an awareness of the potentialities for certain actions.

The use of alienation in political studies is not new. In many cases, the word itself was not used and was involved as a *post facto* rationale for some political act or event. More recently, there have been significant efforts to explain political behavior on the basis of alienation. Prior to dealing with political behavior and alienation, a brief foray into other uses of alienation and political studies will be undertaken. Since the modern study of politics has many important roots in the historic studies of law and political philosophy, it is useful to cite a few examples of the uses of alienation in these fields, even though the use of alienation may be different from the one proposed in this chapter. For example, among the earliest uses of the term itself was alienation related to the exchange of property. One became alienated from one's property when it was sold. In this sense it was a legal use of the term which, of course, could have sociopolitical overtones.

In dealing with political philosophy, some writers look for examples of estrangement in early recorded history. The Bible is one source for this kind of approach. The relationship of Biblical (cultural) themes to Marx's theories of alienation has been made by a number of authors in dealing with the origins of the concept. For example, Mészáros (1970) writes:

> The first aspect we have to consider is the lament about being "alienated from God" (or having "fallen from Grace") which belongs to the common heritage of Judeo-Christian mythology. The divine order, it is said, has been violated; man has alienated himself from the "ways of God" whether simply by "the fall of man" or later by "the dark idolatries of alienated Judah," or later again by the behavior of "Christian alienated from the life of God." The messianic mission consists in rescuing man from this state of self alienation which he brought upon himself [p. 28].

It is at this point that Mészáros (1970) and some other writers dealing with this subject matter raise the issue of social struggles developing from these forms of alienation. A similar approach to alienation was taken by the writers of the Middle Ages who dealt with both theological and secular conflict.

However, with the development of modern political philosophy—especially that dealing with social contract theory—the notion of alienation has received more extensive utilization. In a recent study of the philosophic and sociological bases of alienation, Richard Schacht looks at social contract theory and deals with the conceptions of Grotius, Hobbes, Locke, and Rousseau. In discussing Grotius, Schacht (1970) writes:

> Grotius conceives "sovereign authority" over oneself, or the right of determining one's actions, as analogous to property rights. This enables him to use the Latin *alienatio* in connection with the transfer of "sovereign authority" over oneself to another person. "As other things may be alienated so may sovereign authority." (DeJure Belli ac Pacis 9, Vol. I, 342).
>
> Grotius further suggests that such alienation provides the basis and justification of political authority. In his view political authority is constituted when a group of men relinquish the unrestricted right of each to determine his own course of action, and transfer sovereign authority over themselves to some one man [pp. 8-9].

Hobbes, Locke, and Rousseau—each with his own thrust—develop ideas similar to those of Grotius. Alienation is especially pivotal for Hobbes (1958, see esp. Ch. XIV) and Rousseau (1960). The last mentioned uses the word itself and discusses it in terms of one of his central themes, the general will. It is evident that prior to Hegel and Marx, Rousseau's treatment of alienation is the most fully developed of any political philosophies.

It is clear that for Hegel alienation was central to his thought. Recognizing the complexity of his philosophy it would be inappropriate to discuss it here.[5] In an excellent study which focuses on Hegel, Herbert Marcuse (1941) summarized a basic point when he wrote:

> The history of man was to him (Hegel) at the same time the history of man's alienation (Entfremdung).
> "What Mind really strives for is the realization of its notion; but in doing so, it hides that goal from its own vision, and is proud and well satisfied in this alienation from his own essence *(Philosophy of History,* p. 17)." The institutions man founds and the culture he creates develop laws of their own and man's freedom has to comply with them. He is overpowered by the expanding wealth of his economic, social and political surrounding and comes to forget that he himself, his free development, is the final goal of all these works; instead he surrenders to their sway. Men always strive to perpetuate an established culture, and in doing so perpetuate their own frustration. The history of man is the history of his estrangement from his true interest, and, by the same token, the history of its realization [p. 246].

This clearly indicates a modern use of the concept of alienation which was then utilized by other prominent political and social thinkers including Marx.

Unlike Hegel, when one turns to Marxian theory, economic and political questions are dominant within his whole system. In the study of political philosophy, Marx's theory of alienation is central to his thinking. Of course, students of Marx, both hostile critics and followers,[6] have been concerned not only with his intellectual arguments, but also with utilizing his ideas to explain political behavior. Alienation is central to his discussion of potential political behavior. Again, a full treatment of Marx's theory of alienation is beyond the scope of this chapter. However, a brief discussion of his ideas in this area is necessary, since alienation for him leads to antisystem behavior. At this point he is close to using alienation as it is being used in this chapter, although in a narrower fashion.

As with many of his ideas, Marx borrowed from others in his use of the concept, alienation. This borrowing seemed to serve only as the basis of a search for rigorous redefinition. In the case of alienation as noted previously, Hegel had an influence on Marx, as did Feuerbach. However, there is no denying that Marx applied the concept in an original way. Although, subsequently, his ideas were used to explain alienation in all kinds of societies, he directed himself specifically to

[5] It will be discussed elsewhere in this volume. The reader should also consult Schacht (1970, pp. 17-64).

[6] For a recent discussion of Marx's theory of alienation by authors with an avowedly Marxist outlook see Herbert Aptheker (1965). The book includes an extensive bibliography. Another rich bibliography on the subject of Marx and alienation can be found in the aforementioned book by Mészáros (1970). Here the bibliography includes mostly works published in Continental Europe. Mészáros was a student of George Lukács.

the critical analysis of a bourgeois society.[7] More specifically, he treats alienation as originating in the work ethic and labor process present in a Capitalist system. The following lengthy quotation from Marx (1959) explains his use of alienation in this area:

> What, then constitutes the alienation of labour?
> First, the fact that labour is external to the worker, i.e. it does not belong to his essential being; that in his work, therefore, he does not affirm himself but denies himself, does not feel content but unhappy, does not develop freely his physical and mental energy but mortifies his body and ruins his mind. The worker therefore only feels himself outside his work, and in his work feels outside himself. He is at home when he is not working, and when he is working he is not at home. His labour is therefore not voluntary, but coerced; it is forced labour. It is therefore not the satisfaction of a need; it is merely a means to satisfy needs external to it. Its alien character emerges clearly in the fact that as soon as no physical or other compulsion exists, labour is shun like the plague. External labour, labour in which man alienates himself, is a labour of self-sacrifice of mortification. Lastly, the external character of labour for the worker appears in the fact that it is not his own but someone else's, that it does not belong to him, that in it he belongs, not to himself but to another [pp. 72-73].

The worker becomes a commodity losing his dignity and his individuality.[8] As technological progress advances, the alienation of the worker becomes more severe. However, it is not the technology which causes the alienation, but, rather, the capitalist classes which increasingly exploit the worker through the new technology. From this point, it must be noted that what begins as a relationship based on economics soon engulfs all aspects of society. In the realm of government and politics, coercion is necessary for the maintenance of the system. Marx's analysis leads to the prediction of a special sociopolitical action, a revolution. In this case, alienation is at the basis of antisystem political behavior. Through the direct action of the alienated, that is, the workers, alienation can be overcome.

Having briefly looked at some of the uses of alienation in precontemporary political philosophy, the whole question of alienation and political behavior will now be raised. However, before this is undertaken a caution must be made. Frequently, writers indicate they are going to treat political behavior caused by alienation, but instead they focus on the conditions which provide the setting for alien-

[7] Addressing himself to his point, Blauner (1964) wrote "The alienation thesis has become the intellectual's shorthand interpretation of the impact of the industrial revolution on the manual worker. Non-Marxists and even anti-Marxists have followed Marx in the view that factory technology, increasing division of labor, and the Capitalist property institutions brought about the estrangement of the industrial worker from his work [p. 2]."

[8] Some contemporary commentators on Marx argue that the modern industrial system may not involve the same kind of alienation Marx described. Rolf Dahrendorf (1959), dealing with what he describes as the empirical consequences of the theory of institutional isolation of industrial conflict, wrote: "In the post-capitalist society, the worker, when he passes the factory gate, increasingly leaves his occupational role behind him with the machines and his work clothes; outside he plays new roles defined by factors other than his occupation. The occupation and the expectation connected with it dominate less and less the life of the industrial workers, and other expectations mold his social personality [p. 273].

ation. In a useful article on alienation and political behavior Joel Aberbach (1969), after discussing Keniston's four questions, asserts:

> While a test of the utility of Keniston's scheme in empirical research is valuable in itself, there is a broader set of questions raised in the existing literature on alienation and political behavior. Basically, these concern the conditions which stimulate the political mobilization of the alienated [p. 87].

The question of these conditions is very important, but they should not be confused with attitudinal aspects of various states of alienation. For example, different societies even with similar social conditions will often be markedly different in terms of the portion of the population which is alienated. This may be partly due to differential awareness in different societies. It should be mentioned again that in the treatment here the alienation of political man involves the conscious rejection of the major components of the political system. Hence, at this point, it is possible to confront the question of how an alienated man might behave in the face of a political system which he rejects.

A signifcant body of literature argues that he will not voluntarily participate in political life. He will endeavor to withdraw, and will eventually become apathetic. This approach is not borne out, unless apathy is, a priori, defined as almost synonymous with alienation. First of all, it is obvious that certain people may not participate in political life because they are satisfied, and, hence, do not deem it necessary to become active. (Some, of course, argue that the politics of happiness brings greater participation.) Second, a large body of persons are inactive, and, according to some, are apathetic, because they lack the minimum political information necessary to act. Certainly, neither of these groups can be considered alienated in the sense in which the concept is being used here. Furthermore, the alienated man may not be apathetic in any way; in fact, he can be an activist. As another option, the alienated man may physically depart from the political system. This is certainly a critical political act, whether or not in his self-exile he works against the system which he left. This is an area in which insufficient research has been done in spite of the large number of political emigres and refugees in the past four decades. On the other hand, if the alienated man chooses to remain in the political system (or if he has no choice but to remain) he may become committed to antisystem behavior. In this case, his alienation may cause him to develop a new identity with and a commitment to a political movement or party dedicated to the overthrow of the system from which he is alienated. Although, contrary to the approach taken in this chapter, it is noteworthy that some see alienation being overcome through the very act of identification with a leader, a movement, or a party. In other words, these subsystems become substitutes for the entire political system.[9]

[9] In a very perceptive essay entitled "Anxiety and Politics" Franz Neumann (1957) focuses on some aspects of substitute identification. He wrote, "The cement which holds the mass together and ties them to the leader is thus a sum of instincts that are inhibited in their aims. In this manner, I believe, the logical connection between alienation and mass behavior has been established. Since the identification of masses with the leader is an alienation of the individual member, identification always constitutes a regression and a two-fold one. On the one hand, the history of man is the history of his emergence from the primal horde and of

It should be acknowledged that empirical research is in its nascent stages in this area. Measurement of antisystem involvement is obviously difficult. In addition to the problem of getting people to acknowledge their role in antisystem activities, there is the additional difficulty that the activities may be very diverse and intermitten. Furthermore, while some of the alienated person's activities may be antisystem, some of his other activities may take place within the system.[10]

The increase of peaceful protest in the United States and other democracies has accentuated the question of how alienated persons, acting within the "rules of the game," can go about to defeat or destroy the system. It may be useful at this juncture to make a distinction between political protest within the rules of the system, and clearly antisystem behavior. The line between the two is not always clear or firm. Usually, political protest involves disagreement with certain policies, and, possibly, some of the norms identified with the system. Protest is undertaken to bring attention to what the protestor considers inequities. Generally, the protest aims at reform, but not the outright destruction of the entire system. However, an activity which begins as political protest within the rules of the system (or even to demand the enforcement of the formal rules of the system) can quickly change into demands for radical, instant systemic change.[11]

A summary using general categories of political action based on system and antisystem attitudes will now be presented. Table 12-1 endeavors to visually delineate those who are alienated toward politics in any system. It represents a dynamic model in which change can come rapidly for individuals, groups, and the overall system itself. In terms of the system, itself, suffice it to say that as the rules change, the reaction to them will be different. Also, in the table, a range of other variables, which affect activity or inactivity among persons are represented in the four quadrants. Among these are changes in the level of political information, participation

[10] Kenneth Keniston (1968) addresses himself to the problem of alienation and activity primarily within the system. After studying a limited number of American radical students, he wrote, "It is always possible, like Humpty Dumpty, to make words mean what one chooses them to mean. And so it is possible to define 'alienation' in such a way that the civil rights marcher, the peace demonstrator, or the Berkeley activists are by definition 'alienated.' But after having worked for several years with a group of undergraduates who are intensely repudiative of American culture, I am inclined to see most student protest not as a manifestation of alienation (as I have used the term) but rather of commitment to the very values the alienated students reject [p. 34]." Clearly some persons involved in the activities Keniston cites are alienated and antisystem in their attitude, while others are not.

[11] After many years when the emphasis in the social sciences was on equilibrium, order, and consensus, conflict and items like political protest are receiving increasing attention. Some of the writers in the conflict area have endeavored to work out a general theory for the study of protest and violence. However, the line between system and antisystem behavior and the perceptions of the participants which goes with this behavior has received insufficient attention. Ted Gurr (1968, 1970), a prominent scholar in this area, writes about what he calls illicit violence, but he does not probe deeply into its importance to the whole system.

his progressive individualization; the identification with a leader in a mass is a kind of historical regression. This identification is also a substitute for a libidinal object tie; thus a psychological regression, a damaging of the ego, perhaps even the loss of the ego [p. 277]."

**TABLE 12-1**

*Attitudes toward the Political System and Potential Political Behavior*

| Prosystem | Marginal cases | Antisystem |
|---|---|---|
| I.  Active modes<br>Activities within "the rules of the game."<br>A.  Conventional. | | I.  Active modes<br>Activities within and outside "the rules of the game" aimed at overthrowing the system. |
| Voting. ⇒<br>⇐ | ⇒<br>⇐ | ⇐ |
| Political party work⇒  ⇒<br>interest articulation<br>work in the public sector.<br>Political communication.<br>B.  Unconventional. | ⇐ | ⇐ |
| Strikes. ⇒<br>Demonstrations. ⇐ | ⇒<br>⇐ | ⇒<br>⇐ |
| | ⇒ | Violence.<br>⇐ Revolution.<br>Coup d'etat.<br>Clandestine activity. |
| II. Inactive modes<br>A.  Satisfied with "the rules of the game" and "the game."<br>B.  Uninterested in "the rules of the game." | ⇒  ⇒<br>⇐  ⇐ | II. Inactive (alienated) modes<br>A.  Apathetics who reject both "the rules of the game" and "the game." |

*Left margin (vertical): Change from active to inactive or vice versa.*

*Right margin (vertical): Change from active to*

opportunities, level and nature of governmental repression, nature of political movements, and economic conditions, to cite a few.

As indicated in Table 12-1, the activities within the system would fall into two basic categories. The first might be called conventional politics. These are activities within the usual channels, such as voting, political party efforts, government work, voluntary and professional (occupational and nonoccupational) work, traditional interest group articulation, and a wide range of efforts that comprise what can be described as political communication. The second category includes activities which are predominantly within the system but outside traditionally accepted channels. Hence, they can be described as nonconventional. These include sit-ins (or other types of take-over of property), marches and mass demonstrations, politically motivated strikes, lockouts, some property destruction (such as farmers destroying their own crops), mock trials, public oriented, nongovernmental hearings, etc. All these activities are aimed at bringing about reforms. While the predominant element which participates in these activities is committed to the continuance of the system, it is undoubtedly true that some of the activists are alienated from the system and dedicated to its overthrow. They are involved in these activities in order to embarrass public or quasipublic authorities and, in some cases, to stimulate further action, generally of a violent nature, which would undermine the rules of the system, and, hence, the system itself. In the area of unconventional politics, situations change rapidly and the activities (or the counter-activities by public authorities) become, in effect, antisystem behavior, or very close to it.

In this table, the changed nature of unconventional politics is represented by the area between system and antisystem activities and is identified as marginal cases. It is here that people committed to working through the system, at times, move outside of its rules. However, the sporadic and temporary nature of their antisystem behavior does not indicate that they are alienated.

Participation in the system through voting and its relation to alienation require a special discussion. The alienated voter is the title of a well-known book and is a phrase used extensively in the literature of political science. However, for the purposes of the present discussion, most of the voters who are described as being alienated would not fit that description because their very act of voting is a commitment to the system. Levin (1960), in his study of politics in Boston, discussed the attitudes of voters which, according to him, made them alienated. He specifically states:

> Political alienation is the feeling of an individual that he is not part of the political process. The politically alienated believe that their vote makes no difference. This belief arises from the feeling that political decisions are made by a group of insiders who are not responsive to the average citizens—the outsiders [pp. 61-62].

Levin (1960) concludes that a large proportion of the electorate of Boston is alienated since survey data indicated that the people felt powerlessness and that elections were meaningless. From the point of view of a statement of attitudes, this situation would seem to qualify for the use of the concept of political alienation. However, when it is recognized that in most cases these so-called alienates are troubled by one phase of what they perceive as democratic politics, the use of alienation does not quite hold. In this case, a subsystem, that is, local government and local elections, did not work in a way in which they would have liked. However, most of these people are generally satisfied with the total system. Furthermore, these are the very people who, in other large American cities, have been active within the "rules of the game," working to develop reform movements to overthrow bosses and political machines in order to make elections more meaningful. The Levin position is cited only as an example of many studies involving voting in the United States which seem to equate dissatisfaction with competing candidates, parties, or a special subnational government unit with alienation. If some of these studies were placed in a transnational context, and nations with meaningful antisystem parties were studied, a term other than alienation (in the conventional meaning of the word) might better be used to describe the American voter.

The point should be made clear, then, that it is not being argued here that either the act of voting or that particular voting behavior cannot be motivated by alienation. Obviously, voting for parties which are dedicated to the overthrow of the system can be a behavioral manifestation of alienation. Here again is a case where the political act (voting) is undertaken strictly within "the rules of the game"—albeit with the desire to overturn the system.

To continue a description of Table 12-1, the lower portion is concerned with depicting participants in politics who are either satisfied, or without knowledge necessary for participation. It also includes others who are alienated and against the system. Rosenberg (1954), in what has become a basic work for the study of apathy, states "Whether one measures apathy by the criterion of political involvement, knowledge or activity, the number of people who also satisfy the culturally defined desiderata of participation is small [p. 349]." As noted previously, apathy, like alienation, has been defined in a variety of ways. This is less important here than the point that in most cultures political participation is low, and, hence, the number of persons who fall below the horizontal line in the table is very great. The group represented in the lower left quadrant of the diagram consists of the nonparticipating but satisfied. Some are not only satisfied with the system, but also with the rewards they take from the system. They feel no need to participate, and do not do so as the result of a conscious decision. Others may not be satisfied with the rewards which the system affords them, but they feel no motivation to participate. Still others feel that participation could be costly to them is some way (Rosenberg, 1954).

Some people (and, generally, a significant part of the population in most nations) withdraw from participation simply because they are alienated from the political system. These are the persons represented in the lower right quadrant of the diagram. Rejecting the system, their perceptions lead them to believe that it is futile to engage in any political activity. For some, even if they acknowledge that there may be rewards which might result from participation, they nevertheless consider these minor and not of the kind promising to meet direct and urgent needs. Large numbers of persons in systems with repressive regimes, or in parochial situations are in this category of alienated nonparticipants. (Some persons may be forced to participate, by a repressive government, in some staged political activity—"voting," demonstrating, etc. Actions of this kind are excluded from our discussion since these persons are not acting on the basis of free choice.)

Special minority status can also lead to political alienation and withdrawal. Examples of such minority groups are those which are based on status, class, race, religion, occupation, etc. (or combinations of these). The political leadership—generally most governmental personnel—and the processes and norms within the system are all alien to these people. They expect nothing positive from them, and have as little to do with them as possible.

The perception of the system of the alienated activists (represented in the upper right hand quadrant of Table 12-1) is similar to those of the alienated non-participants. However, the activists are unwilling to accept their situation without trying to do something about it. As already noted, they may temporarily be willing to participate within "the rules of the game" of the very system from which they are alienated—voting and peaceful demonstrations being appropriate examples of this. In spite of this marginal or prosystem behavior, they frequently belong to a movement, party, or group which is ultimately dedicated to the overthrow of the system. All of their activities, within the system and against, are aimed ultimately at its radical change and overthrow. Outside and against the system, they may fulfill clandestine roles poised to undertake violence, illegal strikes, assassination, revolution, *coup d'etat,* and civil war: in fact, anything to achieve their ultimate goal.

It should be noted that on the far right there is a vertical line with arrows pointing up and down. This is to indicate that alienated nonparticipants can become involved in intermittent political activity against the system. What generally happens here is that, as the result of a specific issue or governmental or private policy decision, the alienated nonparticipants become motivated to act. Frequently, their response to the thing they do not like is spontaneous and violent. This kind of anomic behavior (in Merton's sense) often involves an assault on persons or property related to the authority imposing the extremely unpopular measures on these politically alienated people. For most of these individuals this constitutes a single, impulse foray into the world of political action. For others it begins a new commitment to a sequence of actions. Sometimes these individuals may have formally broken laws, and, in the process of being pursued by the authorities, undertake on-going political action as a way of protecting themselves. For some, their originally impulsive individual actions may become identified with a party or movement, as noted before. Often the nonparticipant, alienated person who is ready to become active is moved by a charismatic leader. However, if this leader passes from the scene or deludes his followers, the alienated person generally reverts back to the status of nonparticipation. Many become even more embittered and resolve not to become involved again in political activity. Clearly, the nonparticipating alienated must be considered as potential supporters of revolutionary movements.

In summary, it is well to repeat that the lines of this diagram are not rigid and cannot be considered barriers to changing positions. However, most of the movements across lines is vertical, from active to inactive, or vice-versa. It should be noted that this vertical movement, both up and down on the diagram, takes place among prosystem as well as antisystem people. When the movement is horizontal (meaning that a person or persons moves from an alienated to nonalienated category, or in the other direction), usually a radical change occurs either in the system or in the individual's life. Forays across the system/antisystem line are often brief and impulsive. Alienated persons who momentarily overcome their alienation are prone to revert to their original attitudes, especially when new found rewards are not lasting or of the nature which was anticipated. "Horizontal" movement from nonalienated to alienated status generally has a more lasting effect, unless, again, radical change within the system occurs.

Having described some possible actions and inactions in the political realm based on political alienation, the attitudes at the foundation of this behavior will be examined in greater detail than was previously undertaken. Earlier in the chapter it was stated that Melvin Seeman's (1959) work—in which he endeavors to clarify the use of alienation—would be utilized to explain the attitudinal basis of political behavior.[12] In spite of the limitations of Seeman's work, his categories (powerlessness, meaninglessness, normlessness, isolation, and self-estrangement) can be useful for the understanding of political behavior. Several of the categories have been touched on briefly but now the first four will be discussed more fully. (The last, self-estrangement, is being omitted because, as noted earlier, this area was excluded from the scope of this chapter.) Powerlessness, meaninglessness, normlessness, and isolation can clearly be identified with antisystem attitudes. The discussion which follows is not limited completely to Seeman's meanings of the categories as he sets them forth.

Political powerlessness involves the alienated person's perception that he does not have the ability to influence decisions in the political area which have a significant impact on him. His perception of the rules of the game and the operation of the system are such that he believes that he has no role in the control of his political destiny. His expectations are at complete variance with outputs in the political system.[13] It is well to remind the reader that the question of perception is critical here. Objective political conditions may not be what the alienated political man perceives them to be. The perception of powerlessness may lead to an antisystem attitude.

Meaninglessness relates to a lack of understanding of the political norms of the system. In part, it may result from imperfect political information. This is of-

---

[12] Although Seeman's (1959) article has been used extensively, there has been much discussion about the achievement of the author's goal of clarifying the use of alienation. Seeman (1961) himself raised a telling point in responding to some criticism of his article. He wrote, "I agree that one of the difficulties in the original presentation resides in my failure to deal with the articulation among the five categories of alienation. I took it that the variants of alienation were tied together, at a minimum, by the traditional sociological interest in them as common products of a mass society. Beyond that I left (and would still leave) the empirical relations among the categories an open question—i.e., the paper does not present a theory of alienation but is an effort to make such a theory possible [p. 781]."

[13] Seeman (1959) states the same point this way: "In the case of alienation I would limit the applicability of the concept to expectancies that have to do with the individual's sense of influence over socio-political events (control over the political system, the industrial economy, international affairs and the like) [p. 785]."

ten the case in parochial or certain subcultural settings cut off communicationally as well as politically. However, a highly divided political culture may have norms that are perceived as confused and confusing by large numbers of persons. Something close to this situation is approached as follows by Seeman (1959):

> We may speak of high alienation, in the meaningless usage, when the individual is unclear as to what he ought to believe—when the individual's minimum standards for clarity in decision making are not met [p. 786].

This often can lead to alienation in the political sphere and withdrawal from participation.

Normlessness is often used as if it were synonymous with alienation. Generally Durkheim's description of anomie, which refers to normlessness, is utilized. What is implied is that the traditional norms of the society have broken down. This means that to be effective at all persons have to go outside these norms to achieve their end. For political purposes we can liken these norms to the written and unwritten rules of the game. If these rules of the game break down and are rejected as providing a base for political behavior, by the definition used here, the individual involved in this situation would be alienated. In this case, however, the system which was being opposed would, itself, be a very weak system.

According to Seeman (1959) "The alienated in the isolation sense are those, ... who assign low reward value to goals and beliefs that are typically highly valued in a given society [pp. 788-789]." It seems particularly appropriate to speak of isolation on the basis of the political use of alienation in terms of rejection of the unwritten rules of the game more than the written. Customs, conventions, and traditions are critical to governance and are generally accepted by most persons or a large portion of the population in any given system. However, they are given little value by most alienates. And when people are cut off from commonly accepted cultural norms (in this case those which have political overtones), they can readily become alienated.

The emphasis on the acceptance of norms which has pervaded the discussion to this point—especially the above treatment of Seeman's (1959) multidimensional approach to alienation—must perforce bring us to a discussion of the transmittal of these norms. This process is generally called political socialization.

A useful definition of political socialization has been set forth in the Introduction to a recent reader on the subject. Sigel (1970) wrote:

> Political socialization refers to the process by which people learn to adopt the norms, values, attitudes, and behaviors accepted and practiced by the ongoing system. Such learning, however, involves much more than the acquisition of the appropriate knowledge of a society's political norms and more than the blind performance of appropriate political acts; it also assumes that the individual so makes these norms and behaviors on his own—internalizes them—that to him they appear to be right, just and moral. The socialized human being, in other words, develops an affective commitment for the system [p. xii].

It obviously follows from this that if the individual does not develop an affective commitment for the system one of two results occur: either the individual has developed no attitude toward the system generally as a result of having no knowledge about it, or he becomes alienated from it.

Students of political socialization have focused on the impact of the family, schools, and social groups (such as churches, leisure time groups, and special interest groups) as well as political parties and those norms of the political culture in which the individual lives. Clearly, the learning process is both of a formal and an informal nature. In other words, perception in everyday life related to class, social, or religious attitudes, for example, has a very significant socialization effect on people, even though no special rules of behavior or formal instruction are involved. Obviously, a great deal of learned political attitudes do not relate to the formal political process or events which are generally described as political events or acts.

It is clear that as a learning process, political socialization works to inculcate the values and operative norms of the status quo (Greenstein, 1968, p. 555). While there is generally sufficient transgenerational flexibility to facilitate a certain amount of adjustment to new conditions, radical change is not associated with traditional political socialization. As a conservative force identified with the system, the alienate becomes separated from the socialization process, as well as from the overall system itself. From a generational point of view this means that the alienated people may endeavor to see to it that their offspring are not socialized into the system. In fact, some alienated persons go so far as to openly attack the forces, both governmental and nongovernmental, which are involved in the socialization process, if repression in the system does not preclude this. In this area, the transgenerational heritage of some antisystem attitudes are clear.

Thus, many of those persons who are not socialized into a conventional system, by default develop a subsystem or subcultural political identity. Often these subcultures have norms and values which are in basic conflict with those of the total system. Hence, some young people can be brought up in a national or ethnic social group (or minority political movements of various groups) which have among their norms a dedication to the overthrow of the total system.

Since political socialization deals with the transmission of values, it is a process closely related to the concept of political culture. Even before giving a definition of political culture, the connection between political socialization and political culture should be noted. A recent textbook on political socialization states: "political socialization shapes and transmits a nation's political culture. More specifically, political socialization maintains a nation's political culture, insofar as it transmits that culture from old to new constituents [Dawson & Prewitt, 1969, p. 27]." Obviously, the relationship between political culture and alienation is a direct one, as in the case of political socialization. The following definition of political culture by Almond (1966), who wrote extensively on this subject, demonstrates the relationship between alienation and political culture.

> Political culture is the pattern of individual attitudes and orientations to
> politics among the members of the political system. It is the subjective realm
> which gives meaning to political actions. Such individual orientations involve
> several components, including (a) cognitive orientations, knowledge, accurate
> or otherwise of political objects and beliefs; (b) affective orientations, feelings
> of attachment, involvement, rejection and the like, about political objects;
> and (c) evaluative orientations, judgments and opinions about political objects
> which usually involve applying value standards to political objects and events [p. 50].[14]

In explaining this paragraph in greater detail. Almond (1966) cites attitudes
for all the individual orientations which may provide the basis for alienation
of a political nature. An individual can be alienated either as a result of a lack of
information or through possessing incorrect information. As another possibility,
he may reject the system because of familial or other group hostility to it. Alternatively, he might have some evaluative attitudes that are in conflict with the
norms of his society: that is, a particular moral evaluation may cause him to be
antisystem in outlook. For example, he might have no faith in the masses, and,
hence, reject a democratic system or reject a corrupt system that impinges on
his democratic outlook.

Still, in its infant stage, in terms of systematic study in political science, the
entire concept of political culture remains somewhat amorphous. Its complexity
has brought a wide variety of approaches to its study. Some scholars in the field
have endeavored to be systematic by using instruments employing large scale cross-
cultural opinion surveys. Others have done in-depth community studies, usually
based on lengthy interviews. Still others have done content analysis of books, magazines, newspapers, etc. Illustrative literature utilized in conjunction with discussions of political culture often does not include the phrase itself.[15]

[14] Almond gives credit to Talcott Parsons and Edward A. Shils for the origin of the
categories he cites.

[15] One example of this is the well-circulated autobiographical book by Carlo Levi (1947).
This book is an account of Levi's internment as an anti-fascist in southern Italy during the Mus-
solini regime. A very vivid picture of a subculture in Italy is presented. Many of the people described are alienated, at least in part, for political reasons, as the following paragraph details:

> The gentry were all Party members, even the few like Dr. Milillo who were
> dissenters. The party stood for Power, as vested in the Government and the
> State, and they felt entitled to share it. For exactly the opposite reason none
> of the peasants were political party members; indeed it was unlikely that they
> should belong to any political party whatever, should by chance another exist.
> They were not Fascists, just as they would never have been Conservatives or So-
> cialists, or anything else. Such matters had nothing to do with them; they be-
> longed to another world and they saw no sense in them. What had the peasants
> to do with Power, Government and the State? The State whatever form it might
> take meant "the fellows in Rome don't want us to live like human beings. There
> are hailstorms, landslides, draughts, malaria and . . . the State. There are inescap-
> able evils; such there always have been and such there always will be. They
> make us kill off our goats, they carry away our furniture, and now they are
> going to send us to the wards. Such is life [p. 76]."

One dimension of political culture that has, in recent years, received a significant amount of attention is the issue of political participation and nonparticipation, as well as attitudes toward the outcomes of participation. Students of democracy have long wrestled with normative questions related to participation. Some recent endeavors in this field have shifted from the normative approach to raise empirical questions about the amount of participation in a given system or systems and the reasons for participation and nonparticipation. In this area, one of the best known and original studies is *The Civic Culture* by Almond and Verba (1963).[16] Utilizing a general theory of political culture, Almond and Verba endeavor to explain the relationship between the individual's perceptions of the major components of the political system and government behavior.

Using the individual orientations of cognition, affect, and evaluation, Almond and Verba (1963) indicate:

> . . . the political orientation of an individual can be tapped systematically if we explore the following:
>
> (1) What knowledge does he have of his nation and of his political system in general terms, its history, size, location, power, "constitutional" characteristics and the like? What are his feelings toward these systemic characteristics? What are his more or less considered opinions and judgments of them?
>
> (2) What knowledge does he have of the structure and roles, the various political elites, and the policy proposals that are involved in the upward flow of policy making? What are his feelings and opinions about these structures, leaders, and policy proposals?
>
> (3) What knowledge does he have of the downward flow of policy enforcement, the structures, individuals and the decisions involved in these processes? What are his feelings and opinions of them?
>
> (4) How does he perceive himself as a member of his policy system? What knowledge does he have of his rights, powers, obligations, and of strategies of areas to influence? How does he feel about.his capabilities? What norms of participation or of performance does he acknowledge and employ in formulating political judgments, or at arriving at opinions [pp. 16-17]?

These questions spell out in greater detail the points made throughout this chapter about attitudes toward the political system. Obviously, the answer to questions like these will indicate if a person is alienated or not. Almond and Verba (1963) focus on the sense of civic competence and civic obligation, and in their findings they make distinctions according to types of political cultures. This material in turn is related to socioeconomic status, education, voluntary association, participation, and certain basic social attitudes, such as "trust in people."

Almond and Verba (1963) see the need for a balance between citizen influence and citizen passivity for the successful operation of a democratic system. Of greater importance for the present discussion, these authors have indicated that

[16] This work is based on opinion survey research done in five countries.

when issues become intense and remain intense, the system may be made unstable. It can be assumed that intense issues protracted over time will give rise to political alienation and antisystem attitudes. These in turn will bring about some withdrawal and limitation of that kind of involvement necessary for a stable democratic system. Eventually it will also bring about some actual antisystem behavior. In the *Civic Culture,* the need for a mix between consensus and cleavage in a stable democratic system is handled in a way similar to the need for a balanced type of involvement. Obviously, for our purposes, extreme cleavage within the political culture will bring about various forms of alienation.

One place where extreme cleavages have been evident is in the political conditions in many newly emerging nations. These nations have been the focus of studies of political culture, socialization, conflict, and their resultant states of alienation. The study of attitudinal concepts is profitably directed at nations undergoing rapid change. Identifying alienation based on political outlook is more difficult in a developing nation than in a modern industrial state. As Lucian Pye (1963) states: "In non-Western societies the political sphere is not sharply differentiated from the spheres of social and personal relations [p. 657]." Also, as modernization goes on, the conflicts of maladjustment are often severe. The move of the peasant to a new society in an urban area often causes alienation, as the traditional ways of his life are swept away. Political communication, so necessary for the understanding of new government policies, is often lacking. Revolutionary zeal—for a long period directed at colonial rulers—can easily be redirected at the postrevolutionary regime if there is widespread dissatisfaction with economic and social conditions. Youth often becomes impatient with older, ruling generations and can easily become antisystem in attitude. The charismatic leader can often find followers among alienates. The movements that these kinds of leaders head frequently attempt to overthrow the political system. Just as frequently, the social and religious complexity in a newly emerging nation results in the presence of alienated minority groups. Hence, we can conclude that the sweeping away of traditional societies (and their stable belief systems), the physical movement to cities, the recruitment of large numbers of new participants to politics, the existence of communication problems, the generational conflict problem, and the susceptibility to charismatic leaders make the populations of modernizing nations particularly prone to alienation. The problems connected with these factors are aggravated by the fundamental social and economic factors incumbent on rapid culture change in those societies undergoing radical development.

Obviously, in newly emerging nations, one of the major crises faced is one of the assumption of a new identification. The phrase "nation building" has a component of identification with the newly developed system. However, identity crises, while more obvious, are certainly not unique to modernizing nations. Alienated groups of persons can cause identity crises (and other important systemic crises) in any nation. Three vivid examples of alienated populations in developed nations make this very clear. The violence directed at the political systems of Canada, Belgium, and Northern Ireland can be seen as resulting from alienated people who behaved not unlike dissident minorities in the newly emerging countries. One need not study only the overt acts of violence to ascertain alienation in these three nations. An excellent study of the attitudes of French Canadians toward all aspects of the Canadian political culture and the political system giving graphic evidence of the reasons for alienation among these people is available *(Report of the Royal Commission,* 1968-1970).

Much has been written in recent years about urban alienation, specifically revolving around life in the ghetto. Since this subject will be treated elsewhere in this volume, it will not be discussed here. However, one point should be made. Persons living in the ghetto who react to it through violence in their own community, or in the larger urban setting, are generally alienated from the total system rather than alienated from any local condition or subpolitical system. This point may be obscured since their immediate reactions to political alienation are directed at those symbols of the total system which are most proximate, that is, commercial and civic institutions within their own (ghetto) communities.

The subject of mass society, which normally would fall within the purview of the political uses of alienation, is also dealt with elsewhere in this book. The implications of "mass society" for possible political alienation is a vast subject in itself. However, alienation, as used in this chapter, can in no way be considered unique to the mass society. First, if a mass society is considered a modern phenomenon, it is enough to say that people were alienated from political systems as long as they have existed. Second (as noted in the discussion of newly emerging nations), alienation exists in many areas where the conditions of mass society are unknown. However, it should be acknowledged that the conditions of mass society do accentuate the possibilities for alienation as do other general factors, for example, modern technology and overdevelopment of bureaucracy.

To summarize briefly, the foregoing discussion of the political uses of alienation has centered on attitudinal states accompanying various experiences of political alienation. Furthermore, although there is little consensus about the political use of the term alienation (or a general sociological term for that matter) one cannot dispute the use of the term in political science where a focus (or foci) of alienation is defined and delimited. It has further been argued that where politics is concerned, the focus involved is the political system. Moreover, in this chapter it has been observed that the rejection of any political systems (or "the rules of the game") leads some alienates to withdraw from the system and others to move toward political behavior which is aimed at overthrowing the system. Admittedly, the specific nature of the feelings or attitudes accompanying these conditions have not been considered in detail. A review of various empirical studies of the political uses of alienation has not been undertaken here. Unfortunately, it has been noted that the disagreement concerning the term, arising out of the investigations,

TABLE 12-2

*Contemporary Empirical Research on Alienation: A Summary* [a]

| Scholar | Term | Indicators | Hypothesized behavior |
|---|---|---|---|
| Aberbach (1969) | Alienation | Political trust | Vote for Goldwater, 1964 |
| Templeton (1966-1967) | Alienation | Srole's scale, modified | (Apathy) (Vote of opposition in referendum) (Electoral choice) |
| Levin (1960) | Alienation | Author's interpretation of attitudes about candidates | Voting against the "in" party |
| Litt (1963) | Political cynicism | Political and personal trust Political and personal efficacy | — |
| Agger, Goldstein, & Pearl (1961) | Political cynicism | "Cynicism" scale | Apathy |
| Stone (1965-1966) | Alienation | None; alienation inferred from behavior | Vote of opposition on referendum on fluoridation |
| Kellstedt (1969) | Alienation | Trust Efficacy Civic obligation Policy satisfaction Misanthropy "Black Power" | Riot-Proneness |
| Horton & Thompson (1961-1962) | Alienation | Powerlessness | Vote of opposition |
| Thompson & Horton (1959-1960) | Alienation | Political efficacy & trust combined | Vote of opposition |
| McDill & Ridley (1962) | Alienation | Modified Srole Scale & SRC Efficacy scale | Vote of opposition |
| Dean (1960) | Alienation | Powerlessness Normlessness Social isolation | Political apathy |
| Erbe (1964) | Alienation | Anomia scale | Voting turnout |
| Kirkham, Levy, & Crotty (1970) | Anomic authoritarianism | F scale and anomic scale | "Political vengeance" |

[a]From Nass (1971).

has so far, limited the utility of general theory development.[17] It is obvious, then, that the political uses of alienation constitute a rich field of study. However, the overall utility of the term, alienation—aside from use as shorthand for certain explanations—is only now coming into its own.

## REFERENCES

Aberbach, J. Alienation and political behavior. *American Political Science Review,* 1969, *63,* 86-99.

Agger, R. E., Goldstein, M., & Pearl, S. Political cynicism: Measurement and meaning. *Journal of Politics,* 1961, *23,* 477-506.

Almond, G., & Powell, G. B., Jr. *Comparative politics: A developmental approach.* Boston: Little, Brown, 1966.

Almond, G., & Verba, S. *The civic culture.* Princeton: Princeton University Press, 1963.

Aptheker, H. (Ed.) *Marxism and alienation.* New York: Humanities Press, 1965.

Blauner, R. *Alienation and freedom: The factor worker and his industry.* Chicago: University of Chicago Press, 1964.

Dahl, R. The behavioral approach in political science: Epitaph for a movement to a successful protest. *American Political Science Review,* 1961, *55,* 769.

Dahrendorf, R. *Class and class conflict in industrial society.* Stanford: Stanford University Press, 1959.

Dawson, R. E., & Prewitt, K. *Political socialization.* Boston: Little, Brown, 1969.

Dean, D. Alienation and political apathy. *Social Forces,* 1960, *38,* 185-189.

Duverger, M. *Introduction to the social sciences.* London: Allen & Unwin, 1964.

Easton, D. *A systems analysis of political life.* New York: Wiley, 1965.

Erbe, W. Social involvement and political activity. *American Sociological Review,* 1964, *24,* 198-215.

Galtung, J. *Theory and method of social research.* New York: Columbia University Press, 1969.

Gamson, W. The fluoridation dialogue. *Public Opinion Quarterly,* 1961, *35,* 526-537.

Gould, L. J. Conformity and marginality: Two faces of alienation. *Journal of Social Issues,* 1969, *25,* 51.

Greenstein, F. Political socialization. In D. Sills (Ed.), *International encyclopedia of the social science.* New York: Macmillan, 1968.

Gurr, T. Psychological factors in civil violence. *World Politics,* 1968, *15,* 245-278.

Gurr, T. *Why men rebel.* Princeton: Princeton University Press, 1970.

Hobbes, T. *Leviathan.* Parts 1 & 2. (Republished: Indianapolis, Liberal Arts Press, 1958.)

Horton, J., & Thompson, W. Powerlessness and political negativism. *American Journal of Sociology,* 1961-1962, *67,* 485-493.

Kellstedt, L. Riot propensity and system disaffection. Paper presented at the American Political Science Association National Convention, New York, September, 1969.

Keniston, K. *Young radicals notes on committed youth.* New York: Harcourt, 1968.

Keniston, K. *The uncommitted alienated youth in American society.* New York: Dell Pub., 1970.

Kirkham, J. F., Levy, S. G., & Crotty, W. J. *Assassination and political violence.* New York: Bantam Books, 1970.

[17] For students interested in some of the empirical research done in the United States, Table 12-2 indicates many of the recent works in the field. The use of the term, alienation, in this table is broader than that employed in this chapter.

Levi, C. *Christ stopped at Eboli.* New York: Grosset & Dunlap, 1947.

Levin, M. *The alienated voter.* New York: Holt, 1960.

Levin, M. B. *The alienated voter: Politics in Boston.* New York: Holt, 1960.

Litt, E. Political cynicism and political futility. *Journal of Politics,* 1963, *25,* 312-323.

Marcuse, H. *Reason and revolution: Hegel and the rise of social theory.* New York: Oxford University Press, 1941.

Marx, K. *Economic and philosophic manuscripts of 1844.* (Republished: Moscow, Foreign Language Pub. House, 1959.)

McDill, E., & Ridley, J. Status, anomia, political alienation and political participation. *American Journal of Sociology,* 1962, *68,* 205-217.

Mészáros, I. *Marx's theory of alienation.* London: Merlin Press, 1970.

Nass, M. Political protest and political conformity: A study of attitudes and behavior of blacks and whites in America. Unpublished doctoral dissertation, Maxwell School of Citizenship, Syracuse University, 1971.

Neumann, F. *The democratic and the authoritarian state.* Glencoe, Ill.: Free Press, 1957.

Pye, L. W. The non-western political process. In H. Eckstein & D. P. Apter (Eds.), *Comparative politics: A reader.* Glencoe, Ill.: Free Press, 1963.

*Report of the Royal Commission on bilingualism and biculturalism.* Ottawa: The Queen's Printer, 1963-1970. Vols. I-V.

Rosenberg, M. Some determinants of political apathy. *Public Opinion Quarterly,* 1954, *18,* 349.

Rousseau, J.-J. The social contract. *Social contract: Essays by Locke, Hume, and Rousseau.* (Republished: New York, Oxford University Press, 1960.) Pp. 169-307.

Schacht, R. *Alienation.* Garden City, N. Y.: Doubleday, 1970.

Seeman, M. On the meaning of alienation. *American Sociological Review,* 1959, *24,* 783-791.

Sigel, R. S. (Ed.) *Learning about politics, a reader in political socialization.* New York: Random House, 1970.

Stone, C. N. Local referendums: An alternative to the alienated voter model. *Public Opinion Quarterly,* 1965-1966, *29,* 213-222.

Templeton, F. Alienation and political participation. *Public Opinion Quarterly,* 1966-1967, *30,* 249-261.

Thompson, W., & Horton, J. Political alienation as a force in political action. *Social Forces,* 1959-1960, *38,* 190-195.

# Chapter 13

# The Imagery of Estrangement:
# Alienation in Modern American Fiction[1]

## Blanche H. Gelfant
Dartmouth College

Alienation is the inextricable theme of modern American fiction. For some critics, alienation is the essence of all modern art. They find in the artist's life a pattern of estrangement from the world, and in his work a recreated experience of estrangement from the self.[2] These obverse sides of alienation—separation from the world and loss of self—appear in the first American novel we can confidently call modern, Theodore Dreiser's *Sister Carrie,* published, significantly, in 1900. In this work, the images that will create and express the theme of alienation in American fiction are indelibly clear: the lonely seamless room that shuts one in; the ominous walls that shut one out; the teasing windows through which the self gazes at the world from which he is barred.

---

[1] Adapted from a presentation to the Institute on Alienation, Maxwell School of Citizenship and Public Affairs, Syracuse University, February, 1970.

[2] In an interesting and highly suggestive book, Wylie Sypher (1964) deals with what I call here alienation from the self. Note the title: *Loss of the Self in Modern Literature and Art.* See also Renato Poggioli, *The Theory of the Avante-Garde,* (1968).

That alienation has been our predominant literary theme is implied in another title, *After Alienation: American Novels in Mid-Century.* In this study, Marcus Klein (1964) sets a trend for current literary criticism, and that is to look at the novel for its patterns of "accommodation," the gesture after and beyond alienation. This quest for examples of reconciliation to the world leads various critics currently to examine the theological basis of the modern novel and the motifs of play as conceived in contemporary game-theory.

With *Sister Carrie* we can begin to trace the portrayal of alienation through various emblematic novels up to the present, discerning in them the purely literary patterns that shape experience into art. Images, metaphors, symbols, language, and narrative structure—these formal elements of the novel not only tell us about alienation but make us feel estrangement and loss. Through the art of the novel we are seized and transported into the private inner world of the alienated, a world otherwise inaccessible to us. The data of the social disciplines—questionnaires, reports, demographic charts, and historical surveys—give us ascertainable facts about alienation: the novel recreates an immediate subjective state. In Nelson Algren's *The Man With the Golden Arm,* the changing image of a room takes us directly into the character's consciousness so that we reexperience her fear and her flight from reality as the room changes from a real place to hallucination:

> The room was bare . . . the walls . . . as white as the corridors, as white as the cot, as the sheet, as the ceiling and as the faces that urged her inside. . . . A room with neither window nor door. . . . [She] heard the click behind her . . . and something locked in her heart with that same automatic key. When she looked around . . . she saw no way to tell where the door had been at all: the walls merged into the door in a single whitewashed surface. Her slow eyes followed for some corner that would rest them, but wall merged into wall in a single curve and there was no place for the eye to rest. Around and around and around, on a whitewashed merry-go-round, ceiling to floor and back again. Till the heart grew sick and the sick brain wheeled, around and around and around [pp. 413-414].[3]

This passage goes on, and when it is finished, we have retreated hopelessly with Sophie into a final state of complete alienation—schizophrenic withdrawal —and we know from the oppressive weariness of our eyeballs, roving around this seamless room, that contact with the outer world has become impossible.

The separation between the self and world, imaged in Algren as madness and confinement, belongs within the Romantic tradition. Romanticism descried a conflict between the world and natural man, whose instincts, impulses, and emotions were inherently good and should be freely expressed. One had only to look at the innocent child, the primitive, or the rustic to see the natural goodness of natural man. Corruption stems from the world-as-society which imposes restraints upon the self, frustrating its desires and perverting its drives. The English Romantic poets, Blake and Wordsworth particularly, identified the corrupting world with the rising industrial city. They believed that man and nature had been harmonious and still belonged in close communion, for both were imbued with the same divine spirit. The city, representing all that was artificial and false, kept man separated from nature, from God, and finally, from the deepest resources of the self. To redeem his self, the Romantic rebelled against the world and sought escape. The prototypical literary figures representing an alienated self in search of freedom are the rebel, the

---

[3] I have tried wherever possible to quote from popular and available editions.

exile, and the vagabond, figures who weave their way through American fiction under various guises and with various intent. Sometimes they seek their liberation and express their alienated condition through violence and revolutionary activities, sometimes through withdrawal, sometimes through spatial dislocation and wandering. In some novels, the rebel appears as a wise child, in others, a madman. Always he is apart from and opposed to the world.

The traditional style for the alienated Romantic was established by the dashing and demonic Lord Byron, who dramatized the part of the rebel in his life as well as in his poetry. He created the "Byronic pose" still recognizable today (particularly with capes in fashion again), the pose of the man alone against the world —the poet, lover, demonic, revolutionary, wanderer, impulsively free, and, ultimately, with the help of opium, self-destructive. Two stanzas from his *Childe Harold's Pilgrimage,* give famous expression to his dramatic creed:

> I have not loved the world, nor the world me;
> I have not flattered its rank breath, nor bowed
> To its idolatries a patient knee,
> Nor coined my cheek to smiles, nor cried aloud
> In worship of an echo; in the crowd
> They could not deem me one of such; I stood
> Among them but not of them; in a shroud
> Of thoughts which were not their thoughts, and still could,
> Had I not filed my mind, which thus itself subdued.
>
> I have not loved the world, nor the world me—
> But let us part fair foes; I do believe,
> Though I have found them not, *that there may be*
> *Words which are things,* hopes which will not deceive,
> And virtues which are merciful, nor weave
> Snares for the failing; I would also deem
> O'er others' griefs that some sincerely grieve;
> That two, or one, are almost what they seem,
> That goodness is no name, and happiness no dream.
>
> [Canto 3, Stanzas 113 and 114].

Of all American novelists, Ernest Hemingway wanted most to believe "that there may be words which are things." For Hemingway, as for many writers, the integrity of language had moral as well as esthetic implications. Morally, words and things should be true to each other; language reflects immoral behavior—lying, deceit, hypocrisy, manipulation—when words do not stand for things, and when things are not what words say. When Hemingway's hero in *A Farewell to Arms* discovers that public words are immoral—in fact, obscene—he separates himself from the world (represented as the Italian army) and goes his own way, a deserter and fugitive: "I was through"; "It was not my show any more"; "I had made a separate peace." Hemingway's hero finds "obscene" the words of the politician and the war poster: sacrifice, honor, not died in vain. These—and not words of sexual connotation—are immoral words because they conceal their true intent and meaning while they lead men to self-slaughter and murder, to war:

I was always embarrassed by the words sacred, glorious, and sacrifice and the expression in vain. We had heard them, sometimes standing in the rain almost out of earshot, so that only the shouted words came through, and had read them on proclamations that were slapped up by billposters over other proclamations, now for a long time, and I had seen nothing sacred, and the things that were glorious had no glory and the sacrifices were like the stockyards at Chicago if nothing was done with the meat except to bury it. There were many words that you could not stand to hear and finally only the names of places had dignity . . . mean anything. Abstract words such as glory, honor, courage, or hallow were obscene [Hemingway, p. 191].[4]

The attempt to purify language of its pretension, artifice, and hypocrisy goes back to the Romantic credo of Wordsworth and Coleridge who believed that the common speech of the plain natural man could provide a poetic medium. Later, Byron was to use colloquial language not only for comic effect but also for sheer honesty of expression. Certain American novelists like Ernest Hemingway, and, before him, Sherwood Anderson and Gertrude Stein, tried to rid the language of its flatulence and hypocrisy and to make it ring clear and true. Their restoration of language represents an attempt to reconcile self and world by reconnecting words of the self to things of the world. A reversal of values concerning language, which makes obscene words clean and honorific ones dirty, intends not merely to shock, but, more important, to criticize. When an alienated character attacks the language of the other, preferring his own obscenity, he establishes a moral position. In *The Catcher in the Rye,* Holden Caulfield's dirty words signify not his corruption, but his innocence. His words, at least, are not false or empty, but his professor recites only flat and flatulent platitudes ("Life *is* a game, boy. Life *is* a game that one plays according to the rules") and falls into rhetorical poses ("I had the privilege of meeting your mother and dad when they had their little chat with Dr. Thurmer some weeks ago. They're grand people [p. 11]"). "Grand," thinks Holden, "there's a word I really hate. It's phony. I could puke every time I hear it [Salinger, p. 12]."

Misused, abused, words become finally meaningless and absurd. This attrition of language appears most striking in contemporary novels of black humor, such as Bruce Jay Friedman's *Stern. Stern* tells the story of a modern suburban man who begins to have a rather comic nervous breakdown when he discovers he is afraid to hit his neighbor who called his wife a "kike." Everyone he approaches for help, mother, father, wife, boss, strangers, friend, speaks nonsense to him, repeating clichés and mechanized meaningless phrases, until all words fail. The failure of language to remain meaningful accelerates his breakdown, and, finally, he must be separated from the normal world and set apart with other alienated characters in a sanatorium. Help comes to him from a most unexpected source, from a little Polish cleaning woman, who makes no pretensions to using language, and who, by her very incoherence, sets him straight: " 'You just can't,' she said, rolling her head from side to side, 'I

[4] See also Gelfant (1963).

mean you just don't go around . . . You got to just . . . sooner or later . . . I mean if a man don't . . . This old world is going to . . . When a fully grown man . . . Rolling up your sleeves is what.' " To which Stern says, "Oh, God, how I appreciate this. I think I'm going to be able to get hold of myself now. . . . Sometimes you just get together with a certain person and it really helps [Friedman, p. 150]."[5] And, in fact, after this purgation of language, he is cured—at least, for a while.

In certain novels, then, the alienated protagonist who refuses to stay with the crowd and share its language is not society's problem, but, rather, its critic. Alienation may thus signify ego-strength, for the hero rejects the world and its words to save his self; but, also, alienation may represent loss of self, ego-disintegration, and death. Two great works of the twentieth century, James Joyce's *A Portrait of the Artist as a Young Man* and Franz Kafka's *The Metamorphosis* dramatize these opposite poles of alienation, and the influence of both works pervades modern American fiction. Joyce's *A Portrait of the Artist as a Young Man,* first appearing serially in 1914-1915, shows the growth of an inviolable self in the person of Stephen Dedalus. Poor but proud, highly intelligent and egoistic, he utters the words of the first rebel, Lucifer—I will not serve: "I will not serve that in which I no longer believe, whether it call itself my home, my fatherland or my church: and I will try to express myself in some mode of life or art as freely as I can and as wholly [p. 291]." Stephen adds that he does "not fear to be alone"; and after his rejection of Dublin and all it would demand of him, so he sees himself: "Alone, quite alone [Joyce, p. 292]." In contrast, Kafka's dutiful son, who gives support and loyalty to his family, sticks to his job, and gives up hopes for personal happiness and romance in order to serve, also remains alone—hideously. This is Gregor, of *The Metamorphosis,* who becomes, literally, what he feels himself to be, figuratively; an insect. The story begins, "As Gregor Samsa awoke one morning from a troubled dream, he found himself changed in his bed to some monstrous kind of vermin." Having lived like a vermin, having felt himself weak and crushable as an insect, he now becomes in fact what he was in spirit, a creature without a self, damned to crawl before his father in fact as he had in spirit, and shut away in his room in fact as always he had been separated in spirit from others and himself.

Flight and confinement, dramatized in these works, represent the opposite kinds of alienation. Imagery of roads, sea, and birds reinforces the theme of freedom. Encapsulating rooms, walls, and windows opening on other walls, or merely on fog, suggest imprisonment of a self already marked for death. Both kinds of imagery recur with an almost inevitable regularity in American novels dealing with alienation, as do both opposite moods (Stephen's and Gregor's) of pride and abjectness. Many American novels establish, also, a rhythm of movement and stasis produced by alternations of flight and confinement, effort and lethargy, or hope and disillusionment. Characters are typically running somewhere, and then stopping, sensing themselves nowhere. Action is not linear and progressive, but

[5] The ellipses are in the original.

circular; and the underlying circular structure of the novel gives mimetic expression to the theme of futility.

Theodore Dreiser's *Sister Carrie* was one of the first important American novels to portray the self-alienating effect of the modern city, and to do so through images and rhythms that I find classic. Carrie, the naive country girl, and Hurstwood, the sophisticated city man, are both overawed, both made to feel their insignificance, vulnerability, and helplessness by Chicago and New York, and both are deprived of identity. Ironically, their loss of self is reflected in an accumulation of new names and guises, all false. Who is the real Carrie: Carrie Meeber, the hopeful waif who arrives in Chicago to seek happiness and fortune; Carrie Drouet, the blossoming mistress of a flashy, good-natured salesman; Carrie Madenda, the aspiring actress; or Carrie Wheeler, the wife of a New York bar-owner? But she can't be Mrs. Wheeler, because Wheeler is really Hurstwood and, moreover, his marriage to Carrie is illegal. The confusion over identity does not lie with the reader, but in the character himself. Carrie regularly studies herself in the mirror, practices a new walk or position of the head, imitates a facial expression she has observed, recreates her "image," trying in this way to make herself into someone, because deep within her she feels she is no one. She is a moth driven to the flame of the city's lights, a will-of-the-wisp drifting on the tide of the city's crowds, a helpless fragment drawn by the magnet of money, fashion, and fame—these are Dreiser's metaphors to express the helpless fascination of an impressionable naive self before the city's power to attract. When Carrie seeks work in the city's business district, she responds to the strangeness of, and feels estranged by, Chicago's towering buildings, granite, stone, "large plates of window glass"—the artificiality of the city. Though the bustling scene interests her, it imposes "a sense of helplessness amid so much evidence of power and force." The great streets are "wall-lined mysteries to her; the vast offices, strange mazes [Dreiser, p. 18]."[6] Preceding Joyce and Kafka, Dreiser anticipates here their essential images of alienation, the maze of streets and the imprisonment of rooms. The city as a maze of labyrinth from which the hero must escape pervades Joyce's *A Portrait of the Artist as a Young Man,* built as it is upon the myth of Dedalus, creator of the labyrinth and of the waxen wings to be used for flight. The city as a seamless room, Kafka's image of separation and, finally, of death, is also a chief setting for Dreiser as he alternates between flight and confinement, movement and stasis. Carrie rushes downtown to seek work and then returns and sits in her lonely room; she goes to theaters and restaurants with Drouet, and then sits and rocks in her room; she rides with Hurstwood, agitatedly, excitedly, on the train to New York, and then sits in the furnished room; she mingles happily with the crowds in streets and lobbies, rides in carriages, rushes to and from her theater, but always, and at last, she is alone, rocking, yearning, lonely, shut in her room, her self still eluding her though she has gained the world. "In your rocking-chair, by your window, shall you dream such happiness as you may never feel [p. 57]."

[6] See also my discussion of the impact of the city upon Carrie (Gelfant, 1954, Ch. 3). Ch. 3).

This fictive movement is analogous to that in a recent movie, "Midnight Cowboy." Like Carrie, the Cowboy comes from a small town to the city, hoping to make his fortune, though in a sordid way, and find happiness. Like Carrie, he thinks that clothes are the key to a meaningful identity, and he stocks up on Western outfits, studies himself in the mirror, as she often does, and invents a posture for himself. Like Carrie on the train, he is on the move (on the bus at the beginning and the end of the movie) and in between he alternates from the loneliness of his hotel room to the loneliness of the crowd in the streets, the automat, the far-out parties —unlike Byron, wishing to be not only *among* the crowd, but *of* them. The Cowboy at least connects in one meaningful relationship; Carrie merely drifts.

In the end, though Carrie has money, clothes, and some fame, the things she wanted, she is a victim of the city, as is Hurstwood who becomes pauperized in New York, a "nothing," retreating finally to that dismal room where in his utter aloneness he turns on the gas and dies. Why does this happen in the novel? Why must Hurstwood, who starts out in such brilliance, die? Why must Carrie dream of a happiness she can never feel? The answer is complex—and that is part of the novel's beauty—but there is one intransigent fact: these people and this scene lack authenticity. The city glitters, dazzles, glows, and gleams (and this also is the way Times Square appears to the Cowboy), but it is false. The lights are unreal, and when Dreiser compares them to natural phenomena, the stars, he shows their speciousness and their harmful, destructive power. Speaking of the false lights of the "lighted chamber," the "lure" of the restaurant and fancy bar, Dreiser says, "the love of light and show and finery . . . to one outside, under the serene light of the eternal stars and sweeping night winds, what a lamp-flower it must bloom; a strange, glittering night-flower, odour-yielding, insect-drawing, insect-infested rose of pleasure [p. 53]."

Ironically, of all American novelists, Dreiser, himself a naive newcomer to the city, was most captivated by the city's glamour, most fascinated by its show, most yearning for its rewards. His characters grapple for money, clothes, power, and pleasure in novel after novel: *Sister Carrie, An American Tragedy, The 'Genius,' The Financier, The Titan;* but always, whether or not they get what they want, all that the city offers them turns out to be inauthentic. And because the values of the city and its glitter are inauthentic, so are they. Carrie achieves her dream of becoming one of the crowd; she enters and is taken into the world; but she never finds a self. Her dream of happiness is illusory and the novel describes a pattern of hope and disillusionment, of movement and stasis, that is fundamental to the portrayal of alienation.

Another novel of city life, *Manhattan Transfer* by John Dos Passos, published in 1925, begins with various characters entering the city in an aura of hopefulness and expectation. It ends in dejection as Jimmy Herf stands by the road, his symbol of escape, thumbing a ride out: "Say will you give me a lift?" "How fur you going." "I dunno . . . pretty far [Dos Passos, p. 371]."[7] The image of the vagabond

---

[7] See also Gelfant (1961).

emerges, his costume carefully chosen to symbolize his alienation from the world
of business. In Dos Passos, the theme of historical betrayal, so indigenous to our
times, becomes foremost. Dos Passos writes always with a sense of the past and its
formative democratic ideals. Testing the realities of the present against these ideals
of the past, he describes the only honorable course to be that of alienation, cutting
one's self off from a society that has betrayed its dream. As Jimmy Herf decides
on the costume of alienation—the workingman's shirt—his thoughts of personal
escape intermingle with historical references: "Young man [he tells himself] to save
your sanity you've got to do one of two things . . . one of two unalienable alternatives: go away in a dirty soft shirt or stay in a clean Arrow collar. But what's the
use of spending your whole life fleeing the City of Destruction? What about your
unalienable right, Thirteen Provinces [*Manhattan Transfer,* p. 335]?" In his next
novel, *U. S. A.*, his masterpiece, Dos Passos uses a cinematic technique and a stream
of consciousness to superimpose the past on the present, to make a previous idealism
comment on modern corruption. In some of the finest passages of his work and our
literature—the Camera Eye sections in *U. S. A.*—he traces the growth of a young
man's sensibility and social awareness. Set apart from the main fictional narrative,
these fragmentary passages imply the theme of alienation. The novel's structure—its
division into four distinct and alternating sections—dramatizes separation of the self
from the world. The world, war-bound and money-mad, is represented by the fictional
narratives and reinforced by the Newsreel sections (selected excerpts from actual newspapers suggesting a kind of cosmic social insanity). A third panel, on famous historical figures, real contemporaries of the fictional characters, exposes the critics
of society, those who, separated from the world, would not play assigned parts,
and consequently were broken. Finally, the autobiographical Camera Eye section
moves into the inner consciousness of a sensitive observer who concludes that he
must categorically declare his separation from a country that has betrayed its original avowed ideals. In particular, the Sacco-Vanzetti case, to which current history
resonates,[8] alienates the young man. When he sees the miscarriage of justice, the
coercive blind power of the judge and the courts, the sanctioned murder of the
two men, he declares himself like Hemingway's hero "out of it."

In Camera Eye (50) he dramatically repudiates the world. This section is
worth looking at, not only because its subject is still timely, but also because it
recapitulates some of the points already made about literary form, and introduces
others. Notice that the speaker deplores the defilement of language: "the clean
words our fathers spoke . . . [are] made . . . slimy and foul." Notice also that the
stream of conscious technique in itself, as an expression of a private inner world,
denotes a separation of the self from others. The writer who keeps us limited to
the point of view or consciousness of a single character, who shows us, as Joyce does
in *A Portrait of the Artist as a Young Man,* only what that character sees, feels,

[8] I wrote this at the time of the Chicago Seven trials.

and knows, keeps us shut away from a public reality—indeed he may be implying that there is no objective public reality at all. If, philosophically, this is so, then alienation is inevitable: a person will be as much locked in his own consciousness as in a closed room, and alienation will be not a result of "social causes," but an intrinsic fact of existence. These are possibilities to consider. Meanwhile, here are Dos Passos' words:

> they have clubbed us off the streets they are stronger they are rich they hire and fire the politicians the newspapereditors the old judges the small men with reputations the collegepresidents the wardheelers (listen businessmen collegepresidents judges America will not forget her betrayers) they hire the men with guns the uniforms the policecars the patrolwagons
> all right you have won you will kill the brave men our friends tonight there is nothing left to do we are beaten
> . . .
> America our nation has been beaten by strangers who have turned our language inside out who have taken the clean words our fathers spoke and made them slimy and foul
> . . .
> all right we are two nations
> America our nation has been beaten by strangers who have bought the laws and fenced off the meadows and cut down the woods for pulp and turned our pleasant cities into slums and sweated the wealth out of our people and when they want to they hire the executioner to throw the switch ["The Big Money" in *U. S. A.,* pp. 461-464]

After such impassioned words and feelings, after such a sense of betrayal, what can the character do but break away? The final section of *U. S. A.* recapitulates the ending of *Manhattan Transfer.* The young man becomes a Vag (vagabond) and takes to the road. That is the last word of the book—Road.

The failure of radical activism in the thirties and forties to affect the course of historical events helps to explain why the Road-novels of the next generation simply ignore the political scene. In the thirties, characters joined the Communist Party, circulated pamphlets, let themselves be clubbed by the police, enlisted in the Lincoln Brigade in Spain to stem the tide of fascism—to no avail. Dos Passos' *Portrait of a Young Man,* like Hemingway's *For Whom the Bell Tolls,* has an American hero volunteering his life in the Spanish Civil War for the cause of political freedom. Both heroes die; the cause is defeated. The hero of the next generation has so definitively made his "separate peace," he does not even have to mention it.

In particular, the beat characters of Jack Kerouac's series of Road-novels do not explain why they have dropped out of the scene, out of politics, out of the scramble for money, fashion, and fame. They do not rationalize why they retreat to the mountain to meditate in *The Dharma Bums,* or to Mexico to get stoned in *Tristessa,* or to San Francisco to move into the underground world in *The Subterraneans.* They take for granted the failure and the devaluation of everything the world represents. For them, the exaltation of the self through impulsive Romantic release is the only, the highest, good. Sheer movement replaces meaning; movement becomes meaning. "We were leaving confusion and nonsense behind and performing our one and noble function of the time, *move,* [p. 111]," says the hero of Kerouac's *On the Road,* a hero who defined a new style of life still imitated today.His costume, carefully abnegating his social class, seems casual, copied from working-class and minority people: Mexican sandals, sailor's peacoat, railwayman's cap, hunter's shirt, Indian's blanket—beads and feather to come later. All dressed up, busy with plans and schedules to go to New Jersey, meet in Denver, push on to San Francisco, drop down to Mexico, head for Virginia, then to New Jersey, and back to New York—the beat hero discovers two strange things: he is running out of room so that he has to move in circles, and as soon as he stops running, he does not know who he is. "Here I was," says Sal Paradise in *On the Road,* "at the end of America—no more land—and now there was nowhere to go but back. I determined at least to make my trip a circular one [p. 66]." Insofar as the novel's structure reveals its theme, the circular movement of *On the Road* suggests futility, just as the disjunction of parts in *U. S. A.* suggests social alienation. Kerouac's hero literally goes in circles, to the effect that he never gets anywhere, and whenever he arrives at his immediate destination he can barely wait to get on the road again because wherever he is things begin to fall apart. (Another contemporary movie, "Easy Rider," dramatizes the same pattern: going somewhere, getting there, going again, and discovering, at last, "We blew it.") There are times Kerouac's hero knows that drugs are estranging him from himself, but his most awful moment of loss of self comes from the sheer fatigue and futility of constantly being on the road. Again, loss of self is imaged by the small room, the cheap hotel room in which Sal awakens not to know who he is:

> I woke up as the sun was reddening; and that was the one distinct time in
> my life, the strangest moment of all, when I didn't know who I was—I was far
> away from home, haunted and tired with travel, in a cheap hotel room I'd
> never seen, hearing the hiss of steam outside, and the creak of the old wood
> of the hotel, and footsteps upstairs, and all the sad sounds, and I looked up at
> the cracked high ceiling and really didn't know who I was. . . . I wasn't scared;
> I was just somebody else, some stranger, and my whole life was a haunted life,
> the life of a ghost [Kerouac, *On the Road,* p. 16].

When he says this is the only time he did not know who he was, he is merely forgetting other occasions. In truth, it would be hard for him to know his own identity, for his deepest and most lasting experience is that of inner emptiness. He tries to compensate for this emptiness—perhaps to run from it—by keeping on the move. Drugs blot out his aching awareness of emptiness, or, rather, suspend him in a different kind of nothingness; but neither drugs nor movement provide any permanent escape from the fears that pursue, the irrational fears of madness and death. Madness does overtake Kerouac's protagonist of a later novel, *Big Sur,* a character who, despite his extravagant surface emotion, lives in dread. Kerouac's mood, with which he imbues his rushed heroes, is fundamentally ecclesiastical (as reflected in the title and theme of his last novel, *The Vanity of Duluoz*). While his generic hero's underlying feeling is that all is futile and vain, he still struggles to create a life for himself and an identity; characteristically, he adopts the life-style of the social outsider, the member of a minority group, the criminal, the madman, the outcast. Whereas Dreiser's Carrie tries to establish herself within the accepted crowd, Kerouac's hero tries to join the "subterraneans" and finds his identity in the outcast. This reveals his Romantic disposition to believe that there is a primitive being, and that he, rather than the highly civilized man, knows how to tap his deepest resources for pleasure and joy. He wants to be someone other than he is because, typically, he feels "like a speck on the surface of the sad red earth."

> At lilac evening, I walked with every muscle aching among the lights of 27th and Welton in the Denver colored section, wishing I were a Negro, feeling that the best the white world had offered was not enough ecstasy for me, not enough life, joy, kicks, darkness, music, not enough night . . . I wished I were a Denver Mexican, or even a poor overworked Jap, anything but what I was so drearily, a "white man" disillusioned . . . [I wished] I could exchange worlds with the happy, true-hearted, ecstatic Negroes of America [Kerouac, *On the Road,* pp. 148-149].

Now, Kerouac's generic hero knows better than to believe in the myth of the black man's ecstasy, because in *The Subterraneans,* as Leo Percepied, he has an intimate affair with a black woman and comes to know of her fears, paranoic hallucinations, and her simple everyday problems about money, friends, and lovers. While Mardou Fox is hip—and for this Leo loves her, her hip walk, clothes, speech, sense of jazz—she is also dismally and profoundly unhappy, and she too suffers a loss of self through a schizophrenic break. Nevertheless, in a typically Romantic preference for illusion over fact, Leo persists in his dream of an ecstasy that only the other, the nonwhite, feels:

> I feel that great hepness I'd been having all summer on the streets with Mardou my old dream of wanting to be vital, alive like a Negro or an Indian or a Denver Jap or a New York Puerto Rican come true, with her by my side so young, sexy, slender, strange, hip, myself in jeans and casual and both of us as if young (I say as if, to my 31)—[Kerouac, *The Subterraneans,* pp. 96-97].

Remembering that he is thirty-one of course touches a nerve in the hero, is a bit of fact interjected into his fantasy. And yet his fantasy has a certain rationale that the disaffected youth of today share, for with an assessment that the world is not good, but corrupting, the self shifts its identification from the insider to the outsider. If the world is wrong—money-mad, death-driven, strait-jacketed, and lie-packed— why, then, the perennial outsider might be right. As a consequence, the novel presents a new prototypical hero who wishes to be a black man or a suffering Jew (as in Bernard Malamud's *The Assistant*) because he thinks that in this identity he might have a more valid moral being. In the novels of the late thirties, casting off the middle-class business suit and joining the working-class showed moral integrity; in contemporary novels, moving underground with hipsters, criminals, and addicts (or circumcising one's self) becomes a symbol of moral self-recreation.

"All Americans are in a sense members of minority groups," Ralph Ellison wrote in an essay, but it takes his nameless protagonist in *Invisible Man* time and arduous experience to discover the real meaning of being a minority person, a black man in a white society. If he is alienated, he does not really know it at the beginning of the novel, because he has stayed where he has been told he belongs and has never had occasion to overstep his boundaries. His troubles begin in a characteristic way for an alienated hero: he believes the words that someone says. When Mr. Norton, the white founder of a Southern black college, tells the young hero he wants to know the notorious Trueblood, the boy obeys, makes the introduction, and from then on is engaged in a series of misadventures from which he escapes barely with his life. His identity from then on becomes unstable; he changes name and costume, and, even when he is himself, others consistently mistake him for someone else. He is a walking case of mistaken identity, or of nonidentity, because he says, "people refuse to see me." His invisibility is in their eyes rather than in his substance. Nevertheless, he tries for a long time to live up to the image others project for him: "I was pulled this way and that for longer than I can remember. And my problem was that I always tried to go in everyone's way but my own [p. 433]." Whether he realizes it or not, in his own way he repeats Stephen Dedalus's words: "I will not serve." After years of trying to adopt the opinions of others [exactly what Stephen fought against] I finally rebelled. I am an *invisible* man [p. 433]." Invisibility is his road, his escape from the importunities of the world; if he is not there to be seen, he cannot be made to conform. His escape from the crowd, both figuratively and literally (for a mob is after him) is farcical and fortunate. Running, he falls into a manhole and finds himself underground, entombed in a room from which there seems to be no exit. But unlike Kafka's room that grew more disorderly, cluttered, and dark, this one is flooded by light, and here at last the hero begins to see. He sees the way to a new and better relationship between the world and the self. His world has become "one of infinite possibilities": it can permit diversity and difference; it can allow the self to make its own choices; it can assure the survival of both the self and the world through "division." Considering the invisible man's experience, his conclusion is generous and humane, transcending racial barriers. Moreover, it is not—at least not completely—unrealistic. He recognizes that the world will not change miraculously:

> No indeed, the world is just as concrete, ornery, vile and sublimely wonderful
> as before, only now I better understand my relation to it and it to me. I've come
> a long way from those days when, full of illusion, I lived a public life and attempted
> to function under the assumption that the world was solid and all the relationships
> therein. Now I know men are different and that all life is divided and that only in
> division is there true health [Ellison, p. 435].

He has yet to test his conclusions, and the book ends with his decision, "I must come out. I must emerge." The final image of a man rising from underground to life again expresses a universally shared hope—that a man can be reborn, and that, to use the title of a Malamud novel, he can start "a new life."

This perennial hope seems to motivate the fiction of Saul Bellow, a writer whose themes include, but transcend, that of alienation. Again and again Bellow writes of a character in extremity who seems, somehow comically as well as courageously, on the verge of final breakdown. In *Seize the Day* Tommy Wilhelm's case is ultimately neat. In one day he is wiped out; the man he trusted disappears; the money he gave him is lost in the stockmarket; the hotel bill is due and he is to be evicted; the relationship with his father, such as it is, is broken irretrievably as his father calls him a torturing slob; the hope of relief from his ex-wife is destroyed by her demanding phone call; the chances for a decent new job are dim. All in all, it is, as he says, "a day of reckoning"—a reckoning that ends with zero and cancels him out. He loves the world, but the world clearly does not love him. There is no rescue, no miracle—except that, in the very depths of his despair, through the very knowledge of his own foolishness, stupidity, sheer wrong-headedness, Tommy Wilhelm manages to affirm a love for his self. The self, stripped of pretension, realistic hope, all validation from the world, can still affirm its value, can still love its own humanity. Bellow's hero, like many of Malamud's heroes, is the perennial loser, the schlemiel—an object for jokes and derision, shabby outsider, loner—but he glows with the translucence of art and the artist's love for him as an emblem of bare, unaccommodated man—perhaps not much, but the only thing we have.

At the end of *Sister Carrie,* Carrie sits and rocks and yearns, still alone and unfulfilled. Hurstwood is dead. At the end of *Manhattan Transfer* and *U. S. A.,* the sensitive dislocated protagonist puts on his workshirt, his symbol of vagabondage, and takes to the road, without destination. At the end of *For Whom the Bell Tolls* and *Portrait of a Young Man,* the politically committed protagonists are killed, betrayed by their idealistic dreams of living within the world. Young Holden Caulfield, who dreams of saving the innocent children from the world in *A Catcher in the Rye,* is headed for a mental hospital. Kerouac's heroes chaotically and compulsively review their frantic efforts to achieve union with others and self-communion, and at the end report inanition, madness, and "the vanity of all human wishes." Ellison's invisible man is last seen about to arise from a manhole —to what uncertain future?

Only recently, in the fiction of Bellow and Malamud, for example, does the protagonist transcend his condition, his loneness and loneliness, his estrangement from the world and self, to effect a tenuous but real reconciliation. However farcical, pathetic, or harrowing are the adventures that carry him to this reconciliation, they import, always, the same time-imbued healing message of love. In the end, characters who love—themselves, another, the world—can move beyond alienation (and beyond mere resignation) to affirm the value of the self and the struggles it must engage in to establish its place in relationship to the world, either firmly within it at last, or outside as its concerned if self-contained observer.

What of the writer, the creator of the alienated characters and the images of estrangement and loss? Traditionally, at least in Romantic literature, the writer as artist has separated himself enough from his world to become its conscience, its critic, its recreator. If the serious novelist had no complaint against the world, why should he write? For money, fame, sheer pleasure in story-telling? These are legitimate motivating ends, and certainly we can envy Philip Roth, say, for apparently achieving them all. But telling his story is also the novelist's means of mastering his experience, of re-forming it, controlling, and redeeming it, and thus of creating his self. Through his alienated hero and his images of estrangement and loss he effects a communication, and, perhaps, also a reconciliation with the world. He affirms his reality and his life by affirming his art. In the end his art objectifies both self and world, and becomes part of the world we live in. This thought, that art validates and transcends the self, however ignoble, decadent, or futile it may be, that art survives and is, consoles Byron's melancholy hero withdrawn to his romantic cave. There, dramatically alone, battered and battering against the world, he reconciles himself to his own nothingness by affirming the immutable worth of his art:

> 'Tis to create, and in creating live
> A being more intense, that we endow
> With form our fancy, gaining as we give
> The life we image, even as I do now—
> What am I? Nothing: but not so my art.
>
> [Canto 3, Stanza 6]

REFERENCES

Algren, N. *The man with the golden arm.* New York: Pocket Book, 1951. (Originally published: 1949.)

Bellow, S. *Sieze the day.* New York, Viking, 1961. (Originally published: 1956.)

Dos Passos, J. The big money. *U. S. A.* New York: Modern Library, 1937.

Dos Passos, J. *Manhattan transfer.* New York: Penguin Books, 1946. (Originally published: 1925.)

Dreiser, T. *Sister Carrie.* New York: Modern Library, 1917. (Originally published: 1900.)

Ellison, R. *Invisible man.* New York : Modern Library, 1952.

Friedman, B. J. *Stern.* New York: New American Library, 1962.

Gelfant, B. H. *The American city novel.* Norman, Okla.: University of Oklahoma Press, 1954. (2nd ed.: 1970.)

Gelfant, B. H. The search for identity in the novels of John Dos Passos. *Publication of the Modern Language Association of America,* 1961, *126,* 113-149.

Gelfant, B. H. Language as a moral code in *A Farewell to Arms. Modern Fiction Studies,* 1963, *9*(2), 173-176.

Hemingway, E. *A farewell to arms.* New York: Scribner's, 1957. (Originally published: 1929.)

Joyce, J. *A portrait of the artist as a young man.* New York: Modern Library, 1928. p. 291. (Originally published: 1916.)

Kafka, F. *The metamorphosis.* New York: Chocken, 1968. (Originally published: 1937.)

Kerouac, J. *On the road.* New York: New American Library, 1957.

Kerouac, J. *The subterraneans.* New York: Grove Press, 1966. (Originally published: 1958.)

Klein, M. *After alienation: American novels in mid-century.* New York: World Publ., 1964.

Malamud, B. *The assistant.* New York: Farrar, 1957.

Poggioli, R. *The theory of the avant-garde.* (Transl. by G. Fitzgerald) Cambridge, Mass: Belknap Press, 1968.

Salinger, J. D. *The catcher in the rye.* New York: New American Library, 1959. (Originally published: 1953.)

Sypher, W. *Loss of the self in modern literature and art.* New York: Random House, 1964.

# Chapter 14

# A Theology of Alienation[1]

## John Macquarrie
University of Oxford

The term alienation is widely used nowadays by many groups of people and bears many senses. Psychologists, sociologists, existentialist philosophers, educators, politicians all make use of the concept, and it is frequently the theme of artists and literary men also.

In this paper I shall talk about the theological employment of the idea of alienation. Perhaps the theological sense of alienation stands closest to the sense in which the term is used by existentialist philosophers. In theology, the modern concept is used to explicate some of the traditional symbols of the Judaeo-Christian heritage. These symbols, many of them originating from or still embedded in mythological narratives, tend to become unintelligible as the historical cultures out of which they came slip into the past. Hence, the theological task is to bring them into contact with contemporary ideas which can throw light once more on the ancient symbols. But in such an act of interpretation, there is a remarkable reciprocity. The concept employed as the hermeneutical tool on the one hand illumines the symbolic material, but, on the other hand, this material itself reacts upon the interpretative concept so as to bring out new dimensions of meaning that may have hitherto escaped attention.

[1] Adapted from a paper presented at the Institute on Alienation, Maxwell School of Citizenship and Public Affairs, Syracuse University, February 1970.

I think this has been especially true in the case of alienation. If, on the one hand, this modern concept of alienation is able to refurbish and bring to life such traditional ideas as the fall of man, sin, and atonement, these ancient ideas and stories reveal a depth and intensity of alienation which is overlooked in accounts which confine themselves to the viewpoints of psychology and sociology.

Actually, the expression "alienation" is used in several ways, even within the context of theological discussion. I shall distinguish four senses of the term, and I do not believe that even these distinctions cover all the varieties of usage.

1. According to Biblical theology, the very existence of man involves a duality. This duality is basic to humanity itself and makes the difference between man and animals. It appears in the Genesis creation story in symbolical and mythological form: "Then the Lord God formed man of the dust from the ground, and breathed into his nostrils the breath of life."[2] Other mythologies tell similar stories. There is, for instance, a Latin myth which describes how Cura (Care) formed man (*homo*) from some earth (*humus*) and how Jupiter then bestowed upon the creature spirit (*spiritus,* literally, breath). It should be noted that although such stories point to a fundamental duality in man, they are not necessarily dualistic in their underlying philosophy. The existence of such myths makes it clear that from the earliest times man understood himself as a complex being standing in a tension between two component elements. This is taken to be true of his original condition, even before there is any mention of a fall into sin. But the two component elements are embraced within a unity, and both belong equally to the primordial humanity. In a genuinely dualistic philosophy or mythology—the various forms of Gnosticism, to which reference will be made later, are examples—body and soul are utterly foreign to each other and are in irreconcilable conflict. Only the soul is recognized as truly human, and salvation is understood as the escape of the soul from the imprisoning body. In the Biblical view, the matter is understood quite differently. Body and soul are equiprimordially constituent of the whole man, and salvation is understood as a resurrection of the body—a renewal and transformation of human existence in all its dimensions.

However, the use of the expressions "body" and "soul" is inadequate to reflect the meaning of the Genesis story and imports into it a later (Hellenic) metaphysic. Originally, we may suppose, the story had a purely existential import—that is to say, it expressed a self-understanding prior to any attempts to find a metaphysical basis for this, for instance, in a theory of independent soul-substances existing alongside material substances. The "dust of the earth" symbolizes the "given" in human existence. To be sure, this "given" is most obviously the body, but it does not coincide with the body. But as well as the given, man is constituted also by "possibility" (symbolized by the "breath of life"). Man differs from any other creature in not simply having a given nature, but in having essentially a changing, dynamic nature so that he is always on his way to becoming something other than

---

[2] Genesis 2:7.

he is at any particular moment. In the case of man, existence precedes essence, to use Sartre's expression.

A classic analysis of the fundamental duality of human existence is provided by Soren Kierkegaard. He relates it to the phenomenon of anxiety and sets it in the context of an exegesis of the Biblical narrative of the creation and fall of man. What emerges in Kierkegaard's analysis is not yet alienation in the full sense, but rather what makes alienation possible.

Kierkegaard asks, "What makes sin possible?" (Later we shall consider the relation between sin and alienation.) In seeking to answer the question, he turns to the Genesis story which he regards as one describing an event or development in the life of every human being—the passage from innocence to sin or from the unbroken wholeness of a merely given existence to the felt tension between a given state and an unrealized possibility. What makes this event of a transition possible is the mood of anxiety.

Kierkegaard describes the primordial anxiety of existence in at least three ways: first, it is already inherent in the state of innocence. Already in dreaming innocence there is something like an instability, an uneasiness, a presentiment that disturbs the tranquility of bliss. "This is the profound secret of innocency, that at the same time it is anxiety [Kierkegaard, 1946, p. 38]." The illustration which Kierkegaard uses is the awakening of sexuality and of sensuality in the individual. There is a malaise not properly understood, a premonition which finally issues in the sensual act, and so in the loss of innocence and in a changed quality of existence. This is a loss—not to be described analytically but known only in experience.

Second, anxiety is also linked to freedom. Again, it is a kind of instability prior to action. Kierkegaard describes anxiety as the "dizziness" or "vertigo" of freedom. For freedom means possibility, and to stand on the edge of possibility is like standing on the edge of a precipice. One is standing on the firm if not very exciting ground of the given, but to leave the given and cast oneself into possibility is to let life become, all of a sudden, fluid and changing. The stirring of possibility in primordial freedom is experienced as anxiety, the awareness of complexity, differentiation, and possible alienation within the very depth of one's being.

Third, Kierkegaard associates anxiety also with the traditional philosophical doctrine that man is constituted of body and soul. This is taken to mean that in the very way he is constituted, man is subject to the tension of anxiety. The human task is to accomplish the synthesis of body and soul (notice that this is precisely the opposite of a dualistic point of view) and this task is, from the beginning, laden with anxiety. Anxiety is a peculiarly human phenomenon, related to the peculiar duality of the human condition. An animal knows no anxiety, for its life is purely sensuous; an angel likewise would know no anxiety, for an angel is said to be a pure intellectual essence. But man in his "middle state," conjoining sense and intellect, body and soul, the given and the possible, lives in the tension of anxiety.

This brief summary of Kierkegaard's teaching on anxiety makes it evident that his concept has some rough edges and may not be entirely self-consistent. But this untidiness is perhaps inseparable from reflection on the concrete phenomena of human existence. There is, however, another point that must be made and that may seem to make the concept still more ambiguous. Until this point, I have presented Kierkegaard's notion of anxiety in a fairly negative way—it is the inner mood which lights up the fundamental duality of the human constitution and, as such, it is the precondition for sin, alienation, and even, in extreme cases, for those pathological forms of division described by R. D. Laing in *The Divided Self.* But, strictly speaking, the basic duality of human existence is a neutral phenomenon, and so is the anxiety which it engenders. Thus, Kierkegaard is willing to assign a positive role to anxiety as a propaedeutic to the attainment of selfhood.

This idea is developed further in the thought of Nietzsche. The fact that existence and essence in man do not coincide, and that from the very moment he becomes man there is a gap between the given and the possible is seen on the one hand as the imperfection of man, but on the other as the sole condition that allows for the possibility of transcending his current condition toward the superman *(Übermensch).*

Later existentialist philosophers, such as Heidegger and Sartre, have further explored the fundamental discontinuity or duality at the heart of human existence in terms of the opposition between facticity and possibility, or between "thrownness" (*Geworfenheit*) and "projectedness" (*Entworfenheit*). However, we shall pass over these to a more recent analysis, that presented by Paul Ricoeur. In describing man as "fallible" rather than "fallen," Ricoeur is recognizing that the gap which emerges with human existence itself is neutral—the occasion for sin and alienation but also the necessary occasion for self-transcendence. Ricoeur's analyses are of further interest because of the great use which he makes of Biblical and mythological material, especially in his book *The Symbolism of Evil* (Ricoeur, 1967). Human existence is fallible because it is characterized at its very basis by a fault—not so much in the sense of a fault calling for blame, but rather like a geological fault, a discontinuity. Ricoeur's (1965) terms are richly varied. He speaks of *faille,* breach; *escart,* gap; *felure,* rift; *dechirement,* tearing [p. xiii] , to express what he has in mind. The gap is between existence and essence, or between the self that one is and the self that is projected. But this kind of flaw or fault is not yet a moral fault. It is, rather, the kind of finite being for which morality then becomes possible. However, finite freedom has already, as Origen and other ancient writers suggested, a tragic quality. The possibility of man's rising (self-transcendence) is inseparable from the possibility of his falling.

2. We now turn from that neutral, primordial discontinuity in human existence, which is the condition of the possibility of alienation, to an actual form of alienation. We take up the Biblical and theological concept of sin. We must remind ourselves that sin is not synonymous with guilt. The word sin introduces a religious dimension which is not conveyed in the notion of pure moral guilt. Sin brings along a religious model for the understanding of guilt.

Guilt has, of course, been understood under many images (for a discussion, see Ricoeur, 1967, pp. 100-150). Stain or contamination, missing the mark, breaking the law, and so on. One may ask, then, what is distinctive about sin as a way of understanding guilt? Although there is some debate about the derivation, it seems probable that the English word "sin" (German: *Sünde*) is connected etymologically with the verb "sunder" (German: *sondern*), so that originally talk about sin referred to a situation in which a sundering or separation took place. The word "sin" has nowadays, of course, become so much trivialized that this strong connotation of sundering has virtually been lost.

Recent theology, however, has sought to revitalize the understanding of sin and to restore to the understanding of the word the notions of separating and sundering. It is in this connection that the notion of sin has been brought into contact with the idea of alienation. Paul Tillich, in particular, has interpreted sin in terms of alienation, though he has preferred to use the word "estrangement." Both alienation and estrangement correspond to the word *Entfremdung* which Heidegger (1962) uses to describe one aspect of what he calls the "falling [p. 222]" of man. Man falls away from the possibilities of a more human existence by becoming another object in the world or by losing his freedom in impersonal mass-existence. This means, in effect, that he becomes alienated from his authentic existence, from his true self and his genuine humanity.

The notion of existential estrangement does, in fact, recapture an important element in the traditional idea of sin. However, the ideas are not identical. In existentialist philosophy, alienation implies alienation from oneself, from the possibility of authentic existence. In religion, sin means separation from God, *aversio a Deo,* in the traditional expression. But the two kinds of separation are closely connected, and each is linked also with a third—separation from other human persons. In Heidegger's philosophy, the inward split (which is alienation) from the authentic possibilities of existence does, in fact, destroy authentic relations with other persons, and, even beyond that, produces a sense of alienation from being, from the whole scheme of things. Conversely, the religious concept of sin which sees the sundering from God as basic also sees this as correlated with the sundering from other persons and from one's own authentic self. There is an interesting illustration of this in the New Testament story of the prodigal son. We are told that in the "far country" (a vivid symbol of alienation) he "came to himself," and this coming to himself was also the beginning of his return to the father.

We now see more clearly the specific theological contribution to the understanding of alienation. When the religious dimension is included, alienation is understood in terms that go beyond psychological or sociological accounts. We must speak here of ontological alienation or of cosmic alienation. In religious terms, this is separation from God, that is to say, a separation from that which is understood as the deepest level of reality. It is to this kind of alienation, whether we call it ontological, cosmic, theological, or religious, that we must now give fuller attention.

3. It is a strange but undoubted fact that at various periods of history men have been seized with an overwhelming mood of ontological estrangement, a feeling of being alienated from the universe. A very interesting example of this is pro-

vided by what is loosely called Gnosticism. Partly religious, partly mythological, partly philosophical, Gnosticism flourished over wide areas of the Near East about the time of the rise of Christianity. To the Gnostic, the world was utterly alien and demonic. The gap or discontinuity within the self had been projected upon the whole of reality which was felt to be hostile and stifling. The inner duality became a metaphysical dualism. Light and darkness were the two great Gnostic symbols. The human soul is a bearer of light but it is imprisoned in a world of darkness. Men are lost and alone in a vast alien world. Hans Jonas (1963) has used the expression "cosmic nihilism" to describe the mood of the Gnostics, and it finds eloquent expression in this fragment of Gnostic document:

> A vine am I, a lonely one that stands in the world. I have no sublime planter,
> no keeper, no mild helper to come and instruct me about everything [p. 66].

The nineteenth century ushered in a new age of cosmic nihilism. Again the universe seemed strange and hostile, and we are still living in this new phase of cosmic alienation. It found expression in poets like Hölderlin who wrote of the departure of the gods and the feeling of forlornness on the part of men. Philosophically, it was Nietzsche who brought the new mood to expression, but he was also a poet. The following striking verses express Nietzsche's sense of the alien character of the world after the death of God:

> The world's a gate
> To deserts stretching mute and chill
> Who once has lost
> What thou has lost stands nowhere still.

Since Nietzsche, the same mood has found expression in the writings of atheistic existentialism. According to Camus, we live in a world the character of which is basically absurd so that we can only rebel against it. Sartre's philosophy leads to the insoluble dualism in which the fragile *pour-soi* confronts the nauseating spectacle of the senseless, all-engulfing *en-soi.* In literature, the sense of not being at home in a world which must be adjudged pointless and meaningless has been powerfully expressed in such works as Kafka's *The Castle* and Becket's *Waiting for Godot.*

Theology is not without its understanding for this profound ontological type of alienation. How far this alienation is related to other types and whether it is cause or effect is hard to say. We have already seen that alienation from oneself, alienation from society, and alienation from the cosmos are linked in subtle ways.

In saying that theology has an understanding for cosmic or ontological alienation in terms of its concepts of the creation and fall of man, I am not, of course, saying that theology gives its blessing to them. The Judaeo-Christian tradition is opposed to Gnosticism and its modern equivalents. Alienation is recognized, but atonement and reconciliation are set against it. The doctrine of God and the doctrine of creation deny that dualism is the last word about the world and in the face of cosmic alienation these doctrines teach a fundamental trust or faith in being.

Sociologist Peter Berger (1969) mentions the deep need that human beings have for believing that the world is an orderly and meaningful affair rather than absurd or chaotic. He introduces an illustration which makes very clear what I mean by ontological alienation. I quote the passage in full:

> A child wakes up in the night, perhaps from a bad dream, and finds himself alone, surrounded by darkness, beset by nameless threats. At such a moment the contours of trusted reality are blurred or invisible, and in the terror of incipient chaos the child cries out for his mother. It is hardly an exaggeration to say that, at this moment, the mother is being invoked as a high priestess of protective order. It is she (and, in many cases, she alone) who has the power to banish the chaos and to restore the benign shape of the world. And, of course, any good mother will do just that. She will take the child and cradle him in the timeless gesture of the *Magna Mater* who became our Madonna. She will turn on a lamp, perhaps, which will encircle the scene with a warm glow of reassuring light. She will speak or sing to the child and the content of this communication will invariably be the same, "Don't be afraid—everything is in order, everything is all right" [pp. 67-68].

Berger (1969) goes on to point out that although this is a routine scene, it has a religious dimension. "Everything is in order" is a metaphysical statement. To quote again: "The formula can, without in any way violating it, be translated into a statement of cosmic scope—'Have trust in being' [p. 69]." But to have trust in being is simply another way of saying what religion seeks to express when it talks of belief in God, that is to say, belief in a cosmic order that is not alien or even indifferent, but that is supportive.

As Berger (1969) says, "at the very center of the process of becoming fully human, at the core of *humanitas,* we find an experience of trust in the order of reality [p. 69]." But the question at once arises whether this "trust in the order of reality" is an illusion, induced by our need to overcome alienation and ontological insecurity. And we have at once to acknowledge that the world has an ambiguous face. Some things do indeed point to an order that can be trusted, but others to dark, chaotic, threatening forces. One may eventually decide that there are better reasons for taking the order as fundamental rather than the chaos, but this can never be proved and involves an act of faith, albeit a reasonable faith. It seems moreover—though the reasons for this are obscure—that there are periods of history when the sense of cosmic alienation erodes the faith in order and produces such phenomena as Gnosticism and nihilism.

One's theological or metaphysical stance is not merely an academic question but, obviously, has profound existential consequences and affects the whole "feel" or "tone" of life. If the final reality is alien to human aspirations, then man has a profound sense of alienation pervading his whole being. If the final reality can be trusted, then there is an equally profound sense of belonging. But it must be made clear that in no responsible religion is this sense of belonging, the so-called "peace" of religion, represented as a facile acquisition or an undisturbed possession. Against alienation is set a theology of atonement and reconciliation, and these ideas imply a costly struggle to overcome the division.

These considerations raise again the question of the relation among the various levels of alienation. Does cosmic or ontological alienation produce, in turn, social alienation and alienation of the individual from himself? Do periods when this cosmic alienation is strongly experienced also exhibit powerful alienations and polarizations within society? On the other hand, does cosmic trust or religious faith build social trust? Does belief in reconciliation to being produce social reconciliation? Is this the meaning of the theological doctrine of grace—that there is a supportive context for man's strivings toward a deeper humanity?

These are difficult questions and we must beware of oversimplified answers. We must even beware of thinking that alienation is always something to be overcome, for even if this is true in the long run there may be occasions when separation and conflict are inevitable stages toward the ultimate atonement. So we now turn to consider some of the implications on the social level of our theological and metaphysical analysis of alienation.

4. In this final section we come back to the social scene and ask about the religious and theological dimensions of alienation in the relations of the community of faith. It is a picture with many variables, making it hard to interpret, and it changes from one historical period to another. The story has been different, for instance, as between Christians and Jews, the former having been, for long, a majority in the West, and the latter a small minority.

However, we may remember that Christianity began itself as a very small minority. For the first three hundred years of its existence, the Christian Church was itself an alienated minority. About that period, historian K. S. Latourette (1954) writes: "From the beginning, Christians felt themselves in opposition to what they called 'the world' [p. 241]." He goes on to detail some of the ways in which the Christians were isolated from the society of the Roman Empire. They did not enlist in the army, as they were opposed to bearing arms. They did not take part in the public sports and amusements. They did not join in the celebration of holidays and festivals, because these had pagan associations. They would not burn incense in honor of the Emperor. On the other hand, the imperial authorities frequently persecuted the Christian minority because it did not conform.

While, however, there was alienation between the Church and society at large, ancient alienations were being overcome within the Church. In particular, differences of race, social position, and sex were being reduced and abolished by a new spirit of reconciliation.

From Constantine and the fourth century, the picture changes. The one-time alienated and persecuted minority became the majority. Now there is identification with the larger society. There is even persecution of the remaining pockets of paganism. Although, indeed, there were many ups and downs, for something like fifteen centuries Christianity was the dominant spiritual force in the West and was closely identified with the whole social fabric. This was the phenomenon which we nowadays call "Christendom." We cannot give even an outline here of the Church's social history in that long period, but it assumed many forms under changing circumstances. Ernst Troeltsch distinguished two major types of religious community, both found in the history of Christendom. The "church-type" is open to the world and tends to identify with the society in general, while the "sect-type" remains alienated and leads a life of its own (Troeltsch, 1966).

How do we see the situation today? There is general agreement that Christendom has been breaking up for more than a century. The days when Christianity, as the majority faith, identified with the Establishment, are almost past. Does this mean that the Church will return to a sect-like type of existence, alienated from the mainstream of secular society, in a situation resembling the one which Christians knew in the Roman Empire in the first three centuries of the Christian era? The question cannot be easily answered and I think one has to beware of a certain amount of romanticism and nostalgia among some enthusiasts who think that we can have a return today to the conditions of the early Church. Having lived through the Christendom period, the Church could never return to the pristine condition of pre-Christendom days. In any case, there is probably no single answer to the question of what is becoming of the Church in contemporary society.

I believe myself that one of the most perceptive analyses is that given by Chicago historian Martin E. Marty (1969) in his book, *The Modern Schism*. This book shows the complexity of the situation, which varies from one area of Christendom to another, and also shows its ambiguities, with some alienations being overcome while others are emerging.

Marty uses the expression "the modern schism" to describe a new condition of alienation that has developed in Western society from about 1630 onwards. During that period, there has been a steadily widening gulf between the religious and spiritual heritage of the West and its newer secular concerns. This is not, indeed, the first time that such a schism has developed. There was a breach at the time of the Renaissance, but it was healed by the subsequent revitalization of religious faith. Another breach took place at the time of the Enlightenment, but again this was followed by a new flowering of religious consciousness. However, no sustained revival of faith has as yet reversed the process of alienation occasioned by the modern schism.

Marty (1969) then proceeds to distinguish three major forms which the schism has assumed. The religious and the secular interests of society are most completely alienated from each other on the continent of Europe, where, in several countries, religious persecution has taken place. England, by contrast, has been the scene of what Marty calls "mere secularity." Religion is ignored rather than attacked, but it is nevertheless driven into a ghetto. The United States offers the most ambiguous picture of all. More than any other major industrialized nation, America has remained nominally religious and churchgoing. In spite of the official separation of church and state, religious symbols crop up all over the place in American life. But, according to Marty, this facade of amity covers over a situation of very deep alienation. What has happened is that American religion has itself been secularized. Attempts to develop an urban spirituality in the United States have so far failed, and spirituality is quietly abandoned. American churchmen have been adept at changing the meanings of religious symbols so that they conform to the realities of the secular order. Whether it has been capitalism, technology, or the secular city, American churchmen have persuaded themselves (in Marty's ironical phrase) that "this is what the Lord always intended [Marty, 1969, p. 102]".

Marty's analysis is penetrating, and, whether or not one accepts it in its entirety, it is impossible to deny the sharpness of many of his insights. Incidentally, however, in spite of all the secularization that has gone on both in society and in the churches themselves, Marty insists that when he speaks of "schism," he means a real division. Religion survives alongside the secular, but the two are alienated. Perhaps one already sees in the American churches an attempt to break out of the role of simply offering passive support to the society, and the beginnings of a social critique which might lead to an open alienation of church and society in America. But this remains to be seen.

As I see the situation, the problem for religious communities is to find the best means (which will no doubt vary from one area to another) of bringing their vision of a cosmic overcoming of alienation to bear on the alienations of contemporary societies.

## REFERENCES

Berger, P. L. *A rumor of angels.* Garden City, N. Y.: Doubleday, 1969.

Heidegger, M. *Being and time.* (Transl. by J. Macquarrie & E. Robinson.) London: SCM Press, 1962.

Jonas, H. *The gnostic religion; the message of the alien God and the beginnings of Christianity.* (2nd ed., Rev.) Boston: Beacon Press, 1963.

Kierkegaard, S. A. *The concept of dread.* (Transl. by W. Lowrie.) Princeton, N. J.: Princeton University Press, 1946.

Latourette, K. S. *A history of Christianity.* London: Eyre & Spottiswoode, 1954.

Marty, M. E. *The modern schism.* New York: Harper, 1969.

Ricoeur, P. *Fallible man.* (Transl. from the French by C. Keeley.) Chicago: Henry Kegney, 1965.

Ricoeur, P. *The symbolism of evil.* (Transl. from the French by E. Buchanan.) New York: Harper, 1967.

Troeltsch, E. *The social teachings of the Christian churches.* Vol. I. (Transl. by O. Wyon.) New York: Harper, 1966. 2 vols.

# Chapter 15

# The Schools and Alienation[1]

## Gerald M. Reagan
Ohio State University

The historian Carl Becker (1955) once said:

> Now, when I meet a word with which I am entirely unfamiliar, I find it a good plan to look it up in the dictionary and find out what someone thinks it means. But when I have frequently to use words with which everyone is perfectly familiar—words like "cause" and "liberty" and "progress" and "government"—when I have to use words of this sort which everyone knows perfectly well, the wise thing to do is to take a week off and think about them [p. 328].

The term, alienation, can, I think, be classed with Becker's "week off" words, being both perfectly familiar and extremely unclear. And after spending most of my youth trying to get out of schools and most of my adult life working to stay in, I still find the schooling process difficult to understand. It may therefore seem presumptuous of me to describe the interrelationships of alienation and schooling, since I find both the concept of alienation and the process of schooling persistently puzzling. This is intended as both a disclaimer and a warning. In writing on this topic I do not claim to understand it, but I have thought about it, and although I cannot guarantee that I will be "telling it like it is" in the schools, I will be telling it as it seems to me to be.

---

[1] Adopted from a paper presented at the Institute on Alienation, Syracuse University (Maxwell School), April 9, 1970. An earlier treatment out of which this paper grew is Reagan and Green (1967).

321

## THE PROBLEM

One frequently hears tautological assertions to the effect that schools are contributing to the alienation of American youth, and that alienated youth are creating serious problems in the schools. The meaning of such assertions is rarely clear. In some cases, it would seem that people making such statements are bothered primarily by the growing conflict between youth and adults—by what one wag has called the generation gap. But even if youth-adult conflict is a problem (and it obviously is), it is not one which will be analyzed in detail here. This paper will focus on the fact that many people—parents and other adults as well as students—are giving up on schools, on those who operate the schools, and on the wider society which the school represents. Perhaps even more important is the fact that many people who have intimate and extended contact with the school are giving up on themselves and are driven to do so by what is happening to them in schools. In short, many people are "turned off." At least some of the time it is the schools and school people who throw the switch. And this will be the central theme of my essay: what happens in schools which contributes to or encourages alienation? This topic will, therefore, focus on what are described in previous chapters as alienating conditions, as opposed to states of alienation.

Any reflective person who has gone through our schools can list a variety of perennial problems of schooling, inappropriate or unnecessary aspects of the curriculum, and the lack of competent teachers. But dull teachers and "irrelevant" subject matter, although problems, still do not by themselves account for all of the contemporary concern with matters of schooling. Nor are they sufficient to account for the schools' contribution to alienation. Some striking changes have occurred in our schools, and some of these changes are such that schools encourage alienation much more than in the past. The particular changes which will be discussed here are:

1. The increased importance of schooling
2. Occupational training and credentialism
3. The upward drift of decision making, bureaucratization of schools, and professionalization of school personnel

These first two factors will be discussed primarily in relationship to how they affect students. In the case of the third, the concern will be in studying the alienating effects of the schools on those who seek to influence or modify educational policy.

## THE INCREASED IMPORTANCE OF SCHOOLING

On the surface it may seem a little strange for an educationist to claim that in increasing the importance of our schools we have brought about an educational problem of great magnitude, but that is my claim. That we as a group have contributed to making schooling more important can hardly be doubted. This increased importance is reflected in the fact that people are writing, railing, and even rioting over what is happening or failing to happen in the schools. One might ask why any society should attribute such importance to those institutions charged with the formal instruction of the young, or, furthermore, what kinds of problems are produced by such attribution? It is comforting to note that many commentators have addressed themselves to this important issue. The number of possible answers cannot be reviewed here. We do, however, need to remind ourselves that increased importance of education and increased importance of formal schooling are not the same thing. One could hold that education is more important without taking the position that schools should become more important, that is, schooling is a particular way, not the only way, that a society may choose to increase emphasis on education. Thus we have exercised an option in placing more importance on formal schooling. And I want to argue here that in so doing we have created a situation in which we, first, recognize no legitimate escape from schools, second, recognize no excuse for failure in schools, and, third, allow judgments made in the school, supposedly on the basis of academic performance, to be used to justify decisions made for and about persons outside of schools. Let us examine each of these assertions.

Schools are more important today than in the past, both for those who succeed (by school standards) and for those who fail. Success in schools is a good predictor of success in society, at least when the latter is defined in terms of higher social status and a greater share of wealth, and failure in the schools is a good predictor of failure in society.[2] The reasons for this are complex, but the important point here is that one cannot escape the school. It is encountered before taxes and death, but it is no less inevitable. In the school judgments are made—judgments generally not about how well the school serves the client, but about how well the client serves the school. And these judgments, once made, follow the person long after he leaves the school. One can, at least under certain conditions, leave the school. One may graduate, drop-out, or be expelled. But although one may leave the school behind, one cannot escape the judgments made about him by the school.

Hence, there are two factors here. One cannot avoid the school: he must, for a time at least, attend. And one cannot escape school judgments even when one has escaped the school. Now if only just one of these things were true, the problem might be less severe. Having to go through school would be much less threatening if one could choose to leave the judgments of the school people when he left the school. And being unable to escape school judgments would be less disturbing if the schooling itself were a matter of choice. But for many the combination of having to attend school and having no escape from judgments made during the period of schooling makes the school a frightening institution.

[2] This is of course oversimplified. Schools have often operated in such a way that those likely to achieve have certain ascribed characteristics, that is, there has been a systematic socioeconomic bias in the operation of the schools.

It has not always been this way. Schools in the past, in addition to being good or bad, were benign for many in the sense that school judgments had little to do with life chances. Historically, American schools have, in sociological jargon, functioned more to transfer status across generations than within generations, that is, the schools have operated in such a way so as to grant the young status comparable to that of their parents, and when one who was not expected to succeed in schools did succeed, other aspects of the society might render that success meaningless. For example, when employment of blacks was limited to menial occupations, the black who succeeded in school found that school success did not lead to equal success in the world of work. In such a case one can assert that schooling is benign. Schools were benign for others in the sense that nonschool factors, such as affluence, could render failure in schools as unimportant. In short, historically, a person's life chances have depended much more on ascribed characteristics than upon school achievement.

Now, schools in the past did afford a route to upward social mobility for some of their more careful and industrious clientele. And there were other routes in the society as well, mainly entrepreneureal, that did, in fact, allow a significant number of individuals to achieve high status and fortune, and these other routes have disappeared. Now, however, the frontier is closed, and Horatio Alger, if he exists at all, is a scholarship student working for a graduate degree in business administration, supported by a nationally subsidized assistantship in a tax supported university. The school, by and large, is the route to upward mobility; it is the new frontier where each is sent, and where he is judged on his own merits before being placed in society on the basis of those merits.

This new frontier that is the school is not an option. All are sent and all are judged. There is no escape and no excuse—except to claim that the school is a bad school, not in the sense that it is doing the wrong thing, but that it is not doing well what it is supposed to be doing, for example, it is making mistakes in its judgments of merit. And when by reform of schools we mean changing them so they do better what they are already doing, that reform has the effect of removing the "bad school" excuse. Making schools better in this sense may lead to higher college board scores, but it can hardly be expected to lower anxiety or reduce alienation.

Perhaps I should here note certain claims that I am not making. First, I am not simply criticizing compulsory schooling. Indeed, the fact of legal compulsory school attendance is, in my opinion, of little importance. I suspect that we could do away with the legal requirements of school attendance without altering the problem. Some would leave schools earlier, but this would mean only that they would get their failure label earlier. There are many factors other than laws which make schooling virtually compulsory. Second, I am not saying that the problem is miseducation. Now, of course schooling is required by law and schools frequently do engage in miseducation, but the problem I am talking about here centers on the fact that life chances are increasingly determined in schools, and, hence, schooling becomes a deadly serious business. Success in school breeds success outside schools, and school failure virtually guarantees that other failures await the person.

This problem is exacerbated when the person is encouraged to see the school judgment as a judgment of himself as a person, and not merely of school achievement. He comes to see himself not just as a "D" student in math, but as a "D" human being. And we are encouraging this both inside and outside our schools. Judgments made in schools are used to screen persons outside schools, for example, for jobs, and when a person is screened out of a job, he is encouraged to believe that his failure is due to some deficiency in him, and not because someone had to be screened out. Drop outs, for example, are encouraged to believe that if they are unemployed it is because they are not worthy of holding jobs and that they are not worthy of holding jobs because they have not finished high school. Seldom do we encourage them to recognize that in our economy we have more workers than jobs and, hence, some workers will be unemployed, periodically or forever, no matter what their educational background.

Hence, one could argue that school judgments, no matter how accurate, are sometimes misinterpreted, and that the misinterpretation is one with destructive consequences for the person judged. One task of the school is to help students achieve a sense of personal identity and worth. A second job of the school has to do with training for and allocating to occupations. Each of these tasks is important, but the two are not the same. And we may unnecessarily emphasize the latter at the expense of the former. Let us look at this in more detail.


## OCCUPATIONAL TRAINING AND CREDENTIALISM

Schools in our society perform several functions. One of these functions is that of training persons for occupations. Another is screening for or allocating to occupations. Now there is a common argument to the effect that, due to the technological revolution, our society has an insatiable appetite for talent, and that the schools must therefore identify and train the talented. This means, the argument continues, that judgments in the school must be based on achievement rather than ascription, on what the student can do rather than on who he is. Identification and mobility of the talented, long heralded as a social ideal, has become a necessity. So the argument goes. And school people have responded to the argument. In performing the training and allocation functions, they are attempting to place more emphasis on achievement and less on ascription. Thus, it appears, on the surface at least, that we have accepted in our schools and are making operational that slogan of the French Revolution, "Careers Open to Talent."

But is the opening of careers to those successful in schools the same as opening careers to talent? Let us pursue this further. The training function and the allocation function are converging in the school, but they remain two functions, not one. There are many occupations which require no special training. Others do require special training, but it is training best given on the job. Still others require special training which can perhaps best be given in the schools. Allocation for the first two sorts of occupations can occur without reference to what persons have done in schools. (What has or has not been learned may be important, but it is not important in the sense of the technical job skills.) In the case of the third kind of occupation, the judgments about how a person has performed in school are clearly relevant, for the content of the schooling is designed as training for the occupation.

In the minds of educators and employers, the distinction between occupations of the first two types and those of type three are too often blurred. The result is that in many cases we allocate to occupations on the basis of the number of years of formal schooling completed, even when the content of the schooling is irrelevant to occupational performance. This has been widely recognized and has been variously referred to as the "sheepskin psychosis" (Keats, 1963), the "emphasis on certification" (Green, 1972), and "credentialism" (Miller, 1964). To get a particular job one must have the right credential. And the credential is given for the successful completion of a number of years of formal schooling. Too seldom do we distinguish between those occupations for which credentialism makes a great deal of sense and those for which it is sheer nonsense. Thus, in many cases, formal education is used as a screening device even though the school skills are not directly related to occupational skills.

Some have argued that schools in our society have become the preemployment arm of industry and that liberal or liberating education has been sacrificed for vocational training. This may or may not be true. But the point here is that failure in schools, no matter what the content of the schooling, works against the person in the allocation process. If the person wants to be a nuclear physicist, schooling offers the appropriate training. If one wants to be an insurance salesman, factory worker, or many other things, the relationship between schooling and job performance is not at all direct. But even though there are many occupations where one may need little formal schooling to perform satisfactorily, he may need many years of schooling to get the job.

What does this all mean? It suggests that those trained to perform high level technical skills constitute but a part of the "diploma elite" or "meritocracy." Many gain admission to this group partially because they have been successful in schools, even though the content of the schooling is irrelevant to the job. Thus we may need to question whether schools are, in fact, emphasizing achievement rather than ascription. It may be, I am arguing, that schools emphasize a kind of academic achievement, and that this academic achievement has become, in some cases, simply another kind of ascription in the allocation process. In some cases the merging of the training and allocation functions in the schools makes sense, for the training is technical training aimed at job performance. But there are many occupations for which educational or intellectual achievement may be neither necessary nor relevant. When a person is judged and allowed access to one of these occupations only on the basis of success in schools, then academic achievement has begun to function as an ascribed characteristic.[3] And when one looks at the relationship between other ascribed characteristics and educational success, present practices seem even less defensible.

These observations should not be construed as an argument that schooling is unimportant, nor even that it is less important than is generally believed. Schooling is, in fact, as important as people believe it is, and that is true partially because they believe it. But it remains true that training for occupations and allocating to occupations are different things, and that educational credentials are today used for allocating to occupations even when the credential makes no claim to represent training for the occupation.

Of course, the process of allocating people to various occupational roles must be performed in some way, and relating it to formal schooling is one way to do it. But we need to understand that in doing it this way we go far beyond merely allocating trained people: the allocation process becomes the allocation of status or "life chances." Only when allocation is based on training is it really tied to the demands of the occupational structure.

But what does all this have to do with alienation? Youth today cannot escape the school. Within the school they may choose to pursue technical or professional training or they may elect the "general" education. But in either case they face the allocation process. Success in either will speed them to other successes, but failure will follow them quite as tenaciously. The risk is high, and in many cases the battle is lost by the student before he realizes that it is not just a game. Indeed, many students are deluded, many hurt.[4] We ought not be surprised if many withdraw, rejecting both those who operate the schools and the society which would use schools in this way, and our attempts to improve schools, to make them continue to do the same thing more efficiently, can hardly be encouraging to students. Improved schools, after all, will be more threatening, not less, for the only defense the student has at present is to claim that the school has made a mistake.

[3] There is an argument to the effect that success in schools is always relevant to occupational success, even when the content of the schooling is unrelated to the occupation. This is the argument that there is an empirical connection between success in schools and factors other than technical skills which are of interest to employers, for example, various "factory virtues" such as dependability, punctuality, high threshold of boredom, etc. This may be true, but even if it is it seems weak as a justification for using educational success as a necessary criterion for allocation. Surely one can acquire these traits outside the schools as well as within.

[4] Perhaps the most deluded of all is the talented college student who, voicing the ideals of liberal education and damning the growing vocationalism on college campuses, proceeds to graduate school, undergoes some of the most narrow of all training and then moves, Ph.D. in hand, to another campus as a professor.

# THE UPWARD DRIFT OF DECISION MAKING, BUREAUCRATIZATION, AND PROFESSIONALIZATION

The ritual of American education says that the school is close to the people, and that, as a grass roots institution, it reflects community interests and needs. I want to argue here that the ritual is misleading, that when citizens concerned with problems of schooling attempt to influence educational decision making they find that this is, at best, difficult, and that in many cases they are virtually powerless. Among the reasons for this, I will argue here, are the upward drift of decision making, the bureaucratization of schools, and the professionalization of school personnel. These factors have combined to make schools resistant to change; this tends to create a feeling of helplessness. In the preceding section it was argued that the school cannot be escaped. The fact (if it is a fact) would seem to encourage those who find themselves or their children failing in school to try to modify that school. In this section I will attempt to show why they are unlikely to succeed, and thus show why schools may, for them, be alienating agencies.

## The Upward Drift of Decision Making

> An important axiom in political science is that when one level of government
> is unable or unwilling to meet the desires and needs of people, assistance is
> sought from the next higher level of government [Chandler, 1962, p. 6].

There is abundant evidence to support this axiom in the case of educational decision making. Increasingly, the authority of state and federal government has been used in setting and implementing educational policy. Local political units, including school systems, have been charged with being resistant to change and have often been bypassed as the concern for educational reform has grown. Educational policy has come to be seen as a problem properly, and more effectively and efficiently, dealt with at the state and federal levels. And many forms of the traditional demand for local control and local autonomy of schools seem to have lost their persuasiveness.

Increased activity on school matters by state and federal governments has wrought some substantial changes in schools. Yet these changes have not been accompanied by a decrease in the demand for reform. Indeed, in some quarters the demands seem to increase with increasing reforms. Why should this be? A partial answer may be that many are convinced that even though the changes made thus far are important, they have not improved substantially the educational opportunities available to members of minority groups, and part of the answer may be that some groups have become convinced, rightly or wrongly, that it is within the power of the school to improve their social lot. The increased demands can also be viewed as a reflection of a growing ability and willingness of traditionally silent groups to articulate their educational concerns. But there is an additional factor with which I am here concerned. For some groups, and particularly those in the inner city, many of the changes made in schools have seemed, like Cinderella's carriage, to turn into a pumpkin. Promising much and providing little, the attempts at educational reform have focused attention on the question of how those outside the school can bring about change in the school. Let us now turn to this question.

We tell ourselves in our political ritualizations that our systems of government and of education allow for diverse interest groups to contend, and that in the crucible of public debate and discussion political and educational decisions are made. Such decisions, our ritual continues, represent majority rule with a healthy and firm respect for minority rights. Of course we know that the ritual is misleading, and that the appeal to majority rule is often misleading unless we specify the governmental level at which the decision is to be made. In speaking of majority rule we generally assume that the majority to which we refer is the majority of those most directly affected by the decision. Clearly, we do not intend that every decision, or even most, should be made by a majority of all the people in the society, or even the majority of people in a state or city. For example, when we think of a family operating on the basis of majority rule we presuppose that there is a range of decisions properly made at the family level, and that for these decisions the majority is the majority of the family. Similarly, we hold that there are ranges of community decisions, city decisions, state decisions, and national decisions. Now if we make such assumptions about levels of educational decision making, why do we sometimes move a decision from a lower to a higher level?

In turning to higher levels of government to bring about changes in schools, we may appeal to either of two assumptions. First, we may assume that the problem which the reform is intended to solve has become a more general problem. If we turn to state governments to help solve the problem of prekindergarten education, we may do so because we hold that the problem is no longer merely local but is one which directly affects all people of a state and, hence, should be the concern of the entire population. The second assumption is that there is a local problem calling for reform but that the local government, or the local majority, has been either unable or unwilling to act. In such a case, requesting that action be taken at a higher level is a kind of appeal to the wider majority at the next higher governmental level.[5]

When we demand that a higher level of government step in because a lower level either can not or will not deal adequately with an educational problem there

---

[5] We may be encouraged to accept this second assumption because we have come to understand that tyranny, as well as democracy, can exist at any governmental level. The notion that local government guarantees democracy and that a strong central government insures tyranny has apparently been rejected by many as sheer prejudice. Certainly there is compelling evidence to show that local governments can be as tyrannical as those at any other level, and one safeguard we have against local tyranny is the possibility of having protective and/or corrective decisions made at a higher governmental level.

is no claim that the problem is not local. It is rather, a kind of appellate demand, an appeal to a wider majority to solve a problem that is local. Such an appeal may be appropriate when, for example, the local majority fails to take into account minority rights, or when the local majority attempts to decide on problems which are not local in nature, or when the local community does not have the resources necessary to deal with the problem. In short, the appellate strategy is brought into play when it is held that decisions at the local level are being made which should not be made or when local decisions are not made when they should be made. In contrast, the new problem level strategy discussed earlier is used when the problem is perceived as one which is more general or requires greater resources than are locally available.

Neither of these strategies for change suggests that there are no decisions to be made at the local level. Indeed, it is doubtful that anyone would make such a claim. We give at least lip service to some degree of local control of schools, and most of us probably believe that local control should go well beyond lip service. A common argument is that local decisions about education are desirable wherever and whenever it is reasonable to believe that local units can effectively make those decisions and where the decisions are indeed local, that is, where the decisions do not have great effects on the wider public.

But waving a banner which reads "Grass-Roots Control of Schools" does not change what has happened and is happening. And what seems to be the case is that what passes for local control today is often not very local. For example, in any large city, neither the local government nor the local school system is likely to be organized to give the urban poor or the urban minority group (or any other neighborhood group) very much power with respect to the government or schools within their own community. Their community, if recognized at all, is recognized not as a unit but only as a part of the city and the school system. This is, in a sense, a tacit denial that there are governmental or educational decisions to be made at the community level. Thus, most educational decisions which are labeled as local are made by the wider community (city or school system). The neighborhood groups are to play their part by participating at the higher level.

Of course this problem is not new. The poor, the ignorant, and the minority group never have spoken with the full authority which our ritual grants their number. But what does seem new is that these groups, today, in demanding what many apparently regard as great privileges, are in fact demonstrating a readiness to participate more fully in the democratic process. This readiness is too seldom met with a willingness to allow local decisions to be made locally. Thus, these urban groups have become, in John Dewey's sense, "concerned publics" and are attempting to function as such. Now the very existence of such concerned publics could be seen as potential for a more fully democratic society. Unfortunately, these groups have donned the dress clothes of democracy and are now discovering that they have no place to go.

Let us focus on the case of schools. Citizens may together work to influence policy of the school system, but they are often virtually disenfranchised at the level of the community school. In a city with a relatively homogeneous population, this may create no great hardship because there may be substantial sharing of educational interest and purposes. But very often such harmony of interest does not exist, and in the larger American cities it may never exist. Interests and needs are not homogeneous, and in many cases the interests and needs of a neighborhood within a city do not need to be sacrificed for the general welfare. In short, there are problems which concern the local community and which could be solved at that level without great effect on the wider public. But even though such problems exist and concerned local communities are addressing themselves to those problems, there is generally no unit, political or educational, through which these people can effectively work. In short, at the community level in the city, no matter how local the problem, to influence school policy decision making through governmental processes is generally to work through the larger school system.

## Bureaucratization and Professionalization

Even though, typically, there is no local political unit corresponding to the local school, some will argue that the school systems are generally organized so that the influence of a local public is effective at the local school level. In other words, it may be asserted that freedom is granted to school personnel in order that they may be responsive to the wishes and needs of those served by the school. This may indeed be a possibility, but there are certain trends in the development of contemporary schools that may make this responsiveness less likely than in the past. Bureaucratization of schools and professionalization of school personnel have tended to encourage the educational establishment to reinforce the tendency outside for decisions to drift away from the grass roots.

Let us look more closely at this problem. Some have argued that the most important change in American schools during the last half century has been bureaucratization. Ronald Corwin (1965) speaks of this importance as follows:

> The world of the public school teacher is a world of organizations. Indeed the job of teaching as it is known today scarcely exists apart from the organization. It is the perch from which teachers see their students, it is the barrier that teachers erect between themselves and the public, and it is the hierarchy in which they must make their way in order to perform their jobs [p. 3].

Complex organizations are bureaucratized and schools are no exception (Corwin, 1965, p. 38).

At the outset, it should be noted that in speaking of bureaucratization I do not mean simply that schools are increasingly marked by inefficiency and red tape, even though this may be the case. But the intent is not to make bureaucratization evil by definition. Indeed, some writers avoid the term bureaucracy simply because of such connotations. Etzioni, for example, uses the term organization rather than bureaucracy (Etzioni, 1964, pp. 3-4; see also Hodgkinson, 1967). But whatever terminology is used, the process with which we are concerned is the same:

> In contrast to earlier societies, modern society has placed a high moral value on rationality, effectiveness, and efficiency. Modern civilization depends largely on organizations as the most rational and efficient form of social grouping known. By coordinating a large number of human actions, the organization creates a powerful social tool. It combines its personnel with its resources, weaving together leaders, experts, workers, machines, and raw materials [Etzioni, 1964, p. 1].

If rationality, effectiveness, and efficiency are the organizing principles in bureaucratization, what would we expect to find happening in schools if they are becoming bureaucratized? Some of the factors to be considered are (1) size, (2) extent of centralization, (3) extent of specialization, and (4) extent of standardization (Corwin, 1965, pp. 40-43). To these we may add (5) a hierarchical pattern of authority (Campbell, Cunningham, & McPhee, 1965, p. 241). To what extent are these factors evident in contemporary schools?

*Growth in Size*

Clearly the growth in size of the total public educational institution has been phenomenal in terms of the number of people involved. More students are going to schools and are staying in schools for longer periods of time. This requires more teachers, more administrators, more schools, and, of course, much more money. This growth is widely recognized and is a frequent topic for discussion in the popular press. We need not dwell longer on this factor.

*Centralization*

Increased size of the formal schooling enterprise has been accompanied by a rather rapid centralization of schools. Nearly 80% of the students in the United States are educated by one-fourth of the nation's school systems. Furthermore, the number of school districts in the U. S. has been reduced by 50% since 1957 (Corwin, 1965, p. 41). This centralization of schools has long been encouraged by both professional educators and by some of the critics of American public education.[6] And there are other indicators of growing centralization. The growing tendency to have more educational decisions made at higher governmental levels pro-

---

[6] James B. Conant, for example, in his *The American High School Today*, strongly recommended that small high schools be eliminated wherever possible. For a good account of the development and changes in school districts see Campbell *et al.* (1965, pp. 80-109). The decline in the number of school districts, a good indicator of the rate of centralization, is even more marked than Corwin's figures indicate. In 1947-1948 there were 94,926 school districts in the United States. In 1963-1964 this number had declined to 31,319.

duces a greater degree of centralization, that is, the influence of state and federal agencies on the operation of schools is increasing, and this is a centralizing influence (Campbell *et al.*, 1965, pp. 20-79). State and national interest groups have also shown a growing concern with educational matters, and this too represents a centralizing influence (Campbell *et al.*, 1965, pp. 463-492). The fact of increasing centralization of schooling seems clear.

## *Standardization*

Educators are fond of expressing their interests in individualization of instruction and their concern for individual differences. Nonetheless, as one moves from one classroom to another, or from one school system to another, or from one state to another, the similarities in schooling are likely to be more striking than the differences. The infinite variety sometimes attributed to the American schools is difficult if not impossible to find when one begins to examine what actually may take place in the schools. For example, if it is indeed the case that the Iowa tests and the Stanford Achievement Tests are becoming standard instruments, if procedures of administration and of grading in the curriculum are fairly uniform, and if class size is about the same nation over, then one may well ponder where that infinite variety is to be found. Indeed, in any society where geographic mobility is as great as in the U. S., it is probably desirable that there be a high degree of uniformity from place to place in school administration, curriculum, and assessment.[7]

## *Specialization*

Specialization of work, or division of labor, a part of the process of bureaucratization, is clearly a characteristic of the modern school. One indicator is departmentalization of high schools and junior high schools, now extended into the so-called "middle school," and making sizable inroads into the elementary schools. Another indicator is the proliferation of courses and curricula. Accompanying both of these developments is the rapid expansion of "supporting staff" in such fields as guidance counseling, school psychology, reading, physical education, instructional media, and administration. Given the present state of specialization, the modern educational establishment could hardly be seen as following the model of Mark Hopkins on one end of a log and the student on the other. The implementation of

[7] Standardization, of course, takes many forms. When many people express their fears of standardization and centralization, they seem to envisage a situation in which, at 2:32 p.m. on October 18, every fifth grade teacher in the country will be reading question 19 from page 68 in the government prescribed social studies text book. There may be some grounds for such a fear, but such idiocy is not the inexorable result of centralization and standardization. Nor, we might notice, is such stupidity necessarily avoided with increased decentralization or less standardization.

such a model today would require a very long log if all the "instructional support personnel" were to have a place to sit.

### Hierarchical Authority

This bureaucratic characteristic is especially important for those who attempt to influence school policy. Let me begin here with a summary of Burton Clark's discussion of authority in schools. We can, according to Clark (1962), distinguish three principles of authority in schools.

There is, first, the principle of authority as public trust:

> The principle of authority most widely accepted by Americans for the administering of schools and colleges is one of public control vested in a board of laymen. The lay board is empowered legally to direct the organization and is held responsible for its welfare; it is to have final authority over the work of the employed staff. This principle relates to a wider belief, long a part of the American tradition, that schools and colleges should be directed ultimately by community interests rather than by professional personnel or government departments [p. 152].

This does indeed seem to be a widely held belief. But it does not seem to describe what in fact happens. Clark (1962) notes this as he goes on to discuss a second principle of authority which he calls "bureaucratic":

> The legal provision that authority rests ultimately with the lay board does not insure that laymen will determine policy. Schools and colleges are organized in an hierarchy of personnel and staffed with full-time, paid officials; operating authority is either delegated to senior officers by the lay board or is assumed in the course of affairs. The board members, part-time and amateur, are removed from actual operation, while the officials—full-time, expert, informed—are on the spot, making the daily decisions. Even though the board is supposed to make policy and the hired staff to execute it, much policy determination falls into the hands of trained officialdom. The organization assumes, to some degree, the form of a bureaucracy, with a hierarchy of officers assigned to positions that have fixed jurisdictions and duties [p. 153].

Growth of bureaucratic authority, along with the continued belief in authority as public trust, presents a serious obstacle to those laymen who attempt to modify the school.[8] Given any person within the administrative hierarchy, to whom is he responsible? He is likely to see himself responsible not to the public he is supposedly serving—at least not directly—but to his bureaucratic superior.[9]

It may thus appear that educational power and authority are decentralized; that, for example, the principal of a local school has power delegated to him so that he may respond to what he views as legitimate community pressures in such

[8] A good general discussion of bureaucratic authority can be found in Etzioni (1964, pp. 75-93). Discussions of bureaucratic authority in schools are found in Campbell *et al.* (1965, pp. 226-255), Hodgkinson (1967), and Corwin (1965, pp. 217-300). See also Presthus (1965).

[9] Polley (1962) argues that even with attempted decentralization, the lower bureaucrat tends to make decisions to please higher bureaucrats, not to please the "public" served by his unit.

a way that the local school does serve local interests. But the formal delegation of power does not guarantee this responsiveness. The principal may not view his own authority so much as a "public trust" as a "system superior trust." He is likely to feel that he is, in fact, accountable not to the citizens of his community so much as to his bureaucratic superiors. For, after all, insofar as his own power is concerned, the superintendent giveth and the superintendent taketh away.

The principal may well believe that schools ought to serve the public interest, but it is also likely that he will behave in a way which suggests that the public interest is best served by following the rules, by going through channels, by letting the decisions concerning public interest filter down from those persons in bureaucratic positions where they can see the "big picture." He may listen to those who describe for him the "little picture" of the local community; he may empathize and sympathize, but this does not guarantee that he will view community citizens as those who legitimize his decisions. Given a bureaucratic authority system, the principal is often encouraged to look above him in the bureaucratic hierarchy for legitimization of decisions. Hence, one ought not be too surprised, and, perhaps, ought not treat the principal too harshly, if the decisions of the principal are made not so much to please his constituents as to please his superiors. Thus, the hierarchical structure of authority is likely to frustrate attempts by those outside who attempt to modify the workings of the organization. In other words, given a bureaucratic authority structure, lay attempts to influence school policy at the level of the local school are likely to be met by (1) kicking decisions upstairs, or (2) making decisions at the local level, but with the important reference group being bureaucratic superiors rather than the members of the community.

Bureaucratic authority is being challenged by those who regard it as departure from public trust, but it will perhaps be challenged more strongly within schools by what Clark (1962) calls "colleague authority":

> Overall, the long-run trend in American higher education has been for authority to move from external to internal sources, with faculties increasingly contending with the administration about who has authority over what. The faculties march under the banner of self-government and academic freedom, emphasizing equality of relations among colleagues and de-emphasizing administrative hierarchy [pp. 156-157].

Clark (1962, pp. 159-160) goes on to say that this notion of authority has not been strong in public schools, partially because teachers have been more subject to lay control and partially because the freedom implied by colleague authority has not been thought to be necessary for the effective performance of teachers.

But there are trends which suggest that teachers will, in the future, demand more and more colleague authority. Clark (1962) says that authority patterns in schools will change as follows:

> Trustee authority will undoubtedly continue to be recognized legally and formally as the dominant type of authority; schools and colleges will continue to have lay boards as their highest formal element. But in actual operation we may

expect bureaucratic administrations on the one hand and self-constituted groups
of teacher colleagues on the other hand to assert themselves increasingly and contend more actively for decisive influence in school matters. We know that the influence of the expert administrator will increase because the administration will
grow in size and will become ever more specialized and expert. Everything we
know about bureaucratization and managerial technique points in this direction
for the decades immediately ahead. At the same time, the influence of the teaching staff will continue to increase, because the faculty grows in size and also gains
influence through its growing expertness. This is most apparent in the case of physical scientists and mathematicians in the universities, but even first-grade teachers
are now privy to theories and techniques—Gesell on the "fives" or the "nines"
for example—known generally only within the ranks [p. 160].

Thus, Clark expects there to be growth of both bureaucratic and colleague authority. It is clear that if both grow, there will also be growing conflict between the two
(Campbell *et al.*, 1965, p. 253; Corwin, 1965, p. 229).

As conflict grows between bureaucratic and colleague authority, what happens to the notion that schools should be responsive to the public? Increasing either bureaucratic or colleague authority will produce the potential for increased
conflict between school personnel and laymen. The conflict between bureaucratic authority and colleague authority is an intrainstitutional conflict—an increase
in either constitutes a decline in the extent of *de facto* trustee authority, even though
a general belief in trustee authority may be continued. Thus, it may be that the
whole notion of authority as a public trust will well become ritual, while the bureaucrats and the professionals contend over control of the schools. In the meantime,
both the bureaucrats and the professionals are asking who the best trustees are—
with neither group seriously considering the possibility that, for some educational
questions, perhaps the public is the best holder of the public trust. The failure to
consider this possibility may be one of the major reasons that educational profes-
sionalism is sometimes viewed by the public as a kind of educational paternalism.

Many who have urged increased professionalization of teachers would disagree
with the preceding paragraph. But the point not to be overlooked is that professionalization does not necessarily lead to a greater concern for the clients, unless one
makes this true by definition of "profession." The growth of professional or col-
legial authority does not guarantee that the professionals will be any more responsive to attempts to change schools than are bureaucrats. Authority may be vested
more in teachers and less in administrators without insuring that decisions are made
with the welfare of the students or desires of the parents in mind. Indeed, giving
increased powers to teachers may, in some cases, merely replace one bureaucracy
with another, that is, the administrator-bureaucrat may make decisions on what is
best for the organization or school system while the teacher-bureaucrat may decide
on the basis of what is good for the teachers in the system.[10]

[10] This does not make the administrator-teacher battle any less real or less important.
Colleague authority is different from bureaucratic authority, and changing from one to the
other, or placing increased emphasis on one, will make a difference in how a school operates.
But the point here is that changing the emphasis from one to the other does not necessarily
make the school easier to modify or more responsive to the public.

But in any case, advancing the domain of either bureaucratic or professional authority represents a drift away from meaningful lay authority. This is perhaps most clear at the level where we would expect the greatest lay control—the neighborhood school. And if the neighborhood school proves to be invincible, it should not be surprising that many parents have little hope of bringing about significant educational change. Whether intentional or not, too often we seem to accept the paternalistic assumption that educational decisions at the local school level are best made by those who might be considered outsiders.

The urban poor, and particularly the black urban poor, have pointed out again and again that their attempts to modify schools are quickly blocked. And, in a sense, these citizens are, in their objections, paraphrasing an oft-quoted and oft-criticized statement of John Dewey (1927):

> The man who wears the shoe knows best that it pinches and where it pinches, even if the expert shoemaker is the best judge of how the trouble is to be remedied [p. 127].

Dewey's analogy is, of course, weak. It is not always the case that the man who wears the shoe knows that it pinches, just as it is not always the case that a local community will recognize its educational problems. But we ought not to conclude as some apparently have, that because Dewey was not all right, he was therefore all wrong. There may be all sorts of educational pinches which local communities do not feel, but there are some pinches they do feel, and they are real pinches. And we as educators continue to give them answers to questions which they are not asking, and as we do so we are much too busy to hear the questions which they are asking.

Thus, the upward drift of decision making, the bureaucratization of schools, and the professionalization of school personnel are three changes which are transforming the schools. Although all three have promised reform, they seem, rather, to have made the school more distant from parents, more protected from those who seek to modify it. Large numbers of children are not succeeding in school, and the school in which they are failing is a centralized and bureaucratized one, largely controlled and operated by a group which calls itself professional. In short, professionalization, centralization, and bureaucratization have all been urged as improvements, as means which can be used to minimize the risk of failure which faces every student. The means have not led to the predicted end and lay critics are, in effect, saying "show us." Thus, those in authority are being asked to demonstrate how these changes are improving the chances that children will succeed in schools. But professionalization and bureaucratization also make it less likely that those in authority will hear. And if the authorities do hear, they may ignore the demands, for with professionalization and bureaucratization there is apparently less pressure to produce evidence which would answer a parent-critic's claim one way or the other. It has become, in the words of Charlie Brown, "one man against an institution," and, as Charlie observed, "There's always a tendency for the institution to win." Those who run the institution, after all, make the rules.

What I have attempted here is a brief discussion of some aspects of contemporary schooling which may encourage or contribute to alienation, both of student-clients and of those who attempt to modify the schooling process. There are, of course, many other aspects of formal schooling which may be of equal or greater importance in this regard. And, clearly, the schooling process represents but one example of a social institution contributing to this malaise.

## REFERENCES

Becker, C. L. What are historical facts? *Western Political Quarterly*, 1955, *VII*, 327-340.

Campbell, R. F., Cunningham, L. L., & McPhee, R. F. *The organization and control of American schools.* Columbus: Merrill Books, 1965.

Chandler, B. J. Forces influencing urban schools. In B. J. Chandler, L. J. Stiles, & J. I. Kitsuse (Eds.), *Education in urban society.* New York: Dodd, Mead, 1962. Pp. 152-162.

Clark, B. *Educating the expert society.* San Francisco: Chandler, 1962. Pp. 152-162.

Corwin, R. G. *A sociology of education.* New York: Appleton, 1965.

Dewey, J. *The public and its problems.* New York: Holt, 1927.

Etzioni, A. *Modern organizations.* Englewood Cliffs, N. J.: Prentice-Hall, 1964.

Green, T. F. Citizenship or certification? In S. Diamond (Ed.), *Anthropological perspectives on education.* New York: Free Press, 1972. In press.

Hodgkinson, H. *Education, interaction and social change.* Englewood Cliffs, N. J.: Prentice-Hall, 1967. Pp. 25-47.

Keats, J. *The sheepskin psychosis.* New York: Dell Publ., 1963.

Miller, S. M. The outlook of working-class youth. In A. B. Shostar & W. Gomberg (Eds.), *Blue-collar world: Studies of the American worker.* Englewood Cliffs, N. J.: Prentice-Hall, 1964. Pp. 122-134.

Polley, J. W. Decentralization within urban school systems. In B. J. Chandler, L. J. Stiles, & J. I. Kitsuse (Eds.), *Education in urban society.* New York: Dodd, Mead, 1962. Pp. 117-128.

Presthus, R. *The organizational society.* New York: Vintage Books, 1965. Pp. 27-58.

Reagan, G. M., & Green, T. F. *Polity, profession and the urban public: The dynamics of school reform.* Syracuse, N. Y.: Educational Policy Research Center, Syracuse University Research Corporation, 1967.

# Chapter 16

# The Specters of Technicism[1]

## Robert W. Daly
State University of New York

This chapter has two parts. The first section is a review of three contemporary orientations toward technical phenomena and technical activities: a traditional view, a modern view, and a spectral view. The second part of the paper contains fragments from several lives which illustrate how spectral orientations toward technology become "affectively anchored in people . . . by utilizing and altering the instinctual apparatus [Reich, 1949, p. xxiii]."[2]  This section of the paper contains notes on the psychology of possession, obsessive paranoia, and modern religious identification. My intentions are twofold: (1) to report clinical evidence which tends to support the conjectures of social psychologists and culture historians that there are potent, impersonal, and abstract forces at work in the modern world, forces which assume the forms of phantasms or specters, and (2) to call attention to the variety of ways in which these forces are represented in modern lives.

The peoples of many historical and cultural periods have experienced the press of demonic and benevolent spirits. The images and effects of these forces are revealed by artists (Rowlingson, Goya, Henri Rousseau) and by students of

[1] Reprinted from *Psychiatry: Journal for the Study of Interpersonal Processes,* 1970, *33,* 417-432, by permission of The William Alanson White Psychiatric Foundation, Inc.

[2] Reich's introductory remarks to the First Edition of *Character Analysis* furnish the psychiatrist with important clues to the nature of the relationship between social-historical processes and the organization of personal traits. My understanding of the persons described in this article was also aided by a rereading of Tausk (1933) and Sachs (1933).

man and his behavior; by ordinary experiences and expressions; and by the conduct and behavior of those who are perplexed, distressed, and disordered. A sense of the operation of such forces arises when men find that they cannot account for emotionally significant events by ascribing them to the conventional sources of power and efficacy (e.g., human, natural, divine) which are believed to make things happen in the world. When such inexplicable events persist and are experienced by numbers of persons, agencies are created to account for these events. These agencies are given names, made into realities, and adapted to as powerful things—such as The Furies, The Anti-Christ, Death, and The System. When such powers are known to be imminent in the world and are widely acknowledged to be capable of shaping the destinies of persons and society, these agencies are called phantasms or specters.

We now live in an age of technological innovation. Traditions of thought, feeling, and work have developed and coalesced during the past millennium[3] in such a fashion that the men of the twentieth century—particularly in the so-called advanced nations—are almost everywhere found to be extremely busy with the busyness of designing and meeting specifications which will bring about certain finite states of affairs. They are busy building technological environments. Men now spend so much of their time producing, maintaining, and adjusting themselves to the environments which they create that students of Western culture now believe that men are entering a "technetronic age" (Brzezinski, 1968) which is to be dominated by a worldwide "scientific-technoculture" (Nelson, 1968).

But can the study of man and technology in the latter half of the twentieth century be concluded with this sort of statement?

> My thesis, then, is that much of the spiritual meaning of technological culture is found in the realm of communication. Through technology, man has recovered the dimension of sound. With the recovery of sound, man has found a new interior orientation as well as an emphasis on his time-bound nature. From these two dimensions have come man's increasing concern with personal and responsible decision making. As man exercises his decision making capabilities he affirms and reaffirms his own humanity [Ong, 1967, p. 3].

The case fragments reported in this paper suggest otherwise. Some men, at least, behave as if the spirit of meeting specifications in many discreet, limited, and finite human ventures had taken flight from the hands of responsible human agents and become an independent reality—a reality which has come to overhang the modern world and to enter into the dynamic processes of personality—as a spectral object. Before citing ways in which these objects have been experienced by particular men, it is desirable to examine some of the attitudes which men display toward technical phenomena and activities. The following discussion is intended to clarify what I mean when speaking of the specters of technicism.

---

[3] Valuable bibliographies on the history of technology may be found in Mumford (1963, pp. 359-363), Mumford (1966), Ellul (1964), and Nelson (1968). See also Derry and Williams (1961).

## THREE VIEWS OF TECHNOLOGY

Usually there is little difficulty in understanding what is being referred to when the term "object" is used in psychoanalysis (Guntrip, 1961, pp. 28-31): other people, aspects of other people, bodily parts, artifacts, animals, images, an ego state, a process—anything which has some distinguishing features and is found to be meaningful, "cathected," and thereby "utilizing and altering the instinctual apparatus." Objects, as such, are not often discussed in the psychoanalytic literature. Instead, the focus of interest is on the connection(s) between the object(s) and the drives, traits, personal histories, or symptoms of particular persons. Knowledge of the object per se is left to the reader's general information or, occasionally, to his imagination. But which objects are being referred to when one speaks of the specters of technicism?

An abstract sense of these objects can be attained by examining the ways in which the technical activities of men have been represented in thought. Since the time of Aristotle it has proved useful to comment on the following elements when describing a technological situation:

1. The tool-user (efficient cause).
2. The tool (or implement resource).
3. The technique for using the tool correctly—that is, using it in the most effective and efficient way precisely in the sense that it is a tool.
4. The resource substance (stuff, or material cause), or that upon which the tool acts.
5. The specific goal or outcome (formal cause) which is sought through the correct use of the tool and the resource substance.
6. The ends-context (personal, social, natural, cosmic, etc.) in which the tool is used as a means to an end (final cause).[4]

With this scheme in mind, I shall examine a traditional view, a modern (or technicist view), and a spectral view of technical activity and phenomena.

### A Traditional View

The author's experiences and activities in writing this paper can be used to illustrate the traditional orientation of man toward technology. A man (tool user) strikes (a technique) the keys of a typewriter (tool), and writes (another technique), on paper (resource substance), a communication to colleagues (goal), with the intention of enriching clinical science, thereby improving patient care (ends-context).

---

[4] Aristotle, *Physics* II, 3. This scheme is used throughout the paper as a device for examining technical activities and phenomena. Expanding on a definition offered by Peters (1962, pp. 30-32), I shall consider that the technical activities of men have to do with designing and meeting standardized specifications which bring about finite, predetermined states of affairs.

In this illustration an identifiable man uses a tool as a means to achieve a goal in a comprehensible ends-context. He will be held accountable, as a human agent, for the foreseeable consequences of using the techniques at his command. Innumerable examples of men acting as tool users in this way can be found in the modern world.

The traditional view of technology entails the following beliefs and values: first, technical operations should be performed by discernible men acting in accordance with their talents, skills, experiences, and interests, as agents in a society of human agents. Within this context it is recognized that the routine use of tools and of symbolic technologies (as contrasted with their invention or with the mastery of their use) is, typically, a semiautomatic, habitual kind of activity. It is impossible for individuals to conceive of, decide upon, intend, and monitor all the discrete activities of everyday living. Second, it is generally accepted (although not always recognized) that technical innovations should be limited (as well as encouraged) in various ways by ends-contexts which in effect subordinate and order the use and innovation of technologies to "higher human values"—for example, loving, playing, warring, accumulating wealth, worshipping the gods, child-rearing, contemplating, politicking, doing deeds, expressing emotion, soul-saving. Techniques have traditionally been employed by men to enable men to pursue their goals. Third, there is the expectation that the values and beliefs inherent in the innovation and use of techniques will be integrated with values and beliefs pertaining to the nontechnological environment (nature, other men, the gods), as well as with the existing inventory of techniques.

The traditional orientation toward technology suggests that technical activities and events are to be dominated by definitions of reality which are ultimately nontechnical—that is, by human passions, and by various "interests." This view of technology contrasts sharply with another view of the place of technology in human affairs, a view which has been called "technicism" (Stanley, 1972).

## A Technical View

A technicist view of technology suggests that participation in the creation of technical innovations should be the principal end of human activity.

This outlook on the place of technology in human affairs is currently being expressed by the ruling elites of major civilizations with a fervor as intense as the enthusiasm which marked efforts to realize the eschatological visions of earlier ages.[5] Why? Because in the democratic-liberal societies of the United States and Western Europe, in the democratic-communistic societies of Eastern Europe and

[5] For the cultural changes in the theory of practice associated with the transformation of these visions, see Lobkowicz (1967, esp. Parts 2 and 3).

the Soviet Union, and in the monocratic-communistic state of China, the ruling elites appear to be fully convinced that a secular and saving form of life for the collectivity can be brought about by centrally inspired and controlled technological innovations.[6]

At least five important cultural alterations pertaining to the role of technology in human affairs are entailed in this new perspective. First is the dictum that there are no problems which men might experience that do not admit—at least in theory—of a technical solution. This dictum is being applied not only to man's struggle with nature but also to the problematics of war, politics, economics, law, organizations, and to every hint of human suffering and disease. Second, men are being declared to be as malleable as many things in the environment. Therefore, it is reasoned, they can be construed as objects, or "factors," to be studied and manipulated. When hazards to life, human development, and freedom occur as byproducts of technical innovations, it is suggested that such untoward effects of technology will be corrected by further technical innovations. Third, it is thought to be urgently necessary to make men as adaptable as possible, through education, so that they can accept a world characterized by ceaseless technological change (Ellul, 1964). Through education, it is hoped, men will learn to renounce their particular powers, passions, and interests whenever these conflict with "technical requirements." Fourth, it is believed that as technological progress becomes automated, social progress can be planned and made inevitable, allowing men everywhere to receive the manifold benefits of modern technology.

The fifth, most recent, and most important alteration of belief consists in the view that men, qua persons, are no longer responsible to other men, qua persons, for the states of affairs which are produced by technical activities. One is responsible only for seeing that the technical act is done correctly. There are no enduring visions of the ends of human action which serve to selectively restrain the development and utilization of technologies. In this view, the possibility of an innovation in technology is sufficient to warrant its development and use. Ultimately, the correct rules of practice become devoid of coherent reference to the social contexts in which the technique is used. Thus, when atomic weapons were used near the end of World War II, it was said, "It was possible, therefore, it was necessary."

These beliefs, assumptions, declarations, and hopes have led the elites of the major civilizations to spread the good news concerning the benefits of technology within their own societies and, of course, within the societies of the so-called underdeveloped countries. Though the emerging visions of each civilization differ to a considerable extent, one result of this set of beliefs is that the three major civilizations are assuming a quasitechnological form.

[6] See, for example, Shanks (1967) who advocates this outlook on the role of technology in human affairs.

## The Spectral View

The traditional view of technology suggests that technical innovations should be ordered by men according to nontechnical definitions of reality, the vicissitudes of the passions, or according to some human interests which are related to a nontechnical definition of reality. The modern view of technology is that technical innovation itself is the principal source of legitimation for the conduct of human affairs, for it is this activity which is believed to be capable of saving men from themselves, from nature, and from the clutches of the gods. According to this modern view, men must adjust themselves to technology.

The spectral view of technology is not a perspectival, polemical, or ethical view of the proper place of technology in human lives. It is not a view which is explicitly advocated. The spectral view of technology arises, instead, from a sense of domination by mysterious agencies or forces which are, or were linked to technological enterprises but which are now apprehended as being beyond the control of any particular man or collection of men. The following case fragments indicate that nonpsychotic individuals believe in such specters. These cases also illustrate the fact that the role of such specters in the lives of individuals is quite varied. Belief in these specters may even prove to be "adaptive."

## CASE STUDIES[7]

## The Specters of Technicism as Internal Objects

In the first three case fragments, the specters of technicism appeared as the products of neurotic creativity. These phantoms were constructed from what is everywhere "in the air." A spectral force located in the patient's body served to goad the individual into making decisions about his conduct. The therapist was initially cast as the keeper of both the specter and the patient. One wish of these patients, it was later revealed, was to transfer decision-making from this potent force to the therapist. These phantoms also served to screen episodes in the individual's personal history from immediate recall. In addition, the ascription of power to spectral forces proved to symbolize conflicts about omnipotence and the patients' capacities for action in their social settings.

[7] In the study of personal individuality and psychopathology, the "mechanisms of defense" are thought of as personal techniques for avoiding anxiety. The idea that the defenses of particular persons have the forms of techniques should not be confused with the fact that the specters of technicism appear as ideational components of defense arrangements (Cases 1-3), as a set of social realities which must be defended against (Cases 4, 5), or even, at times, as the ultimate reality to which the ego may belong (Case 6).

*Case 1*

Dr. A had ceased to attend tne Anglican Church in his early teens. He was a brilliant student of art history in graduate school and had just accepted his first teaching appointment when he sought treatment. Initially he claimed to be anxious and depressed, believing that he might have heart disease. His long-standing and relatively satisfying pattern of homosexual activity had recently been undermined by a heterosexual experience with a woman whom he had known for several years. Confused about his sexuality, alternately lonely and then pleased to be living alone, uncertain about his capacity to teach and somewhat bitter about his discipline, his main interests in the early hours of treatment centered around his bodily feelings and his attitude of frank hostility toward me. In this context he reported that his body controlled his conduct in the following manner. Whenever decisions had to be made, he monitored his pulse rate. This was done from 200 to 300 times a day with reference to such matters as the following: whether to get up, whether to eat two eggs or one, whether he could masturbate without the risk of raising his blood pressure, whether he could meet his classes, whether he could take a walk, whether it was safe to seek sexual relations with either men or women, whether he should turn on the television set. If his pulse was not exactly 72, the idealized rate, it was too high or too low—in any event, pathological. After discovering a "pathological pulse rate," Dr. A began the immense and time-consuming task of interpreting the results of his findings. Prior to coming into treatment, the patient had devised an elaborate set of correlations between pulse rates and performance abilities. These correlations usually suggested that he could not perform the tasks in question. Indeed, it made nearly every form of self-mediated activity extremely problematic. Dr. A, by his own admission, was possessed by powerful, mysterious, and impersonal forces which the therapist, as physician, was supposed to control.

*Case 2*

Professor B, who was from the Southwest, was also a teacher in a university. He had left the Roman Catholic Church in high school and had married after completing his graduate studies. Our relationship begain after a sudden disabling episode of anxiety prior to his return to the Southwest to attend a wedding. In the course of treatment he, too, reported the use of his pulse rate as a built-in decision-maker. Again this device operated like a switch—Yes or No, Go or No Go. Later in treatment, the regularity of his bowel movements became the principal source of information about what he could do next. He claimed to be unable to control many ordinary aspects of his daily life. His body, construed as a mechanism, controlled his life, forcing him to be sick and to deny his capacity to act in the world. Professor B believed he was possessed by mysterious and powerful forces.

*Case 3*

Mr. C, who was also highly educated, was married, an executive in industry, and a practicing Lutheran. He entered my office with a mathematical set of explanations for his depression. This account concerned a matrix of neural nets and their schedules of firings and misfirings, which were interpreted by means of trend analyses. The firing of these neural nets created small shifts in mood which dictated the untoward elements of the patient's social behavior. He demanded to be experimented upon to see if the nets could be brought under rational control. He felt unable to make many critical decisions affecting his life. Things repeatedly happened to him which were brought about by extremely powerful and impersonal segments of his brain, an organ which operated like an automaton. Mr. C's wife resented her own sexuality and looked upon the patient's sexual frustrations as a sign of "weakness." In the patient's view, mysterious forces conducted him to fates not of his own making.

**Notes on the Psychology of Possession[8]**

Repetition compulsions characterized the behavior of the patients who claimed to be possessed. Pulse-taking and detailed assessments of evanescent body feelings occurred hundreds of times each day. These rituals were performed in order to obtain decisions about proper conduct in various private and social situations. The patients had only vague fantasies related to that which produced these decisions. No colorful, culturally-prescribed descriptions of the sort usually associated with accounts of possession by devils were given; instead, decisions were given in a form which was imitative of the languages and logics of modern actuarial techniques.

[8] The patients who claimed to be possessed displayed traits of character which have been the subject of commentaries by other authors. Comments on these cases are limited to the phenomena of being possessed (see also Freud, 1956b). His description of the psychoanalytic approach to possession is worth repeating here: "Cases of demoniacal possession correspond to the neuroses of the present day; in order to understand these latter we have once more had recourse to the conception of psychic forces. What in those days were thought to be evil spirits to us are base and evil wishes, the derivatives of impulses which have been rejected and repressed. In one respect only do we not subscribe to the explanation of these phenomena current in medieval times; we have abandoned the projection of them into the outer world, attributing their origin instead to the inner life of the patient in whom they manifest themselves [pp. 436-437]."

Should the claims that these individuals were possessed be taken seriously? I believe so and for the following reason: analysis of the defensive function of the compulsions revealed a common theme, a theme which is found in reports of possession by spirits.[9] This theme is: (1) the powers of the ego are experienced as ego-alien, and (2) are acknowledged to be "on consignment" to a spectral agency, which (3) is located on "the inside," manifesting its influence on the life of the victim through his bodily processes.

The patients who claimed to be possessed placed their painfully acquired powers to test reality and their wish for omnipotent control over themselves and others in the protective custody of an ego-alien specter. The unconscious purpose of these defensive arrangements was to avoid the anxieties inherent in accepting any responsibility for choosing between unpleasant alternatives in the management of a variety of sexual (Cases 1 and 3) and aggressive (Case 2) impulses and wishes. The directives issued by the specters permitted masturbation (Cases 1 and 3) and numerous expressions of aggression and hostility via sadomasochism (Case 2). The fantasies associated with the sense of being possessed involved the use of denial, projection, and reintrojection of that which was projected. To wit, "if I am no longer in command of my faculties, and if I deny that my omnipotent wishes are my wishes, I cannot expect, or be expected, to be responsible for my conduct. I will assign my capacities for decision-making and my wishes to another agency. In exchange for my loss, I will be protected from realities which I cannot master, but I will keep this agency with me." Other fantasies, in which wishes for omnipotence were clearly expressed as the patients' wishes, suggested that these individuals were even more powerful than the specter. They could, for example, recover their capacities for decision-making if these capacities were "misused" by the specters.

The security and satisfactions afforded by these arrangements did not last. Having placed their capacities for wishing and for decision-making in the hands of specters, these patients became fearful of disobeying the dictates of "deviant pulse rates" and the messages which were adduced from actual and imaginary alterations in blood pressure, auditory acuity, and gastric functioning in an attempt to contain this anxiety, bodily processes were consulted about an ever-increasing number of items. When severe symptoms of anxiety and depression appeared, these individuals sought assistance from a potent exorcist—the professional psychotherapist.

While it is possible to trace the origins and development of the personal conflicts which led to the fabrications of these specters, it is more to the point of this communication to focus on the construction of the specters per se. Why were specters created to serve a defensive function? Why did the operations of these phantom agencies resemble the operations of modern calculating machines and mimic developments in modern decision theory?

[9] See the similarities in diverse reports of "possession" from such sources as Dodds (1951, esp. Chs. 3 and 4), Michelet (1939, esp. pp. 41-45, 326), and Firth (1960, pp. 299-332).

The patients' accounts of their early lives provide one answer to the first question. For example, Dr. A entered treatment with negative attitudes toward his body, fears of expressing his feelings toward other persons, and doubts as to whose feelings his feelings actually were. The model for these attitudes, fears, and doubts was acquired in childhood and entailed references to spectral forces. Dr. A's unwarranted (from his parents' viewpoint) interest in the form and social meaning of his body and the bodies of others was regarded as being "the work of the devil." He was instructed in the art of employing ritual formulas to enlist the assistance of benevolent phantoms—guardian angels—to help him in combatting the malicious specter who "urged" him to evil thoughts and to the pursuit of "exotic" investigations of himself and others. The combats of these spectral agencies also accompanied his conflicts with siblings and parents. As a rule, the expression of strong feelings of any kind was seen as a triumph for the malevolent phantom. If Dr. A became angry about his father's domination of the household, he was at fault not only for disobeying the imperatives of the father but also for permitting the devil to seize hold of his emotions. Had not his feelings been expressed in an unbridled way? When he failed to control his passions and speech in an acceptable manner, he was urged to seek assistance from his protecting angel—a figure who was, at times, indistinguishable from his mother.

Professor B and Mr. C were also reared in homes where they learned to believe that demonic and benevolent specters influenced one's thoughts, feelings, and decisions. The personal history of all three patients indicated that the operations of these agencies served as vehicles for expressing, and then for overcoming (in part), childhood problems of omnipotence, narcissism, and fears of destruction. With further biological, social, and cognitive development, these persons gave up (i.e. gradually forgot about) their beliefs in devils and guardian angels, but the form of the struggle between the powers of good and evil persisted as an introject. When, in adult life, these individuals had conflicts which could not be mastered because of the fear of accepting the implications of unpleasant ideas—such as giving up elements of either a homosexual or heterosexual identity (Dr. A), or divorce (Professor B, Mr. C)—the devils-versus-angels style of decision-making was resumed in a condensed and ambiguous form. They masked their inability to accept their failure to make reality conform to their desires by recreating the type of agency which, in childhood, had been implicated in learning that one's thoughts and actions are conditioned by external realities.[10] Spectral agencies were again made meaningful, but in adulthood they were given a new technological content and cast in a different dynamic role—as the source of all imperatives. The commands of the pulse

---

[10] Freud and Ferenczi give clear descriptions of how the thinking of the individual progresses from the "omnipotent" outlook of the child to the acceptance of "unpleasant ideas" about reality by the adult. They also explore the persistence of omnipotent thinking in cases of obsessional neuroses. See Freud (1956a, pp. 13-21), Freud (1962, pp. 75-99), and Ferenczi (1952, pp. 213-239).

could not be questioned or understood. They could only be followed. Through such devices these individuals sought to reassert their omnipotence and the primacy of pregenital (physiological) cues. Through these cues they sought to control themselves, the therapist, and the world.

Having considered one answer to the question of why specters were created for defensive purposes, we are in a better position to answer the second question. Why did the operations of these specters resemble the operations of modern calculating machines? One answer to this question is that the final language and logic utilized in modern decision theory takes a form which appears to be very similar to the automatic commands of the superego. The Off versus On of the switch, the Yes versus No of the empirical test, the True versus False of modern symbolic logic, have carried on dramatically to the world of Go or No Go. But recognize that Go and No Go are commands to act in a certain way. The command is compelling and urges compliance; it is precisely at this point that it corresponds to superego conflicts: Do it versus Don't Do It. Given contemporary symbols of power, efficacy, and heroic human action, can one wonder that troubled persons employ these symbols of power in their neurotic constructions?

Now one can see why the fantasies concerning the specters were vague, why attachments to compulsions were so strong, and why the conscious orientations toward these compulsions were so ambivalent. Explicit recognition of spectral forces was impossible for these highly educated persons. The compulsions hid the remnants of pregenital and oedipal conflicts and provided a solution to the problems of current lifeways.

## The Specters of Technicism as External Objects

The specters of technicism do not always appear in obscure, disabling and malevolent guises. Rather than appearing as part of a defense, they may appear as elements of reality against which one must erect defenses. Obsessions and paranoid feelings are the most common results of encounters with the phantoms of technicism. The next two cases illustrate relatively common experiences.

### Case 4

Major X was married, irreligious, and deeply committed to his work in the Air Force. He had served his country for seventeen and a half years and was a combat veteran who held the Distinguished Flying Medal. He entered the office despondent and enraged, claiming that he was unable to work. Recently, he had received notification from Washington that he would not be promoted to Lieutenant Colonel and instead was to be discharged from the Air Force four months before becoming eligible for a pension.

He had spent the latter portion of his military career in the relative isolation of a missile complex, and was without friends in high places. His skills could not be readily deployed in the civilian economy. Major X was unable to assign responsibility for his fate to himself (he was quite competent) or to any known agent or collection of agents. As far as Major X was concerned, unseen forces had sorted the cards and moved the machines to speak.

### Case 5

Sam was 21, recently married, irreligious, impulsive, and a school dropout. He was a friendly young man who had bummed around the country for several years prior to his marriage. At the time of consultation his wife was pregnant. He was brought to a psychiatric hospital with the following story.

Upon learning that his wife was pregnant, Sam had decided for the first time in his life to get a job. He worked alone six days a week in the sorting room of a nationally known tire manufacturer and distributor. The job was outlined in a manual of instructions given to him by his boss, a man ten years his senior. After working for several weeks, Sam came to imagine that he was in charge of the tire room.

The patient was a mystery to the regular company employees. They did not understand his impulsivity, his occasional outbursts of hostility, or his attempts at friendliness.

When Sam's boss began to insist that he follow directions other than those which appeared in the manual, and simultaneously be responsible for maintaining the standards suggested in it, Sam became angry, frustrated, and frightened. He did not want to lose his job or his new level of self-esteem. When his superior became vituperative and critical of him for not following verbal instructions, Sam "blew his cool," smashed his superior in the nose, and began to cry and to speak incoherently. The police then brought him to the hospital.

Sam had little knowledge of the larger system in which he worked. He was low man on a largely invisible totem pole. He had expected to maintain a right to his own feelings and ideas on the job. Sam left the hospital as an enemy, not of other men, but of "The System." His narcissism took on a darker hue.

## Belief in the Specter as a Component of External Reality

These cases illustrate that the effects of an ensemble of technological enterprises can be experienced as being beyond the control of responsible or even identifiable human beings. The contrast between this orientation toward technological phenomena and the traditional orientation toward such phenomena is striking. These men sensed themselves to be the victims of technique—not the masters of technique. Major X, for example, considered himself a victim of The System. Let us see how this communication can be understood in terms of the Aristotelian scheme outlined above.

The essential tool was a computer. There were many techniques employed in the correct use of this tool. Of greatest importance (for present purposes) were the administrative and logical-mathematical techniques which centered around the construction of an algorithm for the selection of lieutenant colonels. Some of the factors considered in writing this algorithm were: numbers of majors eligible for advancement, standards of selection, performance reports, number of lieutenant colonels being "made" in the third quarter of fiscal 1968, and the length of time allotted for the selection process by Pentagon officials. The goal which officials were striving to reach was the identification of individuals to fill service needs for various functional role categories occupied by individuals with the status of lieutenant colonel. These officials were attempting to prove that cost-benefit analysis was an efficient way of maintaining "an effective deterrent force" (the ends-context).

Major X, like the other men of the command, knew that this was how The System operated. The ultimate purpose of these deterrent forces, he observed, was "to make the world a safe place for the exercise of freedom." In this context of tools and techniques, Major X pictured himself as a resource substance. He was a "human factor" who was content to be used by The System if he were used in an equitable manner—that is, if he would be given a pension following a prescribed period of honorable service. He had never sought to identify who used him as a resource substance. He was content with this set of arrangements until the time when he was notified that he would not be given a pension. He then felt that The Whole System had let him down—that is, had not treated him in an equitable manner. In Aristotle's vocabulary, he could not identify a tool-user, 'the efficient cause" of his state of affairs.

We can now formulate a series of steps which lead to the belief that the specters of technicism are objects which should be defended against:

1. An emotionally charged claim (e.g., that one should be loved or given his due), which is usually satisfied by a form of human interaction involving cognizance of the life-ways (including the personal defenses) of a particular claimant, is not met.

2. The frustration of the claim is experienced as a mere event or outcome. There is, in the context of that event, no recognition from others that the individual is a person—the person experiences himself as a resource substance.

3. The frustrating events are associated with the specific operations and manifestations of technological enterprises. The events in question cannot be ascribed to the caprices of nature, for these events are visibly linked with human artifice.

4. There is a failure on the part of the claimant to identify an agent or collection of agents who are aware of the effect of their actions on the claimant. For example, the claimant cannot identify an enemy.

5. A personal disposition exists to ascribe untoward events to the "state of the world." Personal responsibility for the existing state of affairs is, characteristically, denied.

6. A second frustration follows upon the first frustration. There is no object against which one may direct feelings of anger.

7. A spectral agency is created in order to account for one's condition and to integrate one's experience.

### Obsessive Paranoia

Neither Major X nor Sam was unique, of course, in finding himself functioning as a resource substance—a thing—to which a technique was applied. It is also true that there is more than one way of experiencing and responding to such events —for example, by attempts at mastery through understanding and personal actions, by forgetting, by identifications (see below), and by counter-identifications (see, e.g., Adler, 1968). But a common response to being treated as a resource substance in modern technological environments is to create a specter and to interpret the situation in the paranoid mode of perception and cognition. How does this orientation to technological environments come about?

As a result of their experiences, Major X and Sam felt that they had been persecuted as well as rejected. Major X contended that he had "given up" (denied) many of his own potentialities as an individual human agent in return for guarantees of security given by The System. When The System rejected him, he felt that a promise had been broken—that he had been betrayed. But by what? By whom?

Sam had proceeded along life's way in a spirit of youthful innocence. He had consciously and unconsciously avoided learning many basic habits of social cooperation—habits which are requisite to living as an adult with other adults. Throughout late adolescence he had continued to play with the world and had anticipated that the world would continue to play with him. The treatment he received from his employer and his own hostile aggressivity were, for him, as frightening as they were incomprehensible. The experience of being used as a resource substance confronted him with social realities which he could not master by attempting to play the child. Sam felt that he had been singled out and hurt—but by what and by whom?

Both men relieved their anxieties by creating spectral agents. Major X and Sam fabricated ego-alien phantoms which were capable of producing the untoward events described above in the presentations of Cases 4 and 5. They located these agencies in the world—beyond the integument. Then, fearing the effects of the phantoms they had created, they became obsessed with their operations. The System was viewed as if it intended the future and was responsible for one's fate. Major X and Sam adopted watchful and suspicious attitudes toward this phantom.

Elements of reality which were denied and then ascribed to The System were:

1. The patients' capacities to act as human agents.

2. The responsibility of other human agents for their actions vis-a-vis the patients. Neither of these individuals faced the implications of acknowledging that

other persons had decided, as a matter of "technical necessity," to regard them (and a great many other people) as resource substances.

3. The anger and frustration which Major X and Sam felt as a result of the untoward events described above. These feelings were now experienced as being directed at them by the phantom agents—the efficient causes of their states of affairs.

This set of arrangements accentuated long-standing traits of immature, hostile dependency in Major X, and led Sam to withdraw in fright, anger, and depression from his adventurous encounters with the world. Through the expedient creation of a spectral agent, each man avoided a confrontation with himself and with current social realities. These conflicts were bound together and cast into the air —beyond the reach of the emotions, reflection, and coherent action.

Hence, belief in the specters of technicism, construed as external objects, is sometimes held in association with obsessive and paranoid traits of personality. Such beliefs are also held in conjunction with other personal traits. The reader should not conclude, however, that such beliefs are always held in connection with the personal defenses of individuals.

## Social-Cultural Transmission of Belief in Specters

Belief in the specters of technicism—The System, The Establishment, It, They—is so prevalent in the technologically advanced nations that these beliefs are now transmitted from one generation to the next as a regular part of social learning. Belief in the specters of technicism may simply be part of a person's "cultural baggage," and may display no special connection with the development of personal traits of character. For example, young men and women entering highly organized work environments are initiated, often in a secret fashion, into the culture of the taboos surrounding the autonomous specter known as The System. Nuances of posture, speech, dress, and orientations to time, space, and office are often held to be desirable and necessary because The System demands it. If inquiry is made as to who is responsible for The System, it is said that no person or collection of persons is; it is just The System.

It is common knowledge that failure to appreciate the potent nature of this spectral force (in part, a by-product of the omnipotent wishes of the managers of public and private institutions) has led some doubters to considerable grief. It is also true that some believers have found their way to positions of authority and power, in part because they knew all about The System and how it influenced human interaction.[11] It is not surprising, therefore, that when men fall victim to an ensemble of techniques, the spirit of these enterprises tends to become objectified

[11] In these troubled times, it is necessary to add that not all persons who hold positions of power and authority do so because they are "machines" or believers in The System.

and perceived as a demonic force. The visible objects (e.g., computers, manuals of instruction, files, and various officials) associated with these mysterious forces become the symbols of such specters. Advocates and opponents of rule by The System exhibit their differences by struggling to maintain or to destroy these objects.

I have alluded to these facts in order to highlight two of the important clinical implications of the findings reported in this paper. First, it is likely that the lives of numerous people are touched by the specters of technicism. Second, it should be apparent that belief in these phantoms is not necessarily a mark of psychopathology. The essential task for the clinician, and for the patient, is to come to some knowledge of the place of these beliefs in the context of his life and in the conduct of his affairs.

## The Specter of Technicism as an Internal and External Object

Belief in the specter of technicism may appear in still other forms in the lives of individual persons. Instead of being a force which one must dread and defend against, this specter may become that ultimate reality in which one trusts and from which one draws hope and meaning. It may assume the semblance of a faith in the life of the individual. The specter of technicism may become, in Paul Tillich's (1958) words, "a matter of ultimate concern," and may show an "unconditional character [p. 2]" which is the "integrating center of the personal life [p. 106]." In the language of the French social critic, Ellul (1964), such individuals ". . . would hurl themselves gladly and without regret into a completely technological mode of being [p. 411] ." This life-way and the communities of faith which make it possible deserve the close attention of practitioners and scholars who would understand the religious meaning of many lives in the modern era.[12] The following case history provides an example of a person who travelled this life-way.

### Case 6

In Colonel Z, faith in the specter of technicism found its ultimate expression.

Colonel Z was in charge of training all the men in the command who processed, stored, maintained, and repaired nuclear weapons. His ultimate concern was for the techniques which permitted this work to go forward. He did not want the world to blow up by accident. If it were decided that it was necessary to blow up the world—a determination which he left to the supreme experts at headquarters—his attitude would be, "That's the way the cookie crumbles." His ultimate fulfillment was found in reviewing the documents which objectively and factually

---

[12] For a study of some of these faith-perspectives, see Luckmann (1967, esp. Chs. 6 and 7).

showed the bombs and missiles to be safe and in good working order. The maintenance of their working order was the ultimate demand which he placed upon himself.

Colonel Z's inferiors in the ranks found him insufferable as a person but admired his dedication to duty. His peers and superiors were scarcely prepared to question his integrity, good intentions, or technical adequacy. They shared in the work of the mission, but with less passion. His wife and family lived within the society of the military reservation. Though Colonel Z and his son were terrified of the civilian world, his troubled wife found some respite from her husband's urgent and ultimate concerns in the life "beyond the gates."

Colonel Z laughed and danced, played golf, and told dirty stories at the Officers' Club. He enjoyed sexual intercourse when it did not interfere with his work. Families, he knew, were functionally desirable. Colonel Z's brothers in faith were largely abstractions. They were the officers of the nuclear establishments of the other great nations. According to Colonel Z, the lives of such men were devoted to saving all the nations. They were the most misunderstood elite in the world.

Colonel Z's faith survived disputations with his wife, rejection by his son, a severe episode of anxiety, psychotherapy, and the threat of death. He never expressed a wish to be anything other than a competent "human factor." He knew his place in the new Alpha and Omega of things and stayed there. It was clear that his feelings of well-being and self-esteem were predicated upon a feeling of union with omnipotent forces in the external world, impersonal forces which had issued originally from the minds, hearts, and hands of other men. The names of these forces could not be spoken. No one could question their awful power.

### Religious Identification

Greenson (1954) has offered this concise definition of identification:

> Identification with an object means that, as a result of introjection, a transformation of the self has occurred whereby the self has become similar to an external object [p. 201].

Identifications have variable and complex relationships to each other, to personal traits, and to individual psychopathology. When a person has a feeling of "an indissoluble connection, of belonging inseparably to the external world as a whole [Freud, 1958, p. 2]," the person has achieved a religious identification. Such identifications have implications for behavior and conduct, and for society.

In this connection, a number of writers (e.g., Mary W. Godwin, Ernst Junger, Aldous Huxley, George Orwell, Mumford, Ellul) have anticipated the development of the fully technicized man, that is, a man whose most profound and positive identifications are with those forces which I have called the specters of technicism. It has been suggested that all of the important activities of such a person would be informed by the imperatives of a vast assemblage of techniques. His ultimate definitions of self, the world, and the meaning of his activities would be founded upon an unconditional commitment to technique. Such an individual would behave as if the *summum bonum* were to maximize the technicization of life in all circumstances. He would be a resource substance in a world of resource substances.

It is not uncommon to encounter people who appear to harbor identifications of this sort. But in the course of getting to know a person, it usually turns out that what appeared to be a profound identification is in fact an identity fragment which occupies a position in a superficial layer of the personality. However, in the case of Colonel Z, it must be reported that during ten months of intensive therapy, his faith in and identification with the essential benevolence, majesty, and power of spectral forces never wavered. His commitment to the service of phantom entities was limitless. He knew how The System would destroy the world, and how it would rebuild it. His devotion to and belief in the efficacy of the spiritual exercises of his organization (the vanguard of The System) matched his cosmic sense of the mission to which he was dedicating his life. The "personal sacrifices" which he made in the face of the mighty forces which he was helping to perfect transcended any merely human concern. His belief in the ultimate significance of his technical labors defined the context within which he experienced the possible loss of his wife, children, father, and even his position in the military establishment. Through these trials and many others as well, Colonel Z never displayed the slightest doubt about the utility of his identification with spectral forces. Rather than being angered by being treated as a resource substance, Colonel Z was gratified by such experiences. These experiences indicated that self and world were in order.

This remarkable set of identifications developed over many years.[13] The roots of identification with abstract entities could be traced to the patient's preoedipal relationship with his autocratic, austere, aloof, potent, and mysterious father. The emotionally frustrating, sterile, and impersonal qualities of this relationship were repeated in his highly successful memberships in a series of educational and military organizations. His experiences in these institutions continually reinforced the sorts of solutions which he imposed upon himself in response to his problematic

---

[13]Colonel Z sought treatment after experiencing two severe episodes of anxiety. The first episode occurred after he developed abdominal pain and had begun to worry about his health. While contemplating the fact that he might die, he was overcome with anxiety upon having the thought that his children might not love him. The second episode occurred shortly thereafter, while he was in the hospital undergoing an examination for his complaint of pain. "I just happened to be watching 'Queen for a Day.' For some reason it made me feel sad and frightened . . . I couldn't stop crying for two days."

One can speculate that pain, the threat of severe illness, the idleness of life on the ward, and the lack of a work environment to reinforce his typical dispositions, led to a temporary relaxation of Colonel Z's defenses. One can speculate further that under these circumstances, Colonel Z experienced a reawakening of his long repressed desires to be loved, by other persons, and an equally strong feeling of rage at those who had failed to love him.

childhood—maximum social exploitation of his strikingly handsome appearance, loyalty to a cause, the cultivation of a brilliant and decisive manner when called upon to perform, and a high rate of productivity for the benefit of abstract entities. Then, while still a young officer, and prior to the time of his marriage, he came upon the ultimate symbol of supreme power in the modern world—the hydrogen bomb. Colonel Z avidly introjected the life-ways and technoculture surrounding this weapon—as if he had discovered an object which he had always been seeking. By the time he obtained treatment for anxiety attacks, he had completed his identification with the specter of technicism. He had become a son and an heir.

It must be noted that Colonel Z's remarkable identifications allowed him to live his life in a relatively satisfactory manner. From the standpoint of the clinician, Colonel Z displayed a curious form of religious identification. But his set of identifications also arouses one's interest in the study of society and social psychology. Could Colonel Z's life have been so satisfactory or his sublimations so personally convincing to him if external reality in the form of social and cultural arrangements did not, in many ways, support and sustain his faith? If it is assumed that the behaviors through which these identifications were exemplified required a certain measure of support and affirmation from other people, one is struck by a fact of signal importance. A person whose principal identifications are with spectral forces is sustained in this curious identification within a major context of human association in the most advanced nation of the world. Could it be that such identifications will become more prevalent and livable in the future?

## CONCLUSION

I have reported and discussed fragments from the lives of six men whose early instinctive, motivational, and intellectual development led them consciously or unconsciously to continue in adult life to search for omnipotent objects. They fabricated specters from the symbols and events of modern technological environments. Some of these men (Dr. A, Professor B, Mr. C) used the abstract forms of technical enterprises in a magical way as they elaborated ideational defenses; other men (Major X, Sam) believed that mysterious and evil powers were personified in modern techniques of corporate management; another man (Colonel Z) identified himself and his hopes for personal perfection and omnipotence with visions of technical progress. In order to achieve conceptual clarity with respect to these phenomena, I initially contrasted the spectral view of technology with more conventional perspectives.

In the future, attempts to understand ourselves and our patients will often entail an attempt to understand how artificial environments, produced by the mass application of modern technologies, enter into the formation and expression of personal traits of character. If we wish to understand these environments we must be prepared to study our civilization—its contents and its discontents.

## REFERENCES

Adler, N. The antinomian personality: The hippie character type. *Psychiatry,* 1968, *31,* 325-338.

Brzezinski, Z. America in the technetronic age. *Encounter,* 1968, *30*(1), 16-26.

Derry, T. M., & Williams, T. I. *A short history of technology from the earliest times to A. D. 1900.* London & New York: Oxford University Press, 1961.

Dodds, E. R. *The Greeks and the irrational.* Berkeley: University of California Press, 1951.

Ellul, J. *The technological society.* 1954. (Transl. by J. Wilkinson.) New York: Knopf, 1964.

Ferenczi, S. Stages in the development of the sense of reality. 1913. In *First contributions to psycho-analysis.* (Transl. by E. Jones.) London: Hogarth Press, 1952.

Firth, R. The fate of the soul. In C. Leslie (Ed.), *Anthropology of folk religion.* New York: Vintage Books, 1960.

Freud, S. Formulations regarding the two principles in mental functioning. 1911. In *Collected papers.* Vol. 4. London: Hogarth Press, 1956. (a).

Freud, S. A neurosis of demoniacal possession in the seventeenth century. 1923. In *Collected papers.* Vol. 4. London: Hogarth Press, 1956. (b).

Freud, S. *Civilization and its discontents.* 1928. (Transl. by J. Riviere.) New York: Double-day Anchor Books, 1958.

Freud, S. Animism, magic and the omnipotence of thoughts. In *Totem and taboo.* 1919. (Transl. by J. Strachey.) New York: Norton, 1962.

Greenson, R. The struggle against identification. *American Psychoanalytic Association, Journal,* 1954, *2,* 200-217.

Guntrip, H. *Personality structure and human interaction.* New York: International Universities Press, 1961.

Lobkowicz, N. *Theory and practice.* South Bend, Ind.: University of Notre Dame Press, 1967.

Luckmann, T. *The invisible religion.* New York: Macmillan, 1967.

Michelet, J. *Satanism and witchcraft.* (Transl. by A. R. Allinson.) New York: Citadel Press, 1939.

Mumford, L. *Technics and civilization.* 1934. New York: Harbinger Books, 1963.

Mumford, L. *The myth of the machine.* New York: Harcourt, 1966.

Nelson, B. Scholastic rationales of "conscience," early modern crises of credibility, and the scientific-technocultural revolutions of the 17th and 20th centuries. *Journal for the Scientific Study of Religion,* 1968, *7,* 157-177.

Ong, W. J. The spiritual meaning of technology and culture. In *Technology and culture in perspective.* Cambridge, Mass.: Church Society for College Work, 1967.

Peters, R. S. *Brett's history of psychology.* Cambridge, Mass.: MIT Press, 1962.

Reich, W. *Character analysis.* 3rd ed., Transl. by T. P. Wolfe.) New York: Free Press, 1949.

Sachs, H. The delay of the machine age. *Psychoanalytic quarterly,* 1933, *2,* 404-424.

Shanks, M. *The innovators: The economics of technology.* London: Penguin Books, 1967.

Stanley, M. Technicism, liberalism and development: A study in irony as social theory. In M. Stanley (Ed.), *Social development: Critical perspectives,* Chapter 10. New York: Basic Books, 1972. Pp. 274-325.

Tausk, V. On the origin of the "influencing machine" in schizophrenia. *Psychoanalytic Quarterly,* 1933, *2,* 519-556.

Tillich, P. *Dynamics of faith.* New York: Harper Torchbooks, 1958.

# Chapter 17

# Black Alienation and Black Consciousness

*Alvin F. Poussaint*
Harvard Medical School

Much has been written about the feeling of alienation and confusion of identity which has been exhibited by blacks as a result of their membership in an oppressed group in America. The Negro's position is different from that of other minorities because he alone bears the scars of a slave heritage and wears the indelible "mark of oppression," his dark skin. It would be virtually impossible to discuss, in this short paper, the numerous aspects and implications of the Negro's psychological adjustments to white racism. Therefore, I would like to focus on the psychological patterns which have been of special relevance in the black man's identity formation.

The institution of slavery in its original form and its present-day remnants—differences in housing, education, employment and wages—have had dramatic consequences for the black man's identity development. These differences generated a vicious cycle of self-hatred, self-deprecation, suppressed aggression, and nonassertiveness from which the black man has sought to break loose. However, his efforts to do so have unstintingly been opposed by so much of the white society which stood to reap too many psychic as well as economic and political benefits from black oppression.

The black man's alienation began when he was transported as a slave from his native Africa to the alien shores of America. The provisions of slavery turned

[1] Adapted from a paper submitted to the Alienation Institute, sponsored by the Maxwell School of Citizenship at Syracuse University, June 1970.

359

him into a piece of property, a nonperson. To ensure a total break with the cultural institutions which give a man a sense of self, the oppressors not only separated the black man from his family but also from other members of his tribe. The slaves were not allowed to marry, nor were their children allowed to know their fathers. They were not allowed to cultivate their own land, learn to read and write, or meet with other slaves in groups, except for occasional religious gatherings.

Total dependency and subservience were implanted in the minds and behavior of slavery's victims. They were never allowed to acquire the skills of administration and control necessary for successful independence. Thus, once granted their freedom, they were slow to exercise initiative without first checking with the white man. The white master had ministered (however inadequately) to the basic needs of the slave in all areas: financial, social, and personal, and continued to do so after emancipation through the Freedman's Bureau and, today, through the welfare system. The harsh punishments given to "uppity niggers" and the inequitable penalties imposed upon Negroes by the Jim Crow legal system acted as a significant deterrent to independent behavior and the acting out of aggression.

It was quickly learned that any material and psychological comforts to be had could only be obtained by bowing and scraping for the white boss. To be a "good nigger" might mean the denial of his identity as a man, but it also meant his survival. Yet, it was not enough to strip him of his independence; the system dictated that he must also be taught to despise himself and his fellow slaves. Thus, the master's mulatto offspring were favored on the plantation, and, later, under Jim Crow, mostly light-skinned Negroes with fine hair were allowed to achieve material well-being. The lesson drawn from this by dark-skinned Negroes was that their lack of social and economic success must somehow be the result of their Negroid features. Faced with the achievements of "white Negroes" and aware of the premium placed on white blood, the black man sought to emulate Caucasian features while downgrading his own curly hair; broad nose, and full lips.

By the time slavery was abolished, the black man had learned to be unwillingly servile, unwillingly docile, and unwillingly ashamed. Deprived of a rich cultural heritage, his freedom was a token one since a white-dominated hostile environment forbade him to break the bonds of the roles prescribed for him: Uncle Tom, Stepin Fetchit, Amos and Andy, Sambo and Beulah. Just as the master's whip had forced him to comply, so the Southern system of legal justice with its quick and repressive tactics guaranteed that the Negro kept his place. Powerless to fight the system on its own terms, the black man had to arrange his personality in such a way as to not let his legitimate anger and rage penetrate his public facade of compliance.

Here it would seem appropriate to raise the question of why white America has unstintingly and brutally suppressed most attempts at self-fulfillment among blacks. In this highly competitive society with its dog-eat-dog attitudes, the white man's feelings of insecurity and lack of self-esteem found a convenient outlet in racist institutions. Similarly, the inability to confront his irrational drives drove him to project these onto the black man. This in turn provided him with a rationale for his continued violence against and oppression of Negroes. The most current form of oppression, however, is that which is expressed in the scholarly works on the "Negro Problem." Ever since it became fashionable, for political and ideological reasons, to write about blacks, social scientists have done so. The Negro's mark of oppression is no longer only his black skin, or his slave heritage; in addition, it is his pathology (Grossack, 1965; Kardiner & Ovesey, 1951; Kvaraceus, Gibson, Patterson, Seasholes, & Grambs, 1965; Pettigrew, 1964).

In their numerous attempts to show the pernicious consequences of discrimination upon the black man's psyche, social scientists have unwittingly furnished scientific credibility for many white-held stereotypes. They have focussed upon those areas where blacks register highly—crime, juvenile delinquency, welfare, and drug addiction—to bear out the way in which second-rate education, inadequate housing, and unfair employment practices have contributed to the black man's inferior status in this society. It is clear from these statistics, they say, that the black man must suffer from an acute self-hatred and low sense of self-esteem. They argue that for the black man not to have developed a deep-seated wish to be white would have been unnatural in a society where "white is right." They uniformly assume that the black man has internalized on a psychic level the hatred which the white man has directed against him. According to them, the black man is and can only be motivated by negative drives which ultimately spring from his own inferior sense of self. What emerges from this is a picture of the Negro as emotionally disturbed and, therefore, somehow defective and psychopathological (Clark, 1965; Erikson, 1968; Glazer and Moynihan, 1964). Thus, today's whites can dismiss the demands for black self-determination as out-of-hand or paranoid and recommend in their place more welfare and more psychiatric services.

It would seem more pertinent today to study the positive elements within the black personality. Besides the obvious richness of his counter-culture, there are numerous behavioral patterns which warrant our attention. In the 1940s, the noted psychologist, Kenneth Clark, created a minor furor with his famous "doll studies" in which he pointed out that black children exhibit adverse reactions toward their skin color as early as ages four and five (Clark & Clark, 1947). This negative association is one, which apart from being reinforced by racist institutions, also exists in our language—most loathsome activities are identified with the color black. Later studies of black childrens' drawings revealed that they frequently depicted themselves out-of-proportion, without color, or physically deformed, whereas they had little trouble properly depicting their white schoolmates (Coles, 1964). On the basis of these observations, child psychiatrists have tended to perceive a close relationship between color awareness and self-esteem. It has also been their conclusion that among both white and black children, white tends to elicit a positive evaluative response and black a negative one. More recent studies, however, have shed a different light on these findings. For one, it has been found that black children, according to one study, were more cheerful, more curious, more inclined towards leadership, kinder, and more sensitive—none of these seem to be indicative of a pervasive self-hatred (Goodman, 1964).

Another phenomenon observed in black children has been the development, at an early stage, of a high degree of sophistication (Greenwald & Oppenheim, 1968). This may indeed be the result of an early awareness of the bounds of their fate in the white man's world, to which they respond by developing an abiding and often tough sense of what life is all about. This points to another outstanding feature in the black man's psychological make-up, namely his insistence upon "telling it like it is." Having lived in a world of double standards all his life, the black man has not had the luxury of a facade of humanitarian principles behind which to hide. The white man could uphold the courthouse as a seat of justice but could hardly expect the same reverences from the black man for whom it has consistently represented one of racism's most forceful weapons.

Alternate interpretations of black personality adjustments have also been born out by a study conducted recently which used mulatto-colored dolls as well as black and white ones (Greenwald & Oppenheim, 1968). This study showed a considerable drop in the incidence of misidentification among black children, the phenomenon to which Dr. Clark brought our attention. Only 13% of the Negro children misidentified themselves in this study, as compared to the 39% in Dr. Clark's survey.

The refusal to depict himself as black or brown, not to see himself in a picture with white and black children, and not to express preference for either a black or a white doll may be different indications of the same preoccupation, that is, to be heard, seen, and recognized as an individual with a choice, instead of as one marked by his color. Although our language does not allow for such open-mindedness, a child's failure to express preference for black or white may be the result of his cognition of color as not being categorically dichotomized in positive or negative terms, his allowance instead for gradations and shadings.

What have been interpreted as feelings of anxiety, uncertainty, ambivalence, and inferiority may now be viewed instead as manifestations of the Negro's struggle to recover his "surrendered identity" and to forever destroy his status as a second class citizen. To view his boldness and excessive extravagances as only compensatory maneuvers is to misunderstand the defiance implicit in them. To put it crudely, when a Negro rides around in an Eldorado Cadillac with a white-on-white interior and his mohair suit, he is thumbing his nose at Mr. Charlie! Many blacks have been forced to demand their denied recognition by forceful and often flamboyant self-assertion.

The time has come for our society to recognize the black man's achievements and to fully and uncompromisingly admit his presence in the American mainstream. He has always been there, and were it not for his labor, his wisdom, and his genius, as W. E. B. DuBois (1969) once said, America would not be the mighty nation it is today.

Fortunately, the civil rights gains in the past decade, and especially in the 1960s did much to modify the negative self-concepts of Afro-Americans. The civil rights movement brought a new sense of dignity and respect to those blacks most severely deprived by poverty in the ghettoes of the South and North. One factor which was instrumental in bringing this about was the black leadership with which the black masses could identify. The knowledge that they had control over social forces and were not, as has been the case customarily, simply the victims of social forces gave blacks pride in their group and made them feel less helpless. The movement brought the Negro a new sense of power, for it raised his defiance from the level of individual struggle to one of mass resistance. It also served to channel the expressions of self-assertion among Negroes, although they were primarily of a nonviolent kind. The primary goal of the civil rights leaders, however, was to bring about the integration of the black and white races. This, they thought, would end once and for all the black's feelings of alienation.

Their aspirations were challenged when segments of the civil rights movement became disenchanted with the social and psychological consequences of American "integration," for it soon became apparent that, despite court orders and new laws, integration was moving at a snail's pace and was being dictated by whites. Whereas, before, the Negro attended segregated schools, he is now put in the demeaning and uncomfortable position of asking and demanding that the white man let him into his schools and his neighborhoods, even though he knows that the white man does not want him. In the South and North, many Afro-Americans resent the indignity of constantly being in the position of begging for acceptance into the white man's institutions. Further disillusionment set in as it became clear that the recently enacted civil rights laws did not effectively change the patterns of dependency upon whites.

It soon became apparent that integration, especially in schools, was not to be integration in a real sense at all, but merely token placement of Negro children— that is, "one-way integration." Negro parents in the South and North, for example, rarely speak of sending their children to the "integrated school"; instead they say, "My child is going to the white school." It is most rare to find white children "integrated" into black schools. Since integration is only a one-way street which blacks travel to a white institution, it becomes obvious that it is still the black who is viewed as inferior and who must seek out whites to better his position. This suggests that only he can benefit and learn, that he has nothing to offer whites, and that they have nothing to learn from him. Thus, the traditional stereotypes are only reinforced.

Some black parents who fear psychological harm to their children are not anxious to place them as tokens in white facilities. Some of the college-age young people in the movement state frankly that they find this type of integration personally degrading and do not want to go to any school where they have to be "accepted

by white racists." Since the number of Negroes at any white school is usually token, particular hardships are created for these individuals. They immediately find
themselves surrounded by children who are generally the products of white racist
homes. In such a social setting, if the self-esteem of the black student grows, it is
likely to be because he feels he has succeeded in overcoming his blackness and, in
being a "super nigger," has been accepted by his white classmates. Thus, he is either the successful pioneer or the "exception."

It must be remembered that black people are seeking not only social and
economic help but a strong psychological identity. The Negro is not only demanding equal rights, but is also searching for inner emancipation and escape from
the chronic effects of white racism upon his psyche. In this search for peace, many
young blacks feel a need to insulate themselves from the subtle expressions of racism which they experience in their daily encounters with whites. In this context,
the growth of black organizations on campuses takes on a significance notably different from the one of "racist separatism" often imputed to it by the press. Perhaps this isolation serves to protect them from feelings of self-consciousness which
they experience in the presence of whites. Such uncomfortable feelings prevent
them from feeling relaxed and, thus, from being themselves.

Many blacks, including segments of both the old civil rights movement and
nationalists, are beginning to fear that token integration may augment the identity
problems of the black. Such integration as has taken place in the North has not
substantially helped to solve the Negro's identity problems. Assimilation, by definition, takes place into and according to the larger societal (white) model of culture and behavior. Thus, if Negroes are to assimilate, it is they who must give up
their black identity and subculture to be comfortably integrated. Many Negroes
who seek complete assimilation thus become preoccupied with proving to white
people that they are just like all other human beings, that is, white, and worthy of
being assimilated. At the same time, they express their willingness to give up most
elements of their black identity. This in itself signifies that they feel they are giving up something of inferior and negative value to gain something of greater value:
white identity.

It must be remembered that this analysis only holds in a situation where it
is assumed that blacks accept white definitions of themselves. Fortunately, this is
not a phenomenon which extends to all blacks. It is probably more applicable to
the black bourgeoisie than it is to ghetto residents. For the latter, especially because of de facto segregation, it is other Negroes, specifically those of the corner
peer group, who are the sources of identity and esteem. It must also be stated here
that our analysis has assumed a commitment to a value system, epitomized in the
American Dream. Insofar as that's all it's ever been for poor blacks, namely a dream,
we must ask what alternative criteria for success they have placed in its stead. This
is not to say that they are totally uanffected by the criteria of worth expressed by
the dominant majority, but that these have been modified so as to place the burden
of failure on the system rather than on any individual inadequacies.

It is unfortunate, however, that many Afro-Americans still expend a great deal of energy trying to prove that they are all right. This is a vain and fruitless effort because personal acceptability has to be proven anew each time the individual faces another group of whites. Before he can be accepted as an individual he must first prove that he is human. Frequently, one finds blacks who pursue white middle-class status symbols in the hope that this will prove to other whites, as well as to themselves, that they can be successful, worthwhile human beings. Yet, the sense of alienation remains. Most white Americans, in their usual stereotypic fashion, have placed all Negroes in one collective group: "They all look alike." Hence, there can be no "individual freedom" for any one Negro until there is a group freedom for all.

That an individual can achieve individual status only through changing his group's status is, however, an idea foreign to American thought. The Negro, like other Americans, has accepted the belief (descended from the tenets of the Protestant ethic) that individuals succeed or fail mainly as a result of their individual efforts. Thus, an individual's worth is assessed solely on the basis of his merits: he is accepted or rejected because of what he is as an individual. The acceptance by the Afro-American of this idea of individual merit has worked to his detriment, for it has operated to sustain a delusion in the face of a contradicting reality. It would perhaps be more realistic for black people to develop and orient themselves in terms of a sense of community and follow this path as a means of overcoming barriers to them as a group. Only then will acceptance or rejection for individuals follow. Achievement of this group liberation, however, requires undoing racial self-hatred, expending greater group assertiveness for social and political action, and adopting a proud stance—a positive identity.

As we mentioned, an important issue in the identity of black people is self-determination and fate control. As long as Negroes are powerless politically and do not have a degree of control over their own communities, they will remain beggars in a white man's kingdom. For instance, why shouldn't the black community have the final word about the type of policemen that are permitted in their community? Why should a white man downtown be able to send white racist police who shout or think "nigger" into the black community to "enforce the law?" Why can't black communities have some degree of autonomy in governing thier community, particularly since white-controlled urban governments have vested interests in protecting the majority white interests? Who is watching out for black interests? Following the same reasoning, local groups should have some say in deciding who will teach in their schools, who will run local welfare departments, in short, who will control their local institutions. To many blacks this does not represent separatism; it is simply democracy.

Other minorities have attained these goals by developing strong political machines, and there is no reason why blacks cannot and should not do so, as well. However, the establishment, with its traditional acumen, has recognized the potential threat of black unity and has thus set about to destroy it by implanting new seeds of self-doubt in the black community. It has sought to do this by suggesting that blacks are a group of mental misfits who cannot take care of themselves and must therefore be ministered to by the all-knowing white man. It is in view of this latest white strategy that the black consciousness movement has assumed vital significance, for it alone can help blacks to resist this negative psychological warfare.

It is known that such nationalist groups and individuals as the Black Muslims and Malcolm X had positive and constructive meaning for members of the black community. This group has brought greater self-reliance and dignity to hard-core, beaten-down segments of the Negro community. The Muslims were once the one major Negro group (now there are others of the Black Power orientation) that called for separation of the races and black self-sufficiency as an alternative approach for the remedy of the black man's problems of negative identity and self-esteem. Observers generally agree that the Muslims were quite effective in rehabilitating many antisocial and criminal types by fostering in them a positive self-image and pride in their blackness (Haley, 1964; Lincoln, 1969). They helped them to feel less alienated from themselves and their community of black people. This group also afforded blacks a channel for expressing their rage at the "white devils." The significant fact is that the Muslims were able to alleviate much of the individual Negro's self-hatred without holding up or espousing integration or full acceptance of the black man into American white society.

Other black consciousness groups have instilled pride and esteem in Negroes by emphasizing Negro history and achievements. Programs based on this philosophy can build Negro self-confidence and self-assertion by calling upon black men to think and do for themselves. They may also provide the stimulus for more independent thought and grass-roots problem-solving and lead to the development of community leadership. Such programs have the potential for undoing much of the black man's alienation and emasculation.

The question must be raised, however, whether all-black programs will lead to more psychological estrangement of the Negro from society, since such groups would always exist within a surrounding dominant white culture and would run the risk of being considered inferior. Can you really build a sense of community and pride in the ghettoes when these neighborhoods carry the stigma of forced segregation by and from the white community? Can people develop a pride in a neighborhood that consists of dilapidated housing, usually in the most dismal parts of our cities? Definitive answers to these questions cannot yet be given. I would suggest, however, that if Negroes were truly equals in the larger society, a black subculture could exist much in the same way that America has subcultures of other national and racial groups such as the Jews, Irish, Chinese, etc. That is, if community derives from choice and is among people who feel common bonds, it can be a more salutary situation for blacks than if people of disparate interests, abilities, and needs are forced together in a ghetto solely on the basis of a common skin color.

It is clear that despite the drive for racial integration, it is being vigorously resisted by the white population, particularly in the area of housing. Therefore, we can expect to have isolated, predominantly black communities for a long time to come. The potentiality of these communities cannot be ignored while integration is awaited. Whether these can become positive communities, founded on common interests and supported by pride, or will stay run-down ghettoes and encampments of human misery remains to be seen.

Since the black man's need for a sense of identity, self-assertion, and independence cannot be met through token integration, and since assimilation appears to be a remote possibility, it seems logical that both black and white men must turn to the development and rehabilitation of Negro communities. In this endeavor, however, it is crucial that as much responsibility as possible be placed in the hands of black men, since self-development and self-determination lead to a greater sense of self-worth and power.

The white establishment can help to alleviate those problems that afflict black Americans by undoing white supremacy and the oppression of colored peoples. In doing this, white people will have to give up some share of their control and power over black communities. At the same time, the white community must earnestly struggle for open housing so that Negroes can have a free choice about where they will live. With a choice, the many Negroes who choose to live among blacks will know that they have exercised their free will rather than that they acquiesced to powers forcing them into a box.

In our cities, white officials can help to build the status of black communities by making them centers of business and cultural attraction for all people. Why not have major theaters, museums, and trade centers, located in black communities as part of a general rehabilitation program for the ghettoes? There are many other small ways in which the black ghettoes could be made part of the mainstream of our urban centers. Even though much has been said in the past decades about the urgent need for jobs, decent housing, and quality education and training programs, very little has been done to implement these ideas. The society is now paying with urban disorder for this chronic neglect in alleviating some of these basic problems.

It becomes obvious after this long discussion of the alienation of black Americans that this is a subject which cuts across broad social, economic, and political areas. The subject and its implications for social change cannot be considered in isolation. In order to relieve the estrangement of blacks in our society, we must address ourselves to the many ramifications of white racism. The black consciousness movement appears to offer some hope for providing a sense of identity to the black man that may relieve the deep sense of black alienation in America.

## REFERENCES

Clark, K. B. *Dark ghetto: Dilemmas of social power.* New York: Springer, 1965.
Clark, K. B., & Clark, M. P. Racial identification and preference in Negro children. In T. M. Newcomb & E. L. Hartley (Eds.), *Readings in social psychology.* New York: Holt, 1947.

Coles, R. *Children in crisis.* Boston: Little, Brown, 1964.

DuBois, W. E. B. *The souls of black folk.* New York: New American Library, 1969.

Erikson, E. H. *Identity, youth and crisis.* New York: Norton, 1968.

Glazer, N., & Moynihan, D. *Beyond the melting pot.* Cambridge, Mass: MIT Press, 1963.

Goodman, M. E. *Race awareness in young children.* New York: Macmillan (Collier), 1964.

Greenwald, H. J., & Oppenheim, D. B. Reported magnitude of self mis-identification among Negro children—artifacts? *Journal of Personality and Social Psychology,* 1968, *8,* 49-52,

Grossack, M. M. *Mental health and segregation.* New York: Springer, 1965.

Haley, A. *The autobiography of Malcolm X.* New York: Frove, 1964.

Kardiner, A., & Ovesey, L. *The mark of oppression: A psycho-social study of the American Negro.* New York: Norton, 1951.

Kvaraceus, W. C., Gibson, J. S., Patterson, F., Seasholes, B., & Grambs, J. D. *Negro self-concept: Implications for school and citizenship.* New York: McGraw-Hill, 1965.

Lincoln, C. E. *The Black Muslims in America.* Boston: Beacon Press, 1961.

Pettigrew, T. F. *A profile of the Negro American.* Princeton, N. J.: Van Nostrand, 1964.

# Chapter 18

# Alienation: Some Concluding Observations

## Frank Johnson
State University of New York

This final chapter is concerned with presenting recommendations concerning the delimitation of the term, alienation. A table depicting a hierarchy of social relationships will be shown in regard to varying states of estrangement which occur at these levels of association. Some comments will also be made about the reification and negative mythologizing currently associated with the meaning of alienation.

## DELIMITATION OF THE TERM

Although questions concerning the scientific usefulness of the term alienation continue to be asked, there is little consideration given to the idea that the term lacks significance. Alienation has been linked by numerous authors to Neo-platonic, ontological conceptualizations which are of central significance in the interpretation of experience within Western cultures. Embellished by Judeo-Christian writings, these conceptions received a later transliteration from post-Enlightenment writers whose depictions of human experience again emphasized the ontic separateness of discrete things, ideas, and selves. Hence, from both theological and later scientific sources, themes concerning separation, disconnectedness, and fragmentation are central to the explanation of individual and group existence in the Western World. Although the moral, theological, existential, and cultural meanings of the term find ready acceptance, a number of commentators have discussed the delimitation, or even eradication, of the term in scientific discourse. Joachim Israel (1971) comments:

> . . . I would suggest that the term *alienation* be discarded from sociological and social-psychological theorizing and that other, more clearly delimited terms be used in its place. For example, I find it difficult to understand why one defines alienation as powerlessness, normlessness, meaninglessness, etc. Would it not be just as easy to use terms such as *powerlessness, normlessness,* etc. [p. 259]?

Arnold Kaufman (1965) arrives at the same opinion:

> Though it is impractical to recommend the elimination . . . of a concept which has a strong hold over men's imaginations, it might be quite reasonable to recommend that it be replaced within the language of sociology by more clearly specified, more empirically relevant senses of terms which denote only one variant situation or another [p. 162].

The problems which ensue when alienation is used as a specific *construct* in the social sciences (rather than as a metaphorical, metaphenomenal term) were examined in Johnson (see this volume, Ch. 1). Denise (see this volume, Ch. 5) has also argued for its delimitation in philosophical work on the basis of the terrible paradoxes and inconsistencies which are inextricably embedded in its meanings.[1]

Similarly, within psychiatry and psychology, the term alienation seems useful mainly for stressing the melodramatic and humanitarian connotations which are fused in its meaning. Those particular human conditions which are distinguished by severe estrangement, loneliness, and tension—nowadays described as varieties of "schizoid personality"—are more incisively defined by humbler epiphenomenal terms which capture the specific experiences of particular persons (e.g., isolation, despondency, vacillation, "pathological splitting," autism, etc.).

## ALIENATION AND CATEGORIES OF SOCIAL RELATIONSHIP

The extraordinarily rich and confusing applications of the term, alienation, have been critically described throughout this book by commentators from a variety of disciplines. Hopefully, these descriptions have contributed to the clarification of the term. A concluding attempt to clarify usage will be made in this chapter. Table 18-1 displays how the term is used to refer to various experiences of alienation occurring in different types of social relationship.

[1] The analysis of Richard Schacht (1970), has been cited before and contains an excellent discussion of the multiple meanings of alienation in the philosophical writings of Hobbes, Hegel, Marx, and others.

TABLE 18-1

*The Experience and Character of Alienation in Terms of Level of Association*[a]

| Level of social relationship (or association) | Experience of alienation | Example of alienation |
|---|---|---|
| I. Segmental encounters | There is a high potentiality for alienation, but usually of an insignificant nature, since the character, meaning, and quality of these interactions are ordinarily utilitarian, trivial, and perfunctory. | The indifference and inattention that exists between persons in diffuse public encounters (in crowds, public transportation, shopping, etc.) |
| II. Primary relationships | There is a low potentiality for social alienation in relationships to family, friends, co-workers, clergy, teachers, etc. Alienation which does occur, however, assumes graver personal significance. Commonly, this would be associated with states of psychological estrangement (e.g., isolation, depression, madness). | Rejection or change in affections between marital partners, and "significant others." |
| III. Institutional relationships | The potentiality for social alienation is related to the quality and type of role in institutions, the credibility of the value systems, and stability of statuses in organizations. The significance of alienation would vary with the degree of identification and participation in these institutions, value systems, and organizations. If these are positive, little or no alienation would ensue. | Political disenfranchisement on the basis of restrictive, local legislation and custom; or the frustration experienced in repetitious work on assembly lines. |
| IV. Mass associations | Alienation is inherent in the social and personal relations of individuals and groups in relation to aspects of the mass society. Relationships are conducted on an actuarial basis, where the individual possesses a numerical, nonpersonal identity. | The sense of insignificance that accompanies communicating with mass organizations through punch cards, computers, and form letters. |
| V. Reified (projected) relationships | The latent awareness of both social and psychological alienation constantly threatens these fictional pseudorelationships which individuals imagine they have with reified (imaginary) entities, for example, "Technology," "Society," "Culture." | The personalized feelings that "The 'Establishment' is crushing me!" "The Communications Media are poisoning me!" "Pollution is strangling me!" etc. |

[a]The construction of a table, by its very condensation, usually presents some conceptual problems. For example, this table contrasts certain categories of social relationships with various types of alienation. The description of alienated states, however, is not confined to

## Segmental Encounters (See Table 18-1)

Segmental encounters (or associations) consist of relatively simple interactions between persons who are involved in casual, fractionated, and incidental connections with each other—ordinarily over a short period of time. These relationships have been variously defined as "secondary" or "segmented." J. Clyde Mitchell (1966) has used another term, "categorical relationships," to describe those encounters that "arise where, by the nature of things, contact must be superficial and perfunctory [p. 52]."[2] In these encounters, the expectations for personal meaning are minimal. The interactions are usually fragmentary, delimited in time, and conducted in an atmosphere of relative personal and social remoteness. Such interactions are guided by informal conventions based on custom and courtesy, carried out in an oblivious manner.

By definition, relationships at this level involve a calculated degree of both social and psychological estrangement. Persons do not expect to find much meaning in the brief associations enjoined in buying a package of gum, boarding an airplane, or riding in an elevator. Psychological and social alienation, therefore, are not only expected, but also, in a sense, are necessary. An attempt by an individual to infuse such fragmentary encounters with a quality of personal relatedness often generates anxiety and suspiciousness on the part of one or both participants. This is not due simply to a defensive paranoia engendered by living in crowded urban settings, but is connected with the necessity of conserving energy. It is unthinkable that all encounters in a complex society could possibly be suffused with an immanent potential for personal significance. Of course, the proportion of time spent in segmental relationships varies from one individual to another, both in regard to the attributes, functions, and needs of individuals, and according to the social and

[2]Mitchell's (1966) presentation of segmental-type ("categorical") relationships in a multiracial setting is cited here because the setting which he studied makes the perfunctory, instrumental nature of these relationships particularly vivid. In interracial encounters of a segmental type, the underlying rules for social distance are more glaring than in segmental associations where racial and class differences are not as indelible.

---

the structural characteristics of these associations alone, but, of course, includes functional characteristics that inhere in such structural relationships. Furthermore, in a table of this sort, certain conceptualizations, for example, "role," "segmental relationship," etc. are presented in their commonly accepted meanings, ignoring the subtleties and nuances attributed to them in critical writings concerning their meanings. The author is aware of the controversies concerning the use and meanings of sturctural-functional terms, but feels that these arguments are not consequential for the current presentation.

Also, in assembling a table of this sort, the different definitions and shades of meaning between "associations," "relationships," and "relations" are partly ignored. For example, I use "association" to categorize secondary and mass connections (because they ordinarily are discussed in this way). As is obvious, my intention is not to depict a tight and consistent social system, but, rather, to illustrate qualitatively varying experiences of alienation.

The five categories of social relationship (and "association") presented in this table could easily be extended, but would unnecessarily complicate this presentation.

cultural climates in which these individuals live. Using the concept of "overload," Stanley Milgrim (1970) has recently reported on the preponderance of segmented relationships in big city life in contrast to life in towns and villages.[3] His study has documented what has been poignantly reported in popular and scholarly literature for the past several hundred years in regard to disconnectedness and loneliness extant in large urban centers.

The point, however, is not the amount of such alienating contacts, but the inevitability of alienation which is inherent in segmental ("categorical," "secondary") associations.

## Primary Relationships

In contrast to the vagueness inherent in segmental associations, primary relationships are conducted on the basis of some kind of mutually explicated status. In such encounters, the specific characteristics of the persons who interact are condensed into relatively fixed, single or plural designations (roles), for example, "friend," "brother," "teacher," "doctor."[4] In these primary relationships, individuals encounter each other in a social context and atmosphere which by virtue of the clarity of statuses, has a relatively low potential for social alienation. Most people are able to navigate within the various simple and complex roles inherent in these diverse encounters. With little difficulty, they are able to respond to the implicit norms that guide the expectancies in these interactions. Furthermore, they can be reasonably sanguine about the stability of their own statuses and those of others with whom they relate—at least at the time of the encounter.

While social alienation may be low in these associations, the potential for psychological alienation is much higher. Vacillations in the character and quality of the relationship are perceived through subtle changes of mood, context, and language. Considered in this way, one of the clearest operational differences between social and psychological alienation becomes apparent. Psychological alienation, by and large, is cued by emotional reactions to others, in situations of specific role playing occurring within the context of reasonably explicit primary relationships. In other words, it tends to occur in situations where social alienation is not present.

[3]Milgram (1970) adds to the observations and studies of Simmel and Wirth by advancing a social psychological explanation for the mechanisms which enhance the remoteness, aloofness, and hostility evident in the behaviors of individuals living in large cities. He uses the concept of "overload" as a psychoeconomic, energic explanation of the necessity of such ubiquitous alienation. Another kind of commentary concerning the aloofness extant in city life is described by Blanche Gelfant (1954).

[4]The term, "role," is selected here because of its popularity and simplicity. Regrettably, such simplicity may almost seem tautological, (1) "roles are (partly) based on mutual expectations," (2) "mutual expectations diminish social alienation," therefore, (3) "roles diminish alienation."

## Institutional Relationships[5]

This order of social relationship is used here to describe those associations between individual persons and various discrete organizations to which they belong, that is, in their relations to the company for whom they work or in their schools, churches, service, political, and recreational organizations.

The term, institution connotes that such associations are conducted against the background of certain common purposes (common functions, norms, identifications, etc.). The term also suggests that the purposes, goals, and norms of such social organizations are at least partly explicit, that is, public and enduring (in contrast to inexplicit, secret, and ephemeral).

One other distinction is necessary here. Although persons conduct their associations within these institutions on the basis of primary and secondary orders of relationship, they relate to the overall institution as a collectivity of role relationships within an aggregated social organization—parts of which they never directly experience. To be more concrete: a copywriter working in the advertising department of a large manufacturing concern has primary relationships with his immediate coemployees, peers, and supervisors, as well as with incidental people who may work in adjacent divisions. Furthermore, he obviously has many secondary associations throughout the organization based upon nodding acquaintance with individuals who are peripheral to either his own acquaintance or professional functioning within the company. His organizational and institutionalized association to the company, however, consists of the relationship of his professional performance to a remote complex of instrumental and functional activities of the entire institution (product development, manufacturing, accounting, marketing, etc.). The point of this category is to emphasize that the individual has relationships within his various social institutions which differ from those specific primary and secondary associations in which he is involved in his everyday work, family, and recreational life.

As is suggested in the above description, the experience of alienation in institutional and bureaucratized associations is inevitable. One is both personally, and, to a certain extent, socially disconnected from the gamut of complex motives, directives, purposes, procedures, and persons involved in large social organizations.

[5]The category of Institutional Relationships subsumes the area in which much of the sociological literature about alienation is centered. Many of the citations included in other chapters are concerned with the variety of experiences that individuals or groups encounter in being differentially separated from elements of social organization at these institutional levels of association. In addition to the sources already cited, a theoretical social system developed by A. C. Higgins (1964), is particularly adaptable to a discussion of the differential experiences of alienation. His system relates the structures of social relationship, the characteristics of roles within these structures, and the values which are inherent in the functions of relationships at these various levels. Although too complicated for inclusion in the present table, the author is indebted to the insights and advice provided by Professor Higgins.

This kind of alienation—based upon the structural complexity and size of the organization—is, however, only one aspect of such alienation. This basic and inevitable estrangement is either amplified or minimized by the degree to which the individual participates in and identifies (at a symbolical level) with the overall purposes, ethics, and norms of the larger organization. If one's status and identification within the institution are agreeable, then the experience of both social and psychological alienation would be minimized. Conversely, if one's status is felt to be insignificant, or if one is conflicted about the goals of the institution (or finds such goals meaningless), the sense of alienation will be high.

In discussing primary relationships, it was suggested that vacillations in the character and quality of such relations are perceived through subtle changes of mood, language, and context. It was further suggested that the most poignant experiences of psychological estrangement often occur in contexts where social alienation is minimal—with friends, coworkers, family members. This affords an interesting contrast to the psychological alienation that develops in institutional relations. At a gut level, the alienated person may not distinguish between the feelings of estrangement and rejection which follow disappointing encounters in his primary relationships as compared to those which afflict him less directly in institutional settings. Thus, some confusion ensues when psychological alienation is experienced in encounters (and nonencounters) occurring in the context of social institutions. For example, an individual may feel himself alienated from the institution in which he works if he discovers himself isolated and insignificant (that is, socially alienated) in terms of the overall organization. There is a difference, however, between the mechanism of this latter psychological experience of alienation (encountered as part of social alienation) and the experience of alienation occurring as a result of specific, detectable changes in actual primary relationships. The psychological experience of estrangement in primary associations is directly cued, and immediately reactive, while the experience of social alienation, encountered in institutional relationships, is more likely to be a formulated experience. It is not immediately and directly cued through primary relations, but is implicit in the characteristics of the relationships and nonrelationships inherent in the operations of large, complex, corporate institutions. (For example, on a fantasied basis, an employee may "feel" that his boss "hates him," even though he has never met his boss.[6])

## Mass Associations

At this level of relation, individuals have encounters with organizational structures that are considerably larger, more complex, and remote than the insti-

---

[6]Merton (1963, pp. 261-263) has discussed the varying qualities of alienation in primary and secondary relations in an essay on bureaucratic structure and personality.

tutions listed before. In these associations, the individual relates to governments, commercial institutions, manufacturing concerns, professional groups, or other organizations that are not territorially confined and which are guided by bureaucracies that are remote to the individual. He relates to such bureaucracies only in an actuarial and numerical mode. The encounters at this level of association are depersonalized, automated, and mechanized. Individual persons become numerical entities which interact with machines and systems, although such persons continue to have primary and secondary relationships with particular bank tellers, government file clerks, salesmen in stores, etc.

In addition to being remote, these associations include an aura of inflexible one-sidedness. It is nearly impossible for individuals to escape a feeling of insignificance and helplessness in such associations: "Do not fold, staple, or mutilate"; "A surcharge of 3% per month will be added to your balance remaining on the 15th"; "This card remains the property of Humble (Oil & Refining Company) and may be cancelled by it at any time. . . ."

Both psychological and social alienation are basic to associations at this level. The individual may, of course, attempt in a fictional way to impart qualities of personal relatedness to these complexes. Similarly, these mass organizations, through their advertising, may attempt to foster a feeling of personal relatedness ("The 1973 Buick—something you can believe in!"; "You're in good hands with Allstate."). Such yearnings for personal significance in the context of mass associations are quickly dispelled if one chooses to "fold, mutilate, or tear", challenge the legitimacy of automatic surcharges, or in other ways attempt to "personalize" a basically numerical "relationship."

### Reified (Projected) Associations

This category of reified associations is intended to depict those fictional and projected relationships that individuals abstractly formulate and create, rather than directly experience. ("Reified" is used here in its ordinary meaning; that is, to denote the artificial concretization of an abstract category into a definite "thing." A somewhat broader discussion of reification will follow, shortly.) The preceding categories of association have been based upon real encounters and actual interactions between the individuals and others at several levels of social relationship [with other roles, other persons, other (real) groups]. Even in those instances where the association is on the basis of a nonencounter (such as the projected animosity from a boss whom the employee has never met), such fictional encounters are at least theoretically possible and might take place in an actual larger organization.

Relationships in this present category, however, are *pseudo*relationships insofar as they are reifications of the individuals' feelings, attitudes, symbolical representations, etc. In these pseudorelationships, individuals may feel as if they were involved in actual social associations, or may describe their own actions as if they were encountering "their Culture or their Society." Needless to say, they do not interact with the abstraction "Culture" except in a projected, idealized, and fictional way. It has become commonplace not to differentiate between these idealized modes of reified relationship. In the same way, the words "Society" and "Establishment" are readily reified and used in an imaginary way to projectively create psuedorelationships with abstractions. Through the mechanism of reification, the individual creates the fiction that he has primary relationships with abstract entities—much as individuals entertained relationships with spirits, spectres, and ghosts in the past.

(If the thoughtful, fastidious reader objects to the inclusion of the category of "reified associations" as a final element in a hierarchy of social relations—all to the good! Many problems evolve from the fact that most people do not pause to make these distinctions, either colloquially or in some scholarly work. In brief, they do not differentiate between the actual social relationships and the subjective, gut feelings concerning social relatedness. The fact that a rhetoric against society flourishes in such an unbounded way today attests to the confusion which occurs when reified expressions are used in largely polemical and, frankly, mystical ways.)

## The Reification and Negativization of the Concept of Alienation

At several junctures in this volume the question of the amplification and promotion of both the fact and "badness" of alienation has been raised. It is quite evident that the term has become a generic expression for diverse anxieties, violence, imperfections, discontinuities, and separations in Western life. The extraordinary flexibility and vagueness of the term plus its (mainly) negativistic constructions and connotations make it a term very similar in nature to the panchreston, sin, which was similarly taxonomized and codified in Medieval Christianity. It has been suggested here that alienation has both supplanted and supplemented sin as a generic concept for depicting a series of defective aspects of human existence. One must ask, therefore, to what extent do those who codify, describe, and broaden the definitions of alienation contribute to the experience of alienation?

In contemporary demonology, the "witches," "wizards," and "satanic forces" of the past have been replaced with what Robert Daly (see this volume, Ch. 16) has called the Spectres of Technicism. Diverse discrepancies in idealized existence are accounted for not through the Fall of Man, but through Man's loss of a natural paradise, which has been sullied by the avariciousness of capitalism, technology, and acosmism. Alienation also readily subsumes disaffiliations in the family, disorganizations in national and international relations, and those ubiquitous experiences of indifference, violence, and prejudice occurring between different classes, cultures, and individuals. Finally, in its amazing comprehensiveness, alienation is easily applied to all manner of individual existential experiences—especially those which illustrate loneliness, malaise, idiosyncrasy, and madness.

The manner in which these various species of alienation have been reified by psychologists, psychiatrists, theologians, and sociologists is the subject of an analysis by Joachim Israel (1971).[7] He points out that empirical theories in the social and psychological sciences are preceded by models of an implicit, normative nature, whose covert presuppositions delimit the ways in which various "theories" in these disciplines are formulated. These basic underlining (normative) presuppositions are concerned with an idealization of a covertly postulated "natural existence of man." Such implicit postulates strongly affect the positing of values underlying human existence. Such values are implicitly assumed, but not clarified in most models. These unexamined assumptions, implicit in much psychological and sociological work, quite obviously affect both the outcome and the interpretation of scholarly work. This is even more evident in social philosophic commentary about alienation in which the fact of alienation is held as given, just as the fact of man's Fall from Paradise and Grace were held as basic assumptions in previous centuries. One must wonder, therefore, about the status of "empirical" research concerning alienation—research which implicitly assumes that the character of such alienation is already present and "given."

Israel (1971) comments on some of these implicit, normative presuppositions:

> . . . we maintained that theories concerning man's alienation usually presuppose assumptions or theories concerning conflicts, or contradictions, between the individual and society. These contradictions are usually considered to be antagonistic. Either the individual has to renounce some of his basic strivings in order to subordinate himself to society, or society's demands have to be changed in order to allow individual self-realization. Implicit in these theories, usually, are notions concerning balance or equilibrium, either being strived for by the individual or being a precondition of the "normal functioning" of a society [p. 267].

Later in his book, Israel (1971) continues his argument, also citing the work of Berger and Luckman:

> Reified theories have . . . been characterized as cognitive processes whereby human activity and the products of human activity are not experienced as typically human, but as having their own reality. Reified theories are a peculiar phenomenon: "Even while apprehending the world in reified terms, man continues to produce it. That is, man is capable paradoxically of producing a reality that denies him" [pp. 337-338].[8]

Israel describes "reification" as a cognitive process that provides an inexplicit normative base upon which the superstructure of many social, psychological,

---

[7] Israel's (1971) chapter, "The Problem of Reification," culminates a finely developed argument concerning various aspects of alienation. His use of the concept of reification is extraordinarily rich although it is basically concerned with applying the concept to economic and social theory. He is not specifically concerned with the psychiatric aspects of alienation.

[8] Israel (1971) includes the quote from Berger and Luckman (1966, p. 83).

and economic theories are built. His purposes are very complex and suffer from these brief quotations. The point of citing him here is that his suggestions concerning the existence of reified theories in psychology and sociology would indicate that, without intending it, scholars within these fields ineluctably perpetuate the notion of a negativized separateness and discontinuity. Having implicitly done this, they then propose to discover and analyze the empirical and logical order of things in the real (Western) world. Not unexpectedly, they frequently discover "alienation." This analysis suggests a further question: Do social scientists, psychiatrists, and culture critics, who, while intending to inform, describe, and exhibit certain salient characteristics of Western Society, actually create, reify, and reenforce the existence of the very phenomena they purport to study?

I am not suggesting that there is no significant evidence for malaise in contemporary technological societies. The fact of such abundant malaise and disconnection is all too evident. It cannot be an autistic creation of those historians, scholars, and empiricists who set out to discover what existed in their heads. Rather, it is the case that such commentary and research may inadvertently add to a fatuous and idealized depiction of existence, which makes all human behaviors discrepant, deficient (and "bad").

This same situation holds true in psychiatry where the conception of normality ordinarily is not empirically or statistically investigated, but, rather, is concerned with implicit idealized models of "personality functioning" against which actual adaptations are invidiously compared. (Fortunately, the subject of what constitutes normality is belatedly receiving interest within psychiatry from both logical and empirical standpoints. However, much work and explication of these issues remains to be done.)

As a corollary to the reification of "alienation," the prominent negative connotations of the term continue to suggest that the "real nature" of social and psychological man is both evil and denaturalized. If the normative (idealized) standards underlying such formulations are not made explicit, many "scientific" descriptions of the nature of man will continue to implicate him as being hopelessly "bad" and estranged. As under the previous rubric of sin, the discovery of imperfection and badness will be ubiquitous. By reference to either the categories of "sin" or "alienation," nearly all aspects of human behavior can be seen as unideal, disconnected, and fragmented in some way and, hence, "bad." Using the rhetoric of alienation, man (individually and in groups) can then be implicated in the same way that he was during previous centuries with the concept of sin.

There is one other corollary of this parallel between sin and alienation which should be noted. Out of frustration, perhaps (insofar as none can achieve the normative and ideal), some contemporary social philosophy, literary, and psychiatric writings have fallen back on the position that negativity and evil are inevitable and might as well be enjoyed. This position suggests that contemporary existence is so fragmented and isolating that one may as well seek his own form of isolation. This kind of negativity operates as a backlash which is similar to those mechanisms which mimicked the power and magic of Christianity in the early centuries through the creation of such reaction formations as the Black Mass or the profanation of Holy Objects. A philosophy of despair is not an uncommon human response when idealized cultural forms demand compliance to unreachable standards of ideal conduct and experience. Out of frustration, reachable but negative ideals may be sought as alternative goals.[9]   But this leads to a further difficulty. States of vacuous normality and "adjustment," therefore, may be rejected (since they are so patently "unideal") and, instead, a private, isolated state of idiosyncrasy is sought as the only sane alternative.

However, whether one opts for mindless conformity or radical existential separation, both solutions are reductionistic and fail to examine the implicit reified normative basis that posits that states of separation and anguish are inevitable in the first place. Both reactions, therefore, tend to continue the perpetuation of the notion that life in the Western World is inevitably disconnected, fragmented, and separated. Failure to take this into account, therefore, involves those scholars, experimenters, investigators, and commentators in inadvertently lending weight to the general cultural supposition of a fragmented, alienated life in the Western World.

Earlier in this book, the arguments of McDermott and Feuer were reviewed. These concerned the unconscious complicity of social scientists in their acceptance of basic social and economic tenets which supported the presence of alienation. Their arguments mainly were concerned with failure—both in the East and West— to face the need for economic reconstruction. The argument which I am sustaining here would locate the problem at a more general and basic level. It is my contention that the basic ontological belief in separation from idealized existence is so fundamental and pervasive in Western life, that it continually leads to the reification of alienation—just as it served as a base for the ubiquity of sin in previous centuries.

## Alienation as Sin

Concepts related to sinning in Medieval Christianity gave rise to sophisticated rationalizations and casuistries which extricated individuals and groups from a sense of anxiety, guilt, and culpability. The current use of the concept of alienation (in its manifold meanings of loss of social Paradise, and of a Fall into depravity and

---

[9]I have deliberately used the relatively neutral word "negativity" in this section rather than "evil" or "bad." As used in Johnson (see this volume, Ch. 2), the word "negativity" here refers to the lesser or lower pole of choices between dichotomies of (etymologically) opposite terms, for example, "good-bad," "positive-negative," "warm-cold," etc. "Negativity" in this sense is defined conventionally and operationally rather than morally.

Partly, the term alienation lacks much of a moral bite because the connotations of negativity and deficiency are not considered bad or evil. They are instead looked on as specific points on a continuum of experience where value may only be established relativistically, rather than morally.

negativity) does not usually require such complex manipulations. The process of alienation usually refers to a passively achieved isolation and estrangement. That is to say that alienation ordinarily presumes that such ravages are performed on passive individual and collective social objects. The question of culpability is simplified, therefore, by the creation of a series of social categories which implicate "social forces" as the causal agents of such unfortunate conditions. These generally locate the sources of all depravity in nebulous social systems, or in conditions which exist at levels of abstraction that semantically and etymologically have the (meta-phenomenal) status of Witches, Devils, Furies, and Spectres.

Interestingly, even those theologians writing about the issue of alienation and sin tend to perpetrate this identical rationalization. Influenced by the same implicit presuppositions that their scientific contemporaries use, these theologians also concede that those conditions which cause alienation are mainly due to projected social configurations which inexorably act to dehumanize human encounters, deteriorate the environment, and demoralize the character of individual existence (much as Devils worked in earlier times).

Among contemporary writings on the subject of alienation, only a few authors have made connections between the concept of sin and alienation. Fromm (1961, p. 46) refers to these in the introduction to Marx's *Economic and Philosophic Manuscripts*. Also in his inquiry into the psychology of ethics, the notion of individual responsibility for alienating conditions (and for that matter, the act of succumbing to alienation) is also suggested (Fromm, 1947). Tillich (1957) is concerned about estrangement from God in connection with sinning, but, as Schacht (1970) observes, this conception is merely one of a number of ideas that Tillich entertains concerning the manifestations of alienation.[10]

In contrast, Ernest Becker (1967) has paid very serious attention to the conception of sin in relationship to the contemporary meanings of alienation. He writes:

> It is almost impossibly difficult for the individual to assume the responsibility for his own meanings; he must, by his very nature as a creature immersed in the infinite, try to ground his acts in superordinate authority, in self-transcendence of some kind. The weight of sin, then, is the weight of meanings that are not related to a broad and self-transcending framework; they are meanings that do not justify the individual in the light of the eternal significance of the universe. With sin, man is cut off, *he* stands *alone with meaning*, separate from the ground of things, uprooted in his own finitude. This is what gives sin its deep anxiety. As Pascal and Kierkegaard so well knew, sin is existential anxiety, because it is man standing alone with the full burden for the meaning of life. Few men can stand this; and if even these men would stand truly erect, they could not stand it. Man can only stand sin by limiting his perspective, by narrowing his questions, by bending his gaze. Even those who would be strong—say, a Sartre or a Camus —take refuge from the burden of private meanings by claiming that life is "absurd" [p. 275].

[10]Richard Schacht (1970, pp. 212-217) has summarized some of Tillich's (1957) conception of sin.

Despite the vagueness, bipolarities, and ambiguity of "alienation," Becker attempts to rescue the term from its cosmic generality. By way of historical and logical analysis of the significance of the term, he presents the contention that the concept of alienation is of central consequence in seeking a fusion and synthesis between the technological (economic, scientific, bureaucratic) and the humanistic aspects of contemporary life. He sees education as both the context and the process through which such a synthesis must occur.

In a highly creative insight, Becker (1967) transforms the significance of individual sin, as perceived in previous centuries, to the contemporary scene: "When man said that the idea of sin was absurd, they were right: sin is absurd because it means that man is alone responsible for the meaning of life [pp. 275-276]."

The contrast is this: much of the current moral rhetoric concerning alienation would suggest that meaning, significance, and transcendence have been subtracted from human existence through the ravages of a corporate technological society (and the mentality which accompanies such social arrangements). Becker's (1967) formulation would suggest a more active accommodation to, or even, responsibility for this state of affairs. It is suggested from his writings that the presence of alienation, or the depiction of alienation, is a symptom of individual malaise and culpability. The suggestion is that man must consciously and actively strive to create new meanings and significance in his individual and corporate life.

The problem that I have attempted to expose here is that the concept of alienation at a metaphenomenal level has supplanted the concept of sin which flourished as its earlier prescientific predecessor. With the concept of alienation, then, the various species of human (individual and group) depravity, badness, imperfection, separateness, etc. have been effectively subsumed in the multiple meanings of alienation. In startling contrast to the concept of sin, however, the phenomenal Furies, Spectres, and Devils have all been replaced by a series of modern, reified social abstractions which are now held responsible for the baleful nature of collective social life in civilized communities: Technicism, Capitalism, Industrialism, Nationalism, etc. The glaring omission, however, has been the loss of any notion of individual human responsibility. The process of alienation instead is seen as a series of actions by collectivities (or even reified abstractions) against single individuals or groups.

Along with this reductionistic, unidirectional formulation goes the truly immense connotations of the inevitability of the human experiences of negativity and joylessness and estrangement. Furthermore, this negativity itself is unexamined and seems to constitute a reified presupposition which underlies both the psychological and social description of man similar to the pessimistic formulations concerning human nature adumbrated by the notion of sin. This is rarely acknowledged. Even as the most passionate social critics and theologians expose the awful incongruities and schizoidal separations in contemporary society, they, themselves, inadvertently amplify the sense of despair and inevitability by falling into this same, unconsciously negative rhetoric. Along with the contemporary social scientists and psychiatrists, they seem absorbed in describing a Twentieth Century *Inferno*.

Also, the phenomenologists and existentialists have done little to mitigate the everpresent despair. This is particularly paradoxical since, of all groups, the existentialists show a high degree of awareness concerning the synthetic nature of meaning and authenticity. It is worth noting, that, given their understanding of the possibilities for the human creation of human meaning, existentialists often choose negativity and schizoidal isolation as ways of transcending the abundant disconnectedness and depravity in contemporary existence.

Kenneth Keniston (1960) has written brilliantly about this proclivity to despair:

> The reasons for this shift are complex, and to consider them fully would take us far afield. Most fundamentally, this shift is part and symptom of a more general "loss of faith" in the West, seen in the movement from "positive values" (ends which men should seek) to a "negative morality" (which elucidates the evils and terrors men should avoid), and in our widespread doubt as to whether there are *any* values which can be legitimately and passionately held. This transition has often been discussed: it begins with the breakdown of medieval certainty, progresses through centuries of increasing rational skepticism and "demythologizing" of religion, and culminates in the cynicism and sense of ideological defeat that have followed our two world wars. Nietzche's "transvaluation of values" has taken place. But the old creeds have not been replaced, as he hoped, by values more adequate to what man might become, but by the value nihilism against which he explicitly warned. The hammer has been retained, but not the concept of a transcendent man above all men so far envisaged [pp. 182-183].
>
> . . . . Every age, too, has its characteristic balance between positive, eductive, hortatory, constructive, imperative, visionary, utopian myths, and negative, deterrent, cautionary, warning, direful, destructive and counter-utopian myths. In some periods of Western history, images of violence, demonism, destructiveness, sorcery and witchcraft have prevailed; in others, myths of blessedness, justice, co-operation, and universal concordance with divine order have dominated [pp. 185-186].
>
> . . . . Few would disagree that our own time is one of predominantly negative, deterrent or even satanic myths. Our dissociated fantasy is fantasy of violence, cruelty and crime, presented ostensibly as a warning, but often acting as a stimulant [p. 186].

As discussed before, various sectors within psychiatry (traditional, psychoanalytic, behavioral, and existential) also regrettably promulgate this same inevitable negativistic rhetoric. Both the (instinctual) internal mechanisms of the human and the (corporate) social groups with which he interacts, are pictured as negative, destructive forces that somehow must be controlled and/or compromised. Although the ethic of "creative" individual adjustment is explicit in psychiatry, generally such results are looked on as outwitting certain social realities or cleverly rearranging one's internal defenses in order to maximize personal, narcissistic rewards. A corollary to this is that in each of these therapeutic achievements, the implication is that these modifications have been accomplished either at the expense of others, or in spite of others. Furthermore, although it is appropriate to consider psychotherapeutic practices as having technical (scientific, objective) characteristics, there is a tendency to conceptualize procedures and ends of various psychotherapies only in technical, rather than ethical or moral terms. Fortunately, there are notable exceptions to this, but there is an increasing popularization of behavioral techniques that would treat large collectivities in mechanistic ways based, again, on what one would suppose is the belief in the inherent badness of both man as an individual and man in his social organization.[11]

This entire volume has been devoted to an exposition of the historical, etymological, and operational ways in which the word alienation is used—primarily in Western societies. This concluding chapter has been concerned with suggesting some limitations of the scientific uses of the term. A table (Table 18-1) describing alienation in various social relationships has been presented. A brief commentary has been made on the unconsciously emphasized negativity of the term as it is used by many contemporary writers. It is my opinion that culture critics, theologians, social scientists, and psychiatrists inadvertently amplify and reify the negativism, cynicism, and despair associated with the word, alienation. The antidote for such negativity—in addition to the simple exposition of it—resides in the kind of analysis and synthesis given to "alienation" by such writers as Ernest Becker (1967) and Kenneth Keniston (1960). If notions concerning the declining personal agency (Stanley), the human control over meaning (Becker), or the need for positive mythologizing (Keniston) go unheeded, then the future appears apocalyptic and terrifying—possibly even the near future. If we continue to grant totemic significance to the new "Spectres of Technicism" (Daly), we may well find ourselves poised on the eve of a new Dark (technological) Age. Worse yet, through our own fears and pessimism, we may indeed have assisted in reifying the very monster (Alienation) which we all deplore!

## REFERENCES

Becker, E. *Beyond alienation.* New York: Braziller, 1967.
Berger, P., & Luckmann, T. *Social construction of reality.* Garden City, N. Y.: Doubleday, 1966.
Fromm, E. *Man for himself.* Greenwich, Conn.: Holt, 1947.
Fromm, E. *Marx's concept of man.* New York: Ungar, 1961.
Gelfant, B. *The American city novel.* Norman, Okla.: University of Oklahoma Press, 1954.
Higgins, A. C. The use of sociometry in the description of social organization. Unpublished doctoral dissertation, University of North Carolina, 1964.

[11] The moral, humanistic, and ethical bases of psychotherapy have fortunately received a continuing examination, particularly since the 1950s. The contributors to this tradition are many and come from various schools of psychotherapy. A recent book concerning the relationship of ethics to psychotherapeutic practice is by Roy Waldman (1971). A recent example of a more mechanistic approach to the solution of human difficulties is found in B. F. Skinner (1971).

Israel, J. *Alienation: From Marx to modern sociology.* Boston: Allyn & Bacon, 1971.

Kaufman, A. On alienation. *Inquiry,* 1965, *8,* 141-165.

Keniston, K. Alienation and the decline of the utopia. *American Scholar,* 1960, *29,* 182-186.

Merton, R. K. Adult roles and personality. In N. J. Smelser & W. T. Smelser (Eds.), *Personality & social systems.* New York: Wiley, 1963.

Milgram, S. The experience of living in cities. *Science,* 1970, *167,* 1461-1468.

Mitchell, J. C. Theoretical orientation in African urban studies. In M. Banton (Ed.), *The social anthropology of complex societies.* London: Tavistock, 1966.

Schacht, R. *Alienation.* Garden City, N. Y.: Doubleday, 1970.

Skinner, B. F. *Beyond freedom and dignity.* New York: Knopf, 1971.

Tillich, P. *Systematic theology.* Vol. 2. Chicago: University of Chicago Press, 1957. Pp. 44-94.

Waldman, R. *Humanistic psychiatry.* New Brunswick, N. J.: Rutgers University Press, 1971.

# Author Index

Numbers in italics refer to the pages on which the complete references are listed.

## A

Abegglen, J., 199, *202*
Aberback, J., 278, 291, *292*
Adelson, J., 11, *24*
Adler, N., 352, *358*
Agger, R. E., 291, *292*
Algren, N., 296, *308*
Almond, G., 273, 286, 287, 288, *292*
Anagnine, E., 131, *139*
Aptheker, H., 276, *292*
Arendt, H., 240, *248*

## B

Barakat, H., 16, *24*
Barnes, J. A., 190, *203*
Barrett, W., 9, *24*
Becker, C. L., 321, *338*
Becker, E., 14, 15, 17, *24*, 381, 382, 384, *384*
Befu, H., 196, *203*
Bell, D., 111, *124*, 228, *248*
Bellah, R., 188, *203*
Benis, W. G., 100, *109*
Bennett, C., 187, *203*
Berger, P. L., 225, 227, 246, *248*, 317, *320*, 378, *384*
Binkley, L., 144, *160*
Black, M., 225, *248*
Blau, P., 227, 246, *248*
Blauner, R., 175, *180*, 277, *292*
Bleuler, E., 61, 62, 74, *81*
Bloch, M., 128, *139*
Böök, J. A., 63, *81*
Boler, J. F., 245, *248*

Bott, E., 190, *203*
Bourke, V. J., 226, 245, *248*
Bowers, M., 73, *81*
Brand, M., 227, 245, *248*
Brinkman, C., 31, *51*
Bruyere, P., 187, *203*
Brzezinski, Z., 239, *248*, 340, *358*
Buber, M., 147, 148, *160*

## C

Campbell, A., 170, *180*
Campbell, R. F., 332, 333, 334, 336, *338*
Camus, A., 87, *109*
Cather, W., 70, *81*
Caudill, W., 201, *203*
Chandler, B. J., 328, *338*
Chenu, M. D., 128, *139*
Churchill, L., 227, 246, *248*
Cicourel, A. V., 227, 233, 246, *248*
Clark, B., 334, 335, *338*
Clark, K. B., 361, *367*
Clark, M. P., 361, *367*
Cohen, A. K., 84, *109*
Cohn, N., 131, *139*
Coleman, J., 169, *180*
Coles, R., 361, *367*
Commons, J., 228, *248*
Converse, P., 242, *248*
Corwin, R. G., 331, 332, 334, 336, *338*
Covert, C., 13, *24*
Crotty, W. J., 291, *292*
Cumming, R. D., 158, *160*
Cunningham, L. L., 332, 333, 334, 336, *338*

387

# Subject Index

## A

Abdication, 208–209
Acceptance, in primary alienation, 214
Accountability, in policy science, 227–228
Achievement, academic,
  powerlessness and, 169
  relevance of, 326–327
"Acid," effects of, 95
Actions, inauthenticity of, 68–72, 75–76
Activity, political, 278–284, 288
Adaptation, schizoidal mechanisms in, 78–79
Adolescence,
  development of identity in, 89–92
  introspection in, 60
  subculture of alienation of, 92–96
Advantage, comparative, 264
Affect, in alienation, 31–34
Albigensians, 130
  attitudes of,
    toward family, 134
    toward marriage, 132, 134
    toward property and authority, 133–134
Alienation, *see also* Self-alienation
  ambiguity of, 144–160
  analytic schema for, 16
  in anthropology, 17–18
  of blacks, 168–170, *see also* Blacks
  categories of social relationship and,
    370–374
  definitions of, 3–24, 84–85, 114, 145–146
    159, 166–167, 272–274
  denotative and connotative, 29–34
  derivative, 216–219
  economic, 251–252, 253, 257–258,
    265–266
    of consumer, 258–259
    definition and applications of, 18–19

educational, 19–21
ethical, medieval, 131–132
in ethnography, 17–18
fallacies associated with, 150–151
forms of, 113
in history, 10–12
inconsistencies in term,
  etymologic, 34–39
  as scientifically testable, 40–41
  structural, 39–40
intellectual, medieval, 132–133
in literature, 22–23, 295–300, 302, 303
measurement of, 167
ontological, 315–318
in philosophy, 6–10
political,
  definition of, 21–22, 273–274
  empirical research on, 291
  in novel, 303
  socialization and, 286
  usage of, 21–22, 275–277
primary, 208, 210–213
  rejection of, 213–216
in psychiatry and psychology, 12–14
reification and negativization of, 377–380
relationship to identity, 89–92
religious, medieval, 128–131
sin and, 80, 379–383
social, 46–50, 126, 186
  in Black integration movement, 122
  compared to psychological, 373
  definition of, 117
in sociology, 14–17
sources of, 112, 117, 149–150, 166
  real versus potential, 37
subculture of, *see* Counterculture
surrogate, 214–215
in theology, 6–10, 311–312

internal, 344–346, 354–355
Objectification, 209
of knowledge, 223
of labor, 113
self, *see* Introspection
Objectivity,
alienation as, 30–31, 33
metaphors of, 224–227
cybernetics as, 227–236
Obligation, reciprocal, Japanese, 194–197, 199
Obsessive paranoia, 352–353
Occupation(s), *see also* Job; Work
of Japanese-Americans, 200
orientation and value differences and,
174–176
school training for, 325–327
self-image and, 175
Okinawans, social network of, 194
*On,* 195–196
Ontology, 68, 315–318
Opinion(s),
pluralism of, 243–244
validity of, 244
Opinion polls,
of blacks, 168–169
powerlessness in, 168–169
of youth, 171
Organism, as metaphor of objectivity, 224–227
Orgasm, in self-affirmation, 95
Orientation,
class and occupational differences in,
174–176
collective, 210–219
Japanese-American, 186, 188, 189,
197–199, 200, 202
individualistic, 210–219, *see also* Individualism

**P**

Panchrestons, 3–4, 27
alienation as, 28
Paranoia, obsessive, 352–353
"Peak experiences," 88, 89
Pearl Harbor attack, effect on Japanese-Americans, 201
Perception, of powerlessness, 284
Periodicals, analysis of alienation themes in, 120
Personal agency, 105, 223–224, 275, *see also*

Individualism
Personality, 210
black, 361–363
classifications of, 56
schizoid, 62, 79–80
splitting of, 61
Phantasms, 339–340
Philosophy, alienation in, 6–10
Pluralism, social decisions and, 242–244
Poetry, alienation in, 296–297
Policy sciences, criticism of, 222
Politics,
alienation in, 21–22, 282
in novel, 303
definition of, 272–273
of subculture of alienation, 96
Poor, *see also* Economy, dual
alienation of, 259–260
consumption technologies of, 260–262
Population, medieval growth of, 128
Possession, psychology of, 346–349
Possessionlessness, 155
Postalienation, 210–216
Power, 211, 273
in defining politics, 272–273
Powerlessness, 16, 36, 166–167
in attitude surveys, 168–169
political, 281, 284
of blacks, 365
of poor, 259–260
school achievement and, 169
Precision, in models of society, 234–235
Predictability, *see also* Control
effect on identity, 102–103
Price structure, 263–265
Primary relationships, 373
Prisoners of war, death rates among, 177
Privatism, 210, 217
Production, effect on laborer, 113
Professionalization, in schools, 331–337
Projected associations, 376–377
Property,
alienation from, 275
attitudes toward,
Albigensian, 130, 133–134, 136
Waldensian, 130, 133–134
Protest, political, 279
Pseudoworld, 49
Psychiatry,
alienation in, 12–14, 41–46